# The Great
# Edwardian
# Naval Feud

# The Great Edwardian Naval Feud

## Beresford's Vendetta against Fisher

### RICHARD FREEMAN

Pen & Sword
**MARITIME**

First published in Great Britain in 2009 by
**PEN & SWORD MARITIME**
An imprint of
Pen & Sword Books Ltd
47 Church Street
Barnsley
South Yorkshire
S70 2AS

ISBN 978-1-84884-083-6

Typeset by Concept, Huddersfield, West Yorkshire
Printed and bound in the UK by
CPI Antony Rowe, Chippenham, Wiltshire


Pen & Sword Books Ltd incorporates the imprints of Pen & Sword Aviation, Pen & Sword Maritime, Pen & Sword Military, Wharncliffe Local History, Pen & Sword Select, Pen & Sword Military Classics, Leo Cooper, Remember When, Seaforth Publishing and Frontline Publishing.

For a complete list of Pen & Sword titles please contact
PEN & SWORD BOOKS LIMITED
47 Church Street, Barnsley, South Yorkshire, S70 2AS, England
E-mail: enquiries@pen-and-sword.co.uk
Website: www.pen-and-sword.co.uk

# Contents

# List of Illustrations

# List of Plates

# Dramatis Personae

Titles and ranks are those held at the time of the enquiry in 1909. Posts are those held in 1909 or, for retired persons, the last post they held.

**The protagonists**
Admiral of the Fleet Sir John Fisher, First Sea Lord
Admiral Lord Charles Beresford

**The judge and jury**
Herbert Asquith, Prime Minister
Viscount Morley, Secretary of State for India
The Earl of Crewe, Liberal Leader in the House of Lords
Richard Haldane, Secretary of State for War
Sir Edward Grey, Secretary of State for Foreign Affairs

**Secretariat**
Charles Ottley, Secretary to the Committee of Imperial Defence (CID)
Maurice Hankey, Assistant Secretary to the CID

**Witnesses at the enquiry**
Reginald McKenna, First Lord of the Admiralty
Rear Admiral Sir Reginald Custance, Second-in-command, Channel Fleet, 1907–8
Captain Arthur Hulbert, Assistant Director of Naval Intelligence
Captain H. Campbell, Assistant Director of Naval Intelligence (Trade Division)

**Some of Fisher's high-profile supporters**
King Edward VII
Viscount Esher, courtier
Lord Knollys, private secretary to Edward VII
William Thomas Stead, editor of the *Pall Mall Gazette*
Sir James Thursfield, *Times* journalist

**Some of Beresford's high-profile supporters**
Commander Carlyon Bellairs, MP and journalist
Admiral Sir Cyprian Bridge, Commander-in-Chief China Station, 1901–4

Rear Admiral Sir Reginald Custance
Admiral Lord Walter Kerr, First Naval Lord 1899–1904
Walter Long, Conservative MP
Admiral of the Fleet Sir Frederick Richards, First Naval Lord 1893–9

# Preface

Lord Charles Beresford admitted that he was always 'fond of a row' and he boasted of his insubordinations as a naval officer. He also revelled in a near half-century of attacking the Admiralty while claiming that he was only seeking to buttress the nation's defences. From April 1875 until his death in 1919, he mounted assault after assault on his employer. He would say that he 'had no desire to criticise' but would then launch into a string of complaints. Although he tried to soften each attack by saying that 'no one was to blame' and that the fault lay 'in the system', he remained hostile and insubordinate to the Board.

First Lords and First Sea Lords tolerated Beresford's antics, as did successive cabinets and Prime Ministers. They were shrugged off as the eccentricities of 'Charlie B', the nation's favourite admiral. But when, in the early twentieth century, Beresford began to attack Jackie Fisher, it became harder to ignore his behaviour.

What had begun as mere frictions between the two men developed into a systematic campaign by Beresford to undermine the First Sea Lord. Sometimes the dispute is referred to as a 'quarrel'. More commonly it is called a feud. I have retained the word 'feud' in my title, but with some reluctance. When I began work on this book I too saw the conflict as a feud, but the more I read the papers of Beresford and Fisher, the less convinced I was. Certainly Fisher found Beresford's behaviour exasperating and sought to tame his excesses. But one searches in vain for evidence of any attempts by Fisher to harm Beresford. At worst, Fisher can be charged with insensitiveness, but little more.

Beresford's part is altogether different. From the moment that Fisher was promoted to Admiral of the Fleet, Beresford began to foster an all-consuming hatred of Fisher. From late 1904 through to the end of 1909 he waged an all-out war to have his rival removed from the Admiralty. Beresford's intention was to take Fisher's place or, even better, bring down the Liberal Government and become First Lord in a Unionist administration. The evidence for this is abundantly clear in his letters to Carlyon Bellairs and Walter Long. It is also supported by comments made by his friends (such as Jessica Sykes) in their own letters. All this leads me to see less of a feud and more of a vendetta.

However one wishes to describe the clash, for each man it only spanned at most one-fifth of their professional lives. For this reason I have sought to also show the greatness of the two men and the fullness of their careers. In very different ways, each was admirable and charismatic. Beresford was warm, impulsive, at ease with all classes of men. Although wealthy, he was generous; although aristocratic, he had an innate empathy for ordinary men and women. He was rash, courageous and dashing. He could always rise to a challenge and was the ideal man to have on hand in a crisis.

Fisher was dynamic with an instinctive reforming zeal. He eschewed society and social life, and worked long hours, goading the Navy to drag itself from nineteenth-century lethargy to face twentieth-century threats. He liked to stay in the shadows, describing himself as a mole, who was only evident through his upheavals. Long recognised as one of the Navy's greatest reformers, he can also claim a place alongside some of the twentieth century's greatest administrators. He was, besides, a remarkably talented letter writer. A mere short memorandum would be spattered with pithy phrases and telling metaphors. His longer letters were astonishing literary performances, even when they had been dashed off at great speed.

While Fisher left an archive of over 5,000 documents, Beresford (or one of his family) seems to have systematically destroyed almost every significant document in his possession. In his will he left 'all MSS, letters, memoranda, and private papers' to his wife, but all that now remains is a mere 200 documents. Most of these are trivial exchanges with the various monarchs of Europe. It would appear that, for all his protestations of innocence, deep down he felt he had much to hide. Fortunately for us, others took care to retain the rich trail of evidence of Beresford's vendetta against Fisher, as this book will show.

Richard Freeman
*Cambridge, May 2009*

# Acknowledgements

I am grateful to the following organisations for their kind permission to reproduce materials in their possession:

Items from the Esher and Wemyss archives are reproduced with the permission of the Master, Fellows and Scholars of Churchill College. The material from the Bellairs archive is reproduced by permission of McGill University Library. The Fisher letters and papers in Bacon *The Life of Lord Fisher of Kilverstone*, Marder *From Dreadnought To Scapa Flow, Vol. 2*, Marder *Fear God and Dread Nought, Vols 1 and 2*, and in the Churchill College Archives are reproduced by permission of the Duke of Hamilton. Material from ADM 1/7450B, ADM 1/7465C, ADM 1/7507, ADM 116/1037, ADM 116/3108, ADM 196/83/86, ADM 50/390, ADM 53/21378, CAB 16/9A, CAB 16/9B and CAB 17/7 is reproduced by permission of the National Archives. Material from Add Mss 49710, Add Mss 49713, Add Mss 49719, Add Mss 50288 and Add Mss 62407 is reproduced by permission of The British Library. Extracts from *Fear God and Dread Nought, Vols 1 and 2* by Lord Fisher of Kilverstone, edited by Arthur J. Marder, published by Jonathan Cape are reprinted by permission of The Random House Group Ltd.

I am also grateful to the following for permission to reproduce photographs:

MaltaVista.net for the photograph of Malta harbour. Stephen Luscombe for the photograph of HMS *Renown*. Imperial War Museum for the photographs: Beresford with his flag staff, 1904–05; Beresford with flag staff 1909; Fisher in *Renown* cabin. Dubris Design for the photograph of the Lord Warden Hotel.

*Prologue*

# The Roots of the Feud

Beresford and Custance were not leaving a stone unturned
to defame and injure me. – *Fisher.*[1]

## Scene 1: No. 2 Whitehall Gardens, 1909

Today, 27 April 1909, all political eyes are on No. 2 Whitehall Gardens in
the heart of London. It is an imposing edifice built in 1808 and now
standing in a jumbled complex of government buildings. On the first floor,
a room has been prepared for a formal meeting; the blotters are laid out,
the carafes filled with water, the chairs are set in position. It is a room
steeped in history. At one time Disraeli had held his cabinets here, a
practice he abandoned in 1877 when he could no longer manage the stairs.
The walls are panelled in rich, dark wood, inlaid with paintings of French
chateaux and rural scenes. Through the tall windows, we can see a
splendid panorama of the Thames, glimpsed through the trees of the
new embankment. Along one side of the room is a marble mantelpiece,
decorated with carved statuary, with a pier-glass above. Between the two
windows, through which pours the early morning sun, flickering as it is
reflected off the river, there is a large mirror. Its twin faces it from the
opposite wall. The space between the mirrors is dominated by an oblong
table, where so many high decisions have been taken – and where the
defence of Britain in both World Wars will be planned – but rarely, if ever,
will the meeting room of the Committee of Imperial Defence see such a
bizarre event as is to begin on this April morning.

   The door opens and the Prime Minister, Herbert Asquith, comes in. He is
a stocky man, careless in his dress (despite his wife's attempts to rectify
this), his silver hair rakishly long. His heavy-jowled face adds to the sense
of a sedentary individual, not given to unnecessary activity.[2] He walks to
the far end of the table and takes his customary position between the two
windows. Next comes a lugubrious-looking man, his face obscured by a
vast moustache, reminiscent of the more famous countenance of Kitchener.
The Earl of Crewe, Liberal Leader in the Lords, is an obvious choice for the
enquiry, being a natural conciliator and said to have 'the best political
judgement in the cabinet'.[3] After Crewe comes his fellow peer, Viscount

1

Morley, Secretary of State for India, a man as careful of his dress as Asquith is neglectful. He is on the short side, with keen, sparkling eyes, betraying his kindly manner, whilst disguising his fastidious nature. Behind him is a tall, imposing man, good-looking to a fault, with an athlete's frame; it is Sir Edward Grey, Foreign Secretary, an arresting presence, not yet showing the effects of his rapidly deteriorating sight. The last to enter is the Secretary of State for War, Richard Haldane. To Grey's sporty appearance, Haldane offers the physique of the couch potato; he is short, tubby and is chatting away in his squeaky voice as he sits down at the table with his colleagues.

Around the table are just some of the cream of one of the most illustrious Cabinets that Britain has ever known. Yet they are not here to discuss high state business, but have been summoned with indecent haste to form an *ad hoc* subcommittee of the Committee of Imperial Defence. They are to 'Inquire into Certain Questions of Naval Policy', but they know little of the background, beyond the gossip in the Pall Mall clubs.[4] Each man has better things to do with his time, yet here they are, and here they will sit for fifteen days.

After a few brief preliminaries, Asquith opens the proceedings by asking the first witness, Admiral Lord Charles Beresford, to present his case. A man with the rolling gait of a sailor enters; it is 'Charlie B', hero of the public and the *Daily Mail*, recently sacked from his post as Commander-in-Chief of the Channel Fleet. He is tall, handsome, with square shoulders, a firm mouth and a determined chin.[5] Despite his sixty-three years, he has an imposing bearing and the air of a man who was not only born to command, but knows it. His very presence is to prove intimidating to the illustrious men around the table.

Four weeks earlier, on 2 April, Beresford had written to the Prime Minister, making the serious charge that the Navy was not properly organised for war. After barely consulting his colleagues, and without making the least enquiries into the charges, Asquith had conceded an enquiry. The man known as 'Mr Wait and See' had, uncharacteristically, acted on impulse.

The spin for the press was that this was an enquiry into the efficiency of the Admiralty. It was a fiction that Asquith made little effort to disguise. Indeed, his casual approach to an apparently important enquiry was evidenced by his bizarre attitude to its membership. He had, understandably, invited Admiral of the Fleet Sir Arthur Knyvet Wilson, the most respected of Britain's retired admirals, to join the committee. Wilson was the one man above all others who was seen to embody the true spirit of the Navy. Winner of a VC in the Sudan in 1884, he was 'a great seaman, and a masterly tactician'.[6] No man was more qualified to sit in judgement on the efficiency of the Navy. Yet as soon as Beresford objected to his presence, he was dropped. With Wilson, the inquiry might have had some credibility;

2

without him, a handful of politicians, none of whom had ever served at sea, advertised the fact that there was a hidden, less serious, agenda.

In fact, the enquiry was the final round in the Beresford-Fisher feud. For years the two admirals had sparred; for years Beresford had sought to destroy Admiral of the Fleet Sir John Fisher, His Majesty's First Sea Lord.[7] But it would not have been seemly to enquire into a feud between two such distinguished servants of the Crown, so the Committee accepted the fiction of the charge sheet: that the Admiralty was in the dock. In this way, Fisher could be seen as a mere servant of the Board, only there to support his master, Reginald McKenna, MP, His Majesty's First Lord of the Admiralty.

## Scene 2: A decade of mutual jealousy

Accounts of the feud, both at the time and later, have always confused the widespread and intense hostility that many of Fisher's naval reforms engendered with the personal antipathy between Fisher and Beresford. Fisher had become First Sea Lord, aged sixty-three, in 1904, after completing a monumental reform of naval education in the previous year, when he introduced a single system of entry for all officers and a common curriculum. This reform struck at the heart of the class-ridden Victorian Navy. From now on, executive officers would have to treat the engineers as their social equals and accept them on the quarter-deck and in their messes. Few reforms could have been more calculated to arouse the hostility of the upper-class dominated officer corps.

It was, though, as First Sea Lord, that Fisher introduced his avalanche of reforms, which split the Navy from top to bottom. Amongst his many actions, he scrapped over 150 ships that 'could neither fight nor run away';[8] he reorganised the fleets, concentrating ships in areas of vital interest to Britain; he reshaped the reserve in order to make it more ready for 'instant war';[9] he built the *Dreadnought*, the world's largest and most powerful battleship, said by his opponents to have weakened Britain by making the rest of the fleet obsolete overnight. At the time of his great reforms (broadly 1903–6), naval officers (particularly retired ones) could barely find adjectives strong enough to describe their abhorrence of the changes. Each new reform was denounced as more catastrophic than the last, with the ruin of the Navy being ever more imminent.

In so many accounts of this period, Beresford is added as one more (important) voice to the chorus. That is to misread what happened. Like Fisher, Beresford had a gigantic personality; both men sought credit for their works and neither liked to share the limelight. Never in his life was Beresford a member of anyone's chorus. He was a one-man band, but made more noise than all the others put together. What this book will show is that lumping Beresford in with the other admirals and senior officers who opposed Fisher's reforms is to mistake his behaviour and misunderstand his motives. The admirals who fumed against Fisher simply detested his reforms and saw consequent ruin for the Navy. Beresford, once on good terms with Fisher, grew to abhor him *personally* and saw ruin for *himself* in Fisher's vertiginous rise to the pinnacle of the Navy. From 1900 onwards (when Fisher and Beresford served together in the Mediterranean) each man realised that his career was inextricably intertwined with the other's. Both dreamed of the prize of First Sea Lord and each was in a position to obstruct his rival. Put simply, reforms or no reforms, the feud was basically fuelled by the fact that the Navy was not big enough for two such colossal, competitive personalities. Whatever policies Fisher might have adopted, Beresford would have condemned them because they came from his rival, not because of what they were.

As the story unfolds, Beresford will be seen to be driven by his increasingly frustrated ambitions. No man wished more than he (or, to be more accurate, than his wife, Mina) that he should be First Sea Lord. Fisher's taking of that prize in 1904, and his later extension in the post to 1911, released in Beresford a torrent of hate and jealousy that deprived him of what little remained of his capacity for rational thought.

Any attempt to account for Beresford's opposition to Fisher as being based on his calm analysis of policy will be seen to be misguided. As the evidence presented here will demonstrate, at first Beresford supported Fisher's reforms. His later vituperative outbursts against his adversary and his attempts to unseat him from the Board cannot be seen as merely a change of professional opinion. His behaviour only makes sense if we see his later eruptions as a response to perceived personal slights, not to Fisher's policies. Time and again, Beresford would approve of one Fisher scheme or another and then, in later years, violently condemn what he had once lauded. On other occasions, he would accept a Fisher policy as routine naval practice, only later to represent it as a carefully contrived, brutal and personal assault against him.

As the feud developed, Beresford's behaviour became more and more irrational. Admiral Bosanquet, writing to the journalist Arnold White in 1907 told him that 'I am personally convinced that on certain subjects he is not sane.'[10] And in that accusation lies a clue as to how we must interpret the feud. Attempts to read Beresford as a rational man just do not stand up. By the height of the feud he had effectively lost control of his own actions. On one occasion, in 1908, he persuaded the Board to ban newspaper correspondents from joining his fleet for manoeuvres. Having reluctantly accepted this extraordinary breach with precedent – manoeuvres were normally accompanied by thirty or more journalists – the Board found that, just a week later, Beresford had invited all his friends and political cronies to sail with him.[11] Any sane person would have realised that this action would invoke the fury of the Board, but not Beresford; he had reached the point where he was incapable of foreseeing the consequences of his actions – in this case, yet one more official reprimand.

This book will not go into the technical details of Fisher's reforms, which were complex and often tedious for those who are not naval fanatics. Instead, we will note that, 100 years later, the official website of the Royal Navy, in its list of famous admirals, only includes five who served in the twentieth century – Fisher was one of them. Needless to say, Beresford is absent from the list. The modern Navy's verdict on Fisher is that he was 'an outstanding innovator and administrator' whose reforms turned the old Victorian navy 'into a military machine capable of maintaining Britain's naval supremacy in the First World War'.[12] This assessment is matched by a recent academic re-appraisal of Fisher which describes him as 'the most astute and adept First Naval Lord there had ever been'.[13]

As the story progresses and Beresford becomes increasingly caustic in his abuse of Fisher's reforms, it will help to recall that today's naval officers have declined to share his opinion.

This, then, was the man who Fisher faced: a famous, popular and privileged aristocrat who was consumed by ferocious jealousy. He was a man bent on one thing only: to unseat Fisher. This book will tell the story of that feud, from its gentle early frictions to its cataclysmic conclusion.

But first, we need to understand the protagonists, since their backgrounds and personalities were to lie at the heart of their mutual jealousy. Fisher and Beresford first worked together when their ships were despatched to the bombardment of Alexandria in 1882. The first Act of our account will tell the story of how each man arrived there and the baggage each brought with him.

5

*Act 1*

# Giants in the Making

Beresford and Fisher 'had practically nothing in common outside the Service'. – *Bacon*[1]

### Scene 1: From the Ceylon jungle to a glittering command

John Arbuthnot Fisher was born into the Victorian Empire on 25 January 1841, in a ramshackle bungalow in the steaming jungle of Ceylon (now Sri Lanka). His father, Captain William Fisher, had gone to Ceylon in pursuit of his mediocre army career. In 1840 he had married Sophie Lambe, the sister of a coffee-planter, Frederic Lambe. Within three years of his son's birth Captain Fisher followed Frederic's example and set up his own plantation after resigning his army commission. Neither position nor fortune ever came to Captain Fisher.[2] What remained of his modest life brought only debts, poverty and social neglect. His travail came to an early end when he died after being thrown from his horse in 1866.

The Fisher family had been sliding down the social scale for many years. In 1544 the King had handed the manor of Packington in Warwickshire to a John Fisher and the Fishers proudly held the estate until 1729 when it passed into the Aylesford family.[3]

There had also been a baronetcy in the family, but this lapsed on the death of Sir Clement Fisher in 1739.[4] From then onwards, the most the Fishers could boast were minor positions in the Army and a bevy of parish priests in Devon and Bedfordshire – Fisher's paternal grandfather was rector at Wavendon. The family's fortunes fell yet further, to the point where Fisher's father had to abandon his English roots and accept overseas service. By the time of Fisher's birth, the family was paying the price of empire, administrating Britain's possessions in the forgotten corners of Victoria's sprawling realm. They were condemned to live and die beyond its riches and pomp.

Fisher's parents' precarious existence left him with a lifelong insecurity about money. On his entry to the Navy, his father had warned him not to get into debt and that, if he did, there would be no family money to bail him out. Indeed, six years later, his father's estate lost £2,000 in just one year (about £125,000 today) and, at times, Fisher sent his mother an allowance out of his pitiful naval pay.[5] (As a midshipman, Fisher would have been paid £31 a year – around £2,000 today.) For the rest of his life he would keep meticulous records of how much he spent – as did his wife.

As the Fisher parents proudly looked down on the first of their eleven children, they are unlikely to have nurtured any great ambitions for their son. If he were to follow family traditions, his future would be in the minor ranks of the army or ministering in a backwater parish in one of the remoter English counties. Not for one moment would they have imagined that the newborn boy in the cradle would achieve fame beyond imagining. He would hold his country's destiny in his hands in the run-up to the First World War, receive the favour of one sovereign and the friendship of another. He would die a hero and be buried with a pomp that rivalled the funeral of his beloved King Edward VII. As his coffin wound its way to Westminster Abbey, the silent crowds would stand twenty-deep on the pavements of London.

In childhood, Fisher enjoyed a freedom denied to most children today. His father's estate lay in untamed jungle, where the family bungalow was one of just six in a compound which was, said his brother Frederick, 'scattered over a vast semi-wilderness where game, big and small, was plentiful'. The young Fishers revelled in their father's passion for hunting, chasing after him as he ran down elk on his horse. Until Fisher left home at the age of six, he never wore shoes or socks and there was 'no schoolmaster to worry us'. Only the 'voracious' leeches which bit them on their bare legs annoyed the children, but their mother was at hand to soothe them with Friar's Balsam.[6]

Aged just six, Fisher was shipped home to school in 1847, never to see his father again. Where exactly he went to school is unclear, but he spent part of his holidays at Catton Park, the country estate of Sir Robert and Lady Wilmot-Horton.[7] Her Ladyship was Fisher's godmother, and she facilitated his entry into the Navy, aged thirteen. In those days, entry was by nomination, and Fisher proudly boasted that he was nominated by 'the last of Nelson's Captains' (Admiral of the Fleet Sir William Parker) who lived nearby.[8] Clearly Fisher's family were less humble than he liked to maintain in later life.

There is no trace as to what put the idea of a naval career into his head. All we know comes from his father, who, writing from Ceylon, told him that 'Lady Horton tells me it was your own choice to go into the Navy.'[9] His naval career began when he stepped on to the deck of the *Calcutta* on 13 July 1854, dodging the seamen who were vigorously holystoning the boards and darting between the bucketfuls of water being thrown across the deck. Fisher later recalled that first day, writing: 'I entered the Navy penniless, friendless and forlorn.'[10] His father had reminded him that 'I cannot give you much pocket money' since there were many other siblings to support. He went on to tell his son that he was 'never to tell an *untruth*', was to 'make friends with the best fellows and *gentlemen*' and to 'be very clean'. As a final piece of advice, he added: 'never forget your religion and your prayers'.[11] It was a counsel of which the young Fisher had no need whatsoever.

The *Calcutta* was a supply ship, taking stores to sea-going vessels. Many years after Fisher's time on the ship, she was taken out of commission and moored as a hulk for the accommodation of naval cadets in Portsmouth harbour. It was in this reduced state that Tissot immortalised her in his famous painting *The Gallery of HMS Calcutta*, which is now in the Tate Britain.

During Fisher's first four months on board, the ship remained in Plymouth Sound and when she finally left for the open sea in November, she was hurled in every direction by violent early winter storms. Her intended destination was Portsmouth (due east), but by 15 November, she was sheltering in Falmouth harbour (due west). Ever one to reach for his pen, Fisher recorded this first voyage with some advice to other sailors:

Now sailors all take my advice
Let steamships be your motta.
And never go to sea again
In the sailing ship *Calcutta*.[12]

It was his first attempt to reform the Navy and an early indication of his hostility to sails.

In February 1855, the *Calcutta* set off once again, this time to take supplies to ships fighting the Crimean War in the Baltic. In the following year he was in the Black Sea, bringing home the sick and wounded on board the *Agamemnon*.

Fisher was then posted to the *Highflyer* under Captain Shadwell whom he called 'about the greatest Saint on earth', whilst the sailors called him 'Our Heavenly Father'. Shadwell recognised in Fisher a prodigious talent, which he nurtured for three years, at the end of which Fisher recalled 'I learned from him nearly all that I know.'[13]

Fisher had joined the *Calcutta* as a boy; he was to leave the *Highflyer* as a man. It was the Second Chinese War which was to transform his life; after merely smelling the gunpowder and the blood of the Crimean War from safe anchorages in the Baltic and the Black Sea, he was to plunge into the hell of war in a brutal fashion.

His first experience of battle was in a naval attack at Fatshan Creek at Canton on 1 June 1857. In his own account, he recalled that 'We went up a Chinese river to capture a pirate stronghold. Presently the pirates opened fire from a banana plantation on the river bank. We nipped ashore from the boats to the banana plantation.' This was written around 1919, memory playing its tricks, since the banana plantations had been no more than rice fields and the 'pirates' were Chinese sailors and soldiers, resisting British encroachments. Of his own part in the action all that Fisher recalled was being 'armed to the teeth, like a Greek brigand, all swords and pistols'.[14] Meanwhile, his dear Captain Shadwell went into battle with 'a yellow waistcoat, [and] white trousers & a white umbrella'.[15]

Two years later he was in battle again in north-east China where the Peiho Forts guarded the entrance to the river of the same name. By this time – June 1859 – Fisher had begun his prolific correspondence with Mrs Warden, the wife of a P&O shipping company official at Shanghai. Mrs Warden acted as a surrogate mother to young officers, keeping open house for them when in harbour and, at least in Fisher's case, corresponding with them when at sea. After the battle, Fisher sent her a breathless account of the day. He first told her that Captain Shadwell 'has been very badly wounded in the foot' – an outcome that would be advantageous to Fisher's career. Then he told Mrs Warden about the 'killed or wounded that you know', who included Inglis, who died 'smothered in the mud when we landed' and the Chaplain, 'badly wounded in the groin'; Fisher doubted that he would live. Another acquaintance of Mrs Warden's, a Captain Vansittart, had 'had his leg shot off'. Back on the ship, after the battle, 'it was nothing but blood and men rolling about with arms and legs off'. Calmly, the eighteen-year-old went on to tell Mrs Warden that 'No one takes account of dead people inside here, we pitch them overboard as they are killed or dead. One soon gets used to it.'[16]

Fisher was to prove a gifted writer, pouring out vibrant, uninhibited letters for the next sixty years, ceasing only a few days before his death. Oddly, he never appreciated his own talent and once apologised to Mrs Warden saying, 'I can't write nice letters like you' and 'I can't say I am at all great in the art of letter writing.'[17] Amongst those who did not share this opinion was the naval historian and would-be biographer of Fisher, Hallam Moorhouse. He was, she said, 'the most glorious of correspondents ... the very look of his letters was exciting'.[18]

Captain Shadwell's injured foot refused to heal, despite two operations, the second of which Fisher graphically described to Mrs Warden:

> The principal artery of his foot broke adrift and the whole place filled with blood. Courteney had to cut another piece out so as to be able to reach it with his tweezers, and they hauled it out and tied it up. They had not time to give him chloroform, so you can fancy the agony the poor gentleman endured.[19]

As a result, Shadwell was invalided home, his last act being to give Fisher a pair of *Loyal au mort* cuff links and to warmly recommend him to

9

the Commander-in-Chief, Admiral Hope.[20] Shortly afterwards, Fisher was promoted to mate, passing first class. He told Mrs Warden that 'they took three days to pass me . . . you have no idea how very jolly I feel'. Hope then took him on as flag mate. It was hard work, since the Admiral 'hardly takes his boots off without sending for me and informing me officially of it', and the hours were long: 'I have to call him at 5.00 am, be in his cabin dressed, by 7.00 am ready to receive orders as to what the different ships are to do.'[21]

In the same year he was promoted to lieutenant, allowing himself four exclamation marks when writing to Mrs Warden: 'March 30th. Made a Lieutenant. Lieut. Fisher!!!!'[22] He turned down an appointment to a small vessel, only regretting that he was not able to ask Mrs Warden to address her letters to 'Lieut. J. Fisher, R.N., H.M.S. *Esk*'.[23] He revelled, though, in the fact that the midshipmen who before called him 'Jack', now 'come up very respectfully and touch their caps and say "Sir"'.[24]

From then on, Fisher distinguished himself in post after post. On returning from the China Sea in 1861 he became a full lieutenant after completing his shore-based exams at Portsmouth, passing with the highest marks ever attained: 968 out of 1,000.[25] This led to various appointments as an instructor at the gunnery school, HMS *Excellent*, at Portsmouth and short postings on several ships from 1862–9.

It was at the *Excellent* that Fisher first came to the attention of the Board, although in an unconventional manner. Their Lordships, recalled a colleague of Fisher's, were on an inspection tour and, pausing to watch a gunnery drill, an admiral asked: 'Is this Lieut. Fisher as good a seaman as a gunnery man?' Fisher stood up and responded, 'My Lords, I am Lieut. Fisher, – just as good a seaman as a gunnery man', at which they bowed their heads and moved on.[26]

Their Lordships did not forget him, since he crowned this stage of his career by being selected in 1869 to join a party attending the opening of the new German naval base of Heppens (now Wilhelmshaven). At lunch he sat next to Bismarck, who apologised to Fisher for the local Burgomaster's boring speech, saying, 'I didn't know this was going to happen, or I would have cut him short.'[27]

For the next seven years, Fisher acted as commander of the *Ocean* in the China Sea, followed by a period at HMS *Vernon*, the torpedo (mine in modern parlance) training establishment. During this time he was promoted to captain, at the age of thirty-three. He was glad to have shore-based appointments, not only because they gave him more contact with the Admiralty, but also because, at sea, he missed Kitty, his wife. He told her in 1870 that, 'I can't get used to the separation at all and feel every day to get worse instead of better . . . I am *always always* thinking of you and feel

10

it so very hard that we should be separated now in the prime of our lives.'[28]

Fisher's choice of spouse was to prove advantageous to his career. Francis Katharine (Kitty) Josepha Delves Broughton[29] came from a modest background – her father was the Rev. Thomas Delves Broughton of St Peter's, Broughton in Staffordshire. From the day they married in 1866 she dedicated herself to supporting her husband's advancement to the glittering goal of First Sea Lord. She was quiet, retiring and self-effacing, but would never allow any criticism of her husband. Her self-sacrifice went as far as to accept that never in the whole of their married life did they own a house. When not in Admiralty accommodation, they rented homes and they were on the move every few years as Fisher's career advanced. Even in retirement, Fisher preferred to shift from place to place, not even being able to settle in the splendid Kilverstone Hall, which his son Cecil had inherited from a wealthy shipbuilder. Possessions were of no consequence to him and, in retirement, when showing a visitor around his son's house, he pointed to two despatch boxes, sitting on the floor of his own bedroom, and said, 'All my worldly possessions!'[30]

It was through Fisher's letters to his wife that he first revealed his intense religiosity. After discovering religion during his first tour in the China Sea, his letters were filled with frequent references to church attendances, sermons and bible readings. Early allusions were mild, but Fisher's religious obsessions began to grow, so much so that he apologised in one letter to Kitty, telling her that 'I am afraid you will soon begin to think that my letters are principally copies out of the Bible and that I ought to tell you more about myself.'[31]

One expression of his religion was through his support for charitable causes. He suggested to Kitty that they should donate five per cent of his pay to charity and should 'note down what we give away'.[32] If the total fell short of five per cent, he would make up the amount at the end of the year. Thirty years later Lady Fisher was still meticulously recording charitable giving in her household accounts book, noting, for example, that she donated three guineas to the Mission to Deep Sea Fishermen and 15s 0d to the local Free School. In all, she had paid out £75 10s 0d (about £5,500 today) in the year.[33]

Reform was in Fisher's blood. For him, every naval procedure could be improved, every piece of equipment could be redesigned, every ship could be made to go faster. When too junior to initiate reforms, he wrote paper after paper setting out his ideas on topics from the electrical detonation of mines to how to sail a ship through a cyclone and putting out fires on board ships.[34-36] Initially these papers seem to have been mere exercises

11

for his own development, but in 1871 he found the courage to send his latest work on naval tactics to the Admiralty. In it, he advocated getting rid of masts and sails – a revolutionary suggestion for the time. The Admiralty approved and the paper was printed and circulated.

His last ship of this period was the *Northampton* on the North America station – the quietest in the Fleet. It was a period notable for one event only, but most distressing for Fisher. The ship received a message from the Admiralty asking her to search for the missing training ship HMS *Atlanta*. 'I regret to say,' Fisher told a friend, 'my young brother is on board her.'[37] He hoped that the *Atlanta* was simply dismasted, but no trace of her or her crew was ever found: Philip and all his fellow seamen had drowned.

As the first phase of Fisher's career came to a close, he had demonstrated an extraordinary capacity for mastering every task he was given. Able, ambitious and focused, his superiors took every opportunity to promote this exceptional talent. The next promotion would find him working side by side with Commander Lord Charles Beresford. They were to meet at Alexandria, where the Mediterranean Fleet had been called to suppress an Arab uprising against the British-supported Egyptian Government. Fisher was to command the Fleet's latest battleship, whilst Beresford would command a humble gunboat. Yet it was not on the decks of their two ships that they were to come together, but on land, two days after the naval attack. There, on that hostile soil, they would labour side by side to triumphantly crush the rebellion and calm the city, an act that would lead to mutual admiration and a bond of friendship, which would last until the early years of the next century.

## Scene 2: From Curraghmore to half-pay

Charles William de la Poer Beresford was born, five years after Fisher, on 10 February 1846, to Christiana and John de la Poer Beresford at Philipstown House, Dundalk in Ireland. Beresford's father was a clergyman, but hardly an average parish priest. He was descended from a long line of Irish nobles and was heir to the Marquessate of Waterford, together with the magnificent eighteenth-century Curraghmore House and an impressive 8,000 acre estate. Within the house, the walls of the corridors and principal rooms proudly displayed the family's 700 years' of residence, with the works of Gainsborough and Reynolds glorifying the family's impeccable lineage of landowners, generals, admirals, and archbishops.[38]

When John and Christiana admired their newborn second son, they would have only been troubled by the multiplicity of options that lay ahead as he followed family traditions. Would he be an archbishop? Or perhaps an admiral? Or what about a general? Or maybe he would marry into yet another great family and acquire yet more lands and houses.

If, on the other hand, a soothsayer had leant over the cradle and said 'Beware, your boy will ruin himself in a feud with the son of a minor army captain' they would surely have dismissed the seer with aristocratic disdain.

Beresford enjoyed an idyllic early childhood on the Curraghmore estate where he acquired his lifelong passion for reckless outdoor pursuits, ever heedless of cuts, bruises and broken bones. In his youth he broke his chestbone and had to have a piece cut out, 'leaving a cavity', he said. Later in life he went on to break his pelvis, his right leg, right hand and foot, to which he added five ribs, his collar bone (three times) and his nose, also three times.[39] On the estate, there was riding six days a week in winter and up to 100 horses in the stables. Destined to be a sailor, the saddle was to remain a favourite berth to the end of his days.

Beresford's daydream ended with schooling at Bayford House in Hertfordshire, but after two years' attendance he was removed on the grounds of weak health, being sent to a tutor at Deal. His health problems soon vanished and he was to enjoy a lifetime of robust fitness, subjecting his body to strains that only the toughest physique could survive. It was at his Hertfordshire school that he initiated his lifelong career of insubordination, a fellow pupil recalling that 'a more unruly young gentleman never defied the schoolmaster's birch'.[40] This was not surprising given that his uncle, the third Marquess, Henry de la Poer Beresford had been 'notorious for his wildness' when a pupil at Eton College.[41]

While Beresford was still preparing for his naval career, Uncle Henry died and Beresford's father became the fourth Marquess. His son could now take up his courtesy title of Lord Charles Beresford, a designation that he would exploit to the full for the next fifty years. The family's inheritance did not, though, result in largesse for Charles, since the new Marquess believed in teaching his children to manage money, keeping them on very small allowances.

Money, though, never worried Beresford. He was spontaneously generous, whether lending money to those who might never repay him or thrusting coins into the palms of the needy and destitute. Equally, he would splash out on his own account, heedless of his capacity to pay. Aged seventeen, with an allowance of just £80 a year from his father he was soon in debt, a state that angered the Marquess who warned him that he would not pay his debts. Should there be further incidents of this type he would 'be dishonoured' and have to leave the Navy.[42] Beresford found early release from this harsh financial regime when he inherited some farm estates in 1866. In due course, his personal wealth gave him the power to defy all comers. He would be able to afford to resign commissions rather than bow to commands and could hint at legal retribution against any who thwarted his will.

Beresford's choice of the Navy as a career needed no explanation, with both an admiral and a vice admiral among his recent ancestors. So, in December 1859, he passed into the service, having been nominated by a relative, Commodore Charles Eden, who was Comptroller-General of the Coastguard. This was not before he had been sent to a crammer to rectify the deficiencies in his education. Despite all this preparation, he still managed to spell his name incorrectly when signing his qualifying certificate. When asked whether he always spelt William with one 'l', he quipped, 'Only sometimes, Sir' – an early example of his flair for repartee masking his lack of intellect.[43] On entering the Navy, Beresford was one of the first recruits to benefit from the then new two-year shore-based training in HMS *Britannia*, moored in the River Dart in Devon.[44] (Fisher had been amongst the last of the boys who were sent straight to sea on entering the Navy.)

Whilst serving on the *Britannia*, Beresford was promoted to the rank of cadet captain – something akin to school captain – but succeeded in losing the rank on the same day.[45] From then on, he was to show a disconcerting tendency to thwart authority and to ignore regulations whenever he found them inconvenient.

After the *Britannia*, he was appointed to the *Marlborough*, the Mediterranean flagship. It was not long before he disgraced himself in the eyes of the ship's officers. At that time, sail-drill competitions between ships were common, and speed was what mattered. Before one particular competition had begun, Beresford had secretly prepared one of the sails, so reducing the time needed for the drill. His underhand action was discovered and he was 'severely reprimanded' for 'staining the character of a ship', being disrated to cadet. Although he was reinstated the next day, the event added to the growing number of reprimands that he received.[46]

His service on the *Marlborough* was followed by a posting to the *Defence*, which he hated so much ('a slovenly, unhandy tin kettle') that he asked his father to remove him from the Navy.[47] In 1864 he was transferred to the *Clio*, a 22-gun ship of 1,472 tons, which took him to the Falkland Islands, Cape Horn, Honolulu and Vancouver.

During this time Beresford proved to be a good sailor, receiving a special commendation on his certificate of promotion to acting sublieutenant in January 1866.[48] It recorded that he had conducted himself 'with sobriety, diligence, attention, and was always obedient to command'.[49] It was perhaps the last occasion when anyone would connect the name Beresford with obedience. It was not in his nature.

Beresford's next significant appointment was as a lieutenant under Prince Albert, Duke of Edinburgh on the *Galatea*. With the Duke, Beresford visited the Cape, Australia and New Zealand, as well as the Far East and India. This was followed by over a year of half-pay and then an appointment as Flag Lieutenant at Plymouth in 1872 and, in 1873, his first command in a gunboat called the *Goshawk*.

Within a year of his promotion to lieutenant, Beresford was to make a move that was to shape the rest of his life: he went into politics. It was an astounding decision. At twenty-eight years old, when he should have been devoting himself to his career and moving through a range of posts to gain experience, he chose to become the member for Waterford. From being a (reasonably) compliant naval officer, he plunged himself into a lifelong conflict of interest between Beresford, the dutiful servant of the Board, and Beresford the Member of Parliament. Ignoring this conflict, he would from now on expect to step off his ship, bow deferentially to their Lordships and proceed to the House of Commons where he would abuse them and their works. His diatribes concluded, he assumed that their Lordships would welcome him back as if nothing had happened.

In a sense though, his move was a wise step, given his mercurial personality. In future, whenever things became too difficult in politics, he simply slipped back to sea. When, at sea, life became too rough or boring, back he would retreat to the soft green leather of the Commons' benches. He was a man with dual bolt-holes and, as he slithered between them, he endlessly evaded the hand of any authority that sought to control him. Not until 1909 would the Board's tolerance snap and Beresford would, metaphorically, be asked to walk the plank.

In his memoirs, he admitted that being an MP and 'on full pay and on active service ... was not in itself conducive to discipline' but he excused himself on the grounds that he did not think that he had 'abused' his position.[50] It was yet another example of his view that the rules were there to be obeyed, except in his own case.

In the story of the feud, Beresford's predilection for erratic and insubordinate behaviour was to play a major part. He had an irrepressible, ebullient and mischievous personality. In his youth this expressed itself in (relatively) harmless pranks; as he matured, it manifested itself in ways that occupied increasing amounts of the Board's time.

From an early age, Beresford seemed determined to outdo his late uncle Henry who was known as wild at Eton and was asked to leave Christ Church College, Oxford. Henry was frequently fined in magistrates' courts following events such as painting 'the Melton Mowbray toll-bar red' and hunting a parson with dogs.[51] Following in this vein, when the young Beresford and his friends were careering round in a cab, shooting peas out of the window, he had the misfortune to hit a woman in the face and landed himself in court the next day, where he was fined £2 10s (about

15

£165 today) plus costs. Left unable to pay his mess bill, Beresford wrote a begging letter to his father. In reply the Marquess expressed his disapproval of Beresford's money-management and his chagrin at the family name being brought 'before the public'.[52]

On another occasion Beresford was sitting at his sewing bench (sailors made their own clothes in those days) when a sailor knocked it over. He recalled that 'I took up the first thing which was handy, which happened to be a carpenter's chisel, and hurled it at the retreating figure.' The blow could well have been mortal, but Beresford was lucky since, as he said, 'It stuck and quivered in a portion of his anatomy which is (or was) considered by schoolmasters as designed to receive punishment.'[53]

Later, in 1867, Beresford and some friends came across a station porter 'whose hair was of an immoderate luxuriance'. Deciding, said Beresford, that the man had no right to such an abundance of locks – being 'neither poet, nor musician' – they lashed him to a railway truck and forcibly cut his hair.[54] It was an act of common assault, yet Beresford still felt able to recount it with pride in his memoirs.

On yet another occasion, returning to Plymouth late one night and perhaps thinking of Uncle Henry and the Melton Mowbray toll-bar, he and a fellow officer found a locked turnpike gate. They attempted to raise the keeper, but on failing to do so, broke a window of his house. Still the keeper kept to his bed. Undeterred, they detached the gate and took it back to Plymouth where they chopped it up for firewood before its presence could be discovered.[55]

Beresford could cause just as much trouble with his pen. He managed to upset the Admiralty with his very first letter to the press. Hearing, in January 1879, that a 38-ton gun had exploded on the *Thunderer*, killing eleven men, he dashed off a letter to *The Times*, giving his own explanation as to the cause of the accident. When the enquiry published its report, his reasoning was shown to be fallacious and the Board vented its anger at his impudence.[56] This would be by no means his last insubordinate letter to the press – one of his most notorious newspaper letters forms Act 4 of our story.

In 1875 Beresford was selected as an *aide-de-camp* to accompany the Prince of Wales on a visit to India, so beginning a very important relationship.[57] Beresford quickly made his mark with the Prince who, on the tedious voyage out recorded, 'Charlie Beresford kept up our spirits when they flagged.'[58] His was not an onerous task, mostly involving helping the Prince to shoot all the wildlife they came across, but at night Beresford had to take his turn in sitting outside the Prince's tent or bedroom, armed with a pair of pistols to repel attempts on the royal life.[59] The Prince could not have had a better bodyguard, since the one quality that Beresford

16

possessed in abundance was physical courage. (He twice received medals for rescuing drowning men.)

For some men, marriage marks a switch from youth to maturity following the restraining influence of a wife. In Beresford's case, he married a woman who was to stimulate him from one excess to another and be generally regarded as a bad influence on him. Ellen Jeromina, daughter of Richard Gardner, MP, became his wife in 1878 and they set up home at the highly fashionable address of 100 Eaton Square in Belgravia. There were to be two daughters – but no son. Throughout their married life the Beresfords remained townspeople, never possessing a country home, although frequently being weekend guests in the shires. Ellen was always 'Dot' to Charles and 'Mina' to her friends. They made an interesting, if not notorious couple, both having dynamic personalities; Beresford's forceful presence and Mina's excessive make-up earning them the joint sobriquet of 'the red admiral and the painted lady' or, less politely, 'the windbag and the ragbag'.[60] Rarely have half a dozen words so appositely described the fallibility of two personalities. Much harsher terms, though, would be in use when the feud reached its peak in 1908–9.

Meanwhile, as a Member of Parliament, life went smoothly enough for four years, with a short period at HMS *Vernon* for torpedo training and then command of the *Thunderer* in the Channel Squadron.[61] Then, without warning, the appointments dried up. The Admiralty were in a huff as a result of Beresford's antics in the House of Commons where he had heavily criticised the Navy. What he had said was prescient, warning the House of the serious threat that torpedoes offered to naval vessels. However, the Board took offence at his mode of expression, when he accused them of 'want of adequate organisation' and his suggestion that his speech would strengthen 'the hands of the First Lord'.[62] He was bluntly told that he had to choose between the Navy and Parliament. In a classic Beresford response, rather than accept the rebuke, he accused the Board of breach of privilege, that is, of illegally restraining an MP in the execution of his duty. Technically he was right, but the Board gave way grudgingly, ensuring that he was kept on half-pay (out of work) for five years.[63] His protector, the Prince of Wales, came to his rescue, by offering him the command of the Royal Yacht. Since the yacht only left harbour for a few days a year, this left Beresford free to live in London and pursue his political career, whilst drawing half-pay.

It seemed, then, in 1878, that Beresford's naval career was over. He was better known as a member of the dashing Marlborough House set that surrounded the Prince of Wales than as a serious naval commander. His surprise recall to service in the *Condor* in 1882 was to open a new phase in

17

his life; there were now to be two years of unadulterated glory for this wayward naval officer.

## Scene 3: Chalk and cheese

On the eve of the bombardment of Alexandria the personalities of Fisher (aged forty-one) and Beresford (aged thirty-six) were firmly set. Both were fanatically dedicated to the Navy as Britain's sole means of defending its shores and its Empire, yet they were each to approach that task in their own way. From now on, their differences were to be as important as their similarities. Whilst it would be wrong to see the feud as being the inevitable product of these differences, nevertheless they were to exacerbate the tensions that the feud threw up. Four factors in particular played a significant part in how the feud developed: money, attitude to authority, politics, and the battle between aristocracy and meritocracy.

Money would always separate the two men. Fisher, the meritocrat, had only his salary to support his wife and four children: Cecil, Beatrix, Dorothy and Pamela. His great fear was to be put on half-pay – a common enough experience since the Navy had a considerable surplus of officers at that time. Beresford, on the other hand, was well-off and, from 1906, rich. He could afford to snub the Board because he could afford to live without his pay. This allowed him to plunge at will from command at sea to agitation at home and to provocation on the back benches. His wealth was his carapace. Fisher was the one who, metaphorically, scanned the jobs' columns of the newspapers.

Fisher's reliance on his position and pay reinforced his tendency to toe the line. No stranger to (sometimes violent) disagreements with his superiors, he pulled back at the point where strong representations might have spilled over into insubordination. Beresford showed no such restraint and he boasted that he had received more reprimands than any other officer. Whilst there are no statistics to confirm this, his claim may well be true; it is possible to identify around twenty-three reprimands and demotions (see Appendix) and there will have been many more that are no longer traceable. For a less well-connected officer, reprimands such as these would have brought dismissal. But not for Lord Charles Beresford.

Politics, also, distinguished the two men. Fisher never seriously contemplated a parliamentary career, partly because he could not afford it (MPs were unpaid until 1911) and partly because he despised the political breed. More fundamentally, Fisher could not imagine life without the Navy. Even repeated job offers at £10,000 to £20,000 a year from shipbuilding companies failed to detach him from naval posts paying a mere £2,000 to £4,000. For him, the Navy was an addiction. When at the Admiralty in the early 1900s he would wake around 4.00 am, his brain seething with plans, reforms and projects for the day. He was often at his desk at 5.00 am, dashing off letters and minutes to colleagues still abed, fired by the adrenalin rush of protecting the Empire. He even worked on Sundays and Christmas Days, simply because he could not stop himself. He just had no time for politics.

On the other hand, Beresford revelled in his political role, whether stomping the hustings, pontificating on the back benches, writing to the press or haranguing huge public meetings. As one officer noted in 1906, 'He does love getting up on his legs and talking.'[64] Whilst the House was often ambivalent in its attitude towards him, he was the darling of the public and, as the years went by, drew ever larger crowds wherever he went.

None of this would have mattered had Beresford given up the Navy. As a knowledgeable seaman, he was an asset to public debate, but his desire to be *both* a political force *and* a naval officer created endless difficulties. Even when at sea and out of Parliament, the Admiralty would daily cower under the fear that he might return to the House to take his revenge on the Board should they seek to constrain him.

Perhaps more than anything else the difference in class between the two men was the fundamental driver of the feud. By tradition, a high proportion of naval officers came from wealthy and aristocratic families. This tendency was partly a snobbish prejudice against middle-class families (there would never have been any question of a working-class cadet) and partly that entry had been by nomination when Fisher joined the Navy. All this was reinforced by the low pay of junior officers – a pay that assumed the recipient also had a private income. The Fishers of this world were unlikely recruits to the Navy.

The practical effect of this prejudice has been described in a much-repeated story of Vice Admiral Sir Reginald Bacon, Fisher's first biographer, recalling how one officer reacted in 1903 to Fisher's plan to unite engineer and officer training. The engineer officer bragged to the ship's first lieutenant that he ranked above him on shore, to which the lieutenant replied: 'I don't care a damn whether you walk in to dinner before me or after me; but all I know, Brown, is that my Ma will never ask your Ma to tea!'[65] The truth embedded in this story is underlined by the certainty that, not for one moment, would the Marchioness of Waterford have considered inviting Mrs William Fisher to tea, even if they had not been separated by several thousand miles of ocean.

In the feud, the fact that Beresford was both rich and an aristocrat was decisive in two ways. First, he could never accept Fisher as his social equal. Privately, he would describe him as 'not a gentleman', as if this invalidated every move that Fisher ever made. Second, and most importantly, successive First Lords and Cabinets shrank from tackling the Beresford problem. As we will see, Beresford repeatedly defied Boards, ignored regulations and, at one stage, defied the House of Commons. There can be no other explanation of the failure of the authorities to act, other than their deference to his aristocratic position and his popularity with the public. As King Edward VII was to note, when faced with Beresford, the Cabinet were 'cowards'.

These two men, with so little in common, were to meet at last and share the lead roles in a drama that Gladstone's Government had struggled to keep off the stage: Egypt. In 1882, the Prime Minister, ever reluctant to become involved in imperial tangles, was forced to act over a rebellious Arab politician. As he ordered the Mediterranean Fleet into action, with it went Beresford and Fisher, as yet barely known to each other and still without major reputations in the Navy. In a few dramatic weeks they were to take centre stage and, shoulder-to-shoulder, show their country that, in these two young officers, there were two diverse, but remarkable talents. Out of the ashes of smouldering Alexandria would come military glory, a firm friendship and a potent mutual respect.

*Act 2*

# Giants into Action

You have always acted all your life (like an Irishman would)
on the impulse of the moment. – *Prince of Wales to Beresford.*[1]

No one knows better than I do what you have done for the
service and the Country. – *Admiral Sir Anthony Hopkins
to Fisher.*[2]

## Scene 1: Beresford's disobedient pen

For a number of years, trouble had been developing in Egypt, largely
arising from its poor government, under the control of the Khedive, Ismail
Pasha, and its mounting debts. Friction between the Egyptians on the one
hand and the French and British on the other, culminated in two mutinies
in 1881 followed, in May 1882, by the Egyptian Minister of War, Arabi
Pasha, declaring himself dictator in a power struggle with the Khedive. He
failed to comply with terms set by the British and French to resolve the
dispute and began to strengthen the fortifications at the port of Alexandria.
It was a hostile act that the European powers could not overlook. It was
effectively a declaration of war.[3]

There was no initial reaction to the occupation from Whitehall, so
Beresford began a campaign to persuade journalists to put pressure on the
Government. Writing to Thomas Bowles from Alexandria he described
how Arabi Pasha was stirring up hate against the British-supported
Khedive, who was telling the Egyptians that 'Egypt will never prosper as
long as she is ruled by a Turk.' Beresford, on the other hand, thought that
the loss of the Khedive 'would be disastrous for Egypt'; he was incensed
that all that the British and French governments had done was to send 'one
small ironclad and two small gunboats each', which he thought was a
supine response.[4]

Whilst his letters to journalists were not intended for publication,
Beresford knew that he was flouting naval regulations by supplying news
to journalists. He appealed to one of his correspondents to keep his name
out of the paper, saying 'you know how particular I am to do everything
strictly according to the Service'.[5] Never one to keep his mouth shut, he

21

bragged to the Prince of Wales about his journalistic antics and passed him copies of the letters. In turn, the Prince passed them to the Foreign Secretary, Lord Granville. Noting that Beresford had admitted to the Prince that he had infringed the regulations, Granville asked the Prince 'to let Lord Charles Beresford know of your disapprobation of the thing itself and of his having informed Your Royal Highness of it'.[6] In turn Granville informed the Admiralty about the episode, whereupon the First Lord ordered Beresford's arrest, intending to court-martial him.[7]

The Prince was stunned by Granville's failure to respect his confidence over the letters, which he had only sent in order that the Government should be better informed about the situation in Egypt. He had not for one moment suspected that action would be taken against his *protégé*. Rising to defend him, the Prince pleaded with Granville to forget the episode 'in justice to the great friendship and regard I feel for Beresford'. He went on to admit that 'He is an Irishman, and in consequence hasty and impetuous, but I feel sure that the Queen does not possess a more zealous and loyal officer than he is.'[8] Beresford escaped his court martial.

And so, as the Government slowly limbered into action over Arabi Pasha's insurrection, Beresford's career lay under a shadow. His courage and daring in the fire and smoke of the imminent bombardment were to overturn his ignominy and leave him a public hero.

## Scene 2: Alexandria, July 1882

At the time of the Egyptian crisis, Fisher was captain of the Navy's newest battleship – the *Inflexible*. He marvelled at his luck, calling it, 'the greatest ship in the world' whereas he was the 'youngest captain in the Navy'.[9] Beresford, junior to Fisher, was in command of a small gunboat, the *Condor*.

The *Inflexible* was special, being a trial ground for the Navy's new technology. She was packed with every novelty going from electric light (the first ever in a ship), submerged torpedo tubes, experimental torpedo launchers, ballast tanks (which were a failure), searchlights and the Thompson compass – a new device, championed by Fisher but resisted by the Admiralty.[10] Fisher's own description of the ship captures some of the excitement that he felt when she first sailed from Portsmouth under his command:

> The *Inflexible* in 1882 was a wonder. She had the thickest armour, the biggest guns, and the largest of everything beyond any ship in the world. A man could crawl up inside the bore of one of her guns ... Endless inventions were on board ...[11]

He also enjoyed the 'whistles in my cabin that yelled when the boiler was going to burst, or the ship was not properly steered, and so on'.[12]

In June, the Mediterranean Fleet concentrated at Alexandria, the French having decided to opt out of military action. Nothing much happened for a while and what little there was seemed rather pointless to Fisher, as he told his wife:

> We appear to be playing a most ridiculous part here. Last night a gunboat came out ordering us to go five miles further in ... What the good of that five miles was no one can make out, as we were equally out of sight of the Alexandrians. Then at 7.00 am we were ordered to go out again five miles, as things were more peaceable, we suppose![13]

Eventually, on 10 July, the Commander-in-Chief, Admiral Sir Frederick Seymour, issued an ultimatum: unless the Egyptians stopped work on their defences, hostilities would commence the next day.[14] Arabi Pasha seems to have sent a 'conciliatory' reply but, according to George Clarke, who later wrote a post-mortem of the battle, the bearer 'spent a great part of the night trying to find the flagship' and in consequence 'it was rejected as being too late'.[15]

The fighting began at 7.00 am on 11 July when the mighty weapons of the Mediterranean Fleet, including the gigantic eighty-ton guns of Fisher's *Inflexible*, poured their shells onto the Alexandrian fortifications. The Egyptians fought back with vigour, despite the intense bombardment, aided by the high proportion of British shells that failed to explode on

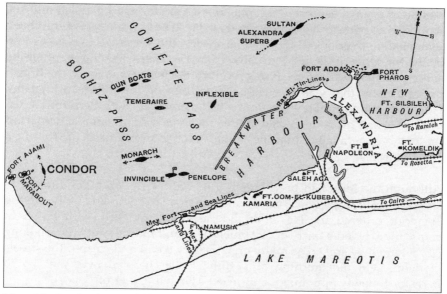

Map of the bombardment of Alexandria. The *Condor* (Beresford) and *Inflexible* (Fisher) can be clearly seen.

impact. However, the British guns made steady progress. An Egyptian magazine blew up at 8.30 am. By 10.30 am Fisher had succeeded in destroying the Mex forts and the *Inflexible* steamed off to attack the positions at Pharos and Ada.[16] Another magazine went up at 2.00 pm and so it went on throughout the day. At 5.30 pm the signal was given to cease firing.

During the day, the *Condor* had distinguished herself, in part due to Beresford's insubordination.[17] Being a small vessel she had orders to keep out of the range of the powerful Alexandrian guns. However, Beresford did not relish the idea of standing by while the bigger ships had all the fun, so he told his men, 'Now my lads, if you will rely on me to find the opportunity, I will rely on you to make the most of it when it occurs.'[18] He did not have to wait long. Shortly after the bombardment started, the *Téméraire* parted from her cable and drifted ashore. Beresford moved in to pull the ship clear and, while doing so, came under fire from one of the Arab forts. As he recalled, the *Condor* 'steamed down at full speed and engaged Fort Marabout', despite the prohibition on exposing his tiny vessel in this way.[19] Admiral Seymour looked on in horror, expecting the *Condor* to turn to matchwood under his gaze. Yet, to the stupefaction of the onlookers, the *Condor* put all the batteries in the fort out of action, earning Beresford and the crew the open signal of, 'Well done, *Condor*.'[20] For the rest of his life, when Beresford arrived at public meetings he would be greeted with shouts of 'Well done, *Condor*.'

At the end of the day, British losses were five dead and twenty-eight wounded against estimated Egyptian losses of perhaps 150 killed and 400 wounded.[21] Beresford's action on that day would almost certainly have remained an overlooked footnote of history, but for one thing: he had on board Mr Moberly Bell, a journalist from *The Times*. Inevitably, of all the actions at Alexandria, Beresford's received the most coverage in the British press, a point that was to weigh against him on his return to England. However, the fortunate presence of Bell, combined with Beresford's disobedience and his courage had made him an overnight national hero. Had the battle gone against him, he would have found himself in front of a court martial.

Although the forts had been largely silenced, many Egyptian guns were still capable of firing and Arabi Pasha remained in command of the city, so Seymour ordered the Naval Brigade ashore on 13 July with Fisher in command. He led a party of 600 bluejackets and marines into the smoking city where they spiked as many guns as they could and cleared the streets of debris. On the morning of 14 July, Fisher handed over the city to Beresford, newly appointed as Provost Marshal (Chief of Police).[22]

Fisher and Beresford faced a perilous few days before the Army could arrive to take over. Until then, the marines were all that stood between holding the city and being pushed back into the sea. In those hazardous days, Fisher, along with Captain Wilson (who later, as Admiral of the Fleet Sir Arthur Knyvet Wilson, VC would be deselected from the enquiry), created the world's first armoured train, mounted with a large gun, which could be readily moved from one place to another, the men being protected by steel plates bolted to the sides of the trucks. The train soon became a sort of tourist attraction, visited by every journalist and officer in the vicinity. By 7 August *The Times* reported its actions in one and a half columns of dense text.[23] Indeed, it had become so important that, once the Army arrived, the generals kept it fully employed. On one occasion Fisher and Wilson built a bridge across a canal 68 feet wide and took the gun across – the General 'was very grateful'.[24] (A curious fact about these few days in Alexandria is that the three main naval players on land – Fisher, Beresford and Wilson – were all to play key roles in the Cabinet enquiry twenty-seven years later. Two as antagonists, and one as a reluctant witness and part adjudicator.)

Meanwhile, Beresford, using his powers as Provost Marshal, vigorously suppressed the rioting, looting and pillage that was everywhere in the city. By 19 July, he wrote, 'I had perfect order in the town' and two days later he had extinguished the fires and buried the corpses.[25] Calm and order finally reigned, partly as a result of Beresford's ruthless methods, which were witnessed by a young army officer, who noted in his diary on 18 July that 'Beresford ... has shot and flogged about 50 or 60 Arab looters.' The next day he recorded that 'Beresford has been shooting about a dozen Arabs a day for looting and murder.'[26] One of the local British traders later commented that 'Lord Charles Beresford saved millions' worth of property, causing the indemnity paid by the European Government [for damage to the city] to be much less than it would otherwise have been.'[27] It was a masterly piece of organisation, improvised in a dire emergency.

On 19 August the *Daily News* announced that 'Captain FISHER, of the Inflexible, was badly wounded on Saturday.'[28] The story was without foundation but Fisher benefitted from royal sympathy when Victoria telegraphed for news of him.[29] Such attention would do him no harm.

Beresford returned home a hero, although he received no decoration for his actions. Instead the Prince of Wales warned him that the huge publicity that he had had in the papers was 'resented in some influential quarters'.[30]

Fisher arrived back in a lower key. In the midst of the fighting, he had contracted dysentery, which at one stage looked as if it would prove fatal. As he later said, the *Inflexible* 'brought me to death's door'.[31] He had no choice but to give up his command which, he said, was 'a bitter business'.[32] It was to be months before he could think of returning to work and years before he found a final cure for his condition.

25

## Scene 3: The Sudan, 1884–5

As if 'Well done, *Condor*!' was not enough, Beresford quickly followed up his triumph with another, greater escapade which was once again to capture the public's imagination and so add one more figure to the pantheon of Victorian heroes. Alexandria and the Sudan were to provide him with a public following that rivalled that of the overnight celebrities of today. Beresford's fame, though, would last; twenty years later, still undimmed, it would render him near to untouchable by both the Admiralty and the Government.

Shortly after returning home from Alexandria, Beresford was once more writing to the newspapers, criticising the Government's policy on Egypt. The Prince of Wales thought this unwise, writing, 'Take my advice, Charlie, and leave Egyptian affairs alone.'[33] It was not to be. Before long Beresford was drawn back to Egypt with a vengeance.

Following the restoration of order in Alexandria by Fisher and Beresford, the British Army had landed and given battle at Tel-el-Kebir, routing the Arab forces. The brief period of calm that followed the combats of 1882 was broken by a rebellion in the Sudan, led by the Mahdi. In response, the British Government despatched Colonel Hicks William (known as Hicks Pasha) with a force of 10,000 men. He was to march to Khartoum and restore British ascendancy in the region. Beresford applied to join the force, but Lord Dufferin, the Government's Special Commissioner in Egypt, blocked his participation which he deemed to be a 'hazardous enterprise'.[34] Had Beresford not been compelled to accept that advice, he too would have perished in the deserts of the Sudan on 5 December 1883 along with all the rest of Hicks' force.

In the following year, General Gordon was despatched to Khartoum with instructions to evacuate its garrison. On arrival, rather than evacuation, he chose to dig in, planning to hold out against the Dervishes. By August 1884, it was clear that Gordon was trapped, so yet another expedition was to make the long trek up the Nile. Once more, Beresford put his name forward and this time he was accepted, being attached to General Wolseley's staff to take charge of the huge convoy of boats that was to go up the Nile. The rescue force arrived in the rubble-strewn but now peaceful streets of Alexandria on 9 September 1884. Beresford was about to experience what his biographer has called 'the golden moment in his eventful life'.[35]

The details of the long chain of events that resulted in a token relief force arriving in Khartoum two days after Gordon's assassination need not concern us here, but Beresford's actions more than merit our attention since they so illuminate the complexity of his character. His courage would mingle with his insubordination and recklessness to raise him to heroic heights but, in the process, to reveal his utter incapacity to work under any other commander. Born to lead, he could not be led.

From Alexandria to Khartoum is over 1,000 miles. For much of the journey the Nile is easily navigable and so it was the natural route to follow when the alternative was to march with camels across searing deserts and rocky wastelands. However, the upper stretches of the river contain treacherous cataracts which, in the dry season, are not passable by larger boats. Beresford's role was to assist the expedition in making its way up the Nile, cataracts or no cataracts. Under his direction, nearly 700 small boats, specially constructed in England, began their move upstream. All went well until the second cataract was reached. Wolseley took one look at the low water and declared that the boats would never get through, to which Beresford responded that 'nothing was impossible until it was proved to be impossible'.[36] By 27 November, he had taken 687 boats through or round the cataract. Of these, 166 had been pulled through using an ingenious system of ropes, pulleys, fixed rocks and 4,000 natives. The rest were carried by teams of men along the bank.[37,38] All this was achieved with the loss of just four boats and twenty-seven men.[39] It was, he said, 'unflagging physical work from daybreak till sunset'.[40]

Having rescued the whole expedition from early failure, a doubtless ebullient Beresford was about to disgrace himself in an act which so nearly brought disaster to the whole force.

At Korti there is a huge arc in the Nile with two more sets of cataracts. The shortest route to Khartoum (176 miles) is to cut south-east across the desert to rejoin the Nile at Metemmeh.[41] On 30 December the massive column began the march across the burning, near-waterless desert.

Eighteen days later, at 10.00 am on 17 January 1885, the bugles sounded in the Sudan desert at Abu Klea: Wolseley's force was face-to-face with 10,000 Dervishes, ready to give battle.[42] Quietly the men formed into a hollow square and began the slow, funereal march towards the enemy. Amongst the soldiers was Beresford with his handful of marines and his precious Gardner gun (an early form of machine gun), which he was determined to prove in action.

As long as the square held, it was near to impregnable; if it broke, its defensive power vanished in a moment since the Dervishes could then enter its hollow core and fire at the backs of the outward-facing soldiers. At some point in the advance, a gap opened in the square, perhaps because the baggage camels in the centre were struggling on the stony ground, perhaps because that section of the square included cavalry men (on foot) and marines, neither group having been trained in keeping formation. It was the absolute duty of all those near the gap to fill it without delay. Yet Beresford, oblivious to the mortal threat posed by the breach, rushed out

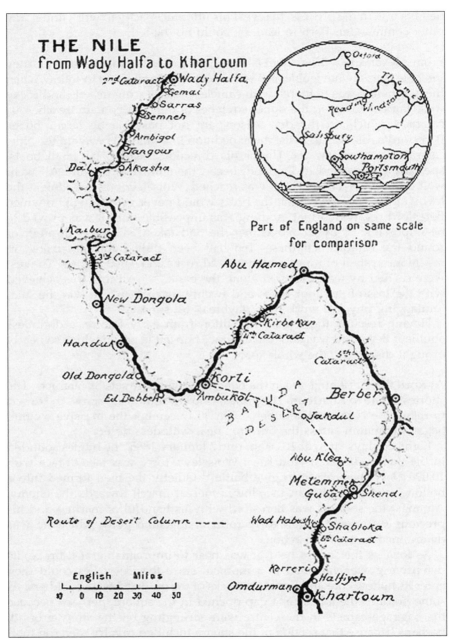

THE NILE
from Wady Halfa to Khartoum

2nd Cataract — Wady Halfa.
Gemai
Sarras
Semneh
Ambigol
Tangour
Dal — Akasha

Kaibur

3rd Cataract

New Dongola

Handuk

Old Dongola
Ed Debbeh — Ambukol — Korti

Abu Hamed

Kirbekan
4th Cataract

5th Cataract

Berber

BAYUDA DESERT

Jakdul

Abu Klea

Metemmeh
Gubat — Shendi

Route of Desert Column ----     Wad Habashi — Shabloka
6th Cataract

Kerreri
Halfiyeh
Omdurman — Khartoum

English  Miles
10  0  10  20  30  40  50

Part of England on same scale
for comparison

Oxford
Thames
Reading — Windsor
Salisbury
Southampton
Portsmouth

Beresford's map of the Sudan campaign showing the route up the Nile and across the desert. Abu Klea, the scene of Beresford's disgrace, can be seen. His triumph in the *El Safieh* took place a few miles from Khartoum.

28

from the broken square with his prized gun and began to pour fire into the approaching Arabs. At first the Arabs fell 'like ninepins' but in no time at all, they were almost upon the marines – and the gun jammed. Nothing now stood between Beresford's seamen and the rapidly approaching enemy. Within minutes, all seven of his marines had been viciously hacked to death. Somehow, Beresford survived, although with a seriously cut hand after deflecting a spear as it was thrust towards him.[43]

Sixty-eight men had been killed in the gap.[44] Beresford was not responsible for the breach, but he had been wilfully negligent in failing to attempt to close it. How many deaths could have been saved had he acted responsibly is impossible to tell. It can hardly be held to be an heroic moment in his life, but the poet Sir Henry Newbolt made it so in the second verse of his famous poem *Vitai Lampada* when he wrote:

The sand of the desert is sodden red,
Red with the wreck of a square that broke;
The Gatling's jammed and the Colonel dead ...[45]


Beresford was to redeem himself though and, for a second time, save the whole expedition. Towards the end of January it was clear that the column was not going to reach Khartoum in time to rescue Gordon, so a small force was sent ahead under Lieutenant Colonel Charles Wilson,[46] who replaced the seriously injured colonel. Once more, Beresford applied to join; once more he was refused, this time on the grounds of ill-health since he was suffering from a large boil on his behind and could neither sit, nor walk more than a few steps. It was a decision that saved the expedition since it was to fall to him to rescue the rescue party.[47]

On 1 February news arrived of the disaster that had overtaken Wilson's force as they attempted to return from the outskirts of the already sacked Khartoum. Their boats were wrecked and the remnants of the party were marooned on the banks of the Nile about 35 miles south of Beresford's position. All that Beresford had under his command was thirty men and the *El Safieh*[48] which was, he said, no more than 'a penny steamer in a packing case'.[49] (That is, a Thames ferry boat encased in an improvised timber casing to turn it into a gunboat.) Later that same day, the tiny boat set off to fight its way south to reach Wilson's stranded party.

Two days later, moving at a graceful 2½ miles per hour, the *El Safieh* soon found itself level with the Arab guns at Wad Habeshi at 7.00 am on 3 February. With nothing else to occupy their attention, the Arabs poured fire into the tiny vessel, which vigorously responded. This went on for hours without any serious consequences, but later in the day, the ship's boiler was hit, making a sizeable hole. Now Beresford, too, was stranded, facing 3,000 armed Dervishes on the riverbank. At this point, Chief Engineer Henry Benbow stepped in and set to work to make a plate to bolt on over the hole in the boiler. It was a long task, carried out in the searing heat of the ship's hold and under the deadly fire of the Arab guns. By 10.00 pm on 3 February the boiler was repaired but, before relighting the fire, Beresford staged a highly visible but fake disembarkation. Then, under cover of darkness, and taking every care not to release sparks up the funnel, the fire was lit. Next morning, when the steamer moved off, the Arabs were furious at the deceit and the ship departed in a final hail of gunfire. By late afternoon, Wilson was safely aboard and the long retreat could begin.[50] Two months later, Beresford had embarked for home.

There were two interesting postscripts to this escapade. According to Beresford he twice applied (once in 1892 and in 1897) to the Admiralty to have his 315 days in the Sudan counted as 'sea-time', given that, technically, he remained attached to his ship.[51] On both occasions the Board refused his request, doubtless delighting in having an opportunity to show their displeasure at the antics of such an idiosyncratic naval officer. It was also typical of Beresford that, in his memoirs, he got the dates wrong: his Admiralty record shows one application as being refused in July 1893; the other was refused in August 1895.[52] What is more, he was still sore about this refusal in 1909 when he raised the point once again at the enquiry. The other outcome was that the resourceful Benbow was promoted to Chief Inspector of Machinery on 31 December 1888.

## Scene 4: Fisher's years of consolidation

On Fisher's return to England in 1882, the Queen was much distressed by his state of health and invited him to stay at Osborne. At the time he was too ill for the royal presence but a few months later he accepted the command. Within hours of arriving he dashed off a letter to Kitty, telling her that he had been welcomed with 'two cups of tea and bread and butter' and had 'a delightful sitting room out of my bedroom, deliciously quiet'. All this, he thought, would 'renovate me'.[53] The next year the Queen summoned him once more and he was astonished to find that he was to be the only guest at dinner: 'The Man-in-black has just been in to my room to say I am to dine with the Queen – no one else here, isn't it awful!' he told Kitty.[54] Just as Beresford enjoyed the favours of the Prince, so Fisher was becoming a favourite of the Queen.

His first posting once he was well enough to return to work was as captain of the Navy's gunnery school at HMS *Excellent*. Little seemed to have changed in the last forty years, but Fisher immediately instituted big changes, including abolishing training in obsolete smooth-bore guns.

It was during this posting (one of several) to the *Excellent* that Fisher first became involved in the political and journalistic aspects of naval reform, playing a key role in a major press lobby discretely aided by the Admiralty. In *The Truth About the Navy* campaign, the front man was William Thomas

Stead (1849–1912), 'the father of modern journalism'. Using his position as editor of the London paper the *Pall Mall Gazette*, he ran a series of articles, beginning on 15 September 1884, alleging serious weaknesses in the Navy and the need for massive Government expenditure. Although his name was never mentioned, Fisher was one of Stead's main sources, acting with the support of the Admiralty itself. Stead later described how 'the rules of the service against giving any information to the press were very strict' and in consequence 'I used to go to Captain Fisher, like Nicodemus, at night-time, meeting him at wayside railway stations.'[55]

Stead's articles were an outstanding success. Within months, the Government had conceded additional naval expenditure of £5.5 million – and Stead had only asked for £3.5 million. Fisher drew his own conclusions: admirals who wished to change the Navy first needed the support of the press, but covertly. From that time on, Fisher courted every trustworthy journalist he could find, plying them with secret documents and outlines for articles.

In 1886, now forty-five years old, Fisher received his first Admiralty appointment as Director of Naval Ordnance. The *Pall Mall Gazette* commented that 'No one is more alive to the deficiencies of the navy, or more competent to lend a hand in correcting them ... His appointment as director of Naval Ordnance will immensely strengthen the personnel at Whitehall.'[56] During this posting he was promoted to Rear Admiral and received the CB.

Despite all this success, Fisher actively sought the advice of two colleagues as to whether he should take up a highly-paid offer of employment at Whitworth & Co., a private armaments company. One colleague argued in favour, the other against; Fisher stayed put.

His next appointment was a brief spell as Admiral Superintendent of Portsmouth Dockyard from May 1891 to February 1892. There he vigorously applied one of his many mottoes:

Build few, and build fast,
Each one better than the last.[57]

Banal as this ditty might sound, it contains an important truth about Fisher, the reformer. Until his arrival, ships were built at a leisurely pace, with perhaps half a dozen of the same type under construction at once. Fisher thought it much better to build one at a time and put each to sea as fast as possible. In that way, lessons learnt in service could be used to modify the design of ships as yet unfinished.

In less than a year he was called back to the Admiralty to take up the post of Third Naval Lord and Controller of the Navy, which gave him responsibility for the building and maintenance of the ships of the Fleet. He plunged into the building of a new form of destroyer, larger and faster than anything hitherto seen. Then he proposed a new type of battleship, recommending that six be constructed. The Board agreed to one – the *Renown* – which was later to be his own flagship on two separate postings.

The most significant event of Fisher's period as Controller was the saga of the naval estimates for 1894–5, fought over against the background of yet another naval scare in 1893. The Board were determined on having its estimates passed; Gladstone, then Prime Minister, was implacably opposed. When the Naval Lords made it clear that they would resign *en masse* if the estimates were not passed, the ageing Gladstone resigned rather than give way. It was left to his successor, Lord Rosebery, to accept the Board's demands. Fisher's participation in the admirals' rebellion did his career no harm, being awarded the Order of the Bath in May 1894.

Having been promoted to Vice Admiral in May 1896, Fisher was appointed as Commander-in-Chief of the North America station in the next year. In this dull backwater, he is most remembered for a bizarre plot to rescue Dreyfus from Devil's Island in the event of war breaking out with France, with the intention of landing him somewhere on the French coast. What contribution this would have made to a British war effort is unclear.

By now, almost to a man, the officers in the Navy had written off Fisher as a desk-bound admiral who knew little or nothing about commanding fleets. The near-universal assumption was that his North American posting would be his last. Their Lordships had other ideas.

In March 1899 Fisher received a telegram from the First Lord, Lord Goschen, appointing him as naval representative to the forthcoming Hague Peace Conference and Commander-in-Chief of the Mediterranean – the plum posting in the Fleet. The scene was set for Beresford and Fisher to meet once again. This time their careers would be inextricably linked by first friendship, then rivalry and then disputes, only to be dissolved by the final feud.

## Scene 5: Beresford's years of indecision

When Beresford came home from the Sudan, he soon got himself elected to Parliament, this time for Marylebone. In the House he showed his independence of both Admiralty and Government by advocating the closing of the Suez Canal should there be war in the Mediterranean. Rather than defend the canal, he recommended returning to 'England's old highway round the Cape which can never be blocked'.[58] He also began a campaign for more ships, advocating an additional £3 million for naval vessels.[59] Two months later he was on his feet to advocate scrapping obsolete naval vessels, of which he said there were seventy-four.[60] It was what he later called 'hammering on the Parliamentary anvil', and he loved it.[61] After battering the Government over the Navy, he voted against

Gladstone's first Home Rule bill in June 1886, and so helped to bring about the end of the Liberal administration.[62]

After Beresford's re-election for Marylebone in the General Election, the Prince of Wales lobbied Salisbury, the new Prime Minister, to find a place for him in his Government. Salisbury sent him to the Admiralty as Junior Naval Lord, which was not a success. Unlike Fisher, Beresford could not work with others and in no time at all had upset all his superiors. His excuse was, he wrote afterwards, that 'I speedily discovered that there was at the Admiralty no such thing as organisation for war.'[63] (He was to level this same criticism against the Admiralty throughout the feud years.) Six weeks after his appointment he presented the Board with a long paper setting out all the faults of the Admiralty. The paper, full of 'schoolboy expletives of the most pronounced character' also appeared in a news-paper, much to the anger of the other Naval Lords.[64] Naturally the Board paid no attention to the opinions of their most junior and newest member, and when he appealed to Salisbury to support him, the Prime Minister advised him that 'you must have more experience'.[65] It was not as if Beresford had not been warned; his predecessor as Junior Naval Lord had told him that, 'Your sole business will be to sign papers.'[66] That was hardly an occupation for a son of the Fourth Marquess of Waterford.

When, in March 1887, he was asked to sign the estimates before they were sent to the Treasury, he refused on the grounds that he had not seen them.[67] The estimates went off without his signature – he was no longer needed even for the most menial of tasks. The rest of his time in the post was undistinguished, except for his irritating habit of bragging to journal-ists about his contributions to all the various reforms then in progress.

It was typical of Beresford that, failing to cooperate with others in the interests of the Navy he professed to love, he could at the same time show quickness of mind when needing to act alone. When visiting a submarine with other distinguished guests in January 1887, the vessel sank to the bottom and stuck in the mud. No one knew what to do and the air supply was rapidly depleting. In his memoirs, Beresford claimed that he promptly suggested rolling the submarine by 'moving the people quickly from side to side'.[68] According to another witness, the rolling was the idea of Beresford *and* another sailor; Beresford had air-brushed the second man out of the scene.[69] Anyway, the trick worked, and they soon surfaced.

Six months later, in July, Beresford exceeded himself in his insubordina-tion, this time flouting the authority of his Sovereign. The event took place on the Royal Yacht at the end of the Queen's Jubilee Review. Beresford's wife was on another vessel so he ordered the Royal Yacht's crew to signal in flags, 'Tell Lady Charles to go at once onboard the yacht *Lancashire Witch* where I will join her.' He had not asked permission from the Queen for this action, no doubt assuming that civilians would not be able to read the signal. An unknown seaman, though, tipped off a *Times* reporter and the signal appeared in the paper the next day.[70] Beresford promptly sent in his resignation to Salisbury, but the Queen refused to accept it.[71] From the Prince of Wales came the comment: 'You have always acted all your life (like an Irishman would) on the impulse of the moment.'[72]

During his remaining months at the Admiralty Beresford repeatedly threatened to resign over trifles, finally doing so in January 1888 over an outcome of the paper that he had sent to the Board in 1886.[73] The paper had led the Board to rethink the structure of the Naval Intelligence Department. A committee was set up and by early 1887 a new department was formed along the lines suggested by Beresford. On Beresford's recommendation, the officers were employed at considerably enhanced salaries than they were previously receiving. Later, Hamilton had second thoughts about the salaries and sought Treasury approval. The Treasury insisted that the salaries should be lowered. Hamilton agreed; Beresford did not and his resignation followed. Within weeks of that resignation, Beresford was claiming that he had resigned over a 'national question'.[74] *The Times* accepted his explanation and was warmly supportive.[75] Salisbury, less convinced, noted that Beresford 'is too greedy of popular applause to get on in a public department. He is constantly playing his own game at the expense of his colleagues'.[76]

There were twenty-one more years of Beresford's naval career yet to come. Never for one moment in that period did the Admiralty consider calling again upon his services in Whitehall. From now on the Admiralty, or as Beresford liked to call it 'the authorities' was to be the object of his scorn, derision and untiring guerrilla warfare.

After his resignation, Beresford continued to speak in the Commons, at one stage asking for an enquiry into the administration of the Admiralty and the War Office.[77] He also continued his campaign for more ships, this time (December 1888) advocating an additional £20.1 million of expenditure.[78] Shortly after there was indeed a huge increase in expenditure, for which Beresford tried to take all the credit, saying 'That was my first shipbuilding programme.'[79] It would not have occurred to him that the deficiencies that he had identified were equally obvious to others, most notably Admiral Sir Phipps Hornby.[80]

A year later Beresford resigned his Parliamentary seat and returned to sea in command of the *Undaunted*, an armoured cruiser in the Mediterranean Fleet.[81] He was, though, to have little chance to think about naval command. Around 1883 Beresford had begun an affair with a Lady Brooke (later the Countess of Warwick but popularly known as Daisy), resulting in his being the father of her second child, Marjorie (born 1884).[82] Although the affair was over, early in 1889 a letter from Lady Brooke to Beresford came into Lady Charles' hands. Unfortunately for the Beresfords, Lady Brooke appealed to the Prince of Wales to help her retrieve the letter, but

Mina refused all entreaties and despatched it to her brother-in-law in Ireland for safekeeping. Offended, the Prince cut Lady Charles in public and a mutual animus developed between him and the Beresfords.[83] Over the following months, pressure was piled on Lady Charles to cede the letter, but she stood firm.

By June 1891 Beresford felt he had to step in and he drafted a letter to the Prince in which he said 'you have systematically ranged yourself on the side of the other person against my wife' and called him 'a blackguard'.[84] On the advice of Lord Salisbury, the letter was never sent, but in December, unable to restrain his outrage any longer Beresford wrote to the Prince threatening to publicise the facts of the case and the Prince's role. As the crisis threatened to explode into the public domain, Salisbury, the Queen, the Prince and the Beresfords entered into a furious week of epistolary diplomacy at the end of which the Prime Minister extracted a low-key apology from the Prince who said, in relation to the accusation of having ignored Lady Charles, 'I have never had any such intention.' If she had had such 'an erroneous impression', the Prince regretted it.[85] Relations between Beresford and the Prince were never the same again. So upset was Lady Charles that the Beresfords left Eaton Square and moved to Park Gate House, Richmond, in early 1892.[86] This incident was to have great significance in the feud years, when, as King, Edward was to prove to be Fisher's staunchest supporter. Had Beresford not quarrelled with Edward, Fisher might well have been less of a favourite.

The one notable event to Beresford's credit during his time on the *Undaunted* was his masterly rescue of a French ship, the *Seignelay* which had run aground at Jaffa on 26 April, 1891. Beresford arrived three days later and organised the removal of 450 tons of stores and equipment to lighten the ship. After floating her off, his men reloaded the freed vessel and the *Undaunted* sailed back to routine duties.[87]

In mid-1893 Beresford was paid off from the *Undaunted* and in June was appointed to the command of the Steam Reserve at Chatham.[88] As ever, he found new opportunities to display the reckless side of his character. Having taken some distinguished guests, including the Commander-in-Chief of the Army in Ireland, Lord Wolseley, to see the trials of the *Magnificent*, he arranged to take them back to Chatham in a torpedo-boat. He took the boat at full speed in the dark, jumping the spit of sand in the estuary. Beresford recorded that 'Lord Wolseley inquired if "we always took short cuts across the land".'[89] On another occasion, returning from a late ball, he was unable to persuade the tug-man to take him home. Unperturbed, he took command of the boat and, in the fog and without lights, 'I found the channel by the simple method of hitting the banks; and cannoning off and on all the way.'[90]

What with writing to the press, quarrelling with the Prince of Wales and making light of the safety of Lord Wolseley, it is not surprising that when, in 1895, Beresford was due to be appointed *aide-de-camp* to Victoria, no appointment came. It would be two years before he was considered acceptable for the post.[91]

The year 1898 proved a good one for Beresford, becoming Member of Parliament for York, enjoying the beginnings of a reconciliation with the Prince of Wales and his recent promotion to Rear Admiral.[92] After Salisbury had refused to allow him to join the force being sent to recapture the Sudan, Beresford settled down to two years of relentless criticism of the Government's handling of the Navy. He attacked the estimates in March 1898, when he said it would take three years to make up the deficit in ships. In the same month he accused the Government of robbing the merchant ships to make up for lack of naval reserves.[93] There was nothing that was right about the Navy, leading him to challenge the promotion system, demand fair pay for officers, call for promotion from the lower deck and higher pay for the First Naval Lord. During this time he fitted in a visit to China on behalf of the Associated Chambers of Commerce, producing a report of hundreds of pages on his return.

In December 1899, against the odds, Beresford was appointed as second-in-command to Fisher, Commander-in-Chief in the Mediterranean.[94] He would probably not have been Fisher's first choice, but Fisher does not appear to have been consulted. Time would tell whether the Mediterranean was big enough for two such oversize personalities.

One of Beresford's last big speeches outside the Commons before taking up his new post was at a Chamber of Commerce banquet in London. After lambasting the Government on a wide range of fronts, he concluded by saying that 'at present he was not on the active list, and was free to say what he liked; but directly he was on full pay ... his duty would be to his commanding officer ... and he would know nothing whatever about politics'.[95] It was a noble ambition, but one that he would struggle to honour.

## Scene 6: On the brink

And so the scene was set for the great feud that was to bring disaster on both men. What was to follow was not inevitable, but it was perhaps predictable, given their almost total lack of anything in common.

Beresford was a colourful personality; he was courageous, reckless, impetuous and high-spirited. He always enjoyed a bit of fun, his life being a trail of pranks, practical jokes and exotic bets. Yet he was still a first-class commander of men and an excellent seaman. He could move effortlessly from a London salon to the House of Commons and then to the bridge of a ship, being equally at home in all three environments. In command he was adored by his men; in the salons he was worshiped by the Marlborough

House set; amongst ordinary people he was a hero who stood up for the Empire.

More a politician than a sailor, Beresford was not, though, a good party man and in the Commons he was ever an oddball, being too careless in his outbursts to command the respect of other members and too casual in his voting to receive the favour of his party. His popularity with the public being near to unbounded he never had the least difficulty in finding a Parliamentary constituency to contest and, he claimed, he had been offered over forty seats at one stage in his career. In his public speaking, he drew capacity crowds wherever he went and received generous write-ups in the newspapers. He was a populist of the first order. Although he rarely had anything original to say and was frequently lacking in coherence and logic, he commanded large and loyal audiences. He was tireless in stomping the country to address political and naval meetings, always providing a barn-storming, patriotic speech, often of inordinate length. As a result, his antics earned him the accolade of 'the biggest of all recorded gas-bags'.[96]

Fisher, too, was big in all but stature. (He put his small size down to the poor naval diet on the *Calcutta*.) He did not, though, seek the limelight, preferring to operate behind the scenes. Even when he became a peer on his retirement he only spoke in the House of Lords on two occasions, and those were to make personal statements. He twice spoke in public yet did not yearn for more. His whole life was focused on his career; apart from dancing, he had no leisure activities; his exercise was limited to walking and he never pursued any sport until he took up golf at the age of seventy. An early riser, he would often be at his desk at 5.00 am, demolishing mountains of paperwork, marking items for his subordinates to handle while answering all his own letters in his inimitable hand – large, clear, flowing, as zestful a pen as ever touched the page. He ate sparingly through the day, returned home for dinner in the evening and, after per-haps reading a newspaper or a light novel, retired early to bed. He rarely dined out, and when he did, he preferred club dinners with his closest friends, Viscount Esher (the courtier) and Lord Knollys (Private Secretary to Edward VII). His family had to fit around him as best they could. On one occasion when he was First Sea Lord, he suddenly announced that he was going to an hotel for a couple of weeks and would shut up the house. The family, he told them, would have to make their own accommodation arrangements.

What perhaps most distinguished the two men professionally was their relative success at the Admiralty. Beresford had been given his chance as Junior Naval Lord, but within six weeks his natural arrogance had taken the upper hand and he had offended the Board through intemperately criticising their work. He could command, but he could not cooperate. Fisher, though, instinctively knew how to work the system. He too criticised, but constructively and with care. More importantly, he showed that he could achieve results. As Director of Naval Ordnance, he resolved a problem that had plagued the Admiralty for over forty years, wresting from the Army their time-honoured right to control the supply of the Navy's ordnance. For Beresford, being patriotic meant making a loud noise; for Fisher, it meant real reforms inside Admiralty House.

It is hard, then, to imagine two more contrasting men.

## Act 3

# Friendship and Rivalry in the Mediterranean

*The tongue is an unruly member, especially when it's an Irish member! – Fisher on Beresford.*[1]

### Scene 1: Commander and commanded

Fisher had taken command of the Mediterranean Fleet in July 1899, fresh from a stunning performance at the Hague Peace Conference where, with the approval of Lord Salisbury, he had successfully blocked every attempt to limit Britain's naval supremacy. His old friend Stead piled superlative upon superlative as he described Fisher's impact at The Hague, where he had been 'one of the greatest personal successes of the Conference'. Stead continued:

> Admiral Fisher with his white hat was almost instantly acclaimed as the heartiest, jolliest, and smartest delegate at The Hague. As the senior officer, who could show forty-five years of service, broken by only two or three weeks of half-pay, he had precedence of them all, but the precedence which he obtained from seniority was nothing to that which he won by the charm of his manner, the frank heartiness of his conversation, and the genuine, unmistakable earnestness with which he applied himself to the task in hand.[2]

Representing as he did the world's most powerful navy, Fisher could sit back in the debates, leaving the minor powers to squabble amongst themselves. At the informal gatherings in the salons and corridors he adopted his famous supercilious air. Stead observed that, as Fisher listened to 'the little Powers which hardly had an ironclad to their back', he 'lay like a great whale watching the gambols of the gudgeon, and marvelling that they should take themselves so seriously'. The Russians adored him (or so Stead claimed) and, despite his sixty years, he 'danced down everyone else in the ballroom'.[3]

The experience, no doubt, had puffed up Fisher's self-confidence, acting for the first time in his life as a world player. With the mighty British Navy behind him he could afford to disdain the representatives of the weaker powers but was falling prey to conceit in himself and in the Navy. This was the man who was to command Britain's premier fleet, and he meant to command it like no one had ever done before.

When Fisher arrived at Admiralty House in Malta he discovered, as he later told Lord Selborne, 'an absence of detailed organisation for war'.[4] This was an understatement. What he witnessed, and indeed would have done so in any British fleet of the last eighty years, was an eye-catching collection of beautiful ships, brass sparkling, decks spotlessly white, guns glistening with fresh paint ... and not much more. It was a time, noted Rear Admiral Sir Percy Scott, when: 'a ship had to look pretty; prettiness was necessary to promotion.' So important was the appearance of a ship that officers frequently bought paint with their own money since the Admiralty supply was never enough. On the *Alexandra*, which Scott recalled as 'the prettiest ship I have ever seen' the officers had spent £2,000 on her paintwork – around £150,000 today.[5]

When it came to a ship's inspection, appearance was the sole consideration. A typical report in 1900 complimented the captain on the men's 'good physique' and the fact that they were 'well dressed'. The inspectors went on to admire the men, who 'moved very smartly' and the ship, which was 'very clean throughout'. Down in the engine room they appreciated the 'appendages', which they found to be 'very good'.[6] At no point, though, did the report mention guns, gunnery or shooting accuracy – the *raison d'être* of a battleship. Not until 1903 was target practice included in the inspection of ships.[7] In fact, in 1900 the Navy was little better than a floating fancy-dress parade.

Of particular concern to Fisher was the state of the gunnery. The quarterly target practice, if carried out at all, was left to each ship's captain to arrange, taking pot-shots at a nearby, stationary target such as an anchored barrel. Beresford recalled that, in the 1860s, gunnery practice on the *Marlborough*, the then Mediterranean flagship, involved manoeuvring the ship to within 100 yards of the Malta shore and firing round-shot into the cliffs.[8] Things did not seem to have progressed much in the succeeding forty years. Often, to save scorching the glistening paintwork of the guns, the captains found it more convenient to steam off out of sight of the Fleet and gently drop the ammunition over the side.

The Navy was living in the past, preparing to fight the French in the style of Nelson: get in close and let off every gun as rapidly as possible. Such an approach to battle had been an anachronism since the day the torpedo had entered the Mediterranean. To avoid these ferocious new weapons, battleships now needed the protection of numerous destroyers and, even with this shield, they still had to keep out of torpedo range of enemy fleets. Fisher reckoned that a battleship had to keep a minimum of 3,000 yards between it and an enemy fleet. There was an obvious corollary to this, as

Fisher quickly recognised: future naval battles would use long-range gunnery; Nelson's close fighting days were over. Yet, when Fisher arrived in the Mediterranean, not one single ship had fired a long-distance shot.

Fleet work was just as bad. When ships worked together, they performed set movements as if they were formation swimmers rather than machines of war. Elaborate routines were laid down for movement in unison. As a fleet turned in a quarter circle, captains were judged by how well they maintained the prescribed distance from the other vessels. In war, such finesse would have no value, but this was a Navy that had long ceased to contemplate or prepare for conflict. Fisher was to change all this with his mantras of 'rush' and 'instant readiness for war'.

From the day he arrived in the Mediterranean, Fisher showed his contempt for arcane and useless customs. Tradition dictated that the new Commander-in-Chief did nothing until he had paid a ceremonial visit to each ship – a task that could take weeks. Impatient to put the Fleet to work on his first morning afloat, Fisher summoned his captains to his flagship, the *Renown*, flamboyantly flying the biggest flag in the Navy.[9] He addressed them for half-an-hour and sent them about their business. A man who could do six weeks' work in half-an-hour was a man to watch – and fear.

This was to be just the start. One officer who arrived six months after Fisher had taken command found that 'the whole fleet was being turned end for end, and every bone was rattling in its socket'.[10] Another noted that, under Fisher's regime, 'many captains, though fine sailors, were out of their technical depth' and that Fisher 'was bent on bowling out the duffers, to expose them, and make them suffer'.[11] A third, writing to his family, told them how, whilst 'the executive branch can say nothing too bad [about Fisher]' it was clear that '[he] is going to shake them up out of their fools' paradise'.[12] A little later he was reporting that Fisher 'has been making a series of experiments in various forms of night attack by torpedo-boats, which are very interesting. This is the *first practical exercise I have seen done out here*'. (Emphasis added.) In the process, Fisher had revealed the weakness of the fleet, since 'in every case the Captains of the "boats" and "destroyers" have shown the most consummate ignorance of the elements of tactics and common sense'.[13] (The author of these latter comments, Maurice Hankey, a marine officer, would, nine years later share the job of writing the enquiry report.)

Although Fisher was much admired for the vigorous way in which he attacked the Fleet's weaknesses, he was not always easy to work with. Captain George King-Hall, his Chief-of-Staff from March 1900, called him 'a gracious master' but also found him 'a difficult man' and 'shifty'. Fisher, he said, was 'jealous of delegating any thing to any one'.[14] In the following year he was to complain that 'he never asks my advice or opinion on anything'. He had, he said, 'never had such an uncomfortable time in the service as I have had this summer on board *Renown*'.[15]

It was into this world of Fisherian revolution that Beresford stepped in February 1900.

After two years as Conservative Member of Parliament for York, Beresford arrived in the Mediterranean as Fisher's second-in-command. He saw himself as a reforming officer so he perhaps looked forward to serving with the man who was determined to end the lax and complacent attitudes of the Navy. In theory, it should have been a meeting of minds. In fact, the partnership would soon turn to rivalry. Some had foreseen this, as when the British press announced that 'Beresford was going to the Mediterranean to teach the Battle Fleet how to manoeuvre.'[16] That could only mean 'teach Fisher how to manoeuvre' and, since Beresford must have been the man behind these words, it was an ominous beginning to his posting.

Shortly before leaving Britain, Beresford received a letter from Lord Balfour, then First Lord of the Treasury and Leader of the House of Commons but, as everyone knew, Prime-Minister-in-Waiting as the aging Lord Salisbury staggered through his last days in Government. The letter was to 'wish you every good luck in your new post', yet Balfour added a prescient last paragraph when he asked Beresford:

> Are you quite sure that you are wise to speak in the sense you propose to do on the 11$^{th}$? Technically, no doubt, you are a free and independent Member of Parl$^t$: practically you are an Officer high in command in the Med$^n$ Fleet.[17]

Beresford was already committed to a speech to the London Chamber of Commerce on 9 January when, he told his audience, the country was 'in a position of danger', and 'would lose the Empire'. It was, he said, all the fault of a 'rotten, false, and misleading system of administration'.[18] However, the next day, *The Times* reported that Beresford had been 'unavoidably absent' from a London Chamber of Commerce dinner on 10 January.[19] He had bowed to Balfour's wise advice. Within eighteen months he would abandon such discretion and so spark an acrimonious controversy that was to occupy press and Parliament for over a year.

On arrival at Malta, Beresford was to raise his flag in the *Ramillies*. Built in 1892, she was a Royal Sovereign class battleship of 14,150 tons and a top speed of 17.5 knots. In 1897 Beresford had written an article for the Navy League's *Guide to the Naval Review* of that year. With its title of *The Resurrection of the Navy*, he lauded the 'splendid' Mediterranean Fleet and, in doing so, praised the Royal Sovereign class, saying 'these vessels were the very acme of what British battleships should be'. He added that 'no measure of admiration can be too great for the ingenuity portrayed by the

Constructive Department under Sir William White [Head of Construction] during the time Sir John Fisher was Controller'.[20] Beresford, then, arrived in the Mediterranean well-disposed to Fisher – a man who could build great ships was worthy of admiration.

The *Ramillies* was indeed an impressive ship ... except that she was in the Malta dockyard under repair, and was to remain there for three tedious months. Much later, listing his 'grievances' against Fisher, Beresford wrote that '[I] had to take a house in Valletta at £180 a year, as *Ramillies* was not ready, she being in Dockyard hands.'[21] Barely stated, this reads like a legitimate complaint, but on closer inspection it reveals a typical Beresfordian duplicity. Time and again he was to contrive retrospective evidence to support his case against Fisher – the Valletta house was just the start. If he truly resented renting the house, why did he and his wife continue to use it throughout his Mediterranean posting? The very fact that Lady Charles was there at all – she rarely accompanied her husband outside England – indicates that she must have found the arrangement congenial. In fact, far from being an encumbrance, it seems to have been the base for an ostentatious social life for the couple and their children. Only later, scouring for grudges to add to his list, did the house feature as a resented imposition.

Lacking an occupation, Beresford filled his time by corresponding with influential figures back home. He did not waste his pen on picture-postcard descriptions of the sun and sea, nor of his game-shooting and social life; there was something much more important to write about – the state of the Navy. He thought the condition of the Fleet to be so bad, that he invited Balfour to come and stay with him on board the *Ramillies*, telling him that 'as the only possible future Prime Minister, you ought to see and know something about the British Navy'. Beresford looked forward to the visit, 'not only for the pleasure that your society would give me' but because there were 'higher reasons'. Reminding Balfour that 'you and the Cabinet are always saying "Trust in the Fleet"', Beresford told him bluntly that 'I tell you distinctly that the Fleet is not ready to fight or nearly ready to fight.' Adding some colour to his accusation, he added that the situation was 'in many ways worse than the Army before S. Africa'.[22] (The latter comment reminds us that, at this time, Britain was still at war with the Boers in South Africa. The successes of the Boer guerrillas against Britain's professional Army had been a humiliation for the country. Fisher and Beresford were determined that, should their war come, their fleet would not be found lacking.)

Beresford considered coming home: 'I have debated with myself,' he told Balfour, 'whether I should not ask to be superseded at once, and go home and warn the country to the state of affairs.' He reinforced his message with a list of eight areas of deficiency, ranging from a lack of coal at Malta (a Beresford favourite) through inadequate cold stores for food to an absence of distilling ships for fresh water.[23] What was never clear in such letters is why he thought it was *his* responsibility to warn politicians and the Admiralty of the state of the Navy. As he admitted to John Sandars (Balfour's secretary) on the same day, 'Fisher the Com. in Chief here has been sending home strong representations as to what he wants, I believe, though he has not told me so.'[24] Arrogance, though, had got the better of him; he was sure he could succeed where Fisher was failing. Ever confident in the strength of his political influence, he told Sandars: 'I am getting up all facts from personal observation & when the country knows the truth, I shall be able to do a good deal.'[25] And, when service in the Mediterranean constrained him from lobbying himself, there was always his wife to bring into play. Back in London for a short visit in April, Lady Charles explained to Sandars that, 'Lord C was so much perturbed by the unsatisfactory condition of affairs in the Med$^{tn}$ that he wanted me to say a great many things he did not like to write being only 2$^{nd}$ in Command.' However patriotic his intentions might have been, Lady Charles undermined his case when she added that, 'he chiefly wanted to convey to Mr. Balfour that in a subordinate position he finds himself unable to accomplish all he had hoped to do'.[26]

The brazen nature of Beresford's inflated view of his own importance even led him to take time off to write letters of advice to the King. Knowing that the Duke of York was about to embark on a royal tour of Australia, Beresford decided that father and son would benefit from his experience. The King told the Prince that he had had 'a lengthy epistle' from the Rear Admiral of which 'the pith ... was that you should associate yourself, in each place you visit, with Trade and Commerce(!)'.[27] The royal exclamation mark summed up Edward's opinion of Beresford as an authority on royal etiquette and polity.

All this, and Beresford had been in post for less than three months. It was the Junior Naval Lord all over again.

At last, on 13 April 1900, *Ramillies* was handed over to Beresford. It must have been a proud moment – and few men were more subject to pride than Beresford – but he still found time to grudgingly note that 'there was wet paint in the Admiral's cabin'.[28]

If, on Beresford's arrival, the phrase 'the Devil finds work for idle hands' had passed through Fisher's mind, perhaps he would have taken more care to keep his subordinate occupied. As things were, it was not long before Beresford discovered that Fisher had little need of a second-in-command. He was later to record that, 'from 5th February to 13th April [I] had nothing to do of any sort of kind of duty'. Fisher, he complained, did not consult him 'in any way whatever on any matters connected with the Fleet, War Organisation, Plan of Campaign, or anything else, though 2$^{nd}$ in Command and Senior Officer out here'. As he rightly pointed out, 'if anything were to happen suddenly to CinC, [I] should be in temporary command of [the] station, but have no idea of any plan or proposal that CinC may have in his head'.[29] (This did not stop Beresford repeating the same mistake when he became Commander-in-Chief of the Channel Fleet. He, too, failed to write down war plans that his second-in-command could have used in emergency. In Beresford's case, the fault was more serious since he was regularly absent through illnesses.)

Beresford's squadron was, indeed, inactive. From the day *Ramillies* became available to him to the end of 1901, his ship was at sea for just 133 days out of 701 – fewer than one day in five.[30]

Beresford's account of his role as second-in-command gives the impression that Fisher deliberately sidelined him. Was this something personal, or would Fisher have treated *any* second-in-command in this way? Beresford himself provided the answer in a letter to Balfour of 8 April 1900, that is, written *before any of the clashes between the two admirals had occurred*. He wrote:

> The *Custom* of the Service prevents him [Fisher] communicating with me (his 2nd in command) on any question whatever, every obstacle is put in my way to prevent me finding out deficiencies in stores or to prepare myself in Signalling, in drills or in manoeuvring, &c. &c. *This is not the C. in C.'s fault, it is the habit of the Service.*[31] (Emphasis added.)

So, what was later to be portrayed by Beresford as Fisher's spite was, in April 1900, merely 'the habit of the Service' and 'not the C. in C.'s fault'. This tells us much about Beresford's capacity to twist quotidian episodes into maliciously orchestrated slights. His own behaviour when *he* became Commander-in-Chief in the Mediterranean also suggests that Fisher was more in the right than his subordinate. As Beresford's Second-in-Command went on leave in October 1906, another officer, writing to his wife, observed that he did not see 'what there is for an Admiral who is 2nd in Command to do when the Fleet is at Malta'.[32] It seems that *both* Fisher *and* Beresford saw the post as largely redundant.

Beresford's idleness also gave him time to fill up his voluminous ledger with his observations. Turning his mind towards what he considered to be the proper role of a second-in-command Beresford decided that, 'He should superintend all Manoeuvres and be in charge of all arrangements as regards drills of all kinds' whereas 'under the present system he does absolutely nothing'.[33] He was also critical of the amount of time that Fisher spent doing paperwork: 'The CinC Mediterranean spends all his time writing, instead of inspecting and drilling, and visiting ships, and carrying out evolutions and manoeuvres.'[34] It must be added, though, that the evidence simply does not support this assertion. When the journalist Arnold White observed Fisher at close quarters in June 1901, he told his *Daily Mail* readers that Fisher rose at 5.00 am and wrote until 7.00 am. After breakfast 'with Chief of the Staff, Flag Captain, Flag Lieutenant, Flag Secretary' he continued with paperwork until 10.00 am, when manoeuvres started.[35] Apart from this eye-witness account, the evidence of Fisher's achievements simply contradicts any notion of a desk-bound commander. Like most of Beresford's grievances, this one has to be deconstructed. He did not have enough to do, so Fisher must be doing too much. The fact was, though, that Fisher could, and did, do the work of two men, not just in the Mediterranean, but throughout his long career.

With time on his hands, Beresford was able to throw himself into the agreeable social life of the small British colony in Malta and the Mediterranean. He was elected to numerous social clubs, such as the *Cercle Européen* and the *Club Hellenique* at Smyrna and the Sporting Club and the Tennis and Croquet Club at Salonika.[36] Even so, he was not content and, in late 1900 he recorded once more that, for two months, 'I had nothing of any sort, kind, or description to do.' He had to be satisfied with 'going out to every field-day on shore' when he should, he felt, have been 'given signalling, manoeuvres with boats, or the countless other drills and exercises'.[37] Rather than firing the Fleet's guns, he was massacring the Mediterranean wildlife. In the two years of his command, *Ramillies*, he said, had bagged a total of 1,359 birds.[38]

It was, perhaps, this inactivity that led Beresford to begin to record his grudges against Fisher. We know of his complaints because, when he arrived in the Mediterranean, he brought with him a gigantic, leather-bound, alphabet-tabbed book. On its pristine pages he recorded administrative minutiae, the wants and failings of the Mediterranean Fleet, notes for speeches, and so on. He also used this ledger to record injustices and slights that he alleged he had suffered at the hands of Fisher or the Admiralty. Indeed, the ledger (which is not chronologically organised and is rarely dated) gives the impression that it started out as an administrative *aide mémoire*, but gradually evolved into the rantings of a deeply frustrated man.

It was sometime during 1900 that Beresford received his first reprimand in the Mediterranean from Fisher. He recounted the incident to his old friend Carlyon Bellairs in an undated letter. 'I was given,' he told him, 'a squadron of 4 ships for 4 days. I at once commenced the only common sense plan for teaching Admirals & Captains to manoeuvre a Squd. i.e. putting each Captain in command for manoeuvring in turn, the Ad[m] reserving to himself the right to negative a dangerous or unclear signal.' On return to harbour, instead of being congratulated for this imaginative piece of training, 'I received,' continued Beresford, 'a reprimand for daring to do anything so "contrary to the system".' Despite this, he still went on to say that he and Fisher 'get on quite exceptionally[;] I do not complain of him in any way'.[39] Nevertheless, Beresford later gave permission to

Bellairs to mention this incident in an article and to say 'that you would not be surprised to hear that Lord C.B. had been censured'.[40]

On three occasions, Beresford claimed, Fisher held 'meetings of captains ... to discuss preparations for war' yet he found that 'I was not invited to either [sic] one of them' but there is no corroborating evidence of these events.[41] Another entry records that Fisher refused him 'permission to obtain information from Store Officer ... as to quantities of coal in store', although Fisher himself later gave him the information.[42]

This particular entry provides us with a hint of Fisher's reasoning. Beresford, before coming to the Mediterranean, had been a provocative, effusive and pretentious 'member for the Navy' in Parliament. Whilst in the Mediterranean he maintained his contacts both with journalists, politicians and with pressure groups such as the Navy League, feeding them ammunition to be hurled at the Government and the Admiralty. One of Beresford's pet subjects was insufficient coal stocks in the Mediterranean. (This may seem an odd obsession, but when Beresford was Junior Naval Lord, coal stocks were one of his responsibilities. He had, as it were, coal in his blood.) Plausibly, then, Fisher controlled Beresford's access to information in the fear that he might injudiciously pass it on to journalists (directly or through his famously leaky wife). King-Hall recorded Fisher's concerns on this point in March 1900 when he noted in his diary that 'Charles Beresford [is] anxious to stir up everyone at home on this [lack of coal at Malta].' Tellingly, he added, 'John Fisher, who is looking towards the same object, [is] not anxious CB should know too much.'[43] This is the earliest recorded evidence of Fisher intentionally withholding information from Beresford. It would eventually become a habit, fed by Fisher's distrust of Beresford's methods. If Beresford had the advantage of aristocratic rank, Fisher was determined to retain the power of information. (Not that Beresford was the only person to feel neglected by Fisher. George King-Hall complained that Fisher 'does not take me into his confidence', which is a remarkable accusation for a Chief of Staff to make.)[44]

The incident over the training of captains and admirals was followed by two occasions when Beresford was, he said, 'refused permission to take T.B. Destroyers and Torpedo Boats to sea in order to practise self and Officers in Signals and Manoeuvres'.[45] On top of this, there was a similar incident at Lemnos. On a further occasion, Beresford was humiliated when '[I] was sent with *Ocean* and *Speedy* to Platea and with *Melita* to Corfu, when all the rest of the Fleet were at Malta.'[46]

By March 1901, Fisher's neglect of Beresford had become obvious to officers of the Fleet, accompanied as it was by tensions between the two men. Both King-Hall and Hankey were quick to note these undercurrents. The former found the relationship between the two men so fiery that he had to act, he said, as 'a kind of a buffer between the two'. At times, some of Fisher's memoranda to Beresford were so acerbic that, said King-Hall, 'I pigeon-holed [them].' In this reciprocal relationship, King-Hall had to handle Beresford, who was prone to 'abusing Fisher to me'.[47] Maurice Hankey put the problem down to temperament, yet he also told his wife that Fisher 'is most vindictive, seizes every opportunity to show his dislike of Beresford'.[48] He went on to detail instances that matched the jottings in Beresford's ledger, telling his wife how Fisher 'refused to give him any ships to play with' and 'refuses to let Beresford take his ship to any decent places'.[49] Amongst all the observers of this period of the Fisher-Beresford relationship, Hankey must be regarded as one of the most reliable, both because he had no personal involvement (he was too junior) and because he was to prove to be a most meticulous recorder of military information later in life. If Hankey believed Fisher to be 'vindictive' then there must be some truth in the statement.

It is likely that Fisher's jealousy of Beresford's powerful connections in Parliament and in society played a part in the chemistry between them. A particularly striking example of Beresford's status at home occurred during the Khaki election of 1900. Goschen, the First Lord, had chosen to retire and suggestions as to his replacement ranged far and wide. One such proposal reached Fisher via the pages of *The Times*, where he read:

> Lord Charles Beresford is beyond doubt the most suitable, the most experienced, and the most fitting man to fill the post. His long practical experience, his pronounced acumen in perceiving instinctively the weak points and the urgent needs of, and the many deficiencies in, our Navy, and his thorough and undoubted capacity to grapple with this subject, clearly indicated that he is the man upon whom should devolve the duties of the First Lord.[50]

Doubtless Fisher noticed, but did not enjoy, the irony of this suggestion. Beresford's 'long practical experience' was actually rather short. In the years between 1878 and Beresford's achieving flag rank he spent just eight years and 250 days at sea, whilst he had spent fourteen years in Parliament.[51] (Although Beresford disputed these figures at the enquiry, the Admiralty insisted they were correct.) As to his 'pronounced acumen' and his capacity to perceive 'the weak points and the urgent needs' of the Navy, many would have disputed this.

But journalism lay at the root of Fisher's distrust of Beresford at this time. Fisher used the press as vigorously as anyone to influence public opinion and Parliament, but he was always discreet and his interventions were always designed to strengthen the Board. Beresford, on the other hand, frequently sought to use the press to undermine the Board.

At a more personal level, Fisher feared Beresford's indiscretions. Writing to White, Fisher complained that 'The tongue is an unruly member, *especially when it's an Irish member!*'[52] Fisher's first biographer noted that

Beresford approached the press 'with more zeal than discretion' – as his *Daily Mail* letter in Act 4 will demonstrate.[53]

Beresford's own journalistic activities were mostly of the self-publicising variety, being part of maintaining his celebrity status back home. On one occasion, the *Morning Post* reported that 'the Mediterranean Fleet of Lord Charles Beresford' had returned from a cruise. Fisher was not amused and asked Beresford to explain this upstaging of his command. In return, Fisher received an insolent reply in which Beresford explained that 'the great British Public are accustomed to the name of Lord Charles Beresford, but as yet ignorant of the name of Sir John Fisher'. He advised Fisher that 'the remedy lies entirely in your own hands'.[54]

Fisher would have been even more concerned had he ever known the full extent of Beresford's correspondence with the Admiralty and politicians. A typical example occurred in June 1900 when Beresford wrote a report on the strength of the Fleet which, he said 'is totally incapable of carrying out those duties which must inevitably be forced upon it in wartime'. He then went on to detail the deficiencies in ships and what needed to be done to put the Fleet into a war-ready condition. So far, so harmless, even if all the points that he made were taken from Fisher. After sending this report to Fisher, in an act of barely credible impertinence, he then sent a copy to the Prime Minister with a covering letter that included the sentence: 'Sir John is an able, clever man and, as he is responsible, he is certain to see the weaknesses I perceive.' He added that he did not know 'whether he [Fisher] has written home on these points ... as beyond an agreement in conversation that the fleet is not strong out here, we have not written or discussed the matter'.[55] This last point was ingenuous to a fault. Every senior officer in the Mediterranean Fleet would have known by heart Fisher's litany of the Fleet's deficiencies since he never missed an opportunity to expound them in his vivid, inimitable language. Also, it is clear both from entries in Beresford's ledger and other sources that they met and talked a good deal. In June 1901, King-Hall noted in his diary that 'Sir John and Lord Charles after dinner entered into a long discussion on naval matters in general.'[56] There was no suggestion that this was an odd or exceptional occurrence. Presumably, Fisher never saw Beresford's patronising letter to Salisbury. Had he read it, he might have been more than tempted to send his second-in-command to the bottom of the Mediterranean Sea.

On another occasion, in June 1901, Beresford sent a seventeen-page report to the First Lord. He began his letter by asking 'leave to submit to you my views about the situation in the Mediterranean' yet immediately admitted that the matter was 'not altogether within my province'. Master of the qualifying adverb, his subtly inserted 'altogether' perverted the truth: the matter was *not* in his province *to any extent at all*. He then treated the First Lord to a typically Beresfordian irrelevance, masquerading as an unassailable justification for his action. Since, he argued, he might have to defend his views in the Commons, he was justified in going over Fisher's head in this way.[57] This was a serving officer and a second-in-command, telling his ultimate superior that, on the prospect that he might one day be a Member of Parliament again, his subordinate status could be set aside and he could bypass his immediate superior, submitting reports over his head. No wonder 'the authorities' found him so hard to handle.

Whilst in the Mediterranean, all this correspondence was clandestine – Fisher doubtless knew very little about it. However, on returning home, Beresford planned, he told Bellairs, to publish the lot 'in the hope that I should be committed to gaol under the Official Secrets Act'.[58] Presumably he thought this would lead to some kind of outcry after which the public and Parliament were to rally to him as saviour of the Empire. A few weeks later, having forgotten his anticipated martyrdom, he was as determined as ever to return home with the message that 'the Navy is [not] properly organised for war'. He saw no problem in putting this message across since 'I shall have all the modern admirals and C. in C. with me now to support me.'[59] In reality, he would repeat and repeat this message until, when presented before the enquiry in 1909, it would be finally rejected.

Writing to journalists was a part of Fisher's daily routine – he had been at it for years. So much so, that some journalists began to echo back his pet phrases in their articles, which led Lord Goschen to warn that White's articles had 'a strong Mediterranean flavour'.[60] Fisher justified his trading with journalists in various ways. One was that articles in the London papers goaded politicians into doing the right thing. As he told Thursfield, when urging him to write yet another article for *The Times*, 'I have no doubt a little "stiffening" from outside in the shape of one of those unmistakable "do-your-duty-or-you'll-catch-it" leading articles in *The Times* will help.' In this case, the 'help' was aimed at Selborne (First Lord 1900–5) who was battling over Navy estimates with 'that unmitigated cold-blooded rude brute Hicks-Beach [Chancellor of the Exchequer]'.[61]

In the early 1900s, the popular press was in its infancy and Fisher had been slow to recognise its potential. Only after twenty years of feeding material to *The Times* and various periodicals did he come to appreciate the value of the *Daily Mail* and its Fleet Street imitators. According to White, it was at a lunch on the *Renown* that Fisher asked him 'why I wrote for a halfpenny paper'. In reply, he told Fisher that 'the price of the paper had less effect upon the future of mankind than its circulation among people who could think and wished to know the truth about things'.[62] Fisher had discovered 'middle England' and, according to White, he 'seized the point like lightning' and from then on was as keen on the popular press as he was on *The Times*.

Fisher's choice of Arnold White and the *Daily Mail* was a risky one. Its proprietor, Alfred Harmsworth (later, Lord Northcliffe) was renowned for his aggressive, underhand and unscrupulous tactics. As a man who would use and discard anyone to boost circulation, Northcliffe was not to be trusted for a moment. In Act 4 we will see how Beresford's supping with the paper backfired on him. It played a rough game and, to paraphrase Fisher, circulation came first, second and third in planning its populist campaigns. Nevertheless, in mid-1901 the paper exalted Fisher describing him as 'this still, strong man'. It was, it said, 'impossible to be in his company for five minutes without perceiving that he is no ordinary personage'.[63] The paper's enthusiasm for Fisher benefitted Beresford, too. Pressing the need for more ships to be sent to the Mediterranean, the paper said that reinforcements 'could not be wasted' on men like Fisher and Beresford who had such 'energy and determination'.[64]

Despite their differences and their mutual lack of trust, Beresford greatly admired Fisher and praised his achievements on numerous occasions. Fundamentally, he recognised that Fisher was a superb fleet commander, from whom he could learn much.

Like almost every officer in the Navy, Beresford had been exposed to precious little practical training in fleet handling in a war-like manner. So little had he learnt, he confessed to his ledger, that 'I was fifty-five years of age and had been forty-three years in the Service before I and my brother Officers discovered what was the proper position for an Admiral in his Fleet in action.' This, he only found out 'by the practical manoeuvring of one Fleet against another – Mediterranean versus Channel in September 1901'. It was, he commented, 'Simply incredible!!!'[65] On another occasion, he said that the exercises organised by Fisher taught 'admirals ... lessons they ought to have known as lieutenants'.[66] He passed on his admiration of Fisher's manoeuvres to White, telling him that 'Fisher deserves the lasting gratitude of the Empire for having started these practical manoeuvres in time of peace.'[67]

Another Fisher innovation that met with Beresford's approval was the prize essay. This he introduced in order to encourage young officers to think for themselves and to argue clearly in defence of their views. Beresford called the essay an 'excellent' practice saying that 'the interchange of ideas ... [was] of educational value'.[68] Indeed, he liked it so much that he agreed to chair the judging panel. (The third prize went to Maurice Hankey.) In his ledger, he recorded that 'The number of things learnt in the Mediterranean by Sir John Fisher's Committees and Writing of Essays is incalculable.'[69] Beresford's experience of judging the essays led him to suggest that the Admiralty would benefit from reading them, recording in his ledger that it would help them find out what ideas young officers had in their heads.[70] The Admiralty did not agree with him on this point and were most unhelpful when Fisher sought their views on his second round of essays. They clearly saw thinking officers as a danger to discipline.[71]

When Beresford came to make notes on his leaving the Mediterranean, he could hardly contain his enthusiasm in praising Fisher. Summarising Fisher's regime he wrote: 'From a 12-knot Fleet with numerous breakdowns, he made a 15-knot Fleet without breakdowns.'[72] He called its efficiency 'admirable'.[73] Later still, when Fisher had left the Mediterranean, Beresford wrote down a list of twenty achievements which he attributed to his superior, including some, such as 'increased stocks of coal at Malta and Gibraltar' that, on other occasions, he claimed for himself.[74] Was this praise 'hypocritical' as Penn claims, or did Beresford really mean it?[75] Given the way that he praised Fisher in the privacy of his ledger, it would seem that Beresford really *did* admire Fisher at this time.

Perhaps, though, Beresford's most remarkable tribute to Fisher was that he chose to stay in the Mediterranean, despite other offers. In September 1900, when he was being enticed back to Parliament, he went to visit Fisher on the *Renown* and, Fisher told his wife, Beresford 'had made up his mind not to re-enter Parliament, but to remain out with the Fleet his whole time!' The reason he gave was a resounding tribute to his commander: 'he had learnt more in the last week than in the last forty years!'[76] It seems that he had changed his mind by the following September, by which time the Navy League was beginning to arrange public meetings at which Beresford was to speak on his return.[77]

Despite all Fisher's reservations about Beresford's agitations Fisher was remarkably appreciative of Beresford's work with the Fleet. At Lemnos, after some fleet exercises he told his wife that, 'Beresford did uncommonly well,' noting that 'he is much pleased at my praising him, which he thoroughly deserved.'[78]

Beresford, who was then fifty-five years old, had fully entered into the spirit of Fisher's realistic exercises. Conservative (both in politics and his personal life) though he was, Fisher had inspired him to achieve, late in life, skills of warfare that had escaped him throughout his naval career. A year later, following joint exercises with the Channel Squadron, Fisher told Selborne that 'both Wilson [Channel Squadron] and Beresford handled their own Squadrons most admirably when working independently against each other'.[79]

In turn, Fisher was sure that Beresford thought well of him, even to the point of being too enthusiastic on his behalf. In May 1902, when Beresford was back in the House of Commons and agitating for naval reforms, he seems to have pressed the case for Fisher's return to the Admiralty rather too fervently for comfort. 'Beresford,' Fisher told his son, 'is so very full of what he thinks my capacity for reform that he keeps on telling people at home how I shall turn them all inside out at the Admiralty, that I am the only Admiral worth his salt, etc., etc.' Despite 'begging him to hold his tongue & he promises to do so but in a few days I hear again of his flourishing me in some Admiral's face!'[80]

Alongside this odd mixture of suppressed antagonism and friendly cooperation, the Fisher and Beresford families mingled happily at Malta. It is hard to reconcile the Beresford who meticulously recorded his grievances in his ledger with the Beresford who dropped this delightfully casual invitation into a letter to Fisher about military politics back in England: 'I have a children's party 4.30 to 6.30 Saturday here. Do come and help me: they would like to see you.' Later in the same letter, the politics being dealt with, he added, 'I hope to send you some fish tonight ... Meet you Saturday.'[81] The tone of this is hardly consistent with the notion that the two men were persistently antagonistic to each other. Rather, it suggests that they actively sought and enjoyed each other's company.

This, then, was the strangely uncertain relationship between Fisher and Beresford in the Mediterranean. In interpreting these two years, we are faced with the problem of Beresford as observer. Most of his carping criticisms come from what he wrote in his ledger, often months after the events occurred. Can we rely on these accounts? Or were they coloured by justifications for his own insubordinations? With no more information, we might incline to the view that things were not so bad after all, and that Beresford chose to colour his accounts to suit his own ends. We do, though, have records of two other highly significant incidents which were witnessed by others and which fully support Beresford's view that Fisher showed a distinct animosity towards him.

## Scene 2: Humiliations by signal

We have already met the petty humiliations that Beresford recorded in his ledger. To these we must add two incidents that were so gross that news of them sped far and wide within hours of their occurrence. The first took place on the naval parade ground at the Corradino Heights, a hill overlooking Malta Harbour.

A curt note in Beresford's ledger records the event. He wrote, on 29 March 1900, '[I] Was ordered ... to discontinue landing *Ramillies* Signalmen whom I had on shore to practise manoeuvring by signal order.'[82]

Beresford, in his memoirs, giving his own account of the episode, explained that 'my interest in signalling inspired me to invent a new drill for the signalmen'. This was to be land-based and involved linking the men together 'with a tack-line' – a piece of rope used with sails. Each man was to represent a ship, the line being used to keep the men the correct distance apart as if they were ships steaming together. In this way, said Beresford, 'the men executed the evolutions of a fleet in obedience to signals'.[83]

Opinions differ as to the value of this eccentric exercise. It has been called 'ridiculous' on the grounds that 'a man can turn on his heel, whereas a ship takes some minutes' – in other words, the men would be learning to signal too late, since ships respond to signals more slowly than sailors on a parade ground.[84] On the other hand, Beresford has also been complemented for devising 'a useful method of training signalmen'.[85] The judgement of history seems to favour the former view, since Beresford's method was never adopted as an official means of naval training. Indeed, even at the time, according to Penn, 'Beresford became a laughing stock' when it became known.[86]

As far as Fisher was concerned it was not the efficacy, or otherwise, of the method that was his issue. It was that Beresford had landed his men without first seeking permission. Such an act was contrary to Fisher's station orders, as his peremptory open signal made plain:

> *Ramillies'* signalmen to return to ship immediately. Report in writing why station order No. ... has not been obeyed.[87]

The signal was an utter humiliation for Beresford. His purpose – the training of signalmen – was admirable and his failure to seek permission to land his men was presumably an oversight. In such circumstances Fisher had no need to act on the moment: a quiet word at a later date would have been sufficient. It would be over-generous to suggest that Fisher did not know what he was doing when he made the signal and what the consequences were likely to be: he was dressing-down his second-in-command in front of the whole Fleet. Hankey later recalled that 'This public affront caused great indignation on board the *Ramillies* and was naturally resented by Beresford.'[88] The indignation was not restricted to the *Ramillies*, as Lieutenant Chatfield noted that 'the Fleet took in the signal and pricked up its ears'. So much so, that later that day, 'Malta was talking of it over the tea-cups and cocktails.'[89]

According to Bacon, Fisher later had a talk with Beresford in which he told him that he:

> [W]elcomed his coming to the Mediterranean Fleet, but he must thoroughly understand that it was as Second-in-Command and not Commander-in-Chief, and that if he was desirous, as most Rear-Admirals were, of taking a portion of the Fleet on an independent cruise, the best way of achieving his object was by paying scrupulous attention to the limitations of his command.

This, said Bacon, 'cleared the atmosphere' and after that they 'were on quite amicable terms'.[90] Bacon gives no evidence for this account, and other observers are of the view that Beresford deeply resented his humiliation and that it was one of many small incidents that provided the basis for the feud.[91]

The second incident that throws light on the Fisher-Beresford relationship occurred later that same year and within walking distance of the Corradino Heights. The bare bones of the incident, which occurred on 7 November 1900, are recorded in the *Ramillies'* Flag Journal:

1.31 pm Fleet arrived at Malta and Ships secured to their respective buoys.

3.39 'Ramillies' and 'Royal Sovereign' slipped and proceeded out of harbour in compliance with Commander-in-Chief's orders.

4.50 'Ramillies' and 'Royal Sovereign' re-entered Grand Harbour and picked up their respective buoys.

Letter to Commander in Chief No. 86. Calling attention to circumstances of 'Ramillies' taking up moorings assigned to her at Malta.[92]

Behind this unemotional account of two ships entering, leaving and re-entering Malta harbour was the second great explosion between the two men. By good fortune, Chatfield left a much fuller account of that day.

In late 1900, he recalled, 'the Fleet was returning to Malta at the end of the first summer cruise'. As usual, Fisher, in the *Renown* had led the Fleet into harbour. After docking, he had gone ashore and climbed up to the Barracca, a vantage point high above the harbour, from which he could watch the Fleet come in.

The harbour entrance at Malta, Chatfield explained, was 'difficult and narrow'. After entering, the ships had to turn sharply in a narrow passage – and the more ships that were in the harbour, the harder the manoeuvring became. It was a task calling, said Chatfield, for 'nerve and skill'. Unfortunately for Beresford, his Flag Captain was not quite up to the mark. Pressed by Fisher to complete every manoeuvre as rapidly as possible – 'rush' was a favourite word of his – he seriously misjudged the passage and 'got his ship stuck across the harbour'. This was bad enough. A more critical consequence was that the harbour entrance was now blocked, leaving a good part of the Fleet queuing in the open sea.

Fisher exploded and issued another humiliating, open signal to Beresford: 'Your flagship is to proceed to sea and come in again in a seamanlike manner.' According to Chatfield, Fisher's staff did their utmost to dissuade him from sending this signal – 'but to no avail'. The signal went out and was read by the entire Fleet. Nor did it stop there. In the new age of wireless, 'news of it spread throughout the Service'.[93] Later, Chatfield was to identify this incident as the moment when the feud started. There is, though, little evidence to support him and, as we shall see, relations between the two men were to remain civil, if not warm, for a few more years yet. In defence of Chatfield, though, Beresford added the incident to the many affronts which he felt he had suffered at the hands of the Board.

Beresford said nothing that day, but lay in wait until a suitable moment arose to take his revenge. He found that opportunity when, some time later, the Fleet was at Lemnos for the annual Mediterranean Regatta. The mail needed to be collected from a Turkish port, a task which should have been assigned to the most junior cruiser present. By mistake, Fisher ordered the *Theseus* to fulfil this task, an error immediately spotted by Beresford. In normal times – perhaps non-existent in the worlds of these two men – Beresford would have simply asked Fisher to reallocate the task. Instead, smarting from the offensive open signals he had received, Beresford responded in kind. From the *Ramillies* his signal spread to the Fleet:

> I regret that after the good work *Theseus* has done under my command during the recent exercises, she is not to be allowed to take part in the regatta.

Fisher realised his error, and reallocated the mail collection, at which point Beresford sent a further signal:

> I am glad that after the good work *Theseus* has done under my command, the Commander-in-Chief has seen fit to allow her to take part in the regatta.[94]

It is no wonder, then, that in October 1901 King-Hall's diary records that, 'Beresford ... detained me for half an hour more or less, having a hit at C.-in-C., ending up by saying he was Asiatic!'[95]

## Scene 3: The Syndicate of Discontent

It was around this time that what Fisher called 'The Syndicate of Discontent' began to appear. He used this phrase to describe a loose collection of individuals, who, motivated by an intense dislike of him and his methods, sought to block his advancement within the Navy. He first became aware of the movement in November 1901, when he told White that 'I hear a syndicate of Admirals (mostly fossils!) has been formed to prevent my future employment!'[96]

One of the chief instigators of the syndicate was Reginald Custance. Born in 1847, he had entered the Navy in 1860 and steadily rose through the ranks, distinguishing himself as a capable naval officer with a passion for historical studies. Although he had a reputation for being of a 'suspicious nature' and 'secretive', Fisher and Custance had worked together from time to time, maintaining friendly relations.[97] When Custance was appointed as Director of Naval Intelligence in 1899 Fisher was delighted. The fact that he was to lodge in Half Moon Street, near the Fishers, was 'excellent' since Fisher wanted to see him 'very often'.[98] The prospect soon turned sour and their friendship was brought to an abrupt end when they clashed over naval strategy. To some extent, these clashes were provoked by what King-Hall called the 'very strong letters' that Fisher sent to the Admiralty.[99] As often as Fisher reported a new fleet exercise in the

Mediterranean, so did Custance (at the Admiralty) find fault with its design or with Fisher's interpretation of its consequences. Custance would write acerbic comments on Admiralty minutes and letters connected with Fisher's Mediterranean command. He was most disparaging of the prize essays and, on one occasion when Fisher asked for more ships, Custance dismissed the request with the comment: 'His ken does not extend beyond his own immediate sphere of operations.'[100,101] By April 1901, when the First Lord paid a visit to Malta, Fisher refused to provide accommodation for Custance at Admiralty House. The breach was total. It was no surprise therefore that, when Beresford finally appeared before the inquiry in 1909, Custance was at his side.

It was not long before Custance set about trying to prevent Fisher's return to the Admiralty. In January 1902, he thought he had succeeded, telling a friend that: 'Fisher has made a great effort to get into the Admiralty as Second Sea Lord, but has, I trust been defeated.' He called Fisher 'superficial and time-serving'.[102] In another letter to Cyprian Bridge (Commander-in-Chief in the China Sea) he said, 'The worst thing I know of is the advent of Fisher with all his wild, superficial ideas. No man has less grasp of principles.'[103]

Another agitator who Beresford tried to draw into his circle at this time was Carlyon Bellairs. He had entered the Navy in 1884 and been promoted lieutenant in 1891. He and Beresford were old friends and had corresponded since 1890, sharing a mutual hostility to the Admiralty and the running of the Navy. In December 1900, Beresford asked Bellairs to become his secretary when he returned to Britain. 'You being a Radical,' (he became a Unionist in 1909) Beresford told him, 'would suit me as all public men ought to have a counterpoise in opinion.'[104] In their correspondence at this time, Bellairs attempted to bring Beresford over to the Liberal Party, but the most that Beresford would promise was to 'write ... when I have had time to weigh the pros & cons as to your proposal'.[105] Bellairs quickly turned down the job offer but, in compensation, recruited someone else to be Beresford's secretary. That Beresford trusted such a task to Bellairs indicates the close bond that existed between the two men.[106] From 1902 onwards, when Bellairs entered Parliament, he became Beresford's principal spokesman in the House.

In the story of the feud there was yet another, discreet player, the Navy League. This was a non-party-political pressure group which, amongst its six 'objects' included:

To enlist, on national grounds, the support of all classes in maintaining the Fleet at the requisite standard of strength, and to denounce any shortcomings in this respect.[107]

On the surface, this statement was innocuous enough but the League was prone, in practice, to spawning naval scare stories as to the weakness of the Fleet and the defenceless state of Britain. Its Executive Committee happily referred to such work as 'agitations' and, since the target of these disturbances was the Government, they were most unwelcome in White-hall. Even Beresford, who had close, if ill-defined, links to the League, noted that, 'There are certain dangers arising from the want of knowledge of its Members.'[108]

Part of the problem for both Fisher and Beresford was that Arnold White was a member of its Executive Committee. White was a colourful character. He had behind him a failed career as a coffee-planter in Ceylon (just like Fisher's father), a managerial post that had ended in redundancy, and a period of helping to colonise the dominions. In 1886 he had attempted to enter Parliament, without success, and had finally opted for a career as a polemical journalist. After first specialising in anti-immigration campaigns, he settled on the specialism with which his name is now for ever linked: the Navy.

When Fisher and Beresford dealt with White, it was hard for them to know whether it was White the journalist or White of the League. No doubt White, too, had difficulties in separating his roles. However, when White and Robert Yerburgh, Unionist MP and the League's President, visited Beresford's squadron in 1901, both came in their capacity as members of the League. This roused Fisher's suspicions and he took the precaution of writing to the First Naval Lord, so giving him the opportunity to prohibit the visit.[109] The visit went ahead, triggering the *Daily Mail* letter, which is the subject of the next act.

Not surprisingly, many observers have dated the feud from the Mediterranean period. Hankey was less convinced. After all, he wrote, 'there was at that time no serious difference of professional opinion between the two Admirals' and 'Beresford always spoke well of Fisher's activities and aided and abetted him to the best of his power.' It was, thought Hankey, just a difference of temperament, but not, at that time, a feud in the making.[110] Even if Hankey were correct in his judgement, the fact remains that Beresford left the Mediterranean with enough material from which to generate grievances whenever he felt the need for them.

Meanwhile, the Mediterranean period contained one other episode that merits an act of its own – The *Daily Mail* Letter.

*Act 4*

# The *Daily Mail* Letter

All persons belonging to the Fleet are forbidden to write
for any newspaper on subjects connected with the
Naval Service ... – *King's Regulations*.

## Scene 1: Beresford writes a letter

At this point in the story we need to return to June 1901 in order to consider
in detail a single event which we have passed over. It is the story of a letter
of just 139 words, which was to give birth to debates and criticism running
to tens of thousands of words over a full year. The *Daily Mail* letter, as we
shall call the incident, deserves our attention because, in writing it, in
failing to defend it and then defending it, Beresford was to reveal to
friends, journalists, colleagues and politicians that none of them could trust
a word he said.

On one of Mina Beresford's return visits to England, she opened her
*Daily Mail* and was horrified to see a letter from her husband. One glance
was enough to tell her that this 'very injudicious & ill worded letter' was
going to be trouble. This is what she read:

H.M.S. Ramillies
At Sea
June 10, 1901

Mr dear ____,

It would be most improper and prejudicial to discipline if I were to give you
details as to why I am so extremely anxious when considering the want of
strength and the want of proper War Organisation of the British Fleet in the
Mediterranean.

I have communicated my views in as strong and clear Anglo-Saxon
language as I can command to the properly constituted authorities.

My duty and business out here as second-in-command are simply to obey
any orders that I may receive to the level best of my ability, and not to offer
any criticism which might become public.

The real point to be immediately considered is not so much the necessity of
expending a further sum of money on the British Navy as the necessity of
allocating the money now voted in a different manner.

Rear-Admiral Lord Charles Beresford[1]

Mina knew at once who to turn to for an explanation and she picked up her pen to write to White. For Mina, the letter could mean only one thing: Beresford must be intending to resign his commission. 'Did you know,' she asked White, 'of his intention to "brûler ses vaisseaux" [burn his boats] at this juncture?'[2] Mina would have to wait a long time for a clear answer to this and many other questions which the letter raised.

As Beresford wrote the letter, did his mind turn back to 8 April 1900 when he told Balfour:

> I cannot write an official letter on these points because I am 2$^{nd}$ in command, neither would it be in the interest of discipline if I were to write a public letter, but I can write as many private letters as I like.[3]

Or was this just a 'private letter'? This was no academic question since serving naval officers were absolutely prohibited from writing letters to the press or entering into public political debate in any way. Yet here was the second-in-command of Britain's premier fleet brazenly telling all the world that it was lacking in 'proper war organisation'.

Beresford's claim that he had communicated his views 'to the properly constituted authorities' was more than justified. We have seen that he had sent Balfour a long list of the deficiencies of the Mediterranean Fleet in his letter of 8 April. Two months later he had sent him the twenty-one page typed report, setting out complaint after complaint. Whether Balfour was one of the 'properly constituted authorities' was another matter. Most readers of the *Daily Mail* letter would surely have thought that Beresford was referring to the Board of Admiralty.

White had told Fisher that the *Mail* was read by 'people who could think and wished to know the truth about things', so what was the truth?[4] Perhaps this was some mistake. Perhaps the letter had been published against Beresford's will. After all, his opening sentence admitted that it would be 'prejudicial to discipline' to publish the details. But even if readers were to set aside their doubts as to the propriety of the letter, what about those reports? Had Beresford actually sent in such critical reports? And had the Admiralty really ignored them?

Answers were going to be demanded, and soon.

Three days later, on 24 June, the Liberal Member for Wolverhampton South, Mr Henry Norman, rose from his seat in the House of Commons to ask Mr Hugh Arnold-Forster, Secretary to the Admiralty, 'whether his attention has been drawn to a letter from Rear-Admiral Lord Charles Beresford, in which he states that he has communicated his views ... to the properly constituted authorities in as strong and clear Anglo-Saxon language as he can command'. Did the Admiralty intend to publish this document?[5]

The House knew what sort of a minister was going to rise from the Government Front Bench. With 'a justifiably high opinion of his intellectual abilities' and a 'schoolmasterly manner',[6] Arnold-Forster, referred to as 'Priscilla' by his colleagues, and author of a wide range of school textbooks, was a fastidious politician.[7] His obituary described him as 'a man of independent mind and strong opinions' with 'a rare power of grasping facts and remembering them'.[8] It was his mastery of facts that made him a powerful and effective debater in the Commons, but at the same time he was never popular, being seen as austere and intellectual. The adjectives that stuck to him were 'high-minded' and 'worthy' – distinctly pejorative terms in the world of politics and the Navy. He found compromise impossible and he was impervious to popular appeal: just the characteristics to make him the ideal man to respond to Beresford's antics. The latter, ever indifferent to the constraint of facts was to meet in Arnold-Forster a man who knew that, ultimately, facts will out. He had the brain, the conviction and the patience to bide his time until proved right.

Arnold-Forster chose to play a straight bat, telling the House that 'there is nothing to show that the letter was intended for publication'. He thought, he added, that it was 'highly improbable that the Rear-Admiral would have taken a step so contrary to the discipline of the Navy as to make public communication with regard to confidential reports' and, in any event, 'any communications from the Rear-Admiral and Captains of the Mediterranean Fleet, which the Commander-in-Chief of that Fleet has sought fit to transmit, have been carefully considered by the Admiralty'. He added that these reports were 'of a confidential nature' and would not be published.[9]

If Arnold-Forster had stopped after his first sentence, perhaps the House and the country would have turned their attention to their forthcoming summer holidays and harvest time. Foolishly, Arnold-Forster had both admitted that the reports existed and failed to deny that they revealed that the Navy was not organised for war. He had said both too much and too little and, as a result, would be answering questions about the letter for the next twelve months.

Of course, no one had any idea as to why this letter had appeared at this particular time. Or, more correctly, no one *admitted* to knowing anything. But one man knew it all – Arnold White.

Early in May 1901, Beresford, sweltering in the Mediterranean heat on the *Ramillies* at Malta, had written to White inviting him to visit and stay 'as long as you like'.[10] This was no invitation to enjoy a leisurely Mediterranean cruise. Rather it was Beresford seeking an outlet for his pent-up, voluminous criticisms of the Admiralty, the Government and 'the authorities'. At the back of his mind was, no doubt, that bulging ledger.

Day by day he entered sometimes a new grievance, sometimes yet another note for a speech, and sometimes another urgently needed naval reform. The ledger overflows and explodes with bile and suppressed dynamism; it is the outpourings of a second-in-command who, accustomed to indulgently attentive audiences in the salons of London and the smoking room of the Commons, found too few outlets for his opinions in the puddle that was the Mediterranean. In White, he had chosen well; he was a man who would happily repeat Beresford's vitriolic comments in the columns of the *Daily Mail* and other journals.

At this time, White was an active member of the Executive Committee of the Navy League and so he had been party to the decision they took on 20 May to 'consider a plan of campaign . . . [for] utilizing the Strength of the League in its Branches'.[11] Campaigns needed ammunition, so it is reasonable to suppose that White saw Beresford's invitation as an opportunity to access naval secrets that were denied him in the Commons and Whitehall. Sometime in June, he boarded the *Ramillies* and began to question, talk, watch and record. He was a reporter in the modern mould. Whereas the typical journalist of that time would dutifully record the measured words of ministers, officials, mayors and aldermen, White delved into the bowels of the ships of the Fleet, seeking out the common seamen and the rising officers, listening to their gripes.

It was not long before a stream of provocative articles was pouring into the offices of the *Daily Mail* and other journals. A typical piece would mix praise for the work of Fisher and Beresford with warnings about weaknesses in the Fleet. For example, on 11 June he wrote that the two admirals 'have made efficiency their cult' and 'have carried the training of their command to a point of excellence never before reached in time of peace'. White went on to warn, that, nevertheless, 'the Mediterranean Fleet is weak'. He could see 'no good reason why a division of the Channel Squadron with half a dozen cruisers should not be sent to the Straits of Gibraltar' to strengthen the Fleet.[12] In reality, these were not White's words – they had Fisher stamped all over them.

In his more investigative capacity, White lived as a seaman for twenty-four hours, sharing their quarters and their food. Writing of his experience he said that 'the sailor does not get enough food from the State in the twenty-four hours to fit him for his work' and complained of there being no meal between 4.15 pm and 8.00 am, except 'a cup of cocoa at 5.00 am'. As to the quality of the meals, he concluded that 'the cook generally knows as much of cookery as of Wagner's music'.[13] This experience led him to begin a long campaign to improve the Navy's diet – but that is another story.

White was back in England by 10 June, when he reported on his visit to the Executive Committee of the League. They were impressed by what he had to tell them and agreed that 'they would endeavour to bring before the public certain information which was thus placed in their possession'.[14] And so we see the tight circle of Navy League–White–Beresford. The League wanted covert details of the Fleet. Who might be sent to collect? None other than a journalist, who just happened to be a member of their Executive. And who might give him access to officers and sailors? Well, why not Beresford, a rear admiral with the closest of links with the League. It was a cosy conspiracy; in public each party kept its distance from the others. Behind the scenes, each played its part in ensuring that the League's 'agitations' hit their mark.

White, of course, needed Beresford – a journalist is nothing without his sources – and Beresford needed White. But writing about cocoa and cabbage was one thing; agreeing to become Beresford's spokesman was something rather different, as White was soon to discover. In publishing Beresford's letter, he had unwittingly unleashed an affair in which the journalist would become bigger than his story.

Readers of the *Daily Mail* letter were no doubt mystified as to its purpose; it is also doubtful whether Beresford was ever clear in his own mind as to his desired outcome. Any attempt to understand this saga is frustrated by the fact that Beresford was a man of little brain. Thinking did not come naturally to him, and when he did think, he often indulged in confused and contorted explanations that neither he nor his listeners could follow. In the case of the letter, the problem for Beresford was that it was White's idea, as White reminded him when the affair was drawing to a close more than a year later. He recalled how he had visited the Mediterranean and how:

> I asked you if you would write a short letter for publication which should contain one sentence indicating that the Mediterranean Fleet was not organised for war ... you wrote the draft of a letter in which I suggested some alterations. You accepted these alterations and were good enough to hand me the letter which was published in the *Daily Mail* on June 21st 1901.[15]

Predictably, this letter describing the origin of the conspiracy was neither made public at the time, nor in the lifetime of Beresford – their cloak-and-dagger operation was to remain a closely-guarded secret until White's archives were opened after his death.

On the day of the letter's publication a triumphal *Daily Mail* leader asserted that the letter 'should be studied by every Englishman' since the Mediterranean Fleet 'has the fate of England in its keeping'. (At that time many people feared a surprise attack from a French fleet, possibly supported by the Russians from the Black Sea.) The paper referred to the on-going Boer War in South Africa where 'experience ... has already shown us the extreme danger of postponing to the last moment the despatch of reinforcements'. It then added a sentence that was soon to be branded as 'scandalous' in the House of Commons:

> That Lord Charles Beresford represents the unanimous opinion of the senior officers in the Mediterranean Fleet is notorious. From Commander-in-Chief to junior commander there is no dissent from what he says.[16]

## Scene 2: Search for the guilty party

Before the Commons next had a chance to debate the letter, Arnold-Forster was to receive an astounding admission from White that was to stir up the furore beyond anything that Beresford could have wished. Writing to Arnold-Forster, White first reminded him that he had said that 'there was nothing in Lord Charles Beresford's letter to show that it was intended for publication'. He then went on to say 'It will be no surprise to you to know that I was the recipient of that letter and am responsible for its publication.'[17]

White assumed that Arnold-Forster would have understood the truth behind the letter since, only two months earlier, he had sought the Minister's permission to visit the Mediterranean Fleet. Writing to Arnold-Forster after the visit, he reminded him that, on 24 April, he had enquired 'whether a respectful application to the Admiralty from the Navy League for an official letter of introduction for a member of that body to the Admiral in command of the Mediterranean Fleet would be likely to meet with success'. In reply, Arnold-Forster had told him that 'it is not the custom of the Admiralty to grant official letters' but that he was sure that his delegation would be given a reception that was 'all that could be desired'. White now released his bombshell, telling Arnold-Forster that he had taken his reply to be in 'the nature of a credential from the Admiralty', had visited the Fleet and *acquired a full knowledge of the facts which you say in your reply to Mr Norman will not be made public*'.[18] (Emphasis added.)

Was this just bragging? Or had White really acquired those facts that the Admiralty had refused to supply to Parliament? Had White even read copies of the reports that Beresford claimed to have sent to the Admiralty? From the evidence of George King-Hall's diary of 21 July 1901, it would seem that White *was* telling the truth, when he noted that 'I do not think Sir John has acted loyally to his superiors, for he disclosed to Arnold White and Mr Yerburgh, at two visits for two at a time, *all our plans*.'[19] (Emphasis added.)

Two days after the Commons questions of 24 June, the Navy League issued a statement in support of the allegation that the Navy was weak. Reminding its readers of their view in October 1900 that Britain was losing command of the sea, it went on to say that, after their recent visit to the

Mediterranean, the same deficiencies still existed.[20] The next day, the *Daily Mail* noted that 'It is needless for the Navy League to go into detail' since 'the fighting fleets of Britain are not ready for war'.[21]

Meanwhile, Beresford was sitting it out in the Mediterranean, saying nothing, although remaining in touch with White. On 27 June he told him 'Be assured that we are all with you … We regard you as a patriot.' Beresford praised White's work, saying: 'you are manipulating things well.' Turning to more practical matters, he added 'You were so wise not to put in the letter who, "My dear" was.' In this omission, he claimed that White had given him a let-out, should the Admiralty call him to justice: 'If they write to me I shall reply that I have written hundreds of the same sort. I do not see that I have done anything short of complete discipline or prejudicial to the Service.'[22] It was a typical Beresford argument: he was not guilty on this occasion, since it was a crime that he regularly committed.

The Admiralty, however, had no intention of investigating how the letter had come to be published, whilst simultaneously bemoaning Beresford's having written it. In a letter to Fisher, the Secretary to the Navy said that he was 'very sorry about Lord Charles' letter' adding that he thought Beresford 'should set an example'. Arnold-Forster went on to point out that Beresford 'would be the very first to condemn … any Officer or seaman under his Command' who behaved in a similar way.[23]

By now, Fisher was becoming concerned about his own position. Already his name had been mentioned in the affair; Beresford was proving hard to control. If things did not calm down, Fisher's career could be under threat. After all, he already held his post on sufferance in the eyes of some at the Admiralty and Custance was actively lobbying to stop his return. When his career had been unexpectedly revived in 1899, Fisher was the subject of much jealous comment. Why him? Having landed the plum job of the Mediterranean Station, his adversaries felt doubly aggrieved at his newly-found preferment. The persistent rumours that he would return to the Admiralty at the end of his posting only further provoked his antagonists.

On top of these problems, following his arrival in the Mediterranean, Fisher had bombarded the Admiralty with letter after letter setting out the Fleet's deficiencies. This did not endear him to the Board, as the Admiralty files of the time show. Lord Walter Kerr, then First Naval Lord (the term 'Sea Lord' did not come back into use until 1904), wrote that Fisher 'has a habit notable in some of his communications of indulging in strong phrases to emphasise his arguments such as "disastrous consequences" – "imperative necessity" – "immediate large increase"'.[24] When Fisher sent in a report asking for more destroyers, Kerr wrote that no one knew better than him that 'sixty-two Destroyers in the Mediterranean is an impossibility under existing conditions – Yet he calmly proposes it'. Of Fisher's endless demands, Kerr said: 'Their Lordships have a right to expect something better than a demand for impossibilities from an Officer holding the position of C. in C. Mediterranean.'[25]

Against this background, Fisher became increasingly anxious about the loose cannon on his station. Referring to White's articles (some of which he knew to be inspired by Beresford) he told an old friend of his: 'It will be of course obvious to you that I have nothing whatever to gain by kicking the shins of the Admiralty! so that the articles (of which, by the way, I have only seen a portion) are certainly not written in my interest! and only serve to aggravate instead of smoothing and facilitating.'[26]

When White cooked up his campaign in the summer of 1901, a central part was an article entitled *A Message from the Mediterranean* for publication in the *National Review*. He does not seem to have told Beresford about this when he visited the *Ramillies*, but he certainly told Fisher, since Fisher's corrected proof lies in his archives. Of course, when Fisher saw the proofs, he knew nothing about the planned Beresford letter. Had he known, he would almost certainly have refused to cooperate with the *Message*. Tactics aside, the article was pure Fisher, full of his phrases and pressing his ideas. It described deficiencies of every type, which White listed using the same words as in the earlier Navy League statement, which were, in turn, Fisher's phrases. But the heart of the article was the message that Fisher had been urging from the day he arrived in the Mediterranean:

> We no longer possess supremacy at sea because we stint our fleets of material, do not concentrate where strength is needed; and yet we require our admirals and captains to act as if they were adequately provided with the best munitions of modern war.[27]

White had written the article in his capacity as a member of the Executive Committee of the Navy League. When the Committee saw it, they were so impressed that they immediately allocated £200 (about £15,000 today) 'for an immediate agitation by hand bills or otherwise'.[28] The following day Yerburgh was able to tell the committee that the Government had 'agreed to make an opportunity for full discussion of the Mediterranean Fleet'.[29]

What is striking about the article is White's use of trade-marked Fisher phrases, such as the Admiralty being 'destitute of a thinking department', 'no breakwater at Malta', 'Egypt undefended' and 'to-day we are strong nowhere, and weak everywhere'.[30] Fisher knew that, with phrases like these, White was running him close to the wind; with the *Daily Mail* letter he was in danger of capsizing the Fisher programme.

## Scene 3: Questions in the House

By early July the navalists in the Commons had had time to think about the contents of Beresford's letter and were ready to attack. As it happened, the naval estimates for 1902–3 were due for debate on 3 July. There was no way they could *oppose* the estimates since they wanted the Government to spend even more. So, to show their disapproval of the Government's lack of support for the Navy, they used the traditional symbolic device: a motion to reduce the First Lord's salary by £100. The sum was puny; the symbolism was potent.

The motion was moved by Yerburgh, as President of the Navy League. In his opening speech he emphasised the Mediterranean Fleet's lack of 'all the auxiliary vessels necessary to make it an efficient fighting force in time of war'. There was nothing *there* to worry Fisher; indeed he would have been delighted that one of his key messages was being made during a debate on naval estimates. The next speaker was another matter.

Mr Edmund Robertson, Liberal MP for Dundee and an ex-Civil Lord of the Admiralty, referred to the *Daily Mail* letter, saying that 'the line taken by Lord Charles Beresford had the support of a more important person – namely Admiral Fisher'. In fact, as he admitted, he had no proof of this, but 'he could not believe, knowing him as he did, that Sir John Fisher would take a line of action inconsistent with his duty'. Later in the debate, Robertson mentioned White's *Message from the Mediterranean* calling it a 'scandal' because, as he put it, 'All the officers from the Admiral in command down to the junior officer, are sending this message to the people of England, not through the Admiralty as they ought to, but through Arnold White!'[31]

Fisher, out in the Mediterranean, read the newspapers (English and French) zealously, so we can be sure that he saw the reports of the debate within a day or two. This was just the sort of publicity that he did not wish to see – and it was all the result of Beresford's indiscretion.

While there is abundant circumstantial evidence that Beresford was closely associated with the Navy League, not much documentary evidence remains to identify the precise nature of the links, all the correspondence of the League from this period having been recently destroyed. However, on 3 July, the League's Minute Book provides hard confirmation of Beresford's direct involvement in its agitations. Later in the day, after the debate was over, the Committee despatched a telegram to Beresford, which read:

Debate in full House, facts admitted by Ministers, promises not satisfactory, Agitation growing, Navy League will do its duty to the Fleet. White.

At the same meeting, the Executive agreed to distribute a copy of *A Message from the Mediterranean* 'to all members of the House of Commons by Friday morning'.[32]

Had Beresford gone too far, even by his own standards? Certainly he was beginning to reflect on the possible dismissal of both himself and

Fisher, although he concluded to White that: 'I do not think they will dare relieve Jack Fisher and myself.' In any case, he was sanguine about such an eventuality, saying: 'If they relieve him I shall resign at once. If they relieve me I can fight my own battle, very easily.'[33] What Beresford meant was that, if he was put on half-pay, he could always return to the Commons. Fisher had fewer options.

Two days after the debate (and probably the day that Fisher would have read the reports on it) Fisher shared with his wife his worries about Beresford's actions: 'Beresford seems to think there is a tremendous row going on in the Cabinet about the Med[n] Fleet & that they would hang me if they could!'[34] In another letter Fisher puzzled over the situation in which he found himself. On the one hand 'the whole Cabinet is most furious over the Mediterranean Fleet agitation' yet at the same time 'every single item demanded is being conceded', a paradox which he described as 'maddening'. Whilst it was true that without White's 'personal articles on me, the agitation would not have gone ahead' this gave Fisher little comfort since it made the Cabinet 'wild with me'. Despondent, he reached the conclusion that it had 'done away with the idea of my going to the Admiralty!' He added, 'Nor do I think it likely that I shall get anything else after this ... I daresay I shall get along all right on half-pay.'[35]

A few days later, Beresford, heaving a sigh of relief when no disciplinary action had been taken against him, opened his ledger to note that 'it would have been fatal ... if I had been ordered home'. Had such an event occurred, ranks would have been closed and 'The *Navy* must and should have sided with the Authorities & quite rightly.' Worse than that, his public would have turned against him since 'The *Electorate* would have thought that all my remarks were the result of personal pique, because I had been ordered home in disgrace.'[36]

On 9 July, the Commons was on the attack yet again, with Arnold-Forster in the firing line. The issue was, of course, those secret reports, the details of which now seemed to be known to White but not to Members of Parliament. Mr John Dillon opened the debate by asking Arnold-Forster, 'whether his attention had been called to the statement of Arnold White in which he said that he received a letter from the Secretary to the Admiralty which was of the nature of a credential' and that this had enabled him 'to acquire a full knowledge of the facts'. Was it also the case that 'the Admiralty [had] sanctioned agents of the Navy League having access to information that was refused to the House of Commons[?]'[37]

In reply, Arnold-Forster told the Commons that his letter to White had concluded 'with a courteous expression, which I imagine cannot, in the opinion of any reasonable man, be regarded as being in the nature of a credential from the Admiralty'.[38] Dillon pressed his point again, but the minister stood firm: there had been no credential and no information had been obtained. On the first point, he was on safe ground; on the second point, he was either being ingenuous or was showing extraordinary ignorance of the press campaigns that both Fisher and Beresford were so actively running from the Mediterranean.

By now it was nearly three weeks since the letter had been published and not a word had been heard from Beresford. White had taken responsibility for its publication, an act which *The Times* called 'dishonourable'. In a letter to White, Beresford said, 'you evidently seem to think I ought to wire home that you published my letter either with my authority or by my desire'. (White's telegram has not survived, so we don't know what he wrote.) Instead of doing the honourable thing, Beresford set out one of his convoluted explanations as he sought to excuse his pusillanimous behaviour. If he were to take the blame for the letter's publication:

> I [would] put myself probably in the wrong with authority ... I [would] aggravate the offence ... and would put a very large number of my brother officers against me who are now strongly in support of my views – why volunteer anything[?][39]

He then came to the crux of the issue, acknowledging that he had authorised White 'to make any use' that he wished of the letter. White had, then, acted within the authority given to him by Beresford, yet Beresford still felt able to tell White that he had kept his and Fisher's name out to avoid 'jealousy and opposition'.[40] Not for one moment did Beresford consider the issue from White's position. It was fine for White's name to be tarnished; quite another for Fisher or Beresford to be derided.

Only two days later Beresford was preparing his defence, presumably for his return to Britain and civilian life, making notes in his ledger for a speech on the letter. Musing on whether he was guilty or not, he concluded: 'it will always be a moot point as to where the line between Discipline and Patriotism should be drawn.'[41]

Quietly, behind the scenes, Fisher was discussing the *Daily Mail* letter with Sir James Thursfield, *The Times* journalist. They knew nothing about Beresford having told White that he could do what he liked with it, so they assumed White and the *Daily Mail* to be the guilty parties. Responding to a letter from Thursfield, Fisher told him that 'As usual you hit off the point exactly in the following sentence: "Of course an officer on active service is fully entitled to express his sentiments on service matters in a private letter to a friend whose discretion he can trust; but if that friend publishes the letter, he shows himself unworthy of the confidence reposed in him."' Fisher was puzzled that Yerburgh and White, in whom he had placed 'absolute trust' should have let him down. As to the *Daily Mail*, 'you may imagine my disgust', he told Thursfield.[42]

In October, a Mr Pearson wrote to the Navy League suggesting that it should agitate for the appointment of Beresford as First Lord. Fortunately for him the Committee agreed that 'to interfere in such a matter, would not only be ill-judged, but mischievous to the prospects of any candidate'.[43] How right they were; the last thing that Beresford needed was any further attention being drawn to his antics.

By November, things were quiet and Fisher assumed that the *Daily Mail* skirmish had run its course. Writing to a friend, he reflected on what had happened, noting that 'no one has more cause than myself to regret all that took place in regard to the *Daily Mail* agitation', especially since 'the personal allusions were most distasteful to me'. Whilst Yerburgh and White, he added, 'were no friends of mine' he believed that they 'were actuated by patriotic motives', so he hoped the affair could now be regarded as closed.[44] Fisher could not have been more mistaken.

## Scene 4: Beresford is free to explain

Beresford, being more a politician than an admiral, was tiring of his life as second-in-command. On 5 February 1902, he had hauled down his flag in the Mediterranean and, within weeks, he was on the campaign trail in pursuit of the Woolwich seat in the Commons. The letter, he explained optimistically to Bellairs, was behind him: 'I do not think he [White] has affected me adversely' although he was less sanguine for White who 'may have done himself harm in his energetic line of conduct.'[45]

Now free to speak his mind, he opened his ledger and prepared to profit from those months of preparation in the Mediterranean. It was not long before Fisher found that Beresford had learnt nothing from the *Daily Mail* incident. In a speech to the London Chamber of Commerce (LCC), he called for a 'War Lord' to be appointed and he seems to have publicly recommended Fisher for the job.[46] Fisher was enraged. Approaching the end of his tour of duty in the Mediterranean, he feared once more for his own career, and took the precaution of writing to Lord Selborne in an attempt to distance himself from Beresford's recommendation. He was, he said, 'very sorry for Beresford's extravagances' coming as they did after 'he promised me he would be circumspect and judicious'. 'Unfortunately,' Fisher continued, 'he has been neither and has personally annoyed me very much by praising me.' As to the post of war lord, he told Selborne it was 'a berth I do not wish for'. Rather, he would prefer to be 'Second Naval Lord' since 'at the present time the most serious questions of all appear to lie in the province of the Second Sea Lord'.[47]

Beresford's LCC speech triggered a lively correspondence in *The Times*, all of it critical. At first, he contained himself but, by 9 April, he could hold back no longer and wrote in anger to the paper. The criticisms were, he said, 'absolutely deficient of any argument whatever on the merits or demerits of the case that I presented to the public'. They were, in fact, nothing more than 'a personal attack upon myself, condemning my "methods", "tone", "bad taste", and the "unwise and unfair" line adopted in my speech'.[48]

Whatever the distinguished correspondents of *The Times* may have thought of Beresford's rantings, he delighted the electorate. Then, as now, the *Daily Mail* represented middle England, and Beresford knew his public. Proof came on 25 April when he was elected unopposed at Woolwich, the sitting candidate, Colonel Hughes, having resigned the seat in his favour.[49] As he recalled in his memoirs, 'I began again to hammer on the Parliamentary anvil.'[50] He must, though, have wished for a more emphatic welcome than the one *The Times* gave him. Whilst the paper embraced the naval expertise that he would bring to the Commons, it opined, with regret, that 'We might desire a man of less exuberant and impulsive oratory and ... of greater sobriety of judgment and expression.' Grudgingly, it concluded that, 'at the present juncture ... he is the only available "Member for the Navy" to be had'. The *Daily Mail* letter had shown him to be a man of 'scant judgement', who was unable to select 'a correspondent who could not be trusted not to disclose a private letter'.[51]

It was just five months since Fisher had hoped that the *Daily Mail* scandal was over. *The Times*, having reopened the matter in a way that cast doubt on Beresford's character, had breathed new life into the controversy. Now, being on half-pay, Beresford had little choice but to respond, which he did in a letter to the paper. It was short, direct, but explosive:

> In *The Times* of the 25th reference is made in a leading article to a letter over my signature which appeared in the public Press last summer. The publication of that letter was a very grave mistake, but all blame (which I own is thoroughly deserved) for that mistake should be laid on my shoulders as the person solely responsible.[52]

How could this be? Was this the same letter that Arnold White said he published on his own initiative? Was this the same letter that Arnold-Forster said was not intended for publication? And where did this admission leave the *Daily Mail*, which had published the letter on the assumption that White was responsible? And, if Beresford really was the person responsible, where did that leave *The Times* that had abused White for his 'dishonourable' behaviour? Someone was not telling the truth. But who?

It was now time for apologies and recriminations all round. First, Beresford apologised to White in a letter of the same date, saying, 'I am so sorry that you should have had any trouble or worry over a mistake that ought never to have [been] made.'[53] It was not much of an apology and White would be back for more.

Next, *The Times* had to eat humble pie. Britain's premier newspaper had vilified a respectable journalist and now realised what a disastrous mistake it had made. There was nothing to be done, other than to unreservedly withdraw the accusation it had made:

> The letter from Lord Charles Beresford which we printed on Tuesday makes it our pleasant duty to withdraw the censure we have passed on Mr. Arnold White more than once for having, as we supposed, made public without the writer's privity or consent a letter which Lord Charles had written to him last summer.[54]

The paper was not, though, going to let Beresford off lightly. After all, he had allowed Parliament and the press to discuss this letter for nearly a year, without ever intervening to admit that he, not White, was the guilty party. This, from a man newly elected to Parliament on a holier-than-thou ticket. Acerbically, the paper suggested that:

> We must leave the writer of that most amazing letter to make such amends as he thinks proper – and as unquestionably the case requires – for placing Mr. Arnold White in so false and mortifying a position and for keeping him there for so many months.[55]

Although Fisher received a letter from Beresford which gave the impression that Beresford and White had 'had a row!',[56] a few days later White was vigorously defending Beresford in *The Times*. After thanking the paper 'for the generous atonement for the wrong you had done me', White then heartily attacked it for accusing Beresford of 'disloyalty to me'. There had been no disloyalty, he wrote, since 'at any moment since the letter was written Lord Charles Beresford was ready to accept full responsibility at all costs to himself'. (A statement that White knew to be far from true, as we shall see later in this act.) White went on to claim that 'The celebrated letter was written, not for private ends, nor to serve a friend, nor to gratify the ambitions of a newspaper.' Rather, it had been written 'because the Mediterranean Fleet was not organised for war'. It was Beresford's argument again: patriotism excused insubordination – and deceit.

Continuing to act as Beresford's mouthpiece, White then went on to make exorbitant claims for the outcome of the letter. Why, he wanted to know, 'if the Fleet under Sir John Fisher was adequately organised for war in June last' had the Admiralty now provided funds for a breakwater at Malta and sent out additional 'stores and munitions' to Malta? It was all Beresford's doing, he claimed, challenging *The Times* with an emphatic: 'This is the man you are pleased to term disloyal ... He has saved the country from possible defeat of its chief battle fleet by a splendid act of insubordination.'[57]

The truth, of course, was that all the matters that Beresford had raised had been the subject of vigorous correspondence between Fisher and Selborne since the former had arrived in the Mediterranean. He had told the Secretary to the Admiralty in January 1900 that there was 'an imperative and immediate necessity to increase the number of destroyers on this station'.[58] A few months later he was telling Thursfield that the number of cruisers and destroyers that he had was *'criminally insufficient'*.[59] More importantly, both White and Beresford disingenuously failed to make any reference to the fact that, as a result of Fisher's endless complaints, an Admiralty delegation had visited Malta in April 1901. Led by Lord Selborne, it had included Lord Kerr, Custance and Pretyman. As a result of this meeting Selborne, against the advice of both Kerr and Custance, had made very significant concessions to Fisher. His war-time battle strength was raised to twenty battleships; his cruisers increased to thirteen, with the promise of up to thirty-six in the near future and forty-two in the longer term; his sixteen destroyers would rise to twenty-four in peace-time and thirty-two in war-time.[60] These and many other provisions showed that Fisher's own campaign against the Admiralty was producing results. Although the letter granting these additions was dated 1 July, the Admiralty files clearly show that Selborne and his Board began discussing their response to Fisher's requests immediately after their return from the April visit. Bluntly stated, Fisher got his ships *before* Beresford's letter had appeared in print. It was no thanks to Beresford that the Fleet was strengthened. In fact, if Beresford's letter had had any effect at all, it was to *distract* attention from the needs of the Fleet to the behaviour of its admirals.

Following Beresford's admission, there were now scores to settle in the House of Commons. On 5 May, Norman challenged Arnold-Forster as to why he had, on two occasions, said that the letter 'was a private communication, not intended for publication'. After Arnold-Forster had defended himself, Beresford rose from his seat and the Speaker called him. He began by asking the House's 'indulgence' so that he could provide 'a little bit more explanation' since 'it affects my own character as a Member of this House'. Well might he have asked for 'indulgence' since he then treated the Commons to one of his outlandish explanations, in which he managed to admit guilt and excuse himself at the same time.

He started straightforwardly enough, declaring that, 'The fact of the matter is that I did write a letter. I ought not to have written this letter under the regulations.' If he had stopped there, with a few words to beg the House's forgiveness, he might have saved his reputation. But the simple, the honest, the direct were never enough for Beresford. Was it his fault? Surely it was all the Admiralty's fault since 'the constituted authorities never wrote to me to ask me if I had written that letter'. As he explained, 'if they had I should have told the truth'. Why could he not have volunteered the truth? He had nothing to say on that point.

Still, the House was not to worry. After all, he had acted honourably, had he not? He reminded the House that: 'When I came home the other day there were insinuations that another gentleman was responsible for publishing this letter, that he had published a private letter which I had written. I was then on half-pay, and I immediately took steps to show that I alone was responsible for the letter.' This explanation did not sound too disgraceful, given that Beresford said nothing of the timing. It would not have sounded so acceptable had he made clear that he had done *nothing* to rectify the situation whilst he was in the Mediterranean – a period of nearly nine months – and that he had been home for nearly three months before he 'took steps' to show he was responsible. A year is a long time to simply say, 'Yes, I wrote that letter.'

Beresford must have sensed that his excuses were rather lame, so he began to embroider his apology, saying: 'If I had written to the authorities before, and while I was on full pay, I think I should have done something very insubordinate.' So, apparently, writing and publishing the letter was not insubordinate, but admitting to his error was. Were his audience still with him? It is doubtful if a single member of the House could follow this line of argument.

Next, he dealt with the content of the letter. 'There was,' he said, 'nothing in my letter about the strength of the fleet that was not of public notoriety.' Nor was there anything 'that I gained in any way through my position'. As an excuse for his behaviour, this was insincere on two counts. First, the regulations forbade writing to the press about naval matters, whatever the contents. Second, irrespective of the facts in the letter, it was what he had hinted at that was serious: 'It would be most improper and prejudicial to discipline *if I were to give you details* as to why I am so anxious at the want of strength and of proper war organisation of the fleet.' (Emphasis added.) He was telling the world at large that there were *details* that were being kept from them – details, which if revealed, would embarrass the Admiralty and the Government.

Having, to his satisfaction, explained away his offence, Beresford then asked the House's leave 'to say that the crimes are of different characters'. What exactly he meant by that is hard to tell, and his own amplification left no one any the wiser: 'If a man breaks his leave by one hour it is a very different crime from that of a man who hits his officer with a cutlass.'[61]

However much Beresford tried to shrug off the humiliation of the Commons taking him to task, he now regretted the episode: '[I] was,' he told King-Hall, 'a fool to trust Arnold White.'[62]

## Scene 5: Breach of privilege

Beresford and the *Daily Mail* letter next surfaced by a roundabout route: that of privilege in the House of Commons. On 14 May, Mr John MacNeill, an Irish Nationalist, claimed in the Commons that 'certain statements in the *Daily Mail*, accusing the Secretary to the Admiralty . . . of a falsehood . . . constituted a breach of the privileges of the House'.[63]

The speaker ruled the request out of order saying that 'such questions must be decided promptly'.[64] This did not prevent, though, an unseemly verbal duel from taking place between Arnold-Forster and Beresford.

Arnold-Forster took the House through the history of his involvement in the affair, demonstrating that, up to the point when Beresford wrote to *The Times* to admit responsibility for the letter, his own assumption that the letter had not been intended for publication 'was a reasonable inference'. Coming to the attack, Arnold said 'The noble Lord made what appeared to me to be a very remarkable speech indeed, because, as I understood him, it endorsed the offensive charges which have been made against myself.' At this, Beresford cried out 'No, certainly not.' What a short memory he had, having said on that occasion: 'When I came home the other day there were insinuations that another gentleman was responsible for publishing this letter, that he had published a private letter which I had written.' There was little doubt that this referred to Arnold-Forster as the person who had made the 'insinuations'; he had every reason to feel offended.[65]

Next came one of those dramatic moments that electrify parliamentary debates – the flourish of a secret document. Arnold-Forster was not the type of man to lay a trap, but he had caught Beresford *in flagrante delicto*, just the same. And what a revelation it was. Arnold-Forster told the House that, on 5 May, when Beresford had charged him in the House with 'insinuations':

> I held in my hand a letter received from the noble Lord two days before on no solicitations of mine, in which he deliberately went out of his way to acquit both myself and the Board of Admiralty of any offence in either of these two matters.[66]

And why had he not used the letter on that occasion? Members were on the edges of their seats as Arnold-Forster revealed that he had not used the letter 'because the letter to me was marked private and when I asked the noble Lord if I was at liberty to state what he had told me, he refused'. As a stunned House heard how one of its own members had sought to silence a minister, he went on, 'Only after I had written telling him that this was intolerable did he accord me the permission I needed.'[67]

Now, as an eager House awaited the sordid details of Beresford's cowardly act, Arnold-Forster read the part that Beresford had so fervently sought to suppress:

> On that letter [White's letter of 25 June to Arnold-Forster, published in *The Times* of 6 July] you were perfectly justified in making the statement you did in the House relative to Mr. Arnold White's being responsible for the publication. As a matter of fact, I told Mr. Arnold White he could do what he liked with the letter when he asked me

75

might he publish it, because there was nothing in it which trespassed on confidential reports. But I was absolutely wrong to do this. The Admiralty never asked me 'whether directly or indirectly I had caused the publication, etc.' Had they done so, I should have told the truth, with the probable result that I should have been ordered to haul down my flag.[68]

Arnold-Forster now had Beresford on the ropes and was not going to let up. He reminded the House that, 'In his recent speech the noble Lord said: "When I came home there were insinuations that another gentleman was responsible."' But, said Arnold-Forster, 'there were no insinuations'. What was more, he added, 'I made a statement in this House in July last year, and the noble Lord has had eight months to repudiate it.'[69]

Now he turned to Beresford's preposterous claim that he had acted promptly to clear the confusion up. As Arnold-Forster reminded the House, Beresford had claimed that, when he hauled down his flag that, 'I immediately took steps to show that I alone was responsible.' He continued:

The noble Lord did not. He sent his letter to *The Times* on April 29th. During the whole of nearly three months, this accusation, which he feels so bitterly as being brought unjustly against another man, remained unanswered ... Not until then was Mr White relieved of the charge which I am accused of having unjustly put upon him. But the only wrong I have done him has been to accept him at his word, and now the noble Lord says that I was under a misapprehension.[70]

Finally, Beresford was able to reply. It was classic Charlie B: first he admitted his guilt, then he absolved himself. He started well enough: 'I must at once preface my remarks by saying that the Secretary to the Admiralty certainly was in a false position, and did get into that false position through an act of mine, which I owned to the other day.' From there on, it was all muddle and confusion. Telling the House that, 'when the Secretary to the Admiralty reads only a part of the correspondence I have sent to him, it is not quite fair to myself' he wrapped himself in knots, since the part of the letter that Arnold-Forster did not read out was merely a sentence or two of abuse of White and not material to the discussion in the House.[71] As he rambled on, an increasingly impatient Speaker finally pulled him up as he digressed into the strength of the Mediterranean Fleet. He was ruled out of order, having strayed beyond the boundaries of the debate.

And so Beresford squirmed his way out of admitting the enormity of what he had done.

On 15 May *The Times* put its seal on the previous day's debate by telling the country that, in its opinion, 'Lord Charles Beresford will hardly be thought by men of sense and judgment to have improved his position, either as a naval officer or as a public man, by the rather defiant and very inconsequent speech which he delivered yesterday.' As the paper rightly added, 'What he really has to explain is not only why he ever allowed the letter to be published, but why, having allowed it to be published ... he nevertheless allowed Mr Arnold White to assume responsibility for its publication and never acknowledged his own responsibility.' His methods were, said *The Times*, 'somewhat peculiar, not to say unbecoming in an officer holding high command'.[72]

For the public, the saga was finally over, but not for White. On 16 May he sat down to write an enormously long letter to Beresford, detailing every step in the story. The letter was never sent, perhaps because, towards the end, White shows distinct signs of becoming increasingly unsure of his purpose. Perhaps he only wanted to clarify in his own mind just what had happened. Perhaps the writing itself was a cathartic act which helped him to reach closure on an incident that had been so painful for him. Whatever its intention, it reads throughout as a letter written by a man who is forcing himself to remain calm and reasonable, desperately stifling a suppressed, volcanic rage – a rage against Beresford.

The bulk of the letter was a straightforward record of the facts, starting way back in early 1901, when 'I was, by permission of the Commander-in-Chief, your guest in Ramillies.' Towards the end, it changes tone, as White recalls a letter that we have not yet seen – a letter of 25 April 1902, the day that Beresford was elected MP. It is most revealing as to the pain that White suffered and the indifference that Beresford had shown to his position:

> You will have seen the *Times* leader to-day representing the offensive insinuation that I have published a private letter of yours.
>
> While you were on full pay or seeking a seat in the HoC I held my hand & suffered in silence under the infamous charge.
>
> Now that you are a free man and in Parliament I am sure that you will see that justice is due to me in this matter.

So, now we know why Beresford had waited so long to speak out. While in the Mediterranean, he dared not confess for fear of being retired. White had voluntarily covered for him. But once home, far from immediately clarifying the situation as he had promised, Beresford had held back until safely elected to Parliament.

White's letter closes with an aggrieved conclusion. First, he straightfor-wardly told Beresford that he thought 'you would have been better advised in your own interests if you had stated categorically that you had given me authority. Your failure to do so has created much misunder-standing and left an unpleasant impression'. But then the letter abruptly switches tone as he returns to the words that Arnold-Forster declined to read out in the House when he quoted Beresford's letter: 'Arnold White is one of the most dangerous of men that I have had anything to do with.'[73] Commenting on this, White wrote:

I am unaware of any episode in our relations which justify you even hinting that I have not exercised proper reticence in regard to either your interests or those of the Fleet.[74]

White had found the courage to say it at last. He lacked the courage, though, to post the letter so Beresford never found out just how badly he had hurt his co-conspirator.

One more letter remained to be written – the official reprimand from the Board of Admiralty. Dated 22 May 1902, it read:

I am commanded by Their Lordships to convey to you the expression of their grave displeasure at the breach of discipline committed by you in disobeying Art 682 of the King's Regulations for the Government of His Majesty's Naval Service, in which it is laid down that 'all persons belonging to the Fleet are forbidden to publish or cause to be published, directly or indirectly, in a newspaper or other periodical, any matter or thing relating to the Public Service.'

I am further to express Their Lordships [sic] surprise that an Officer in whom such confidence has been shewn as to appoint him to an important position in one of His Majesty's principal Fleets, should have set an example to His Majesty's Service so subversive of discipline.[75]

As the saga reached its end, Fisher was preparing to leave the Mediterranean Fleet and return to the Admiralty. He was, though, fearful that Beresford would put him on the wrong side of the Board, as he told his son Cecil. 'Beresford,' he wrote, 'is in great terror! He is so very full of what he thinks my capacity for reform that he keeps on telling people at home how I shall turn them all inside out at the Admiralty, that I am the only Admiral worth his salt, etc., etc., ... I keep begging him to hold his tongue & he promises to do so but in a few days I hear again of his flourishing me in some Admiral's face!'[76]

On the whole, Fisher had come out of the Daily Mail episode relatively unscathed. There is an intriguing note in Arnold-Forster's papers in which Fisher pleads that he is innocent of having withheld letters from Beresford in which he officially informed him that, as 'a public man outside of the naval profession' he might have to 'haul down his flag with the object of letting the public know the true position of affairs'. This followed a letter in The Times of 16 April in which Beresford suggested that Fisher had supported his letters home during 1900–02. Fisher assured the unknown recipient that 'all the Official communications of the R.A. have been submitted to Their Lordships, except of course those items of minor and local interest'.[77]

Meanwhile, Beresford, having parked himself on the back benches of the Commons and disgraced himself over the letter, was left to watch from the sidelines as Fisher's career took off in a spectacular fashion. Beresford's influence was at its nadir, as White told Scott, after noting that only eleven members were present when he spoke in the Commons on gunnery. 'No Cabinet Minister,' he added, 'thought it worthwhile to stay to hear him.'[78]

*Act 5*

# Fisher Takes the Prize

When two men ride on horseback ... one must ride behind.
Lord Charles never could realise that he might be that one.
– *Review of Reviews*[1]

### Scene 1: Beresford untamed

The *Daily Mail* letter, Beresford's reports to the First Lord and his contacts
with the Prime Minister all showed that, even as a subordinate, he was
uncontrollable. Now that he was an untamed back-bencher, Fisher could
only fear the worst. Yet he was torn between his need for publicists whom
he could trust and his fear of Beresford's loose tongue. Conscious of the
risk he was taking, Fisher had written to Beresford asking for his assistance
should he succeed in re-entering the Commons. As a precaution, he told a
friend, 'I have kept a copy, to prevent his, in any way, either quoting me or
using my name in any way in his approaching campaign ... His intentions
are good,' he added, but 'Hell is paved with good intentions.' Whilst Fisher
warmed to 'the great good he undoubtedly could do in educating out-
siders for the good of the Navy' he feared that 'he will put his foot in it' and
make some 'injudicious speech'.[2]

Two months later, Fisher was feeding Beresford with soundbites that
he wanted him to make in his public speaking. Marking his letter *'Private.
No one to see this letter except your own self!!!'* he then poured out 1,500
forceful words of advice and comment. In the end, though, there was just
one message: Britain needed a bigger, better, more powerful Navy.
Beresford was to remind the public that Goschen had maintained that 'the
permanent safety of the country' depended on a Navy that was so powerful that it would cause *'three powers to pause before they attacked England'*. He
added, 'you must hang on to that in your speech like a bulldog'.

The precise detail that Fisher pressed on Beresford is, though, less
important than the tone of this remarkable letter. He reminded his new-
found confidante that 'I am writing to you ... freely' and that the content
was 'of the most secret character'. Fisher was sure that he could rely 'on
your discretion not to haul me into the matter'. Secret as the content might
have been, Fisher went on to recommend Beresford to consult Thursfield

about a forthcoming speech, even suggesting that the latter should revise it for Beresford.[3]

So, here was Fisher, who had cursed Beresford and White for having dragged his name into the *Daily Mail* letter affair and feared for his own career as a result, turning to Beresford and yet another journalist to assist him in his campaigns. Was this a new beginning? If so, how long could it last?

Not long, was the answer. Just one month later, in a letter to Earl Spencer, who had been First Lord in 1892–5, Fisher was bemoaning Beresford's lack of discretion. The problem was, he told Spencer, 'he exaggerates so much that his good ideas become deformities'. What concerned Fisher most was Beresford's 'want of taste and his uncontrolled desire for notoriety'. Nor could he be relied on to keep his word. After yet another episode in which Beresford had referred to Fisher by name in public, Fisher complained: 'He promised me faithfully . . . that he would be circumspect and judicious in what he was going to say to the public' but, complained Fisher, 'he has been neither!' Undoubtedly, though, 'the "oi polloi" believed in him'.[4]

## Scene 2: Fisher reforms and Beresford cheers

At the time that Fisher was losing his battle to control Beresford, he already knew that he was to return to the Admiralty in June 1902. He had been astonished to receive a letter from Selborne saying, 'I want you to take over Admiral Douglas' place as Second Naval Lord.'[5] Although he would have preferred to go to Plymouth and his family hated London, he hastily accepted the offer. Not to have done so risked being put on half-pay which, at his age, would have heralded retirement.

After his three years of bombarding the Admiralty with letters of pleading and complaint, Fisher had not expected to be recalled. Indeed, had it not been for Selborne, he would have been left to plant his roses. The First Naval Lord, Lord Walter Kerr, was horrified at Selborne's choice, warning him that 'he certainly does not possess the confidence of the Service and his appointment as Senior Naval Lord would be universally condemned'.[6] Selborne, though, wanted Fisher because he was the only man who could push through the huge reform programme that lay ahead. It was the engineers that were the trouble. Ever since the first steam engine had been put into a ship, the engineers had been treated like mere mechanics, kept off the quarterdeck and with the mess room door slammed in their faces. Revolt was in the air and agitated press comment was arousing the interest of Parliament. Only action by the Admiralty could stave off outside interference – something the Board always feared above all else. Selborne, at a loss to know what to do, turned to Fisher.

81

The new Second Naval Lord burst into the Admiralty on 10 June 1902 with the full fury of a tropical storm. 'I first arrived at the Admiralty,' he told his son Cecil, 'at 10 minutes to 12, and promptly said "How d'ye do" to Lord Selborne.' By five minutes past twelve he had been, Fisher continued, 'read in at the Board' and within a further five minutes he had 'commenced operations', sending to the printers the first pages of his massive reform of naval education.[7]

In these first few hours Fisher displayed the two traits that were to dominate the rest of his career: a ruthless capacity to design and execute reforms at lightning speed, combined with a growing megalomania. After three years on the front line in the Mediterranean, where he had been daily threatened by an aggressive French fleet in the West and a more timid Russian one in the East, he feared that time was short. Nothing – and, more to the point, no one – would be allowed to get in his way. The least obstruction was to be resented and resisted with fury. Even the Admiralty's refusal to let him have a roll-top desk was met with a promise to 'take it out of them in cabs'.[8]

Working at a furious pace, Fisher soon settled in, finding the job 'very different ... to commanding a big Fleet!' since 'When I leave the office at 7.00 pm I leave all care behind me!'[9] At Admiralty House, though, it was rush, rush, rush. He loved to be told that something was 'impossible' and that there were 'insuperable objections' to carrying it out. To him, this was the signal 'to fight like the devil'.[10] As he used to say, if something was important then it had to be done 'by fair means or foul, foul for choice'.[11]

Although sixty-one years old, his capacity for work was undiminished. One of his assistants recalled that he had 'never met anyone who could dispose of papers at the rate he could'.[12] His vitality was extraordinary, so much so that one doctor remarked that he 'ought to have been twins', to which a colleague quipped, 'What a mercy you were not! Just think of two of *you* in the Navy!'[13]

The whirlwind was a welcome change to those younger officers at the Admiralty who had been stifled by the Kerr regime. Herbert Richmond, one of Fisher's assistants, noted in his diary in March 1903 how wonderful it was 'to have a man at the Head of affairs who can take a matter up' and who was 'absolutely approachable'. He marvelled at the way Fisher was ready to 'listen to suggestions and act on them'.[14]

Fisher's first reforms – a revolution in naval education – appeared in the newspapers in December 1902. At the heart of these measures was one very simple proposition: in future every naval officer should receive the same initial education, starting as a naval cadet at twelve or thirteen years of age.

'Simple' it may have sounded, simple it was not to prove. Under this reform, for the first time in the history of the Navy, engineers were to train side by side with executive officers, initially at Fisher's new Osborne College. The announcement emphasised that 'all will be trained under exactly the same system until they shall have passed for the rank of Sub-Lieutenant between the ages of nineteen and twenty'. Only then would officers be allocated to one of the three branches: the Executive, the Engineer, and the Marine.[15] As far as possible, officers would enter the branch of their choice, but this was not guaranteed under the new scheme.

Fisher was fearful of the reaction that there would be to such radical changes. He knew that criticism would be focused on the equal treatment of executive and engineer officers, so he must have been pleased to see a letter in *The Times*, which vigorously supported the scheme, saying:

Lord Selborne would absolutely wreck the scheme were he to give nominations to any but those who selected all three branches ... If only one single solitary little cadet (standing four feet nothing in his shoes) were allowed entrance to the Osborne establishment on the 'executive' ticket alone, he would forthwith (and for ever after) turn up his dear little nose at the rest and call them 'greasers' and 'lobsters', and probably a big D as a prefix, if his mother hadn't been careful of him in the nursery.[16]

Did he ponder who was behind the signature 'Tria juncta in uno'? Did he not think there was something rather jaunty about the language? Well, no, because he had written the letter himself! For once, not even his faithful journalists could be trusted to put his views across.

In practice, the letters' columns of *The Times* were quite supportive, but Fisher knew well that there was a very good reason for this, as was pointed out by the Conservative MP, George Stewart Bowles. He told his readers that 'Letters expressing dismay at this scheme, and grave apprehensions of its results, are being written every day by naval officers to whose rank and standing you would accord your largest type ... But these letters cannot be published. Their authors are muzzled.'[17] Muzzled, of course, because serving officers were banned from writing on service matters.

Another correspondent, signing himself 'a late captain of a battleship', warned that there was 'a spirit of unrest throughout the service', adding 'I cannot help thinking that this new educational scheme as proposed will intensify it.'[18] The issue was one of class, as Lord Wemyss[19] reminded *Times* readers: 'How can there ever be equality between the engineer officer below and the naval officer above deck?'[20] Engineers were not gentlemen and no amount of reforms from Fisher or Selborne could ever make them so.

But one very senior officer came out with an emphatic, forthright and uncompromising defence of Fisher – none other than Beresford. What makes Beresford's defence particularly important is not what he said, but the fact that, within five years he would deny every word of it. For him, Fisher, the great reformer, would become Fisher, the wrecker of the Navy.

Within a week of the reforms being published, Beresford had given an interview to the *Western Morning News* in which he lauded Fisher's 'brilliant and statesmanlike effort to grapple with *a problem upon the sound settlement of which depends the future efficiency of the British Navy*'. While many officers of Beresford's rank looked with horror on the proposed equality for engineers, Beresford accepted that 'the engineer officer has never received that recognition to which the importance of his duties and responsibilities justly entitles him' and was happy that 'the abolition of distinction regarding entry has settled this point once and for ever'. He embraced the need for more science education for officers which, he said, would 'produce men who will be capable of seeing that the Fleet in its entirety is perfect for its work'. In conclusion he said that 'I am of the opinion that the plan is one that has been thoroughly matured and well thought out.'[21]

As the newspaper campaign against the reforms gathered pace, Beresford sympathised with Fisher, telling him that 'We must remember, however, that all reforms are opposed, generally by those who are too old, or whose brains are not receptive enough, to perceive that 1902 [sic] may require different administrations and systems to 1803.' He added, 'I have often observed that the most obstinate, violent, and passionate anti-reformers are men who in no case whatever have ever even distinguished themselves by adopting the old methods which they wish to leave untouched.'[22] Within a few years Beresford's behaviour would firmly place him, too, in his category of 'the most obstinate, violent, and passionate anti-reformers'.

Further evidence of Beresford's support came in May 1903 in the *Annual Report* of the Navy League. After thanking Beresford for his assistance (presumably financial) during the year, the League turned to the new education scheme, commenting that 'it is difficult to see at present in what manner it could be improved'.[23]

Fisher's educational reforms soon began to split the Navy. His supporters were dubbed members of the 'Fishpond'; Fisher had already labelled his opponents the 'Syndicate of Discontent'. Inside the Fishpond, Captain Reginald Bacon, Captain John Jellicoe, Captain Sir Henry Jackson and Captain Louis Battenberg were notable supporters. Bacon was to go on to be Fisher's first biographer; Jellicoe would command the Grand Fleet in the First World War and then become First Sea Lord; Jackson would be yet another First Sea Lord in 1915; and Battenberg would be First Sea Lord from 1912–14. It was a glittering array of talent.

The principal members of the Syndicate were Custance, Admiral of the Fleet Sir Frederick Richards, Kerr, and Admiral Sir Cyprian Bridge. Custance never rose higher than second-in-command of the Channel Fleet, partly because Fisher blocked his career, but also because he 'lacked the personal warmth' and was 'arrogant and unbending'.[24] Richards had been a highly successful First Naval Lord (1893–9) but was now past his prime. Kerr, as Fisher's predecessor, had taken against him strongly when he was Commander-in-Chief in the Mediterranean. Bridge was then Commander-in-Chief in the China Sea, but rose no further.

This says a lot about the Fishpond and the Syndicate. The latter was entirely composed of men of the past – men who were against change. On the other hand the Fishpond demonstrated Fisher's extraordinary capacity for spotting talent: three out of four of its principal members would go on to be First Sea Lord. When people accused Fisher of packing the Admiralty with his favourites, he at least chose talented ones.

## Scene 3: Muddles and reprimands in the Channel

Fisher's fears of a rampant Beresford subsided in early 1903 when, now a vice admiral, he resigned his seat at Woolwich on 18 February.[25] On 17 April he was appointed to the command of the Channel Squadron. Later in the year, in August, Fisher became Commander-in-Chief at Portsmouth. For the time being both men were away from London and the Admiralty.

It is clear that the two admirals remained on good terms, Fisher having been a dinner guest at the Beresfords' house in South Audley Street in April. Other guests included Prince and Princess Louis of Battenberg, the Russian Ambassador, the German Ambassador and the Italian inventor of radio, Signor Marconi.[26] (Marconi was frequently to be found dining with naval personnel, the Navy being one of his principal customers.) However well they all got on, Fisher never took to social dinners. Only a month earlier, after another dinner at which Marconi was present, Fisher told his son, 'We have about a dozen dinners on hand', adding 'I shall be very glad when we let our house & get out of London.'[27]

It was as a popular hero that Beresford raised his flag in his 14,900-ton *Majestic* in April and perhaps Fisher flinched as he saw the publicity that he received. He would have been even less pleased to read, a month later, how *The Times* commented on Beresford's latest portrait[28] when it was unveiled at the Royal Academy. The likeness, by Charles Furse, was, said the paper, 'so well known' that 'everybody can judge whether his portrait is a true one'.[29]

By this time there were increasing signs that public adulation was going to Beresford's head, as a story told by Richmond illustrates. A lady had asked Beresford in October 1903 'who in war would be what I may call the ''Generalissimo of the British Fleet[?]'' ' to which he replied, 'Oh, I should.' Doubting that things were as simple as that the lady asked whether Selborne really would appoint him 'to this position over the senior men'. In a fine display of arrogance, Beresford retorted, 'Perhaps yes, perhaps no; but the Nation would call for me.'[30]

In his memoirs, Beresford claimed that 'under my command, the drills and exercises were particularly onerous' adding that he made it a rule 'never to go to sea or steam from port to port without practising some exercise or tactical problem'. Ever one to emphasis efficiency, he said that ensured that 'for every pound's worth of coal burnt' there was 'a pound's worth of training'.[31] How rigorous these drills were is open to question. Beresford's flag commander, Henry Bertram Pelly, remembered that life was full of 'all sorts of competitions and drills' including 'racing up the rock of Gibraltar' and mock attacks on Portland Bill. A favourite of Beresford's was 'away all boats' which, when conducted in rough weather, ended up in chaos as the Fleet broke up, each ship searching the waves for its missing boats.[32] Overall, Pelly's impression of Beresford's exercises matches that of Wemyss – both found them fun, but neither made any claims for their relevance to fleet work in war.

Without any sense of irony, Beresford told readers of his memoirs that 'efficiency consists in the maintenance of the most rigid discipline' which meant having to issue 'definite and strict orders'. He would, he said, tolerate 'no mistake or failure, however small'.[33] By the time he wrote this, a fat file lay in the Admiralty files, with the incriminating title *Antagonistic comments of Lord Charles Beresford on Board of Admiralty policy and administration* – a file packed with evidence of his own lack of discipline.[34]

Despite Beresford's claims as to the intensity of his fleet work, a good part of his time with the Channel Squadron (renamed the Channel Fleet in May 1903) was spent touring the British ports to receive the adulation of the populous. At each stopping place, Beresford would land, to be received by the local Lord Mayor and other dignitaries, and join in a round of lunches and dinners, liberally enhanced by self-congratulatory, patriotic speeches. In May 1903, it was Belfast, followed by Dublin, where over 1,000 people visited the *Majestic*.[35] The following month it was Portsmouth; then July saw Beresford entertaining a United States' squadron at Spithead. In August there was a pause in the festivities, with some real work to do, when the squadron steamed off to Lagos for exercises with the combined Channel, Home and Mediterranean Fleets. By September, Beresford was back on tour with a visit to Scarborough. This proved a disappointment since, although the locals 'came in thousands', they were unable to board the ships because 'the weather was so bad'.[36] There was a change of flagship to the *Caesar* in February 1904, to be followed in March by a visit to the Royal House of Portugal and a visit of the German Emperor.

And so it went on. Pelly found the crowds a mixed blessing since, he said, 'my principal job was clearing up the mess they left behind'.[37] He was also left to fix up return boats for the many visitors who, having arrived in a harbour tug, stayed until long after the tugs had ceased to operate.

Despite Beresford's frequent claims about the intensity of his fleet exercises, he seems to have placed far more emphasis on parades. This is underlined by his message to the Fleet when it returned to port in June 1904:

> The Vice-Admiral congratulates the Rear-Admiral, captains, officers, and men on the general smartness of the Channel Fleet while in the company of the combined fleets. The Channel Fleet has every reason to be proud of the smartness and quick times in which all evolutions were carried out.[38]

Whatever the extent and quality of Beresford's fleet management, it no longer satisfied him. The details bored him and, at sea, he missed the adoring crowds and the press. As in the Mediterranean, he sought every possible opportunity to surround himself with admirers. 'Crowds of M.P.s and newspapermen came to see him,' recalled one of his officers, so much so that 'it was difficult to get access to him about Service matters.' Even if an officer could buttonhole him, 'anything arranged was forgotten as soon as you left him'.[39] One admirer, though, did not occupy Beresford's time: despite several entreaties, Bellairs was 'very sorry' to not be able to visit the Fleet.[40]

Amidst all this parading around the British coast, Beresford maintained his capacity for spreading muddles and confusions.

During the visit to Belfast, Beresford lost the piece of paper on which the flagship's course was written. As a result, he gave the wrong order and the Fleet steamed at 90° off from their correct route and was half an hour late arriving in Belfast Lough. Meanwhile, 'the Mayor and Corporation' were kept waiting on the seafront.[41] In January 1904, Beresford suffered yet another hunting accident in which, Lady Charles told *The Times*, 'he sustained concussion to the brain and also injured his back, so that for some days he lost the use of his legs'.[42] Three months later, his barge grounded in mud during a visit to the Royal House of Spain, and he missed the royal procession.[43] It was on this same visit that the King of Spain had invited the crew of the *Caesar* to a reception but, when Beresford arrived, there was no seat for him, so he returned to his ship, 'evidently much annoyed'.[44]

The biggest 'muddle' of them all, though, occurred on the night of 17 October 1903 off Cape Finisterre. As Beresford told the story, 'Two midshipmen of the *Prince George* were relaxing their minds after the strain of the day's work with a hand of cards, when the game was interrupted by the entrance into the gun-room of the stem of the *Hannibal*.'[45] The damage to the *Prince George* was immense, with a gash of 24 feet 8 inches by 6 feet 6 inches in her side and it required one of Beresford's heroic interventions to stabilise the ship and bring her into Ferrol harbour on the following day.

No one can fail to be impressed by the speed, energy and determination that Beresford put into plugging the hole as the water poured in. It was stuffed with anything to hand, including 350 hammocks, nine boat covers, 1,500 yards of deck cloth and 1,000 wooden wedges.[46] It was Beresford at his best. He devoted three and a half pages of his memoirs to the salvage operation – but not one word to its cause nor its consequences.

The cause was that Beresford had been practising night manoeuvres without lights. At the time, he was criticised by the Admiralty 'for the near-loss of a battleship by holding night manoeuvres with lights out' and accused of 'a crazy new-fangled' practice.[47] As a result, the Admiralty ordered that when exercising at night, ships were 'to burn dimmed navigation lights'.[48]

A few months later the Admiralty was typing out yet another letter of reprimand. It was triggered by a comment Beresford had made in a submission to the Admiralty of 3 December 1903. Noting the 'marked improvement in the 12" [gun] firing' he attributed this to 'the recent alterations in the telescopic sight fittings'. So far, so good, but he went on to add: 'if these improvements had been carried out when originally asked for, the 12" firing might well have been three years ahead of what it now is.'[49]

Kerr was furious, calling the remarks 'reckless' and citing Beresford's report as 'another example of the time wasted in getting at the true inform-ation concerning the point raised'. The comment was, said Kerr, 'prac-tically censure of the Board' and 'is wanting in respect'.[50] It was not going to be tolerated; a reprimand was needed. Dated 11 April, the Admiralty told Beresford that the delay 'was only owing to the introduction of necessary improvements and modifications'. Then came the formal warning:

> Their Lordships regret that you should have permitted yourself to comment on their action with so little consideration or knowledge of the facts of the case, and they trust that in future your representations may be confined to bringing to Their Lordships' notice matters that you wish to lay before them, without casting reflection on the administration of the Navy, or making charges that are unsupported by fact, but are disrespectful to the Board of Admiralty.[51]

Just four months later he once again riled the Board with a letter about prize-firing. His remarks were, said the Board, 'neither called for nor necessary and not borne out by the facts'. They took particular exception to his comment on the administration which 'was neither respectful nor in place'.[52]

While serving with the Channel Fleet, Beresford kept up his corre-spondence on naval matters with anyone he thought would listen. In July, Balfour received yet another of his inordinately long and rambling papers, this time on *The Provision of an Admiralty Staff as a Step Towards Imperial Union*. Arguing for what he called 'a thinking department' at the Admiralty, he told Balfour that 'except in the person of the 1st Sea Lord for the time being, there is no one, or no department, who has been given it as a duty to think and realise the relative importance of one branch of the Empires [sic] requirements as compared with the others'.[53]

So much for paying attention to the Board's injunction that he should bring matters of concern to 'Their Lordships' notice'.

## Scene 4: Fisher's triumph

While Beresford had been parading his Fleet around the British Isles and annoying the Board, Fisher had had a short posting as Commander-in-Chief at Portsmouth, primarily to oversee the building and development of his new Osborne College on the Isle of Wight for naval cadets. Then, on 16 May 1904, the First Lord offered him the post of First Sea Lord, the appointment to coincide with the dropping of the term 'naval lord' in favour of the more traditional term 'sea lord'. Fisher accepted the offer, telling his friend Viscount Esher, 'The die is cast! ... I commence work on October 21st.'[54] He told Esher that 'I'm a born ass, as I shall get neither riches, honour, [n]or glory' but, in practice, nothing would have kept him from accepting.[55]

Fisher had feared that his posting as Second Naval Lord would be his last tour at the Admiralty. Others had been of the same view. King-Hall recorded in his diary on 15 October 1903 that '[Admiral Sir Lewis] Beaumont is endeavouring to prevent Fisher from returning as 1st Naval Lord.' However, said King-Hall's informant 'there is not much chance of his doing that'.[56]

It had been a long, hard struggle from the Ceylon jungle to the Navy's most prestigious appointment. Unlike Beresford, Fisher had had few social connections to spur his advance. Instead, he had lived on nothing but his pay, when many officers had private incomes, and he had fought against the prejudiced comments of his not being 'a gentleman'. Those who had supported his advance – from Captain Shadwell and Admiral Hope in the 1850s and 1860s to the current First Lord – had done so because of his talent, loyalty and hard work. Now, he had to justify the faith they had all placed in him.

Although Fisher had feared that he was not to return to the Admiralty, he had still spent most of 1904 furiously developing plans for his next batch of reforms. He kept his thoughts to himself, though, telling Sir Robert Arbuthnot (his Flag Captain at Portsmouth) that 'I'll alter it all! I'm not such a born idiot as to tell all those chaps at the Admiralty what I'm going to do before I go there.'[57]

Fisher's appointment was welcomed in the press, a typical comment coming from the *Daily Telegraph* which wrote 'He is sixty-three years of age, but as active as most men ten or twenty years younger ... Sir John Fisher is regarded as one of the most energetic, far-seeing, and progressive officers of the fleet, and wherever he has been he has ... made things hum.'[58]

On the day after he took office, *Daily Mail* readers were reminded that 'Queen Victoria was among the first to recognise the ability of Sir John Fisher.' Now it would be the King who would 'support the First Sea Lord in the tremendous work'. The paper reminded its readers that 'He has reformed the Army [a reference to his membership of the War Office (Reconstruction) Committee in 1903]; he will certainly complete the reform of the Navy.' He was, the paper said, 'a short, clean-shaven man, with square shoulders and strong arms; his eyes are large and round, the mouth thick-lipped and strong, the nose short, the forehead hard as a rock, the hair stubby and thick'. But it was 'the deep lines running from the curve of the nostrils to the depression at the corner of the lips' which caught the paper's eye. The lines suggested 'scorn and contempt' which, they confided, meant 'scorn for inefficiency and contempt for shuffling'. Having painted a rather hard portrait of the new First Sea Lord, the paper added that 'he is a cheerful and merry soul, a man full of good spirits and filled with zest for life'. He was, they added, 'a laughing philosopher' and 'an excellent teller of breezy stories'.[59]

Fisher had been appointed to reform a sleepy, indolent and self-satisfied Navy that was in no way ready for war. In a frenetic and highly controversial reign of five years he was to bully and cajole the Board, the Navy, the Cabinet and the King into accepting his monumental changes. There were something like eighteen reforms, of which five were major in their scale and impact. The first of the five – the education reforms – we have already met. To this he quickly added his nucleus-crew system, the scrapping of 154 obsolete ships, the redistribution of the fleets, and the creation of the dreadnought battleship.[60]

Aware of the magnitude of what lay ahead, Fisher first armed himself with new powers. Before taking up his post, he had persuaded Selborne to obtain an Order in Council (a form of legislation approved by the Privy Council rather than by Parliament) to extend the authority of the First Sea Lord. It, he told Esher, *'gives the First Sea Lord nothing to do*, except think and send for Idlers!'[61] It was an odd description of his role, given that he sought these powers in order to outdo any previous holder of the post.

Selborne and the King had agreed that Fisher should be appointed Naval ADC to the King on his becoming First Sea Lord.[62] This would mean an extra £400 per year (nearly £28,000 today) and the right of direct access to the King. The suggested appointment caused resentment in some quarters, so the proposal was withdrawn. Writing to Cecil, Fisher re-

90

counted that the King had said 'he would have given anything for me to be his Principal A.D.C. . . . but on reflection he had come to the conclusion that it would do me harm as every one would say it was the King's favouritism'. In compensation the King 'had written a very strong letter' to Selborne asking him to raise Fisher's pay. He concluded, 'The King says so many people are jealous of me & fear me that *He must look out for me!*'[63] Only a month later, it was all change, as Fisher told Esher: 'I have got the A.D.C., and *it all puzzles me beyond comprehension!*'[64]

The issue of pay was a very real one for Fisher. At Portsmouth he had been paid £4,000 a year (including a large entertainment allowance) whereas the First Sea Lord post paid £2,600 (around £185,000 today). He told Esher that he had 'asked for my pay, as a special case personal to me, to be made up to £3,400 a year on account of my giving up an appointment of £4,000 to suit them'.[65] There was strong resistance, though, to making a special case of Fisher's pay, so he relented, advising Esher (who had become involved): 'Don't go fussing, please, about my £800 a year, because if it takes all this worry to get it I would rather go without!' This was despite the fact that 'The King told Selborne *straight* I would save them millions.' Instead, 'they haggled at giving me a few hundreds!'[66]

Fisher's capacity for work, even at sixty-three years of age was phenomenal. He rose at 4.00 or 5.00 am, left his official residence at 16 Queen Anne's Gate without breakfast and walked the couple of minutes or so to Westminster Abbey, where he stayed for a short while. From the Abbey it was a short walk across Horse Guards Parade or along Whitehall to the Admiralty Buildings.

Everything about the First Sea Lord's room reflected the great man. It was, recalled one visitor, vast with 'three great windows looking out on the Mall'. When visitors entered they were struck by the 'immense fireplace at the far end' of the room, the dark wood of the curtainless window frames and the 'huge red and blue Turkey carpet'. To one side stood Fisher's great knee-hole desk, which was 'very orderly, with piled papers, rows of sharpened pencils in racks'. Everything spoke of methodical control, of power quietly reaching out to his immense Fleet. Yet it was not a sombre room, nor military in its aspect. Apart from the vividness of the carpet, the room was illuminated by a 'bright rose and green chintz' screen and a 'red leather couch opposite the fireplace'. The walls were adorned by 'splendid old naval prints' as well as photographs of Fisher's dear King and Queen. Later, as his reforms advanced, he added two huge table-top models of his creations, the *Dreadnought* and the *Indomitable*. With childish joy he would beguile visitors as he 'lifted deck after deck out of the *Dreadnought*'.[67]

By 6.00 am Fisher was at his desk, plunging into a mountain of paperwork. He would mark documents for action by his subordinates, scribble marginal comments on papers and minutes and then handwrite his

91

own letters. Some were a brief one page – an invitation to lunch, an appointment with a shipbuilder – others were mammoth letters of twenty or so pages, filled with his clear, ebullient writing.

At 9.00 am, Fisher left his desk, walked home and sat down to breakfast and the newspapers. Then it was back to Admiralty House for a full day's work, mostly of meetings, pausing only for a biscuit and a glass of lemonade at lunch-time. He would return home around 7.30 pm, have a bath, dine with the family, read for a while and then go to bed at 9.30 pm. The Fishers rarely dined out and never seem to have gone to the theatre or concerts. For Fisher, the Admiralty was a treadmill that he happily accepted.[68] For Lady Fisher, all that mattered was that her husband should hold the highest rank and be recognised for the genius that she saw in him. (The Beresfords, by contrast, never missed a society event which they were free to attend, and Lady Charles was a devotee of the Covent Garden Opera House in season.) Fisher's habit of Sunday working (despite his religiosity) led the King to write that 'Sir John Fisher is to do *no* work on *Sundays* nor go near Admiralty, nor is he to allow *any* of his subordinates to work on *Sundays*.'[69] Almost certainly Fisher paid no attention to this command, despite his dedication to his King.

For all his letter-writing, Fisher was contemptuous of unnecessary paperwork, as he told Winston Churchill in 1912. On his first day as First Sea Lord, he recalled, 'They brought me two feet high of papers.' He ordered his clerks to 'take 'em away' since he intended 'to attend to the Fleet'.[70] On another occasion one of his assistants, Captain Henry Oliver, recalled that Fisher was presented with a huge pile of papers on a long-running, but trivial, dispute: '[He] threw the whole file of papers on the fire and told me that when the Registry asked for them I was to say he had taken the papers to his house. He knew no one would dare ask for them.'[71]

Fisher's choice of personnel caused as much discontent in the Navy as any of his reforms. For men like Beresford and Custance, Fisher was guilty of favouritism and of packing the Admiralty with his chosen men. Fisher was unapologetic since, as he explained to Selborne, 'it's no use whatever attempting to do anything unless we have the very best men, utterly regardless of their rank or anyone's feelings or any vested interests'.[72] He selected men like Henry Jackson, John Jellicoe, Captain Charles Madden and Reginald Bacon because they were *both* good at their jobs *and* in favour of his reforms. He could not see how appointing a man such as Custance – who totally opposed his reforms – could make any sense.

It was during Fisher's early years as First Sea Lord that prominent people began to detect a needless harshness in dealing with officers who either did not agree with him or who sided with his 'enemies'. Battenberg complained to George Clarke, Secretary of the Committee of Imperial Defence, about the 'senseless way in which Fisher insults and alienates our senior men'.[73] Clarke wrote back to say that he agreed with this view, adding: 'However, he shall have my views in season and out of season, from high and low altitudes, now that he has asked for them.'[74] Clarke, no lover of Fisher's methods and often critical of his strategy, learnt to live with the irascible First Sea Lord. Others were less tolerant and sidled off in the direction of the Syndicate of Discontent.

Some were less fortunate and suffered more than just the effects of Fisher's tongue. When Bellairs wrote an article in the *Daily Graphic*, the contents of which Fisher described as 'most unpatriotic and reprehensible', Fisher suggested that he should be 'erased from the Navy List and lose the £300 a year the Admiralty are paying him for fouling his own nest!'[75] According to King-Hall, on another occasion Fisher told an officer that 'You are trying to wreck my plans regarding gunnery' and went on to warn him that, 'Anyone who opposes me, I crush, I crush.'[76] It must be said, though, in Fisher's defence, that the most outrageous stories are the vague ones, with no detail to support them. In this case, the story was recorded by someone who was not present and only heard one side of the case. As we shall see in Act 10, when in 1909 the First Lord investigated a string of complaints of this kind, not one was found to have any substance to it at all.

One of Fisher's initial reforms on becoming First Sea Lord was the re-distribution of the fleets. As Fisher saw it, there were three fundamental things wrong with the existing system. First, the Navy did not have enough sailors to man the ships it had – money was being wasted on repairing and berthing ships that would never be used, simply for lack of crews. Secondly, the Navy had masses of small, underpowered, under-armed ships that would be useless in any war. As Fisher described them, 'they could neither fight nor run away'. Finally, the fleets were neatly spread around the globe rather than concentrated where war might be expected – in the North Sea and the Atlantic. So, in December 1904 Selborne published Fisher's *Distribution and Mobilisation of the Fleet*.

Over 150 old and useless ships were to go and crews from the scrapped ships were to form nucleus crews for the reserve fleet. (A nucleus crew was sufficient to cover all core skills and could be rapidly brought up to full manpower in an emergency.) Commissions were to be reduced to two years. There were to be big reductions in the far-flung fleets, such as the one in the China Sea. In future, the Navy's great fighting strength was to be concentrated nearer home.[77] This would result in a Home Fleet at Dover (eight battleships), an Atlantic Fleet at Gibraltar (eight battleships), a Mediterranean Fleet at Alexandria (twelve battleships), and minor fleets at the Cape and at Singapore.[78]

The abolition of the Pacific, South Atlantic, and North America and West Indies Fleets was to lead Beresford to charge that the Empire's trade routes had been left unprotected. In speech after speech he repeated this message from around 1906 until the outbreak of the First World War. Fisher, though, preferred to abandon expensive fleet stations and protect commerce by *'the dogging, hunting down, and destruction of every enemy's Cruiser. The dogging to continue, if necessary, to the world's end'*.[79] This policy was pursued when war came in 1914 and quickly disposed of every German warship, other than those holed up in ports.

All this was underpinned by Fisher's 'instant readiness for war' philosophy, which explained to Balfour: 'All your fighting ships must be ready to fight and fight instantly! *Our frontier is the coast of the enemy* and we've got to be there the instant or even before war is declared!'[80] The emphatic use of the word 'instant' was to prove a mistake, since such a practice was impossible in reality. And, since there would always be some warning of any significant naval attack, it was also an unnecessary ambition.

Other reforms quickly followed, as we shall see in the next act. The more Fisher reformed, the more Beresford claimed that all the ideas were his. He told his friend Sir William Pakenham, then Naval Attaché in Japan, that, apart from the education reforms 'every one of the new reforms now in progress or effected were all made out, proposed and worked out by me'. This all happened in the Mediterranean, where, he told Pakenham, 'I saturated him with my ideas and gave him my papers.'[81] It was an odd thing to say, given how critical Beresford was to become of Fisher's reign.

## Scene 5: The Russians are coming!

While Fisher was establishing himself as First Sea Lord, Beresford was more or less out of harm's way, sailing with the Channel Fleet. Even so, a vast stretch of blue water was not enough to keep him at bay, so much so that on Fisher's second day in his new post an event occurred which led Beresford to once more incur the wrath of the Admiralty. It all arose over a curious incident involving British trawlers and the Russian fleet.

On the night of Friday 21 October 1904 the trawlers of the Gamecock Fleet from Hull were quietly fishing at Dogger Bank in the North Sea. It was three days off full moon and there was a slight haze, but visibility was good enough for the ships' lights to be seen from a long way off. The sea was calm and the trawlers gently bobbed up and down, their long nets drifting through the cold water, their navigation lights on, while their crews were gutting and cleaning earlier catches. The gentle lapping of the sea against the small ships was the only sound to be heard.

Suddenly, out of the darkness, a section of the Russian fleet roared into view, raking its searchlights over the trawlers before disappearing into the darkness. The bemused sailors shook their heads and returned to their tasks.

About half an hour after midnight, four more huge ships came tearing out of the gloom, searchlights ablaze. A bugle sounded and shells began to fall all around the tiny fishing vessels. Huge plumes of water shot into the night sky, brilliantly lit up by the powerful searchlights. At first the fishermen mistook the action for a sham fight, organised by the Royal Navy, but, as shells began to hit home, they realised they were under a deadly and serious attack. Their instinct was to flee, which was no easy matter given that their boats were weighed down by massive drift nets trailing into the sea. They were defenceless, immobilised, and left staring at the Russian sailors who were clearly visible only 300 yards away. Accounts vary as to how long the bombardment continued. Some say ten minutes, some twenty, some thirty. In the end, though, the firing stopped and the Russians steamed off, having realised their mistake, not even stopping to check the damage or offer assistance. They were on their way to the Russo-Japanese War in the Far East and had, unbelievably, mistaken the trawlers for Japanese gunboats.

The *Crane* had been sunk, her captain and boatswain went down with her. Six other men were wounded and five other trawlers were damaged. Although there were rumours that the whole thing was a British plot to provoke a war, an International Commission of Inquiry in Paris found the British case of an unprovoked attack proven and the Russian Government paid out £65,000 (about £4.7 million today) in compensation.[82]

When the first shell hit one of the trawlers, Fisher had been in office for less than forty-eight hours. No shot had been fired in anger against a British vessel in home waters since the Napoleonic wars, but Fisher was ready to respond as if he were an old hand at war. He was not, though, even metaphorically on the bridge but was lying ill with flu in his bed at the Charing Cross Hotel – his official residence not yet being ready for him. From his sickbed he summoned his Director of Naval Intelligence, Prince Louis of Battenberg, and dictated a telegram to the Fleet:

> War with Russia is imminent. Concentrate your fleet at Station Headquarters. Pay off immediately, all standing, the following ships [list was here]. Send home by first packet and wire date of arrival in England.[83]

Crews from surplus ships were to come home to make up the numbers for Fisher's nucleus-crewed ships – the first test of one of his great reforms.

Later in the day Fisher had another visitor – Sir Charles Drury, the Second Sea Lord. In an agitated state, Drury told him that the Cabinet was in session, busy planning war against Russia. Ill as he was, Fisher dressed in his admiral's uniform, rushed round to Downing Street and demanded admittance to the Cabinet Room. There, claims his biographer, 'He protested, and represented his case with such strength and firmness that different steps were taken, and war was averted.'[84]

For the next week or so the Navy remained on high alert as the British Government wrestled with the Russian Foreign Office. As Fisher told his wife, it had 'very nearly been war'. However, after spending 'all day, morning and afternoon' with the Prime Minister, the Russians finally backed down on 1 November.[85] The crisis had passed and Fisher's Navy had stood firm. Pleased as he was, he had one regret, as he told Lord Selborne: 'I really am sorry we did not mobilise! the excuse was so good!'[86] And there, were it not for Beresford, the incident would have closed.

Off Gibraltar with the Channel Fleet, Beresford was right in the path of the south-bound Russian Fleet, which would reach him a few days after the Dogger Bank bombardment. If war were declared, it would be up to him to send the Russians to the bottom of the Atlantic Ocean. Reinforcements were despatched from the Mediterranean Fleet and by 26 October, *The Times* was able to comfort its readers with the report that, 'The Admiralty has elicited assurances from Lord Charles Beresford that he has ample forces in hand to stop the Russian fleet or send it to the bottom.'[87] Three days later, readers were told that, 'The battleships of the Channel Fleet are in perfect readiness to put to sea immediately.' It is reported that Lord Charles Beresford signalled to the cruisers, 'Situation critical; good luck!'[88] It was a tense time and Pelly recalled that 'one night we cleared for action, and the men slept by their guns'.[89]

All this sounded very jolly and heartening, but then the public had not been told just what plan Beresford was hatching. While British breakfasts were eaten to the news of the great firepower that Beresford would unleash on the cowardly Russian Fleet, he had other ideas, as he told the Admiralty in a later report:

Being quite satisfied with the excellence of the gunnery of the Channel Fleet I should have engaged the Russians at Tangier (in the event of their refusing to proceed into Gibraltar) with four of my battleships, at a distance of 5,000 to 6,000 yards. It appeared to me that this would only be chivalrous under the circumstances.[90]

There was an explosion of anger and incredulity in the Admiralty. Since when, they asked, had naval war been a playground for medieval chivalry? Prince Louis commented that 'If this statement became public property, the taxpayers would probably enquire why they were paying for the other half [of Beresford's Fleet]' and Fisher, in a minute, reminded his colleagues of Nelson's dictum: 'The greater your superiority over the enemy the better.'[91]

The inevitable Admiralty reprimand swiftly followed. Beresford was told that 'your proposed action ... could not have been justified on any ground, and least of all those of sentiment.' He was reminded that 'in warlike operations such considerations cannot be allowed to have any place'. In future he was to remember that he was expected 'to make use of

96

the whole of the force at your disposal'.[92] Whether this reprimand had any impact is doubtful. When writing to his friend Lady Jessica Sykes, he once more conveyed the impression that, for him, war was a casual pastime, telling her that 'when [the] orders came, everything was ready, and we were all smoking our cigars and cigarettes'.[93]

A curious footnote to this episode is that Beresford very nearly found himself in even more trouble with the Admiralty. When the order came to prepare to face the Russian fleet, Beresford entirely forgot that he had sent some destroyers out on an exercise. Only when, in the dark, his ships prepared to fire on an approaching 'hostile' force was the mistake recognised.[94] Fortunately for Beresford, this serious oversight was never reported to the Admiralty.

Meanwhile, the British nation poked wry fun at the Russians by purchasing in 'tens of thousands'[95] a mock funeral card, which read:

---

### IN DISGRACEFUL MEMORY
### OF
### THE RUSSIAN NAVY

The world's stumbling block to civilization: the 20th century savages, who started on the road to destruction on October 23[d], 1904, in their brilliant naval battle when they completely routed nine disarmed Fishing Smacks in British waters.

---

*Act 6*

# An Uneasy Truce

Certainly he holds the record, to use his own language, of
'contempt and insubordination'. – *Hay's comment on Beresford* [1]

## Scene 1: Beresford's command of the Mediterranean Fleet

Fisher felt that Beresford had not been sufficiently punished for his proposed chivalry towards the Russian Fleet at the time of the Dogger Bank
incident, so he decided to terminate his command of the Channel Squadron one month early as a punishment. By some misfortune, Beresford
heard the news, not from Fisher, but from his successor, Sir William May.
In a rage, he wrote to May and told him that 'he would be very glad to give
him lunch or fight him, but he would not be superseded'. He then stormed
into the Admiralty and demanded to see Selborne, who merely referred
him to Fisher. From the latter he learnt that, not only was there no chance
of his retaining his command for the additional month, but that Fisher
wanted him to take the presidency of a signal committee before taking up
command of the Mediterranean Fleet. Beresford told the story to Vice
Admiral Charles Barlow, who passed it on to King-Hall. In the latter's
version, when Beresford refused to join the committee Fisher threatened:
'Well, then, you will not go to the Mediterranean.' [2] He continued: 'All the
pent-up wrath of years between the two men broke out.' In Beresford's
reply, we hear his formal declaration that the feud was now open and
serious. 'You dare to threaten me, Jacky Fisher,' he said. 'Who are you? I
only take my orders from the Board. If I have to haul my flag down on the
7th February, I will resign the Service, go down to Birmingham, get into
the House and turn out both you and Selborne. What is more, I will go to
the Mediterranean and I will not go on a Committee.' [3] Beresford himself
confirmed these events when he wrote to Bellairs much later in 1905.
He confessed to having told Fisher that 'he might take himself and the
Mediterranean Fleet to Hxxl' and he confirmed that he had threatened
Fisher, telling him that 'I would go down to Birmingham, fill Bingley Hall,
and have both of them out in two weeks.' This, he said, had 'made him
pipe down'. Interestingly, Beresford predicted that 'He will never threaten
me again' which, in a sense, proved true. [4]

There is a good case for saying that this meeting marked the true start of the feud. (The exact date of the meeting is unclear, but it must have been in December or January.) King-Hall's account seems irrefutable evidence that relations between the two men were, by then, dysfunctional. Beresford was threatening his superior officer when he said 'I only take my orders from the Board' and his threat to 'turn out both you and Selborne' verged on treason. There had been clashes before this date, but also a good deal of friendly intercourse and mutual support. From now on, the two men were to be most wary of each other. Each now saw the other as an implacable, untrustworthy rival and neither was to feel secure again. Fisher was to avoid direct confrontations with Beresford.

Further evidence of the breakdown in relations comes from the concern that Beresford's friends began to express. Even Pakenham, in Japan, had heard of the ructions and appealed to Jessica Sykes to 'do all you can to smooth over matters'. Fisher, he said, 'is so clever' and was more than a match for Beresford who, he thought, 'may ultimately suffer from the disagreement'.[5]

The last thing Fisher needed was a rampaging Beresford on the back benches. In 1901, when they had been on much better terms, Fisher had found that, as a Member of Parliament, Beresford was uncontrollable. Not surprisingly, then, he relented and the idea of the committee was dropped.

In May 1905, Beresford became Commander-in-Chief in the Mediterranean. It was Beresford himself who, describing fleet life, wrote, 'There is little to record during a sea command except the cruises, exercises and manoeuvres which constantly occupy a Fleet.'[6] Indeed, that would be the case for a less flamboyant and troublesome admiral than Charlie B. As it was, a good deal happened, which occupied an inordinate amount of Admiralty time, and none of which receives a word of mention in the ten brief pages that Beresford devoted in his autobiography to his Mediterranean command.[7]

Beresford claimed that he liked to keep the Fleet busy and was a determined trainer of officers. He recalled that, 'every morning when the Fleet was at sea, except on Sundays and in very bad weather, small tactical and turning movements were executed from 7.30 to 8.00 am'. Many commanders might have been able to claim this much, but Beresford added that 'the movements of each individual ship being carried out by the officer of the watch, all lieutenants taking it in turn to relieve the deck, and being put in charge of the ship for this period of time. The captains did not interfere in the handling of the ship, unless the officer of the watch placed the ship, or a consort, in a position of danger'. Later in the morning, he said, it was his custom to give the charge of the Fleet to 'an admiral or a captain' for the practice of short manoeuvres.[8]

However well Beresford fulfilled his plans, it was his reputation for training officers which had assured his appointment in preference to Wilson. When the posting had been under discussion in 1904, Battenberg had championed Beresford as '[he] trains the Flag-Officers under him, but Wilson does not', adding, 'in fact he is the only Admiral who has ever done this'.[9] His progressive attitude was appreciated by Wemyss, who was Captain of the *Suffolk* in the Mediterranean. In a letter to his wife he enthused over Beresford's training methods, telling her that 'All this morning I have had charge of the Fleet . . . which is capital fun.'[10] After Beresford had left the Mediterranean, Wemyss often referred to how dull life had become, as in February 1907 when he recorded 'A very uninteresting day . . . no amusing tactics such as we always had in C.B.'s time.'[11]

This attention to his Fleet seems to have paid off. Whilst Beresford's service record is splattered with reprimands and notes of his acrimonious correspondence with the Board, the period of his Mediterranean command actually lists three occasions on which the Board praised his performance. In February 1906 their Lordships noted with approval the 'great interest & trouble he has taken & is taking in development of gunnery efficiency of Med$^n$ Fleet'. In October of the same year he again received their praise for heavy gun-laying, where they noted the 'great improvement . . . compared with 1905 results'. In the following month he was congratulated on his battle practice results.[12]

However, there were many level-headed officers who cast doubt on Beresford's fleet management skills. Sir Francis Bridgeman (a future First Sea Lord), when Vice Admiral in 1907, said that 'he never knew much of what was going on'.[13] Captain David Beatty (another future First Sea Lord), was also critical, telling his wife that the exercises were 'Too much of a set piece, where everyone is told where to go and what to do . . . Everything we do is of the most childish description.'[14] This opinion is confirmed by more recent academic analysis, which concludes that Beresford deprived his 'captains of any real authority, while bombarding them with endless orders . . . and setting outdated exercises'.[15]

Whatever his qualities as an admiral, Beresford was near to universally liked by his officers and men. Bacon, who was to be vilified by Beresford from 1909 onwards, was still able to give credit to Beresford as 'the most charming Commander-in-Chief under whom I have ever served', having joined the Mediterranean Fleet because he had heard 'many reports of Lord Charles Beresford . . . as Commander-in-Chief'.[16] He also observed that 'all his subordinates loved him' and found him 'an ideal leader of men'.[17] Pelly found him 'a marvellous man . . . to serve under' who was 'ever thoughtful for all his juniors, and always making things easy'.[18] Wemyss thought him 'extremely civil', especially since Beresford 'perpetually' invited him to lunch and dinner.[19] He could hardly find superlatives enough to describe his fawning appreciation of his commander. He was 'perfectly marvellous'; 'the most indefatigable man I ever came across'; and 'extraordinarily active for his age'.[20] However, few people have suggested that Beresford had much of an intellect. As Bacon noted, 'his mercurial temperament militated against deep study or concentrated thought', which made him 'dependent on his staff'.[21]

Although Beresford had a keen appreciation of his men, his exalted status as vice admiral and then admiral was beginning to distance him from the lower orders. One day, when introducing his midshipmen, whom he habitually addressed as 'Mr Midshipman', to the Duke of Aosta he hazarded an attempt at their names. He started off well when naming those longest serving 'but' recalled Frewen, '[he] ran out of names with Gibson, Power and Chichester', whom he introduced as 'Mr. Brown, Mr. Jones, Mr. Robinson'.[22]

There were also signs that Beresford's attention to detail was beginning to slip, even to the point of upsetting his sovereign. On 11 April 1906, the King arrived at Corfu on a royal visit to Greece, where Beresford was due to meet him. Edward VII, having given notice that he was to visit Beresford's flagship, arrived to find that the admiral had failed 'to take the trouble to change into full-dress uniform'. So affronted was Edward that he ordered his diplomatic aid, Charles Hardinge, 'to bring Beresford's insulting and slovenly conduct to the notice of the Board of Admiralty forthwith'.[23] When the royal party left, Beresford managed to give further offence since only the flagship fired the royal salute, all the rest of the Fleet remaining silent.[24] Like his mother before him, Edward was not amused.

Age and rank were adding to Beresford's natural sense of superiority, which inevitably extended to lauding it over foreigners. Whilst making a speech at a lunch in Spain, he was constantly interrupted by a Spanish general. When he could take no more, Beresford turned to the British Consul saying, 'Please inform his Excellency that his time will come when I have finished.' Recounting this incident to his wife, Wemyss noted that 'He does love getting up on his legs and talking, & certainly likes neither interruptions nor contradictions.'[25]

When serving under Fisher, Beresford had been the victim of his commander's overreaction to various incidents. It was now Beresford's turn to elevate a mistake into a serious incident. On 7 July 1906 Wemyss had had 'a great row' with Beresford all because of 'a very silly mistake' over a signal made 'in a wrong manner'. In an intemperate retort Beresford accused Wemyss of 'disloyalty'. Wemyss stood his ground 'and very strongly objected', at which Beresford backed down and was 'charming'.[26] Wemyss similarly escaped Beresford's wrath in January 1906 when he tried to negotiate the notoriously difficult entrance to Malta Harbour – the very place where Beresford had received his dressing down from Fisher six years earlier. Wemyss, his ship struggling with a strong wind, confessed in his journal that '[I] nearly made a mess of getting out of harbour.'[27]

## Scene 2: The rise of the Syndicate

During Beresford's absence one man remained on the home front to press forward the Syndicate's aims. Described as the 'stimulator and clearing house for the anti-Fisher plots', Custance, at this time without a command, was fanatically dedicated to forcing out Fisher.[28] In August 1905, he told Admiral Sir Gerard Noel that 'It is not at all our duty to accept the decisions of the authorities when we perfectly well know that they are those of one man who has not understood his business and is doing an immense amount of harm.' He went on to prophecy that 'we shall get him out of Whitehall before his five years expire', but complained that: 'Single-handed it is hard work, but I hope that in time others will join in the hunt.'[29] Between them, Beresford and Custance were to fulfil this forecast, despite the extension to Fisher's period of office.

In January 1906, reinforcements, in the shape of Bellairs, arrived. He had won a seat in the Commons, which he was to hold until January 1910. Those four years were to be devoted to serving Beresford as, month in, month out, he asked parliamentary questions drafted by his friend and planted stories in the newspapers on his behalf.

Fisher, who had christened Custance 'the *Blackwood* Balaam' for his contributions to the Tory fortnightly publication, was well aware of the influence of all three men, but was reluctant to act. He knew that Beresford wanted martyrdom and that the Syndicate wanted publicity – he declined to offer such fruits to either party. Instead he poured out his worries to his trusted correspondents such as Earl Cawdor, who was briefly First Lord in 1905: 'I am storing up ammunition for you to fire away in the House of Lords,' he told him in January 1906, but it was only to be used 'should any of these fossils get some noble Lord to speak.' He hoped that necessity would not arise since 'silence is the best weapon' and he did not wish to give them 'the notoriety they seek'.[30]

But as soon as Fisher had fended off a Syndicate member on one side, another would arise from a different angle. In May 1906, Fisher told the naval historian, Sir Julian Corbett, that Bellairs 'has told a friend he intends to have me out of the Admiralty within 18 months!'[31] Yet, if it had not been Bellairs, it might have been Herbert Wilson of the *Daily Mail*, or Spenser Wilkinson of the *Morning Post* or Charles À Court Repington of *The Times*. On the Navy's active list Fisher was opposed by Rear Admiral Sir Hedworth Lambton and Noel, as well as Custance and Beresford. Attacks from the retired list came from Vice Admiral Penrose Fitzgerald, Admiral Sir Vesey Hamilton and Richards. From outside the Navy, Clarke,

Sir William White and Lady Londonderry, the hostess, all vigorously campaigned for Fisher's demise.

It was one thing for Fisher to ignore the Syndicate's agitations, but quite another for the Government to be seen as impotent before its accusations and agitations. Lord Tweedmouth, who took over from Cawdor, was weak and well out of his depth, a point which Wemyss made to his wife, observing that he was 'much torn between the Fisherites & the anti-Fisherites' and unable to judge the rights and wrongs of their respective accusations. 'Poor devil,' he continued, 'he can't possibly know enough of the subject himself to be able to form any sort or kind of opinion.'[32] Esher came to the same conclusion, noting that 'good fellow as he is' he was 'unequal to his task as First Lord'. When, in late 1907, Tweedmouth was a member of an enquiry into the risk of invasion, Esher found his contributions 'almost painful to listen to'.[33] Had Asquith appointed a more competent and forceful man to this post, the feud might well have taken a different course. As it was, Tweedmouth insouciantly presided over an impending disaster, unable or unwilling to act to prevent it.

Both sides in the controversy sought to recruit the Prince of Wales to their cause. Fisher complained to him about the 'poisonous things being said' and cited the accusations made by Hedworth Lambton that he, Fisher, was 'working the Press'. This was, he said, 'about the grossest calumny ever propagated'. Hoping to hoodwink the Prince, he pointed out that he could not possibly be 'working the Press' since many of their articles contained errors. If he had been behind them, 'such errors would never have occurred'. It is unlikely that the Prince was taken in for one moment.[34]

The new education scheme of 1903 continued to attract the Syndicate's particular criticism, ever fearful as they were of having to share a mess room with an engineer. Bridge, Custance and Fitzgerald had refused, said Fisher, his invitation to visit Osborne College 'to see the actual education going on ... They don't want to be converted!' Meanwhile, he continued, 'Beresford is writing *exactly opposite* to what he wrote two years ago.'[35] The extent of Beresford's antagonism to Fisher at this time can be found in a letter to Bellairs of 24 March 1906. He told him that he thought that 'the battle is won' but Beresford warned 'It is a long way from being won ... it cannot be abandoned unless the originator of it is asked politely to retire.'[36] Importantly, this letter predates the creation of the Home Fleet – often said to be the cause of the feud – by at least seven months, thus showing that Beresford's antagonism to Fisher was not rooted in the latter's new fleet, but in much earlier events.

By the end of 1906, Fisher's patience was at the limit. Custance was 'malignant' since he had promised he 'was going to be such a good boy' but had then published 'the most misleading of all his many misleading papers' in *Blackwood's* magazine.[37] When he found that Beresford's secretary was trying to plant a pro-Beresford article in *The Times* he cursed the Syndicate, saying that 'their wives shall be widows; their houses a dunghill'.[38] Two days later Fisher had learnt that the Syndicate 'were about to redouble their efforts'; he was becoming increasingly disheartened and was 'very sick of this "taking it lying down" apologetic line of policy!' Clearly tempted to fight back in public, he reminded himself that 'We don't hit back ... An attack should always be met by a counter-attack.' He then went on to repeat his achievements of recent years and only at the end of his letter returned to what he thought should be done, but he got no further than the vague suggestion of 'Let us, therefore, give up apologizing and support our supporters!'[39]

Fisher was protected from these machinations by his continued friendship with the King. As one of Edward's 'seven highly placed, trusted and congenial friends' (the others were Sir Edward Cassel, Lord Esher, Mrs George Keppel, Sir Charles Hardinge, Lord Knollys, and Louis de Soveral) he enjoyed his sovereign's unswerving support.[40] Without it he would not have survived. Knowing not only the value of the King's endorsement, but also saw the importance of the cabal that surrounded him, he habitually dined with Esher, Knollys and Soveral at Brook's Club.

## Scene 3: Fisher's crowning moment

When Beresford opened his copy of *The Times* of 6 December 1905, his eyes were instantly drawn to the ominous headline 'Promotion for Sir John Fisher'. Those five cruel words struck deep into his heart and needed no further explanation: Admiral Sir John Fisher was now Admiral of the Fleet Sir John Fisher. In those few seconds, Beresford's great ambition (and, more importantly, Lady Charles' great ambition for him) was swept away. No longer could he succeed Fisher as First Sea Lord. The reason lay in the technicalities of rank. As an admiral, Fisher would have retired on his sixty-fifth birthday, that is 25 January 1906, at which point Beresford, at fifty-nine could have taken over. But, as an admiral of the fleet, Fisher could go on until his seventieth birthday, 25 January 1911, by which time Beresford would be sixty-four and within months of retiring.

Whilst *The Times* welcomed the news of Fisher's extended reign saying 'his retirement at this time ... would have been universally recognised as detrimental to the best interests of the nation', Beresford's world fell apart.[41]

Commander Crease, one of Fisher's assistants, later recalled how things stood in the Beresford camp at this time. 'C.B.' he said, 'had made up his mind that he would be the next 1st Sea Lord' and, more importantly, it was the ambition of Lady Charles 'that he would occupy Admiralty House & be a big figure in London & Society.' When Beresford heard 'the bombshell' continued Crease, 'that J.F. was not going to retire', he 'was egged on

104

by everyone round him to try to down J.F.' It was, of course, the only way that Beresford could hope to be First Sea Lord. In Crease's view, Beresford was initially unwilling to bring Fisher down but 'he got more and more drawn in as time went on', with the lead being taken by Custance. But, fundamentally, said Crease, 'the whole Beresford troubles arose from Lady Charles' disappointment and spite'.[42]

Crease's assessment of Beresford's inclinations is borne out by a letter that Beresford wrote to Bellairs just a couple of weeks after Fisher's promotion. 'My inclination now,' he told Bellairs, 'is to leave the Service, and look after my private affairs.' He doubted that he would 'take First Sea Lord if it was offered'.[43] There was no mention of ousting Fisher; instead, Beresford seemed to accept defeat.

It did not take long for him to bounce back. Just a month after appearing to have given up hope of further advancement, Beresford returned to battle. Rather than attack Fisher directly, he decided to make a vicious attack on one of his subordinates – Rear Admiral Battenberg – who was in command of the Second Cruiser Squadron. He was, said Beresford, 'the only Admiral who supports Fisher's wild schemes'. The attack was to be in the form of three parliamentary questions which he wanted Bellairs to table. They were amongst the most vile questions ever to be asked in the House, being an outright racist attack on this loyal, naturalised British citizen. To appreciate the nastiness that Beresford was now prepared to descend to in order to get at Fisher, the questions deserve full quotation:

> Are the Government aware that there is a very strong opinion throughout the Navy as to the desirability of placing a German Prince in the position of Second Sea Lord, thereby giving him an Administrative Appointment over the Naval Service?
>
> Whether the said German Prince is, or is not, a Naturalised British Subject, and if so, for how long time.
>
> Whether it is a fact that during the time this German Prince was Director of Naval Intelligence, he employed German servants, who had charge of Dispatch Boxes, and took them from the Admiralty to the Prince's house, and from the Admiralty to the Prince's estate in Germany?[44]

Needless to say, Bellairs never asked the questions. It would be fascinating to know whether he declined to ask them, or whether he handed them to the Table Office, who refused to permit them to be asked.

There is no evidence that Battenberg ever heard about these questions, but later that year, whilst in Germany, he heard reports that Beresford and Lambton had denounced him as 'a d--d German who had no business in the British Navy'. This was, he said, 'a drop of poison in my cup of happiness of a lifetime devoted truly and wholly to our great service'.[45]

In passing, it is worth noting that, in attempting to attack Battenberg in such a mean manner, he was attacking the very person who had supported him in obtaining his Mediterranean command. At least Battenberg was free from prejudice.

## Scene 4: Fisher's 'espionage'

Aware of the unrest in the Navy, Fisher was keen to obtain grass-roots feedback on his reforms. In a move that was to have disastrous consequences for his reputation, he asked various officers to send him confidential reports on the mood of the seamen and officers, and their reactions to the reforms. Details of three such requests have survived: those to Captain Troubridge, Captain Sturdee and Captain Bacon.

In May 1906, Troubridge received a letter from Crease (then one of Fisher's assistants) asking him to write to Fisher about the Channel Fleet situation. Writing on Fisher's behalf, Crease told Troubridge that 'Sir John would be glad if you would let him know your opinion of this matter. He has already consulted Sir A.K. Wilson on the subject ... but he thinks that you may possibly be able to give him better opinions as regards the Captains + more junior officers.' Fisher wanted no ordinary letter, explained Crease. Rather, he desired a letter that 'he could show to the Prince of Wales' who was concerned about rumours of 'a considerable feeling of unrest in the Service'.[46]

Troubridge replied the next day, outraged at the thought of 'giving my opinions to my subordinate', adding that '[I] do not propose to make any exception in your case.' What he then wrote is very significant in the light of how the 'spying' charge against Fisher was to develop: 'You will be good enough to request(?) Sir John Fisher that I shall be glad to avail myself of an opportunity if he wishes to give him my opinions personally or by letter to him.'[47] True to his word, a week later he wrote to Fisher, telling him that he paid far too much attention to his noisy critics and that 'there are hundreds like me', by which he meant 'sea officers whose guiding principle is – that it is their business to assist to further to their ultimate success such orders or reforms as their superiors are pleased to command'.[48] Troubridge, then, was quite prepared to write to Fisher and did not for a moment consider himself to be a 'spy'. Only later was this word to be attached by Beresford and others to this and similar incidents.

Another 'spy', Captain Sturdee, claimed that Fisher called him to the Admiralty just before his posting to the Mediterranean, asking him to 'keep an eye on Charlie' and 'to write to him privately about my Chief'. Writing much later, he said that 'This request I never complied with' since it was 'a disloyal act ... that ... did not require a second thought.'[49] There is nothing to corroborate this charge. Coming as it does from a man firmly in the Syndicate camp, it may well have been influenced by later events.

Fisher's requests to Troubridge and Sturdee never became public knowledge during the period of the Feud. Bacon's letters, on the other hand, were to become a *cause célèbre*, leading to Beresford's accusation that Fisher had established 'a system of espionage', the purpose of which was to 'report secretly upon brother officers'.[50] It was a charge that would do more to harm Fisher's reputation than any other accusation made against him. What made matters worse was the saga of how the letters came into the public domain. This we shall see in Act 9.

As with Troubridge and Sturdee, Fisher had asked Bacon to write to him from time to time about the state of the Navy in the Mediterranean and the reception of his reforms. There is no evidence that Fisher asked Bacon to comment on individuals and, years afterwards, Bacon, defending his actions, acknowledged that 'It would ... have been highly improper for me to have written home to Sir John any remarks on the professional ability of the Commander-in-Chief' or to have commented on individuals. However, he thought that it would be helpful to the Navy 'to point out to Sir John any weak points in the Admiralty proposals which were being discovered by the brains of those at sea'. As a result, he wrote, he said, 'six or seven letters', although two of these were never posted.[51] In the surviving letters Bacon was true to his word: he passed no comments on any officer's performance, nor were his criticisms based around identifiable individuals. His naming of Beresford and Lambton was solely with reference to the fact that they were agitating against the Board – which was public knowledge in any case. None of this prevented Beresford from repeatedly giving the impression that the letters were diatribes against him and his staff.

Bacon wrote his first surviving letter on 31 March 1906, beginning 'You may like to hear how my three months at sea have altered or confirmed my views *re* education, &c.' In the rest of the letter, the sole information that he gave Fisher about the Mediterranean Fleet concerned the effects of some changes made to the midshipmen's course at Greenwich. 'Quite unbiased Naval Instructors,' had told him, he said, 'that the difference in the way the boys work is extraordinary.' The nearest that he came to mentioning anyone by name was when he (wrongly) predicted that 'I think the present agitation will die out, and as the present Government gets accustomed to office they will pay less attention to agitators and their like!'[52] There was not much there to justify Beresford's accusations of being spied on by Fisher.

The second letter was to be seized on by the Syndicate because names were mentioned, but, contrary to what would be later said, Bacon made no criticism of any serving officer in the Mediterranean. What he did do was to report to Fisher what the Prince of Wales had told him. Passing through Corfu on his way back from India, the Prince 'seized' on Bacon, telling him how worried he was about 'the opposition ... to the new schemes of reform' and the reports that 'the Navy is becoming full of cliques'. What particularly concerned the Prince, said Bacon, was that Vice Admiral Sir Arthur Moore (China Squadron) and Vice Admiral Poe (East Indies Squadron) 'had been wailing and bemoaning the schemes and their exclusion from consultation'. Most unfortunately, Bacon added on his own initiative the phrase 'and probably the two Admirals here'. It was the Prince's contention that the Admiralty only 'issued arguments on their side of the question and never those against'. Bacon pointed out that admirals such as 'Bridge, Custance and Fitzgerald' were doing a fine job in 'providing ... every argument against the scheme'.[53]

As a result of what he heard, Bacon wrote a paper, which he gave to the King at a dinner on board the Royal Yacht. In handing it over he told the King that what 'the Navy was suffering from was want of loyalty ... among the Admirals afloat; that any scheme they did not approve of, although their knowledge could not compare with that of the Admiralty ... [they] thought they were justified in ... agitating privately against their governing body'. He continued: 'The Navy must accept the superior knowledge of the Admiralty and stifle their opposition and loyally support a policy once adopted.'[54]

In his third surviving letter, Bacon set out in general terms, with no names, the main complaints being made against Fisher and the Board. Senior officers, he said, complained that 'the Admiralty never gave them more information than they do the Paymaster of the ship'; they bemoaned 'not being more consulted by the Admiralty'; captains received 'insufficient notice of appointment'; and there was the widespread view that 'the Admiralty is run by one man'. Ironically, given the spying charge, this letter is more a critique of the Admiralty than of the officers and men in the Mediterranean. The one bit of good news that he could offer Fisher was that he retained the support of the King and the Prince of Wales, although they were 'very much disturbed at the Service agitation headed by Lord Charles Beresford and Admiral Lambton'.[55]

The fourth letter, which dealt largely with the problem of the status of engineers, made no references to either Beresford or Lambton.[56]

If Fisher sent Bacon as a 'spy' and anticipated a flow of sharp and pungent comments on Beresford and his activities, then he must have been most disappointed. Bacon offered not one example of a disloyal act on Beresford's part, other than to make general references to his agitations. Since it is unlikely that, so far from home, Beresford had been overcome with a fit of loyalty, we can only conclude that Bacon – whatever Fisher intended – never saw his role as that of spy. Rightly or wrongly, he thought Fisher wanted to know how the reforms were working out, and that is just what he told him.

Beresford knew nothing of this correspondence until April 1909. Had he discovered the letters whilst still in the Mediterranean we can be certain that his reaction would have been of the most hostile nature.

## Scene 5: Beresford and the Home Fleet

Despite Beresford's disputes with the Board it was decided to offer him the command of the Channel Fleet when it fell vacant in 1907. It must have been a difficult decision for the First Lord. On the one hand, Beresford was an able and much admired commander; it would be a popular appointment both at sea and at home. On the other hand, the Channel Fleet would provide him with yet one more base from which to maintain his hostile attacks on the Admiralty, with the added advantage of his being able to attend meetings on land and invite journalists to join him at sea. Almost certainly the First Lord's decision was tipped by the comforting thought that, chained to his Fleet by King's Regulations, Beresford would not be free to re-enter Parliament and attack the Admiralty from the back benches.

It was through press speculation that Beresford first heard of the appointment. 'The papers have it that I am going to the Channel Fleet,' he told Knollys, 'if I go there . . . I shall be very satisfied.'[57] It was therefore no surprise that he accepted the post two days later, after negotiating his terms of command with Tweedmouth. It was agreed that 'he would hold the chief command in home waters and be responsible for "organising the Fleet for War and immediate action"'. He was also to take charge of 'the organisation and training for war of all the torpedo craft'.[58]

All the arrangements for the posting had been smoothly and amicably completed in a few days. The Home Fleet was now to overturn all that had been agreed.

To understand what happened next, it is important to keep in mind that the governing Liberal Party was deeply split at this time between the Gladstonians, the imperialists and the radicals. Only the imperialists (leading members being Asquith, Grey and Haldane) were favourable to paying what it cost to have a strong Navy, while the radicals (led by Lloyd George and Churchill) were determined to see a *decrease* in the estimates. Fisher and Tweedmouth had, at one and the same time, to fight off accusations that the Navy was not strong enough *and* accusations that it was the bloated consequence of profligate estimates. Between them they had to devise ways of spending less (to please the radicals and Gladstonians) while creating a stronger fleet (to satisfy the imperialists). In practice, Tweedmouth was incapable of rising to this challenge, so it was left to Fisher to come up with a scheme. The result – the Home Fleet – was to prove his most controversial reform yet and stimulate Beresford to his greatest excesses.

In August 1906 Fisher had sent a circular letter to commanders-in-chief, to inform them that, the international situation now being quieter, the Board was to withdraw certain ships from the Mediterranean and Channel Fleets. Fisher was adamant that this would give more naval power for less money, but his proposals received a hostile response. At this point there was no mention of a Home Fleet, which did not appear on the scene until October, following a good deal of critical comment about the proposed new fleet distributions.

Fisher, on holiday at Levico, described his plans for the new fleet in a letter to Tweedmouth in which he discussed how to get more defence for less money. He reminded the First Lord that 'we cannot possibly get the Navy Estimates down to the figure which I think the House of Commons will insist upon ... unless we strictly confine our naval expenditure to *absolutely necessary services*'. Reviewing the international situation, Fisher, concluded that 'Germany [is] our only possible foe.'[59] The conclusion was obvious – to reduce ships in quieter areas and to strengthen the fleets in home waters – but Fisher did not mention this until seven days later. Still at Levico, he announced that he proposed to create 'a new Home Fleet and a Reserve Fleet'. He knew that there would be much opposition, but thought that once the public saw 'a new Fleet emerge into being' the changes would be accepted. Then came the ominous bit for Beresford: the new fleet would be based at Dover, the Nore and in the North Sea.[60] To achieve this, seven battleships and four armoured cruisers would be brought home and added to the existing reserve, 'placing them all under one Admiral' and so have 'a homogeneous perfectly constituted *Reserve Fleet* always in "Home Waters"'. Fisher continued: '*I don't know anything that we have done which will more add to our fighting efficiency!*'[61] At the same time, all the submarines and destroyers in home waters were to be separated off into a new command. Whether Fisher was as convinced of this 'acme of efficiency' as he claimed, we shall never know. What is certain, though, is that his new fleet came in for a torrent of critical, and even abusive comment. A typical reaction came from Lord Knollys who wrote to Esher to complain that Fisher 'is as clever as a monkey and has persuaded the King that his nucleus [-crew] Fleet will be as efficient in every way as if it were afloat! To my mind this contention is contrary to common sense'.[62] He was not the only one to take this view. Even the ever loyal Battenberg called it 'simple topsy-turveydom'.[63] Indeed, he went one step further and suggested that Fisher created the Home Fleet in order that 'Beresford would not have so big and honourable a command'.[64]

It is beyond the scope of this book to explore the full mysteries of the Home Fleet, but recent research suggests that it was all part of a secret Fisher policy called 'flotilla defence'.[65] This involved deterring an enemy fleet through the use of a vast number of coastal submarines and torpedo boats. The mere existence of these, he hoped, would deter Germany from sending the High Seas Fleet into the North Sea. Fisher was reluctant to explain this for fear that the Germans would find out about his new strategy. So secret was this that, when in February 1907 Captain Herbert Richmond, one of his assistants, had to reply to a Foreign Office memorandum about the Home Fleet, he noted in his diary that he found the task difficult 'without giving away too much'.[66]

Once the decision had been made to commit to the Home Fleet, Fisher went rapidly into action. Only twelve days after informing Tweedmouth of his proposal, a letter was on the way to all commanders-in-chief setting out the detailed changes.[67]

Although Beresford must have wondered what the relationship was to be between his Channel command and this new fleet, he initially showed few concerns. The full import of what Fisher had done does not seem to have hit him until December. Meanwhile, there was time for just one more gloriously silly dispute with the Board.

## Scene 6: *The Truth About the Navy*

With Beresford's Mediterranean command nearing its end, he provocatively found time to lob yet another pointless broadside at the Admiralty, choosing a matter of unbelievable triviality. His target was not the distribution of the fleets, not the size of the guns, not the sufficiency of their ammunition ... it was that great threat to the Empire's safety: the ship's library.

Late in 1906 the Admiralty despatched one of its routine bundles of books and papers to the fleets around the world for onward circulation to the libraries of the individual ships. Amongst these items was a pamphlet entitled *The Truth About the Navy*, issued by a very reputable company, Chapman and Hall, renowned as the publishers of the works of Dickens.

A few days later, at considerable expense to the Navy, a long telegram arrived at Admiralty House. It had been despatched by none other than Beresford and was a tirade against the Board's impropriety in its circulation of this pamphlet. In his acerbic critique of their actions, he claimed, in telegraphic language, that 'the Admiralty wrapper and official stamp give pamphlet official sanction'. This, he said, combined with 'the letter accompanying the pamphlet [which] orders it to be placed in the ship's library' all gave the impression that the Admiralty approved of its contents. Fisher, in an amusing annotation on the telegram scribbled, 'No more than in the supply of Darwin's *Origin of Species* & the Admiralty thereby don't commit themselves to any official sanction that we are descended from Apes!'

Beresford went on to say that 'the pamphlet is also political in character and has been published in the party press' and that it 'has been violently opposed by the Press of a different shade of opinion'. Objecting to such a partisan document, he added, 'I consider it most insidious for authorities to issue under official sanction one set of views under such circumstances and not to issue as well under official sanction the views of contrary opinions.' He then concluded with a typical Beresfordian excess claiming

111

that 'My special cause for objection is in the interests of authority and its dignity.'[68]

Had Beresford intended to enrage the First Sea Lord and offend the Board in one swoop? Whatever his intention, Fisher was astounded at the effrontery of a serving admiral who sought to tell the Board which pamphlets it could and could not circulate. The next day he sat down and prepared a minute for his colleagues.

He began by recounting for the Board the history of the pamphlet's circulation. It was he himself who first noted the existence of this 'apparently clear and impartial history of Admiralty Policy'. Bringing it to the attention of the Fourth Sea Lord he recalled that he had suggested that 'it might with advantage be circulated like other magazines' although 'it would be unwise to publish [it] officially' since that might cause offence to the German government. In consequence, when the Fourth Sea Lord circulated the pamphlet '[he] no more gave it official sanction than to all the other periodicals'.

If this had been a first offence, doubtless Fisher would have left the matter there. But this was far from being a naïve complaint from an inexperienced admiral: this was yet another pointed and antagonistic stab at a Board and a First Sea Lord who could do nothing to please Beresford. 'The fact is,' Fisher continued, 'that Lord Charles Beresford has consistently and persistently thwarted Admiralty Policy at every opportunity and hardly ever does he receive an order without some private or public representation on his part of an improper character.' Nor had Beresford any right to complain that the Board had been over zealous in its rebuttals of his agitations. Rather, said Fisher, there 'never has an Admiral received such consideration and been permitted such licence for the simple reason that it has been rightly decided in the past that to take the proper steps would have been to make him a martyr'.[69] (In using the word 'martyr' Fisher acknowledged for the first time that the Board retained Beresford, not because he was worthy of his post, but because he would be more dangerous outside the Navy than in it.)

Broadening his attack Fisher explained that 'these remarks would not have run to this length except for the purpose of indicating this questioning and discussing of Admiralty orders is descending from Lord Charles Beresford to those under him'. Bellairs, he said, had letters which showed that Beresford 'had canvassed all the Captains & Commanders of his Fleet against the Admiralty' and 'the tone of his official & private letters is such as to be very difficult to conduct business'.[70]

Noting that 'a crisis appears to be approaching' Fisher told the Board that Beresford needed 'a timely reminder ... of his position' in order 'to avert' further insubordinations.[71]

Beresford may well have been responsible for making sure that the controversy reached the pages of *The Spectator*. By mid-January, the pamphlet's publishers felt the need to defend themselves. The author, said the publishers, had asked them to point out that 'the idea of publishing this brochure was the author's own, and was not suggested to him by anyone'. He had used sources 'drawn from official correspondence issued in this country and in Germany'; the pamphlet, he said 'differs in no respect from other books issued to libraries of His Majesty's ships'. With a neat turning of the tables, the author added that the *Naval Annual* (also circulated to ships) had included an article by Bellairs which was critical of Admiralty policy. If it was considered appropriate to 'circulate Mr. Bellairs's criticisms of their work at the taxpayer's expense' where could be the harm, he asked, in 'issuing a plain statement of the facts as revealed in Blue-books?'[72]

(Four years later, Beresford took up his case against the pamphlet once again. This time, Chapman and Hall found it necessary to write to *The Times* in defence of the publication, taking the opportunity to point out how accurate the forecasts that it contained had proved to be.)[73]

## Scene 7: Beresford disputes terms for the Channel Fleet

We have seen that on 7 August 1906, Beresford had formally accepted the command of the Channel Fleet, which was to consist of sixty-six (sixty-seven in some accounts) vessels. In an interview towards the end of the year, Beresford was to say 'My life ambition is now realised.'[74] As we shall see, though, by the time he gave that interview, Beresford's dream fleet was disappearing over the horizon at an alarming rate. What happened is hardly conceivable, and yet it was all too true.

Eleven days after accepting his new command, Beresford was informed that four ships were to be withdrawn from his sixty-six, taking his fleet to sixty-two. This was all part of the general fleet reductions that Fisher was making worldwide. Two months later, on 5 November, the Admiralty's letter explaining the setting up of the Home Fleet reached Beresford in the Mediterranean. This told him that all his torpedo craft and submarines were to go to the new Home Fleet. His sixty-two vessels now fell to twenty-six.

Nearly two months later, and four months after having accepted the Channel command, Beresford received yet further details of the new Home Fleet. It was to have 244 vessels and the Channel Fleet was to lose a further five. Beresford's new Fleet would now be just twenty-one vessels. So, in the four months from accepting a fleet of sixty-six vessels, Beresford had seen this number cut and cut, until it stood at twenty-one vessels – less than one-third of the original size.[75]

It must have been no surprise to the Board that Beresford now turned down the proposed appointment. Initially, this was done verbally when the Board paid a visit to Malta early in January.[76] Beresford's refusal,

113

though, was probably just a negotiating ploy since he returned to London later in the month for further discussions with Fisher on 20 January. It must have been a heated meeting since, as Fisher told Lambert, 'I had three hours with Beresford yesterday.' Although 'all is settled' (or so Fisher thought) and he had not had to 'give in one inch to his demands', Fisher had been forced to agree 'three things' with his commander:

I. Lord C. Beresford is a greater man than Nelson.
II. No one knows anything about the art of naval war except Lord C. Beresford.
III. The Admiralty haven't done a single d----d thing right![77]

Was the First Lord surprised or disappointed to receive a letter dated 22 January in which Beresford once more turned down the appointment? 'What can I possibly do,' he asked, 'with fourteen battleships and four armoured cruisers, plus three unarmoured cruisers, and no torpedo-boat destroyers[?]' In his view, 'To take command under these circumstances would be to deceive the country.' Beresford particularly objected to the idea that the new Home Fleet could be ready to 'proceed instantly' given that it would be dependent on nucleus crews. 'No story of the "Arabian Nights" is more delightfully impossible,' he told Tweedmouth.[78]

'We appear to be approaching a crisis' Fisher told an unknown recipient a day or two later. The Board could provide full rather than nucleus crews, but that would 'add another four millions to the Navy Estimates' – a politically unimaginable act. The heart of Fisher's complaint, though, was Beresford's attempt to usurp the Board's right to decide. Beresford, he said:

now dictates terms before he will accept the command of the Channel Fleet. He requires that Fleet to be increased by cruisers and destroyers, and that the Home Fleet shall come under his command. If the Board were to give way, it would have to 'abdicate its functions and take its instructions from an irresponsible subordinate'. Beresford, he added 'is only thinking of magnifying his own particular command'.[79]

For Beresford, the situation was difficult, since he was in the Mediterranean and, by March, would be in Mexico. Somehow, despite these absences, he had to manipulate the press in order to put pressure on the Admiralty to improve the terms for his appointment. To do this, he armed Mina with a long memorandum, setting out his terms for accepting the post and put her and Bellairs in charge of leaking stories to the press. Mina explained to Bellairs just how delicate this task was: 'Lord C's professional reputation is at stake if it were allowed to be supposed for a single instant that he has accepted the Channel under the dangerous & absurd conditions under which it was offered him.' That left the two of them with the problem of how 'to give an inspired version' (Edwardian phraseology for planting a story in the press) of Beresford's position 'without laying himself open to "comment"'.[80]

The two of them did not have a happy time of it as they bickered over minor points. When Bellairs placed an article which used the words 'had declined', Mina was 'very much hurt' because Bellairs had not kept 'to what we had decided'. He should, she said, have used the words '*had declined unless*'.[81]

The Mina Beresford-Bellairs correspondence at this time is especially interesting since Mina merely echoed what her husband said. We therefore find through her the very first of Beresford's charges that the Home Fleet was a fraud. In a fragment from a now lost letter, Mina told Bellairs that 'no one (I mean outside Naval circles) has an idea what a fraud the Home Fleet is'.[82] Only Beresford could have provided this phrase for her to repeat. We also find another very early use of this 'fraud' charge in Frewen's diary, where he quotes a letter from Beresford to his father, Moreton Frewen:

> The last proposal about the Home and reduced Channel Fleets is a fraud, as the 244 vessels of the Home Fleet are only half-manned and most of them are under repair and could in no way take their place in the fighting line, as the public are assured.[83]

Both the Admiralty and the enquiry were to take particular exception to Beresford's 'fraud' charge.

The negotiations continued with results which drove the Sea Lords near to resignation rather than to give in to Beresford. The admirals would walk out, Fisher told Knollys, if there were 'any trucking to either Beresford or to Parliamentary pressure to have an enquiry into Admiralty Policy'. Knollys' advice had proved crucial in ending the dispute. Having recommended to Fisher that he should avoid a breach with Beresford, Fisher was able to tell him that: 'I followed your advice and wrote a most cordial letter to Beresford, and I enclose you his reply. It will not be my fault if he resign[s].' As a result, Beresford once again accepted the appointment, although Tweedmouth was convinced that he would still resign. Fisher, too, doubted Beresford's commitment, telling Knollys that 'he wants to get into Parliament and hates the Channel'. After all, he added, 'Fogs and short days and difficult navigation [are] very different to Mediterranean white trousers!!!'[84]

It was just after this that Esher wrote to tell Fisher that he was handling the situation badly. He had allowed the world to see the battle as 'Fisher versus Beresford' when he should have worked to present it as 'Fisher plus Defence Committee plus Cabinet versus Beresford'.[85]

Beresford's acceptance of the command was finally sealed by Tweedmouth offering him powers to detach destroyers from the Home Fleet 'whenever desired for exercise and manoeuvres' and, in a similar way, to detach the Fifth Cruiser Squadron for 'exercise with the Channel Fleet'. He was also recognised as 'the senior Flag Officer afloat' in relation to the two fleets and, as such, would command in war. In consequence the two fleets 'must necessarily be exercised together in peace'; this was to be 'at such periods as will be decided by the Admiralty on the representations of the Commander-in-Chief of the Channel Fleet'.[86] All these additional powers, though, were to be whittled down over the next two years, so adding to Beresford's mounting grievances.

## Scene 8: Death of Delaval Beresford

In January 1907 the time came for Beresford to haul down his flag in the Mediterranean. After a dinner in his honour, at which he broke down in replying to a toast, he sailed for home on 19 January.[87] Within days of arriving back in England, he was on his way to the United States, where his brother Delaval had been killed in a railway accident on 22 December 1906 while journeying from Mexico to Canada. (Oddly, he seems to have told Fisher that he wanted a month off 'to go abroad for his health's sake'.[88] Possibly he wanted to conceal his true business from Fisher.)

Delaval was Beresford's youngest brother and the black sheep of the family. He had substantial ranch interests in both Mexico – where he lived a colourful existence not at all in keeping with his aristocratic roots – and Canada. In Mexico, he had set up house with a black woman called Flora Wolff, but no one has ever been able to establish whether they were or were not married. It is likely that they were *not* married for one simple reason – that Delaval was almost certainly already married before he met her. In July 1907, an unnamed woman was reported as claiming that she had married Delaval twenty years previously, but that he had disappeared two weeks later. She claimed to have papers to prove her marriage and intended to claim her inheritance.[89]

The estate was well worth disputing. In Mexico alone, Delaval was said to have ranches of 160,000 acres and 73,000 acres[90] and the total estate was valued at $2 million according to the *New York Times*. Some accounts say that Beresford and his brother Marcus inherited the lot. Others that $1 million was shared between the three Beresford brothers.[91] Flora, it was said, received just $15,000, which would suggest that the Beresford family never accepted her claim to have married Delaval.

Whatever the exact size and division of the estate, Beresford did well out of the settlement and was able to buy 34 Grosvenor Square on his return to England. In his absence, Fisher found time to joke with White that 'We can sleep quiet in our beds!' After all, he argued, Beresford claimed to be '[the] one man on whom all depends' so the '"bolt from the blue" can't be coming' or he 'would surely ask that some other Admiral should take his place'.[92]

Beresford was out of the country from 30 January to 11 April, despite the fact that his new appointment was due to start on 4 March. He had settled Delaval's affairs on or before 19 March but had made no effort to return to Britain, preferring to tour Canada and the USA.[93] After seven months of controversy, he finally took up his command more or less on Admiralty terms. All was then quiet until he hoisted his flag in the Channel on 16 April 1907.[94]

Overnight, though, Fisher's well-off adversary had become a rich man.

*Act 7*

# Beresford Declares War

Lord Charles displayed a spirit of insubordination
unparalleled in the history of the Royal Navy. – *Magnus*[1]
Hell. By one who has been there. – *Fisher*[2]

## Scene 1: Choppy waters in the Channel

After months of dispute over his terms of appointment, Beresford was
finally settled in a new post. A few weeks earlier, Fisher had written
optimistically to him, saying that he had 'no doubt ... we shall all be
equally satisfied with the way things will work out'.[3] It was to prove a vain
hope as the feud moved into its bitterest phase, driven by Beresford's ever-
increasing hatred of Fisher and his methods. For the next two years there
would hardly be a day when the Admiralty would not feel the animosity of
its foremost sea-going admiral. Nor would it be long before the first
tentative efforts would be made to remove him.

In sending Beresford to the Channel, and in the staff that he chose to
accompany him, Fisher had made a strategic blunder. For once his capacity
to judge men had deserted him, leading him to inadvertently establish a
hotbed of discontent on his own doorstep. Somehow, Fisher seems to have
been taken in by Beresford's promises of good behaviour despite his long
history of bad relations with the Board.

Having made one serious error, two more rapidly followed. Beresford's
second-in-command was to be none other than Custance, Fisher's implacable foe since 1901. According to Marder, Beresford detested Custance, so
Fisher's choice was an attempt at revenge on his adversary.[4] If this were so,
then Fisher was being too clever by half. How could he expect to both buy
Beresford's loyalty and silence him by awarding him the premier fleet, and
at the same time punish him by dumping Custance on him? Whatever
Fisher's complex motives were, the combined appointments were to prove
his undoing. In no time at all, Beresford and Custance had teamed up in a
deadly game of hunt-the-First-Sea-Lord. When Fisher and Tweedmouth
had decided that the 'serious disadvantages' in the two men were 'out-
weighed ... by their good qualities and their record of services in the past'
they were truly deluded.[5]

To add to Fisher's problems, Beresford's Chief of Staff was to be yet another of his antagonists, Sturdee, who had previously served under Beresford in the Mediterranean. Fisher despised Sturdee, who 'returned the feeling with interest'.[6] The only thing that could be said in favour of these appointments is that they gave the lie to the accusation that Fisher promoted his favourites over those who opposed him. Had that been true, not one of Beresford, Custance and Sturdee would have enjoyed a Channel berth.

Later, Sturdee was to recall that 'the relations of us three together were most happy'. This was despite the fact he claimed, that 'many endeavours were made [by Fisher] to break up the trio'. Amongst these endeavours, he cited the planting of Rear Admiral Sir Percy Scott in command of the Cruiser Squadron, where he was, claimed Sturdee, to 'twist Charlie's tail'.[7] This account seems to owe more to Sturdee's imagination than to any verifiable facts, but is a good illustration of the paranoia with which these three conspirators judged Fisher's actions.

Beresford was now a grand man of sixty-one years, who, recalled an officer who served with him, was past 'the peak of his curve' and 'inclined to dwell upon past days' not having 'moved forward mentally'.[8] Love of ceremony and pomposity had replaced the glory days of the *Condor* and the *El Safieh*. Life on the flagship, Sub Lieutenant Dawson recalled, 'centred round the person of the Admiral' so that whenever he appeared on the quarterdeck all stood to attention 'until the well-known and slightly nasal voice graciously commanded: "Carry on, Mr Officer of the Watch"'. He spoke with 'solemnity' as if he were addressing the Commons, while peppering his speech with old-fashioned terms like 'catcher' rather than 'destroyer'.[9]

Beresford's self-importance had reached royal proportions. A mere fishing outing required three men to 'get flies out of weeds or bushes and disentangle knots', whilst in train would be 'the coxswain and two of the galley's crew ... with lunch-baskets, landing-nets, rugs and other gear'.[10] In his cabin, he boasted his exalted connections by adorning the surfaces with photographs of royalty and members of high society.[11]

On board ship, Beresford lived in style. He had a hand-picked group of Irishmen for his stewards and his barge crews, their main role being to 'look smart'. One was assigned to attend to his bulldog, 'his duty being to follow this fat, overfed bitch about the upper deck, equipped with dustpan, brush and cloth to clear up the messes she was always making'. Stowed on board was his car (for which, naturally, he had a driver), which had to be manhandled with slings and derricks onto a barge and taken ashore whenever the ship was within hailing distance of land. No sea was too rough, no terrain too inhospitable for Beresford to command its prompt unloading. In addition, the Fleet was invariably tailed by the Admiralty despatch yacht, the *Surprise*, just as it had been in the Mediterranean.

Often, Lady Charles would be aboard.[12] In fact, he paraded around the seas like a monarch surveying his kingdom.

Pelly, Beresford's flag captain, recalled him as more keen on entertaining and pontificating than on fleet strategy. He loved an audience and, said Pelly, '[was] the most hospitable of men' and 'it was rare for an evening to pass in harbour without a large number of guests being present'. He entertained his admirers with endless stories, never, claimed Pelly, 'repeating himself'.[13]

His hubris extended to providing himself with titles to which he was not at liberty to use. In May 1907 he entered into an agreement with the commanders-in-chief of Chatham and Devonport to address him as 'Admiral in Command of the Channel Fleet'. This was, said Fisher, in a memorandum to his colleagues on the incident, 'in order to show that there is only one Commander-in-Chief present'. Such a designation was contrary to regulations and a reproof from the Board followed.[14]

Within days of taking up his appointment, Beresford wrote to Fisher to complain about something. The letter has not survived, although a clue to its contents comes in Fisher's reference to his intention to provide Beresford with twenty-four destroyers, suggesting that Beresford had written to request more ships.[15] Fisher's staff drafted a proposed reply but Fisher decided that, rather than correspond with his awkward admiral, they should talk. It was not, he said, when writing to Beresford, 'conducive to the harmonious working which is essential, if your Staff are always preparing ammunition for you to fire off at the Admiralty'. It was, he added, 'desirable that we should discuss things personally'.[16]

Beresford replied the same day, saying that he agreed that face-to-face talking was best, but told Fisher that he was mistaken in thinking that his letters to the Admiralty were prepared by his staff. '[A]ll my correspondence,' he confessed, 'good bad and indifferent, emanates in what I am pleased to call my brain.' There then followed an extraordinary passage which illustrates Beresford's uncommon capacity for self-delusion. Saying there was 'not the slightest chance of any friction between me and you' he pointed out that 'When the friction begins I am off. If a Senior and a Junior have a row the Junior is wrong *under any conceivable conditions* or discipline could not go on.'[17] How Beresford could have written this, having been rowing with the Board since 1886 when he was there as Fourth Naval Lord, is beyond imagining. As to the future, it held nothing but arguments between 'senior' and 'junior'.

Beresford's first two weeks in the Channel command passed off quietly. These were to be the *only* quiet weeks of this period. During the rest of the period covered by this Act – that is until the change in First Lord in April 1908 – Beresford was to succeed in dominating Fisher's activities on an almost daily basis. Fisher, Admiral of the Fleet and First Sea Lord, in

120

command of the world's greatest Navy, was to find that day in, day out, Beresford and the Syndicate were driving his agenda. Bacon, who knew Fisher well, marked 1908 as the turning point. Before that time, Fisher had refused to enter into the quarrel which Beresford had started, always attempting to remain calm and to pacify Beresford's persistent attacks and provocations. Only as Beresford ratcheted up his campaign in 1908 did Fisher become 'seriously angry'.[18]

One reason why Fisher reacted less violently than might be expected is that he was under attack from two sides. Beresford and the Syndicate lambasted him for his neglect of the Fleet and for not building enough ships. At the same time, the radical elements in the Government were distraught over the navy estimates which they saw as shipbuilding for aggrandisement rather than for genuine defence needs. Under these contradictory attacks, Fisher, in Esher's opinion, had found 'the *juste milieu*'.[19]

From April to July, Beresford's antics over war plans were to dominate Fisher's agenda; by August, Fisher would be into the long battle to try to prevent yet another Cabinet enquiry into invasion, or at least to stop Beresford from giving evidence to such an enquiry; in November, he would be overwhelmed by Beresford's antics, with the Scott paintwork incident, Beresford's abusive memo about Bridgeman, Beresford's complaints about the withdrawal of officers, and the estimates for 1908–9. And so it was to go on. Hardly an issue was to cross Fisher's desk which was not either driven by Beresford and the Syndicate or did not provide an opportunity for their agitations. Essentially, Fisher was to lose control of the Navy's strategy during this period as he fought a rearguard action to defend his past reforms. New reforms would be near to impossible; he was to become almost a prisoner at the Admiralty.

One issue at this time that was to surface with a vengeance at the enquiry was Beresford's relationship with Bridgeman in the Home Fleet. Although the terms of Beresford's appointment required him to work closely with his colleague, he steadfastly refused to communicate with him, addressing him only through the Admiralty. In May, for example, he asked the Admiralty to direct Bridgeman to keep him 'regularly informed ... of drills and training has been carried out'.[20] Desperate as Beresford was to know week by week how many ships Bridgeman had available, he refused to stoop to asking him for that information.

Throughout this period Beresford was in constant touch with Bellairs, who had become his land-based *alter ego*. He used him to attack Fisher in the Commons over his pay (April), to run the campaign for an enquiry into the Admiralty (May), and to ask questions about absent battleships in the Channel Fleet (June). Having leaked details of these absences to Bellairs, he advised him to 'put in different dates' when he asked the question in the Commons so that he would not be suspected of having provided the details. (Bellairs duly used the figures, with vague dates, later in the year.)[21] Then, in July, he was advising Bellairs on how to use opposition to the estimates as a lever to gain an enquiry. (It is possible that Bellairs' petition to the Prime Minister, signed by around 200 MPs asking for an enquiry into the Navy was a result of this suggestion of Beresford's.)[22] Later in the year he was helping Bellairs to recruit Kipling to their cause 'as he will be sure to make some phrases which will be true, and will take'.[23] In the same letter he offered advice on how to strengthen the Navy League. By January 1908 he was leaking secret details of torpedo boats under repair, an act that paled into comparison with his letter of 13 February 1908 in which Beresford provided Bellairs with a step-by-step guide on how to 'completely upset the Board of Admiralty'.[24] In March Beresford had to explain to Bellairs that he had been unable to get hold of a copy of some book 'as it is so confidential, it has to be signed for'.[25] Effectively, Beresford had recruited Bellairs as a co-conspirator in his drive to oust Fisher.

## Scene 2: War over war plans

After a minor squabble over destroyers, Beresford turned to a dispute that he would sustain right to the end of the feud: war plans or, rather, the Board's lack of them.

Fisher had already told Beresford, in a letter dated 8 March that, when they met, he would tell him about the Admiralty's secret war plans.[26] Whether Fisher or Beresford first raised the issue of a specific war plan for the Channel Fleet is not clear, but by 30 April Fisher was writing to Beresford to offer him the Admiralty's help in preparing these plans. One piece of help, though, was not on offer. Fisher very pointedly asked Beresford, 'as a personal request' not to ask for Wilson's war plans. These plans would, he added, serve 'no good purpose' since conditions had changed since that time.[27]

Two days later, Beresford reported progress, saying 'I am pegging away at my plan of campaign for war with Germany.' He was not happy, though, and told Fisher that, he was 'loath to appear discourteous' but he could not understand why Wilson's plans could not be sent to him since 'such plans must be of infinite utility to me'. In support of his request, he pointed out that he needed them since he was 'the man who would have to do all the executive work' should war break out with Germany.[28] Fisher was not amused at this grand claim, telling his staff in a memorandum that Beresford evidently thought he had the 'plenary powers of an admiralissimo'.[29] Beresford had inadvertently opened up a new line of dispute between himself and the Board: the relative powers and responsibilities of the Board and the seaborne commanders-in-chief. In due course Fisher would have to deal with the matter in a more formal and insistent manner. Meanwhile, Beresford's letter also contained his oft to be repeated charge that the Admiralty was not ready for war.

Annoyed as he was, Fisher yielded a little and on 4 May he sent Beresford a copy of a 188-page Admiralty *War Plans* document which, he said 'embodies all that is useful'.[30] These plans were not quite what their title implied. For some years Fisher, who did not believe in printed war plans, preferring to keep his secrets in his head, had been under political pressure to produce such plans. As a smokescreen, he arranged for his staff to write the *War Plans* paper, but he never showed much sign of giving it any credence. Whatever their merits, the plans found no favour with Beresford.

Four days later Beresford wrote to the First Lord with the very request that Fisher had asked him not to make. Telling Tweedmouth, somewhat disingenuously, that he had been 'unable to find any papers relative to the plan of a campaign to enable the Channel Fleet to take instant action if war had been declared', he asked to be supplied with his predecessor's plans.[31] (He made no mention of Fisher's refusal to supply them.) What had become of the junior-senior relationship that he had pledged to uphold? On 13 May, Beresford turned up at the Admiralty, bringing with him his critique of Fisher's *War Plans* paper. Beresford's comments consisted, said Fisher, 'almost entirely of complaints as to his own position, and abuse of Admiralty administration'.[32] Beresford also handed in a 'Sketch Plan' as his substitute for war plans; it was rejected by Fisher on the grounds that it involved 'more battleships, cruisers, &c., than the British Navy possess'.[33] What was worse, though, was Beresford's inability to produce war plans without at the same time abusing the Admiralty. Fisher commented, in a minute to his colleagues, that 'when the elaboration of such plans for war takes shape in a sweeping criticism of existing arrangements and the whole trend of recent Admiralty policy, the question takes on another aspect utterly subversive of good order and naval discipline'.[34]

At the same time as corresponding with Tweedmouth behind Fisher's back, Beresford was also trying to influence the King by writing to Knollys, his private secretary. He was, he said, 'distressed and alarmed at the complete absence of organisation and preparation for war in the Fleet' which was 'a danger to the State' and repeated his mantra about a lack of war plans and the fraudulent nature of the Home Fleet.[35]

By this time Tweedmouth and Fisher had both had enough and attempted to end the dispute with a firm letter restating Admiralty policy. They first reminded Beresford that 'it is in the nature of things that all such plans must be to a large extent conjectural' since the actual conditions of war could not be foreseen – the Board had no intention of being tied down to minutely detailed plans just to please Beresford. The only assurance that they could give him for an unknown war against an unknown enemy at an unknown date was the Board's statement of policy of 1905, i.e. that

'The fleet which will be placed under [your] command on the outbreak of war will be such as appears to their Lordships most adequate to meet the situation with the resources at their disposal.' They then turned to their fundamental point of disagreement with Beresford. They could not accept the bolt from the blue thesis which so obsessed Beresford. This was the idea that 'a war would come upon us without any period of strained relations or any ostensible cause'. No enemy, they said, would 'perpetrate such an act of black treachery'. Having dealt with the policy, the reprimand followed: 'Their Lordships greatly deprecate statements reaching the press as to any action that may be taken in the fleet as to perfecting war preparations, as they tend to propagate alarmist rumours of national danger.'[36]

Fisher clearly hoped that the matter would be closed at that point, as did the First Lord, who was largely a passive observer of this spat. When Fisher handed him a sheaf of papers setting out, in his usual lively language, Beresford's shortcomings Tweedmouth ruled that they should not be circulated to the Board 'in their present form'. He thought it would 'be a pity to lodge a formal attack ... against him' since it 'must almost forbid his continued employment'. Rather, he preferred to accept that it was 'only human to grind your own axe'.[37] Thus passed the first of what were to be numerous attempts to force Beresford into retirement.

Ignoring Beresford's insistent demands clearly did not work, since only six days later yet another insistent letter arrived from him. This time he demanded that the Board 'should render to me on the 1st and 15th of each month a list of all ships under their command'. This was, he said, 'absolutely necessary in order that I may be prepared at a moment's notice to undertake my responsibilities'.[38]

Tweedmouth's willingness to give Beresford another chance soon led to a further outburst. In response to an Admiralty request to submit operational plans 'under the several contingencies of an outbreak of war', Beresford replied on 27 June that this was 'manifestly impossible ... unless I know what ships are available to carry these plans out'.[39] Within hours, Fisher was penning yet another minute to his colleagues, telling them that Beresford's letter was 'deliberately provocative' and that he had been 'invited to meet the Board' so that he could explain 'his intentions'; this would allow the Board 'to judge whether there is any prospect of his resuming his loyal and amicable attitude towards themselves'.[40]

The attempt to bring an end to the correspondence having failed, Tweedmouth asked Beresford to come into the Admiralty to clarify the situation. This was to be no ordinary meeting since Fisher, despairing over Beresford's endless capacity to defy the Board's instructions and abuse its good name, called in a minute-taker: there was to be a verbatim record of the meeting.

Tweedmouth began by reminding Beresford that he had received his war orders in an Admiralty letter of 14 June. However, Beresford could neither recollect the letter nor his having discussed it with Tweedmouth two days later. He thought that, in his reply to the Admiralty, he had accepted the terms as 'reasonable and fair' yet he was quite unable to recollect his intransigent reply that he had despatched only eight days before. 'What was my answer?' he said to Tweedmouth. The First Lord reminded him that he had insisted that he needed 'a return on the 1st and 15th of each month of ships coming under your orders' before he could prepare war plans. When Tweedmouth referred Beresford to his letter of 27 June, the admiral could not recall its contents. Nor, when he was reminded that the Admiralty letter of the 14th had had Wilson's war plan attached to it, could Beresford recall that plan. For a man who had set himself up as superior to the Board in every possible way, his display of incompetence was astounding.

The meeting then got down to the First Lord's business, which was to put four questions to Beresford in relation to the latter's letter of 27 June. These concerned 'the numbers and types of vessels' that Beresford thought he should have under his command; what further information he needed in order to prepare war plans; why he did not 'cultivate cordial relations with the Admiralty'; and finally, what were his reasons for calling the Home Fleet 'a fraud and a danger to the Empire?' To assist the confused admiral, Tweedmouth handed him a copy of the four questions.

Despite Tweedmouth's careful preparation, within less than a minute, after making an attempt at the first question, Beresford had lost himself in the fogs of the Humber, which was, he said, 'the most shocking place in the world'. He made a stab at the second question on 'further information' but became so confused that, in talking about the ships he needed he ended up by saying 'I want to start at once with every single ship you have in England; then I can send back those I do not want.' Hardly a suitable response from an admiral who was accusing the Board of a lack of precise war plans.

When he got round to question three, Beresford brushed it aside by saying: 'You will allow me to smile for at least ten minutes over Question No. 3.' He then declared that 'There is no question of cordial relations. I do not care about having rows with anybody. I never did.' An odd response from someone who had been disputing every Admiralty decision about the Channel Fleet since the middle of the previous year.

The conversation then turned to Beresford's charge about the Home Fleet. Rather than defend what he had said, he disputed whether he had said it 'officially' or not. He claimed that his letter of 30 June was a 'private letter' and that 'We have all written much stronger things than that on important occasions of that sort.' If he were to say it officially, that 'would be different'. When he complained that such a private letter should not have been placed before the Board, Tweedmouth pointed out that it had not been marked as private – it was typewritten and had the appearance of being a formal communication. Tweedmouth once more pressed that Beresford should not make such charges unless he could substantiate them, but Beresford brushed this off by saying, 'It is a "term".'

There then followed a long technical argument about what constituted 'instant readiness for war' and whether Beresford had sufficient access to the ships of the Home Fleet, but once again this deteriorated into an argument as to whether he had ever said 'officially' that the Home Fleet was a fraud: 'If I said it officially, you would say, "You can go".' When Fisher asked him whether he had ever used that expression in the presence of others, Beresford replied: 'Not that I remember – I may have.' As we have seen in Act 6, he certainly used the phrase in talking to his wife, who in turn passed it on to Bellairs. He also used it in his letter to Moreton Frewen. These are grounds enough for suspecting that he used it liberally.

The conversation then returned to Beresford's request to see his predecessors' war plans. (Beresford had subtly switched from 'predecessor's' in his original request to 'predecessors'' at the meeting.) Fisher pointed out that since Wilson had been in the Channel for six years, there was no need to go back further. Beresford, it turned out, thought Wilson had been there for only three years – a surprising mistake for an admiral who was taking so much high ground. Worse was to come. When Fisher reminded Beresford of his having requested Wilson's plans, he replied 'I did not ask for his plans. I am perfectly able to make plans myself.' Fisher refused to accept this reply, insisting 'But you directly asked for your predecessor's plans.' Instead of apologising, Beresford dismissed the episode, calling it 'a minor thing' and insisting that 'we need not discuss it further'.[41] As Sir Frederick Ponsonby was to note later in the year when he attempted to quiz Beresford on his views on the Navy, 'Whenever I tried to focus the discussion on any point, it only roused him to an outburst of oratory on another point.' It was a mode of behaviour which 'never led to any satisfactory result'.[42]

It was up to Fisher and Tweedmouth to try to salvage something from this bizarre meeting. They had taken the extreme step of calling in a senior commander-in-chief to account for his insubordinate criticisms of the Board's policies and his failure to produce war plans. Instead of contrition, apologies and promises of good behaviour, they had received evasions, denials of proven facts and a clear demonstration that Beresford could barely remember anything about his correspondence with the Board. To bring matters to a close, they offered to make his cruisers up to the six that Wilson had had and to give him two divisions of destroyers, to which Beresford, all too typically, replied: 'I cannot see that thing straight off. I will write to you.' Fisher could not restrain himself from a sly dig, saying:

'You must have thought about it. You have been writing about it for six months.'[43]

Fisher secretly sent a copy of the interview transcript to Vice Admiral Bridgeman, then in command of the Home Fleet, who commented that 'the whole thing is too funny for words'. In writing to Bridgeman, Fisher must have made some allusion to Mina since Bridgeman agreed that 'It is likely as you say that he is *not* master in his own home!', the inference being that if Mina had not pushed him so far, Beresford would not have been so troublesome. More importantly, Bridgeman confirmed what the interview suggests about Beresford's competence at this stage in his career. He recalled that, when in the Mediterranean, Beresford 'never knew much of what was going on' and that now, in the Channel, 'he knows even less & is a complete tool of his subordinates & *their* most obedient servant [Bridgeman]'.[44]

Before the day was out, the Admiralty had written to Beresford to confirm the offer of the additional ships, asking him whether he wished to 'allow the present arrangements to continue' or to take the new ships.[45] The next day, Fisher wrote a personal note to Beresford, saying how they were both besieged by 'mischief makers' who would try to come between them. He was 'most anxious' to return to 'the warmest days of our friendship' in the Mediterranean and would never forget 'how you have stood by me against the whole army of fossils in the past'.[46]

Ten days later, two letters arrived at Admiralty House. The first one, formally addressed to the Admiralty, contained Beresford's belated replies to Tweedmouth's four questions. Denying once more that relations had ever been less than cordial, Beresford continued to maintain his charge about the Home Fleet, neither apologising, nor withdrawing it.[47] The second letter, this time addressed from the *Surprise*, perhaps to emphasise its less formal status, was to Fisher. In it Beresford jauntily reported that 'the Admiralty evidently sees my points, and are doing what they can to meet my views'. It was as if the 5 July meeting had never taken place. He then went on to ask for 'three more armoured cruisers', a request that led Fisher to comment: 'The very day after getting all he asks for, he asks for three more.'[48] Beresford finally closed off the episode with a letter on 18 July when he told the Admiralty that 'I can now make out a plan of campaign on definite lines.'[49] The plans, though, did not reach the Admiralty until June of the following year.

## Scene 3: Triumphs and mediocrity in home waters

While Beresford kept up his running disputes with the Admiralty – pausing to collect an honorary DCL from Oxford University in June[50] – he had a fleet to command. Despite his huffing and puffing about the need for exercises and instant readiness for war, he remained an admiral of the old

127

school, tied to obsolete conventions. Rear Admiral Sir Percy Scott, who joined the fleet in July 1907 in command of the Cruiser Squadron, recalled the stultifying effects of fleet command at that time. A most independent-minded man, Scott was infuriated that 'whenever the senior officer's ship did anything, all the rest of the ships in the fleet had to do likewise'. So rigid was the system that, 'if the senior officer's ship forgot to do what she ought to do, then the other ships must not do it'. In his own case he recalled that, even though he was a flag officer, '[I have] practically no control over [my] squadron when in the presence of a senior officer.'[51] Washing could not be put out unless it was already hanging on the flagship; nor could it be taken in before the same action had been completed on the flagship; tarpaulins were not to be placed over guns as long as the flag's guns were exposed to the elements ... and so it went on.

Beresford saw no reason to depart from such hierarchical routines, which served to emphasise his importance. For him, the Channel Fleet was an appendage to Lord Charles Beresford, not the other way round. It was he who paraded himself from one port to another around the coasts of Britain, not he who accompanied the Fleet. In the summer, week after week the Fleet would visit home ports – whether it were Grimsby, Liverpool or Invergordon – where Beresford would meet the local notables, enjoy civic feasts and make patriotic speeches. His approach would be keenly appreciated as at Grimsby where the local paper applauded the visit because 'it has given us a chance of coming face to face with the brave and dauntless Admiral Lord Charles Beresford, the hero of Alexandria, a man who knows no fear, who never yet struck his flag and never will, whose name is a terror to our enemies and the just boast of our country-men'. He 'has long been', said the paper, 'the idol of the British public' and declared that 'Lord Charles stands alone as the heir-apparent of the great sea-dogs of the past from Drake to Nelson.' He was praised for his 'attractive personality' and lauded for his 'courage, dash, impetuosity, passion, humour, and a magnificent masculinity'. He was 'a leader' who was 'well-nigh irresistible to the people'.[52] Similar views were expressed at Liverpool, where Beresford was described as 'one of the most popular men in the world today'.[53] It was no wonder that he saw himself as untouch-able; no other contemporary admiral commanded such devotion.

As McKenna was to point out at the enquiry in 1909, Beresford's Cook's tour of Britain seemed to belie his assertion that the Fleet had to be ready for instant war. His progress was more reminiscent of the triumphant return of a military commander at the conclusion of a long conflict than of an admiral who had declared that war might descend on the Fleet at any hour.

Beresford's tours around the coastline were not without problems since not all the press attention pleased the Admiralty. When the Board read in *The Times* of 7 August that Beresford 'in conversation with a representative of the Press' had said that he 'sympathised immensely with the people who professed peace principles'[54] but added that he thought they were mistaken because a reduction in armaments would lead to war, he received a telegram from the Admiralty accusing him of giving 'an important interview ... on the subject of armaments'. Although Beresford denied having given an interview, the Board demanded, in a second telegram, that 'In view of the wide publicity given to the alleged interview' he was to 'take immediate steps to have the facts of the interview contradicted.' In a letter to Blumenfeld, a journalist with the *Express* newspaper, he bitterly remarked that 'certain persons in the Ad$^m$ will do anything subterranean[,] malicious, cowardly or vindictive to trip me up'.[55] His reputation was not enhanced when he failed to inform the corporation of Edinburgh of his Fleet's visit to the Firth of Forth. The Lord Provost and other officials were aghast to see the mighty ships steam up the estuary, with no prior warning and no arrangements made for the usual social niceties.[56]

During this early period of Beresford's command, both he and Custance suffered the humiliation of having the poor gunnery scores of their respective flagships singled out for criticism in *The Times*. Of the eleven flagships cited, the *King Edward VII* came eighth and the *Bulwark* was tenth. This led the paper to comment that 'the flagships of the Channel Fleet are very low down in the list', adding 'The position of the flagship is important, as it must be difficult for an admiral to find fault with the other ships of his fleet, if the vessel in which his own flag is flying is low down in the list.'[57] In the Commons, supporters of Beresford tried to argue that the poor score for *King Edward VII* was due to defective gun sights, but George Lambert, Civil Lord of the Admiralty, stated that the equipment was exactly as it was when the ship had achieved higher scores in previous years.[58] Beresford also told one of the King's assistant secretaries, Sir Frederick Ponsonby, that 'Fisher and Prince Louis of Battenberg had been duped' by Beresford's flag captain, Mark Kerr, and that the firing had been done under 'unfair conditions'.[59] What exactly his accusation against Kerr was is unclear, but what stands out is that, once again, Beresford was happy to slur anyone's name in order to clear his own.

On the professional side, Beresford was to have a mixed relationship with the Board. At times he received praise for his fleet work, as in October 1907 when he was congratulated on his night-firing experiments against torpedo craft. Their Lordships expressed their 'appreciation' of the 'able manner' in which this work was reported.[60] In February of the following year another commendation followed for firing experiments.[61]

There was, though, no praise for his larger-scale work, and the autumn manoeuvres of 1907 were to prove a disaster for his reputation. In fact, the manoeuvres had been cancelled as an economy measure and Beresford had been ordered 'to carry out combined tactical exercises only'. Despite this explicit order, he set about converting the exercises into manoeuvres – an action which he later claimed had been authorised by the Admiralty. He chose to divide the Fleet into two sections: one under Custance and one under himself. Bridgeman, in command of the Home Fleet, was placed under Custance. The Admiralty objected to this arrangement, saying it would not give Bridgeman enough experience, which was a key point of the exercises. Refusing to give way, Beresford went ahead using his 'sketch plan', which had been rejected by Fisher earlier in the year. In this way Beresford was effectively refusing to accept the authority of his superiors over the fundamental principles of how the Fleet should be used. McKenna, when First Lord, drew up a report on Beresford's manoeuvres for the enquiry in 1909. He told its members that 'After their experience of Lord Charles's action in 1907, the Board decided to hold no further combined exercises under his command.'[62] (In fact there were further manoeuvres in 1908.) On the surface it would seem to be criminal that the Board retained an admiral in a senior position afloat whom they could not permit to work the combined fleets that were to be entrusted to him in war. Things were not, though, that simple, as we will see in Act 8 when the Cabinet was to block the Board's attempts to remove Beresford.

As a result of the manoeuvres, Beresford sent yet another letter of complaint to the Admiralty. 'I consider it my duty,' he told the Board, 'to bring to the notice of their Lordships the fact that, in my opinion, there is a dangerous shortage of unarmoured cruisers and destroyer forces available for the duties which will be thrown upon vessels of these classes in time of war.'[63] In reply, the Board said that they 'must demur strongly to the opinion you express' and reminded Beresford that they were 'responsible for the strength of the Fleet, its strategic distribution in peace, and the general control of its movements in war'. His language, they added, was 'unnecessarily alarmist'.[64]

In all then, the Admiralty, *The Times* and various notable admirals found Beresford's command of the Channel Fleet to be undistinguished. That would not have mattered – not all admirals can be exceptional – had Beresford not decided to systematically denigrate and dispute almost every Admiralty policy and decision. One decision that he was to attack above all others, was the Board's right to determine the flag officers of the Channel Fleet.

## Scene 4: Beresford's vendetta against Scott

On 15 July 1907 an innocuous event occurred that was to have catastrophic consequences for Beresford and accelerate the termination of his career. On that day, Rear Admiral Sir Percy Scott, aged fifty-four, was appointed to command the First Cruiser Squadron in the Channel Fleet. Short, dapper and round-faced, Scott resembled a frisky gnome. He came with a formidable reputation, and not one that was welcomed in the Channel. First and foremost, he had an unparalleled reputation for his inventiveness, with a string of patents to his name. Such showy enthusiasm was not in the traditions of the Navy, where conformity was more favoured than creativity. His speciality was gunnery, at which, with the aid of his 'dotter' (a device to show gunners how close their aim was to a bull's-eye) and 'deflection teacher' he staggered the Navy on 26 May 1899 when his ship, the *Scylla*, achieved a hit rate of eighty per cent. No one in the Service believed this possible and he had to repeat the operation 'before independent witnesses' before it was accepted.[65]

All might have been well if Scott's reputation had stopped there, but he was also known as a man who knew when he was right and never refrained from saying so. He used to tell the story that, early in his career, he contradicted one of his commanders and, 'as I happened to be right he never forgave me'.[66] He was known as pushy, while 'not cursed with undue modesty'.[67] Quite simply, he did not get on with other officers and, as his biographer, Padfield, has noted, 'His survival to Flag rank was accomplished despite and not because of the top crust of the Service.'[68] All his life, personal relations were less important to him than doing what he thought was right, and doing it better than anyone else. As a result, said Bacon, he was 'rather like the Old Testament seers, who rubbed those in authority the wrong way'.[69] These were handicaps enough for a man about to join Beresford's Fleet, but he came with one disastrous, fatal failing: he was assumed to be a *protégé* of Fisher's. In consequence he was seen as 'a poisoned thorn planted by Fisher in Lord Charles' ample flank'.[70]

In his 1909 account of his clashes with Beresford, Scott recalled that, on arrival in the Channel, 'it soon became apparent to me that the two senior Admirals were animated by a very hostile spirit to the present Board of Admiralty'. Beresford made no attempt to conceal from Scott his contempt for Fisher and his determination to bring about 'his speedy removal'.[71] At first Beresford seems to have been well-disposed to Scott. Indeed, five years earlier he had said that 'there was no man in the Navy ... to whom we owed more'.[72] Not surprisingly, then, Beresford first saw Scott as a possible recruit to the cause and Scott soon received 'certain overtures from Lord Charles Beresford to join in the campaign against the Authorities at Whitehall'. Inevitably, he did not rise to the bait, thereby sealing his fate. From that moment on, Beresford, said Scott, made no effort to disguise his determination to 'weaken my position and, if possible, replace me by an Admiral more in sympathy with the views held by my two seniors'.[73]

In his memoirs, Scott recalled that he ignored the hostility and 'I employed my time in trying to improve the shooting, and I succeeded so well that the *Good Hope* became ... [the] top ship of the Navy.'[74] That is true, as far as it goes, but conveniently suppressed a year of systematic victimisation by Beresford.

The first serious clash between Beresford and Scott occurred on 24 October 1907. Accounts of the feud rarely mention this event, for a reason that will become clear when we see how it ended.

On that day the Fleet was on manoeuvres at Cromarty. Some time on the 23rd, Beresford had ordered Scott to use his cruisers to guard the entrance to the bay, inside which it was presumed that the 'enemy' was holed-up. Scott had no knowledge of where the enemy actually was and, as he noted in his record of the event, his position 'was a very dangerous one' since, if the enemy had already escaped to sea, he could return and annihilate Scott's cruisers, trapped as they were in the narrow entrance.

According to Scott, he had been ordered to maintain his position until he was 'certain the enemy were not there'. And that is just what he did. It was only later that, in a Beresford memorandum issued to the whole Fleet, he found that he had been severely criticised for his actions. A wireless signal, sent from the *Sapphire* at 1.32 am on 24 October was quoted and read: 'Have ascertained for certain that the Enemy's Fleet left Cromarty at 8.00 am on Tuesday, 22 October.' For some reason, none of Scott's cruisers received this message and Beresford took no steps to check whether the cruisers had acted on it. The memorandum went on to censure Scott for remaining in a 'dangerous position' and showing a 'want of appreciation of the facts' which, in war, might be 'fatal'.[75]

As was to be the case in all the clashes between Beresford and Scott, Beresford (a) never asked Scott for any explanation before reprimanding him and (b) broadcast his criticism to the whole Fleet. Later, Beresford was

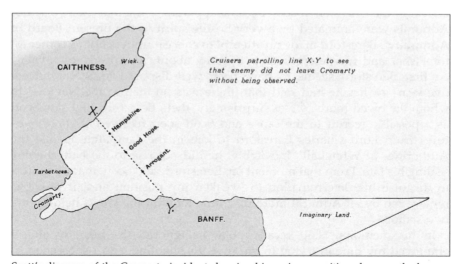

Scott's diagram of the Cromarty incident showing his cruisers positioned across the bay.

to write that an admiral, 'when he feels irritated at seeing something done which appears careless, or opposed to the orders laid down ... should always maintain an unruffled demeanour and be perfectly calm and collected under all circumstances'.[76] In Beresford's case, this was easier said than done.

The episode being closed, Scott sat down to write a letter of complaint to the Admiralty. Putting the draft aside to attend to his duties, he never had time to complete his missive. Another, much more serious persecution was about to fall upon him. This time, it would escape neither the attention of the press nor that of historians. It was the infamous Scott paintwork incident.

On 2 November, the manoeuvres being over, the Channel Fleet moved south to return to Portland in misty weather. Rather than keep the Fleet together in poor visibility, Beresford left the ships to make their own way south. As the *Good Hope* ploughed through the waves, a bearing in one of her engines began to overheat, forcing her to slow down. She fell behind the Fleet and was further delayed by a 'man overboard' on 4 November.[77] By the time she reached Portland later that day, all the other ships were settled in.[78]

When the *Good Hope* moored at 3.20 pm, her sister cruisers were already at work on routine tasks. Amongst these was the *Roxburgh*, which, in Scott's absence, had gone outside the breakwater to practise gunnery, as he learnt from the signal despatched by the ship at 12.10 pm:

Am laying here with banked fires and carrying out towing target practices with aiming rifles ... If it is decided not to send 'ROXBURGH' to Bantry until after the review may we remain in our present position and carry out towing target and also Whitehead [torpedo] practices tomorrow coming in on completion?[79]

All this had to do with the forthcoming visit of the Kaiser, during which he would inspect the Channel Fleet. Beresford had sent round a memorandum advising ships that they would need to repaint for this event. The *Roxburgh* clearly wished to finish its target practice before coming in to repaint. In reply to the *Roxburgh*'s request to continue with its gunnery practice, Scott signalled that 'Paint work appears to be more in demand than Gunnery so you had better come in in time to look pretty by the 8th instant.'[80]

No one on the *Good Hope* or the *Roxburgh* thought any more of this innocent bit of private banter between two officers until four days later when Beresford came to hear of the signal by mere chance. It was 7 November when Sub Lieutenant Lionel Dawson of the *King Edward VII* happened to be on board the *Good Hope*. Having completed his visit, he went towards the deck with the intention of leaving the ship. Suddenly, tempted by the warmth and companionship of the wardroom, he went in, he said, for a 'cigarette and a glass of sherry' with a fellow officer. The conversation was about nothing in particular, but Dawson's ears pricked up when he heard a voice say: 'That was a very typical signal of Percy's.' His curiosity aroused, Dawson asked, 'What signal was that?' and a rather embarrassed officer recounted the whole incident. On his way back to the flagship, Dawson ruminated over what he had heard and decided that 'the Commander-in-Chief had been definitely slighted in his absence'. On boarding his ship, he recounted what he had been told to the Flag Lieutenant and the Signal Officer. 'The effect,' he said, 'was instantaneous!'[81] Within fifteen minutes the *Good Hope*'s signal log was on its way to Beresford's cabin. (Fate nearly saved Scott at this point since the cutter carrying the offensive log book was almost sunk by the *King Edward*'s picket-boat as they collided in the swell.)

The next morning, a signal went out to all flag officers ('negative Rear-Admiral First Cruiser Squadron') instructing them to board the flagship. By good fortune for posterity, Dawson was on the forenoon watch and so saw what happened next and recorded it. (Not one single other witness, except Scott himself, left an account of this monstrous incident.)

It was to be pure theatre, but cruel tragedy, all stage-managed by Beresford. First he went through an elaborate charade of calling all his flag officers to the quarterdeck, where he chatted with them. This was merely to reinforce in the minds of all witnesses what a chummy lot they all were – bar the absent Scott. Having demonstrated his intimacy with his favoured brothers, Beresford dismissed them to the after-end of the quarterdeck and then went below. Now, the vast empty space of white, hard-scrubbed boards was occupied solely by the flag-captain, the commander and Dawson, who naturally stood well to one side. All was silence. The sea lapped against the ship's hull and the gulls yelled overhead, but no one dared speak. Everyone must have known that a momentous event was about to unfold; none could have foreseen what was to happen. No one would forget it.

Meanwhile, Beresford had summoned Scott. Suddenly, recalled Dawson, the 'ominous silence' was broken 'by the piping of the boatswain's mates and the bugle salute as Sir Percy Scott came over the side'. At first his air was 'confident' and 'almost jaunty' but, says Dawson, 'When he saw the group aft his face fell, and a puzzled look spread over it.'[82]

The stage had been carefully set by Beresford, with the flag officers as principals front of stage and the chorus of flag staff in the rear; Dawson was in attendance as chief usher. The accused stood in silence. Unannounced, Beresford appeared, climbing up from below. As he mounted the deck it was clear that he was in a furious mood and, without pausing to allow Scott to utter a word, he commenced a tirade of abuse. In his own report of the episode to the Admiralty, Beresford admitted that he

134

had publicly called Scott's signal 'pitiably vulgar, contemptuous in tone, insubordinate in character, and wanting in dignity'.[83] Dawson continued the story, saying: 'I saw, for the one and only time in my life the "telling off" of a flag officer by his Commander-in-Chief in the presence of his peers.'[84] All those present could have said the same thing.

Having said his piece, Beresford dismissed Scott who was, said Dawson, 'a changed Sir Percy'. Stunned, he crossed the quarterdeck 'silent and white-faced ... his gait was slow and dragging'.[85] Not for one moment had Beresford paused to ask Scott for his account of the incident. He had acted as judge and jury without even allowing the accused to give evidence. Sentence had been decided before the court even opened. It was an outrage of unheard-of proportions. In 1914, Beresford was to write that, when finding fault with an officer the admiral 'should endeavour to send a man away wearing a smile rather than a scowl'.[86] Had he forgotten his own actions of 8 November 1907?

Beresford was not to stop there. His behaviour was to reach depths of despicability that are hard to accept in a sane individual. At 12.15 pm of the same day, a signal went out to the whole Fleet informing them that Scott had sent the offending signal, and quoting the words that Beresford had found most offensive: 'Paintwork appears to be more in demand than gunnery, so you had better come in in time to look pretty by the 8th instant.' He went on to describe the signal as 'contemptuous in tone and insubordinate in character'. As if this was not enough, the signal informed all the Fleet that he had required Scott to issue an order to the *Good Hope* and *Roxburgh* to 'expunge this signal from their signal logs and to report to me by signal when my orders have been obeyed'.[87]

Having humiliated Scott and violated the principles of natural justice all in one short morning, Beresford retired to his cabin and began a letter to the Admiralty. His description of the events was accurate in so far as they could be seen from the *Edward VII*, but the heart of the letter lay not in the facts, but in the action that he was to request on the part of the Board.

As was to be the case with Beresford whenever he transgressed the regulations or the norms of decent behaviour, he could always find a justification. Aware of the grossness of his actions, he now attempted to exonerate himself by saying that, whilst 'in the ordinary case of having to find fault with an officer ... I invariably call for an explanation ... in this case there could be no explanation'. Scott, he said 'had held up to ridicule' one of his orders and was guilty of 'gross insubordination'. Regretting that he was not able to court-martial Scott nor 'to relieve him of his command' he asked that 'Rear-Admiral Sir Percy Scott should be superseded from the command of the First Cruiser Squadron'.[88]

What Beresford did not realise when writing this letter was that he had grievously misrepresented Scott's position. He had accused Scott of ridiculing an order, by which he meant the signal to the Fleet sent on 4 November ordering all the ships to 'come out of routine' and begin painting. (He was not referring to the earlier memorandum.) Yet, Scott always maintained that he did not receive this signal until two hours *after* he had sent his own paintwork signal.[89] In effect, the accusation was that he had ridiculed a signal that he had not yet received.

It was a disappointed Beresford who received the Admiralty's reply dated 13 November, to his request to supersede Scott. Whilst the Board agreed that Scott's signal was 'inexcusable' there was no question of removing him from his post. Indeed, in their view, 'the public censure already administered to that Officer by your general signal of the 8th instant' was more than enough punishment. All that was needed was 'the conveyance to Sir Percy Scott of an expression of their Lordships' grave disapprobation'.[90] The letter was copied to Scott, who also received the further note of their Lordships' displeasure. Yet, still, no one had given him any opportunity to explain his conduct.

The next day, Scott went to see Beresford to offer an apology. In an oddly jokey letter to Arnold White, he first recounted the scene as he had wished it had taken place, telling White:

> With the genial Irish character which his Lordship is known to have, he welcomed my apology, and explained that he had been hasty in action, and regretted that he had not called upon me for an explanation ...[91]

In fact, Beresford's account of what happened was the sad truth:

> Rear-Admiral Sir Percy Scott said, 'I should like to take the opportunity of apologising to you for the incident.' I remarked that I could receive no apology from him, delivered privately on my quarterdeck, relative to an incident where he had publicly insulted my authority by an insolent signal; that if he apologised publicly after the incident, I should have been delighted to have accepted such an apology.[92]

(Beresford claimed in 1909 that he had offered, in April of that year, to accept an apology 'personally, or by letter' but that there had been 'no response on his part'.[93] There is, though, no corroboration of this.)

On 17 November Beresford replied to the Admiralty's letter stating that he regretted that they thought that 'a private admonition is sufficient for so gross an offence against discipline'.[94] According to Frewen, Beresford was all for resigning at this point but Bellairs and other friends dissuaded him, 'pointing out that that is just what Fisher is trying to goad him into doing'.[95] It was a comment that well illustrated how the Syndicate distorted every scrap of news to misrepresent Fisher. It is not clear how Fisher came into this at all, since Scott acted on his own initiative and there is no evidence that he ever communicated with Fisher over the incident. (Indeed, Fisher was rather unsympathetic towards Scott about the whole business.) On the other hand, if Beresford were to have succeeded in ejecting Scott from his fleet (which was the sole purpose of this charade of indignation) he would have undermined Fisher's authority. The goading was clearly from Beresford's side.

The initial phase of the episode reached its end in an ironic way. When the sun rose on 11 November, there was no Channel Fleet – pretty or otherwise – lined up to escort the Kaiser. Instead, its vessels were spread out in thick fog, unable to locate each other, let alone to find the Kaiser's ship, the *Hohenzollern*.[96] The painting, the signals and the public reprimand had all been for nothing.

And there the matter might have ended ... were it not for the press. The first public intimation of the incident came on 11 November, when the *Western Morning News* carried a highly detailed and accurate account, with quotes from the signals, of what had happened. *The Times* reproduced the *News* article in full on the same day. Not surprisingly, the newspaper told its readers that there was 'considerable consternation' in the Fleet and the signal was being 'eagerly discussed among all ranks'.[97] The hunt began for who had leaked the signals.

For Beresford, the source was obvious: it had to be Scott since he had access to the log books. This was to conveniently forget that he himself had had access to the *Good Hope* log book and he (or one of his officers) would have had no difficulty in gaining access to that of the *Roxburgh*.

As it happened, another Beresford affair (which we will come to) was running in parallel with the painting incident. This involved the Syndicate's pressure to allow Beresford to give evidence before an invasion enquiry. Fisher was desperate to prevent this happening, so when the question of an enquiry into the paintwork incident arose, Fisher redoubled his efforts to damp down the press interest. Percy Scott, he told Corbett, was 'as much a "limelight" man as Beresford' and he was determined to deny either of them a public platform. It was for this reason, he told Corbett, that 'we declined any further action'.[98]

It was not until seven weeks after the paintwork signal that evidence came to light to support Scott's claim that at the time of his signal to the *Roxburgh*, he had not yet received Beresford's paintwork order. This was revealed by *The Times*, which stated that 'a comparison of the signal logs' showed that Beresford's signal to go 'out of routine' was despatched two hours *after* Scott's signal. Beresford's reprimand of Scott, said the paper 'appears to have been made under a misapprehension of the facts'.[99]

By early January, the story was still running and Scott was in despair, unable as he was to publicly counter the rumours that were circulating. In a letter to White he mused on taking out an action for libel against the *National Review*. This, he said, 'would unearth all his [Beresford's] crimes'. He thought that, 'if the Admiralty have the pluck of a louse, they will back me up'.[100] (Penn has suggested that Scott should have called Beresford's bluff and 'insisted on a trial by Court Martial', so forcing the Admiralty to act.)[101]

Beresford, too, was feeling aggrieved at the press comment that he was receiving. In a letter to the Admiralty, he drew their attention to the various articles that appeared under pseudonyms such as 'by one who knows' or claimed superior knowledge with titles such as 'authentic statement' and 'the truth about the Beresford-Scott incident'. They were, he said, 'inspired' by his enemies. Pompously Beresford reminded the Board that he could not reply to these accusations because he was 'on full pay'; he requested that 'their Lordships will take steps to have these public charges refuted'.[102]

There was no way that the Admiralty were going to lift a finger to help Beresford out of the hole he had dug for himself. On 9 January they firmly told him that, in their view, 'this matter was finally settled by the drastic action taken by you ... and by the subsequent expression of their displeasure to that officer'. They were 'not prepared to reopen the subject'. Instead, they turned the tables on Beresford and reminded him that the newspaper articles referred to signals which 'must have been copied out of the signal log of some ship present ... [presumably] a ship under your command'.[103]

It has to be remembered that Beresford's persistent demands had but one purpose: to unseat Fisher and install himself in his chair. As a public relations campaign, it seemed to lack subtly and was winning him few converts. On 19 January, *John Bull* said that Beresford was 'suffering from a complaint known as "swelled head"' and, referring to his ambition to replace Fisher, opined that 'Lord Charles has proved himself unfit for this great position.'[104] As far as Beresford was concerned, though, he thought that Fisher had more or less written the article, telling Edward Carson, a leading Unionist MP, that it was 'inspired by the gentleman from Ceylon' and was a 'most determined, audacious, treacherous and cowardly' attack on him.[105] Matters were not helped by the fact that someone had taken the trouble to send a copy of the article to every officer in the Fleet. The news of this circulation caused Beresford to fake an illness, said Esher, and retire to his bed in Claridge's Hotel, where he planned 'to inveigle Cabinet Ministers and others to his bedside'. Esher found it all hilarious as he imagined the ministers around the bed 'interviewing Beresford in a nightcap with Lady Charles holding his hand on the far side of the bed! What a picture of naval efficiency and domestic bliss!'[106]

Once more Beresford turned to the Admiralty for help, requesting them to prosecute 'for the publication of a libel of a nature seriously detrimental to the discipline of the fleet'.[107] Two days later they responded, refusing to assist with the libel action, but offering to make public Beresford's letter of 8 November and their reply.[108]

Nearly two months later, Beresford was still on Scott's tail, as the latter found when he received a letter from his commander, dated 28 February, enclosing a copy of a further memorandum that Beresford was to issue to his Fleet. This incorporated the text of the Admiralty's letter of 13 November and claimed that 'It is their Lordships' desire that the Officers of the Channel Fleet should know that the Commander-in-Chief had the full support of the Admiralty in his severe condemnation of the signal referred to.'[109] It was an odd expression to use, given that the Board had used the term 'drastic action' to describe Beresford's behaviour.

Inevitably, following the intense public curiosity aroused by the endless press rumours, there was a request in the Commons on 9 March to release 'the official correspondence between the Lords of the Admiralty and Admirals Beresford and Scott respecting the signal made from HMS *Good Hope*'. The questioner, H.C. Lea, Liberal MP for East St Pancras, wanted to know 'which Admiral was to blame in the matter; and what action has been taken by the Admiralty'. Declining to publish the correspondence, all that Lambert would say in reply was that Beresford had been authorised to express 'their Lordships' grave disapprobation' of Scott's signal.[110]

And so the incident closed, even though the Admiralty had still not asked Scott for his version of the events. Beresford made no mention of it in his memoirs. Scott, in his memoirs, merely drew his readers' attention to his article in the *British Review*, saying 'There I am content to leave the matter.'[111] Both men, though, left copious documents about the episode, thanks to which it can take its rightful place in the feud. There can be no doubt that it *was* a part of the feud. Beresford used Scott as a means of getting at Fisher. It was clumsy, and it is hard to see how exactly he could have expected to harm him, unless he hoped that some more general enquiry would result in which he could air his grievances. Whatever his intentions, the ruse backfired since it helped persuade many ditherers that Beresford had to go.

The last word should rightly go to Lord John Hay, a retired Admiral of the Fleet of 'rare distinction' (and godfather to Conan Doyle's brother Innes[112]), who vented his anger to Fisher on the sad story.[113] His summary is sufficiently damning to say it all:

A Commander-in-Chief [who] censures an Admiral on the Quarter-deck before other Officers, and makes the censure public to the whole Fleet – without enquiry or explanation. I look upon this display of heedless violence and autocratic behaviour as calculated to lower our reputation for justice in the Navy ...[114]

## Scene 5: Beresford's attacks on the Admiralty

The Scott experience brought about a sea-change in Beresford and only increased his determination to oust Fisher. In the mere seven months from

September 1907 to March 1908 he attempted to usurp the Admiralty's role in fleet management and war, he sought to use an enquiry into invasion as a base from which to attack Fisher, he abused another admiral, he accused the Admiralty of stealing his officers, he called for an enquiry into the Admiralty and he supported the foundation of a new organisation whose admitted purpose was to unseat Fisher. The scope of his antagonisms was breathtaking.

Following the dispute over war plans in April 1907 and Beresford's statements that led Fisher to say that Beresford thought he had the 'plenary powers of an admiralissimo', Fisher felt it necessary to reassert the Admiralty's authority. Not wishing to be over-confrontational with his recalcitrant admiral, the Board sent a letter addressed to all commanders-in-chief. This reminded them that the Board was 'solely responsible for all matters of policy, such as the number and type of ships built, their manning and equipment, as well as their distribution into separate commands' and, in a particular thrust in Beresford's direction, that 'they alone have the responsibility of the strategic placing of the ships for war'. If Beresford read this letter carefully, he would have been greatly incensed to read that commanders 'in foreign waters' had more leeway since they knew more about 'local political and strategical conditions' than did the Admiralty. To rub the point in, they added 'In home waters the responsibility of the Board of Admiralty is more direct.'[115]

Along with this round robin letter, Beresford received a personal reply to his recent criticisms of the home-based fleets. While he was congratulated on the 'activity and energy shown by you and the officers under your command', he was told that the Board could not 'concur in your sweeping charges of inefficiency' and they demurred from 'some of the criticisms you express of units of the Home Fleet'.[116]

None of this was enough to quieten Beresford and, in November, he again challenged the Board's authority and accused them of wishing 'to handicap and hamper me in carrying out the responsibilities connected with by far the most important position within the Empire'.[117] Having laid claim to be above the First Sea Lord, above the First Lord, above the Cabinet, and perhaps even the Sovereign himself, the Board were not amused. In their reply on 21 November, they reiterated their supreme role, saying 'Their Lordships must once more make it clear to you that it is the Admiralty who are responsible for the defence of Home as well as all other Waters in time of War.'[118]

It was, though, all a waste of ink and paper. Beresford had passed the point where he recognised that he was in any way answerable to the Board.

By September, Fisher had become aware that Repington, the military correspondent of *The Times* was agitating for an enquiry into home defence, that is, how the country could be best defended against invasion.

His 10 September article particularly annoyed Fisher since 'Repington calmly and with cool insistence dictates to the Admiralty what the naval arrangements should be to render the problem of invasion impossible.' It was, he said, 'absurd' for a military man to pronounce on naval affairs.[119] This was bad enough, but, as he told Charles Ottley (then Secretary of the Committee of Imperial Defence): 'Beresford is also in business with Repington & Co' and Repington had referred to 'the desirability of Beresford being Admiralissimo'.[120]

Meanwhile, behind the scenes, Repington was attempting to influence the membership of the committee. He was delighted to hear that the Admiralty and the War Office would not be represented as 'that will give much more liberty and freedom'.[121] While beavering away at keeping Fisher off the committee, Repington had been consulting both Beresford and Sturdee and he was insistent 'that these and other practical men shall be examined'. He favoured their evidence since 'they seem to be far from satisfied that they can defend these shores with existing arrangements or rather the want of them'.[122]

The link between Repington and Beresford was very close, and went far beyond what was correct for a commander-in-chief who knew full well that his interlocutor was planning to attack his superior's policy. Beresford, tempted to resign after the Scott affair, consulted Repington about leaving the service, but Repington urged him to stay since, as he explained to Esher, 'I thought the public interest and the inquiry promised would be better served by Beresford appearing in his capacity as C-in-C of the Channel Fleet and Admiralissimo designate in war.'[123] And there it was again, the word 'admiralissimo'. Almost certainly Beresford used it in talking to Repington, yet it was only weeks since he had been rebuked for assuming such powers to himself. That all this was not just casual conversation is demonstrated by the fact that Beresford provided detailed advice on the wording of the papers that Repington was preparing. Repington used Beresford's suggestions and shared them with Lord Roberts, suggesting that 'it would be well to act on his advice'.[124]

The farce of this situation is underlined by the fact that, while Beresford discussed with Repington how to prove that Britain was not safe from invasion, Fisher, Corbett and Slade were drafting papers for the committee to prove that no invasion could succeed, given the Navy's strength. They concluded that 'a serious German invasion of these islands *is impossible*'.[125]

Not content with lobbying Repington, Beresford had had talks with General Sir John French (then in command at Aldershot) to whom he had told 'the whole case against Fisher'. He also told French that he was 'anxious to be called before the Committee'. Esher commented that 'Whether Jackie will cross-examine him is the problem. He may refuse to do so.'[126] Although this proved unnecessary, had the two clashed in such a

141

forum it is a fair guess, based on Beresford's interview with Tweedmouth on 5 July and his later performance at the enquiry, that he would have made such a poor showing that his career would have ended there and then. In the end, though, Fisher was called and Beresford was not.

After the joint fleet exercises in October, Beresford had issued a memorandum to all the officers who had taken part. This included the criticism that 'the destroyers under Commodore Lewis Bayly had not been properly trained'.[127] Since the destroyers were part of the Home Fleet, this was a direct and public attack on Bridgeman's capacities. Once again, Beresford had criticised an officer in public, without giving him any opportunity to put his case. When the memorandum arrived in his ship, Bridgeman was about to go on leave. Seeing that the missive was 'voluminous' he merely glanced at it and approved its circulation without further thought. Later, he regretted his 'hasty action'.[128]

When he returned from leave, Bridgeman read the document more carefully and, enraged at what he found, he immediately ordered that all the copies of the memorandum in his fleet were to be returned to him. It is to his credit that he had the courage to tell Beresford what action he was taking.

Then he sat down to write an exasperated letter to Fisher. The memorandum, he said 'contains criticism on the actions of Superior Officers, most damaging to their authority and reputation'. He added that 'there are damaging remarks on Admiralty shipbuilding policy and these remarks are to be read by Junior Officers of the Fleet!'[129]

In a private letter Fisher sympathised with Bridgeman, saying '[we] all *greatly* resent Beresford's line of conduct', adding that 'he is freely doing it *now* outside everywhere'. Beresford's 'reflections', he continued, 'are totally uncalled for, and the First Lord told me to tell you privately that he is astonished at the moderation of your reply, and would have told Beresford "to go to Hell"'.[130] Two weeks later Beresford received an official reprimand in which he was told to withdraw the memorandum 'and expunge paragraphs 32 and 33 of the Vice-Admiral's letter before it is reissued'.[131]

In November, Beresford picked yet another quarrel with the Admiralty and, since he once again failed to check his facts, he again made a fool of himself.

The heart of his complaint was an accusation that the Admiralty were forcibly (and by implication, maliciously) withdrawing officers from his fleet, in particular Sturdee, Custance and Rear Admiral Montgomerie, in command of the destroyers. He had heard, he said, that Sturdee would 'shortly be removed' so that he could complete his sea command time and qualify for the rank of admiral. This was absolutely true. And who had requested this removal? Well, none other than Beresford! He himself had written to the Admiralty on 14 January asking them to allow Sturdee to count his time as chief of staff as time towards qualifying for the rank of admiral. Then in September he had supported Sturdee's request to be appointed to command of a ship. Now that the Admiralty had finally acceded to the second of these requests, Beresford complained that 'the removal of Sturdee as my Chief of Staff will entail my having to start afresh with a new Chief of Staff'.[132] The most bizarre thing about this complaint was that, far from his having forgotten about his earlier letters, Beresford actually quoted them in the letter. It was typical of him that in 1909 he was still pursuing the issue, asking Bellairs to place a parliamentary question as to whether there was 'a recognised rule in the Navy, that proper sea service must be obtained, other than "Chief of Staff" appointments'.[133]

Next he protested that 'Vice-Admiral Custance . . . is shortly to be transferred to another command' and emphasised how Custance was 'of the utmost value to me'. That left Montgomerie who, he had heard 'has been informed that he might have the option of going on half-pay or remain for the period of one year from date of appointment in his diminished command'.[134]

Beresford bewailed the fact that 'the removal of three such important officers from my command' would 'add enormously to my already exceptionally hard work'. What was more, he accused the Admiralty of picking on him, saying that 'the ordinary etiquette, civilities and courteous dealings which officers of high and distinguished command have hitherto so markedly received from the Admiralty have been entirely absent in my case'.[135]

The Board's reply was pained and perplexed. They pointed out that they had replied to Beresford's letters about Sturdee so they did not understand his remarks about Sturdee being offered a command. He had been offered, and had accepted, the post of Captain of the *New Zealand*. As to Custance, there was no truth in the rumour. And, when it came to Montgomerie, the Commander-in-Chief of the Home Fleet had received two letters explaining the situation.[136] Even so, he had been forewarned in July that Montgomerie's appointment would be 'reviewed at the end of the year'.[137] (More mundanely, it seems that Montgomerie went of his own choice, being in poor health. He died just nine months later.)[138]

It was, though, a more general accusation that the Board found the most offensive part of the letter, when Beresford said:

> It has come to my notice that a feeling has arisen in the Service that it is prejudicial to an officer's career to be personally connected with me on Service matters. This may not be a fact, but the impression I know exists.[139]

This was, said the Board, 'an allegation ... of a very serious character' and they asked him to 'furnish specific evidence' to support this. Beresford did not reply.[140]

Beresford was to resurrect this charge in 1909 after the enquiry. This time he would do it in public through the pages of *The Times*, so provoking a response from McKenna. In a lengthy letter, McKenna demonstrated that, far from being victimised, the officers concerned had received 'an unprecedented number of promotions from one ship'.[141]

In November, Ernest Pretyman called on Fisher to talk about the Channel Fleet. Pretyman was a Tory MP who had served both as Civil Lord of the Admiralty and as Parliamentary Secretary to the Admiralty before the Liberal landslide in 1906. Currently out of office, he had paid a visit to the Channel Fleet and had returned 'much perturbed'.[142] In recounting this to Lord Cawdor, Fisher also told him that 'Beresford and all the malcontents' were calling for an enquiry into the Admiralty. Fisher was convinced that such an enquiry 'would show the Navy to be so strong as to play into the hands of the very strong party in the House of Commons who want to reduce the Navy'.[143] He felt it would also lead to the resignation of all the Sea Lords.

By mid-January the Admiralty was drafting documents to rebut the call. Fisher still lacked any hard evidence of Beresford's involvement; this would be difficult to acquire since others, particularly Bellairs, acted as frontmen for the campaign. Despite the vagueness of the sources, Fisher claimed that he knew 'on reliable authority' that Beresford had asked that a committee 'shall hear him and his witnesses'. It was Bellairs, Fisher suspected, who 'originated [it] rather less than two years ago'. What they wanted to find out was not clear to Fisher, who noted that they just desired to 'advertise as widely as possible ... the failings of the Admiralty'. He thought it was 'a scheme to obtain a "fishing" inquiry in which they hope that facts discreditable to the Admiralty ... would emerge'.[144]

Not long after, Fisher briefed Tweedmouth as to the steps the Admiralty should take to block an enquiry. He was 'certain' that if Grey explicitly stated in the Commons that 'the Government had no intention whatever of holding *any sort of* enquiry' and made it clear that they considered the agitations to be 'most prejudicial to public interests', then 'there would be complete collapse of Beresford'.[145]

On the same day, he wrote to Grey, telling him that it was 'unprecedented' for 'Lord C. Beresford [to be] interviewing Members of the Cabinet and indicting the Board of Admiralty as failing in its duty'.[146] When it came to the Admiralty's evidence to the Government, Fisher was even more obdurate, saying that if Beresford had made 'representations' to the Government then 'it is so flagrantly insubordinate ... he should be relieved of his command'.[147] When sending his letter to Grey, Fisher had copied it both to the King and to Esher. The latter was so horrified that he reminded the King of the treatment that Lord Hood had received in 1795 when he wrote 'a *very* temperate letter' to the Admiralty in which he complained that he did not have enough ships to defend the Mediterranean.[148] He was dismissed forthwith. Why was Beresford allowed to stay, despite endless insubordinations, when one mild criticism was enough to finish Hood? (Presumably Esher was unaware that Fisher had written many similar letters when in the Mediterranean.)

Although Beresford was holding forth 'in every drawing-room in London' in support of his enquiry, it was to no avail.[149] The dying Prime Minister, Sir Henry Campbell-Bannerman, promised in February that there would be no enquiry.[150] Two months later Asquith, as the new Prime Minister, confirmed this pledge.[151]

Fisher had held off the Syndicate once more, but the respite was to be short-lived.

At the end of January 1908 a new organisation announced its arrival. Supported by a ragbag of luminaries ranging from Tory MPs such as Walter Long and F.E. Smith to writers such as Conan Doyle and Rudyard Kipling, it seemed notable for its lack of support from retired admirals of any significance. The Imperial Maritime League, was, according to its founders Harold F. Wyatt and L. Graham H. Horton-Smith, made up of defectors from the Navy League, who were critical of its 'lamentable failure ... to resist and denounce the financial starvation of the Navy by the present Government'.[152] The new league had been born in the summer of 1907, when the Navy League refused to support an agitation against the Admiralty over the strength of the Fleet. Wyatt and Horton-Smith were defeated in a resolution which they had tabled at an extraordinary meeting of the League on 19 July in which they condemned the reductions in Beresford's Fleet and the unreadiness of the Home Fleet.[153] In its first public pronouncement the new league proffered such innocuous aims as the maintenance of 'the sea power of the British Empire' and the need 'to win and hold command of the sea'.[154] However, it made an amazing public relations blunder in its decision to invite Esher to join them. The plan was to enrol him before the League's launch and so use his name – much revered in military circles – to embellish its credentials. Esher replied to the invitation in blunt and savage tones, accusing the new league of asking him to align himself with a group 'engaged in promoting a scheme designed to overturn one of the Prime Minister's principal Colleagues and a Board of Admiralty nominated by him'. Noting that not one of the 'living four statesmen who have held the great post of 1st Lord of the Admiralty' had signed up, Esher then launched into a damning paragraph in which he asked why they had not admitted 'that the object of the

145

Maritime League is to upset Sir John Fisher, and the Naval Policy for which all the world knows, he must bear the chief responsibility'.[155] A version of this letter (but minus the Fisher paragraph) subsequently appeared in *The Times* of 6 February.

Beresford was a strong supporter of the new league, and no wonder since, had they succeeded in ejecting the Board, they would have looked to him to fill the role of either First Lord or First Sea Lord. The new league, though, never got far, perhaps because of the serious blow that Esher had struck it so early on in its career.

Since the paintwork incident Beresford had been lying low. According to Scott, he had 'absented himself from his fleet for almost three months on sick leave'.[156] There is no surviving evidence of Beresford's officially being on sick leave at this time, although Custance stated at the enquiry that he had been in charge of the Channel Fleet in December 1907 and January 1908.[157] Officially ill or not, he was well enough to attend the state banquet on 15 November, a Salters' Company dinner on 20 November, to visit the Whitehead torpedo works on 25 November, to be present at some firing experiments on 30 November and be at a Savage Club dinner on 8 December. After attending some boxing and wrestling champion-ships at Weymouth he and Lady Charles spent Christmas with Lord and Lady Londonderry. Only on 1 January 1908 was there any public acknowledgement of illness, when Beresford contracted bronchitis from which he did not recover until 13 January.[158] Further evidence of illness comes from Beresford telling Bellairs that he had been 'ill with phlebitis' in February.[159]

Sitting in his admiral's cabin in February 1908, Scott reported to White how 'the Channel Fleet has scarcely been to sea' in Beresford's absence. He called this 'unprecedented' but fully realised that the Admiralty tolerated this desertion in preference to facing the trauma of ditching Beresford.[160]

Impossible as it now is to confirm Scott's allegation, he was correct about the low level of Channel Fleet activity. There was no significant activity between 4 November 1907 and 11 March 1908.[161] Beresford's own personal admiral's log would tell us more, but it was never deposited in the official archives. Given that Beresford seems to have destroyed every document of any significance in his personal archive, it is tempting to assume that he also destroyed the log. All in all, the circumstantial evidence suggests that he had much that he wished to hide at this time.

Where the Admiralty feared to tread, serendipity leapt in. Custance's ship was ordered into dock for a major refit. In consequence, Custance stepped ashore, leaving Scott as the senior officer in the Channel. Unless Beresford returned to sea promptly, Scott would be acting Commander-in-Chief of the Channel Fleet! Whatever malady Beresford was suffering from, his recovery was instantaneous. With a triumphant gleam in his eye, Scott told White that Beresford 'cannot be sick any more, because if he is, P.S. runs the show'.[162]

As Beresford's frustration mounted, so his ambitions escalated. While Fisher fumed at Beresford's claims to admiralissimo status, he was still able to maintain a certain level of ironic detachment, jokingly describing to Esher his vision of the future that Beresford and Bellairs were planning for themselves:

> Beresford and Bellairs are going to be First Sea Lord and Parliamentary Secretary of the Admiralty, and there's a statue to Beresford at the Hippodrome (draped! because of his modesty), and Bellairs is allowed to lie without stint![163]

Noting that Charles Beresford and Carlyon Bellairs shared the same initials as Campbell-Bannerman, he wittily added, 'If I was the Prime Minister, I should change my initials.'[164]

Beresford's ambitions were not, though, mere private pipe-dreams; he willingly shared them around the dinner tables and tea salons of London. Rear Admiral Inglefield, newly-promoted commander of the Fourth Cruiser Squadron, reported to Fisher that 'Charlie Beresford is more bitter than ever, and at his dinner table boasted that he had the Admiralty in the palm of his hand – the country was with him, and he was only waiting his time to crumble them up.'[165]

What exactly Beresford planned to do if he were able to usurp Fisher or the First Lord was never clear. In September, when Ponsonby had quizzed him on this point, he was left bewildered. 'Whenever I tried to bring him to the point by asking him what he would have done if he were to be appointed first Lord,' he wrote, 'he never seemed to have any satisfactory answer.'[166]

Those who supported Beresford saw in him only the purest of motives. An unknown correspondent, but one who was viciously anti-Fisher denied that there was a 'duel arising from jealousy or ill-will' and claimed that 'Lord Charles Beresford would hold himself a traitor' if he could not stop 'the demoralisation and dry-rot' in the Navy. As proof of Beresford's disinterested intentions, he added that 'Lord Charles has everything to lose and nothing to gain' from his activities.[167] While it was absolutely true that Beresford did care deeply for the Navy, the naïvety of this author in failing to see his concomitant personal ambitions is astounding.

No discussion of Beresford's motives would be complete without reference to the part that his wife played. Well known to Captain Slade, then Director of Naval Intelligence, he was in position to see her effect on Beresford's professional life. He noted that, whilst 'Lord C . . . will agree to anything', once he got home he fell 'under the influence of Lady C', after which he was 'as bad as ever'.[168] Lady Sykes noted in early 1908 that Beresford had gone into the country, promising to his friends to lie low while the row over the 1908–9 Naval Estimates continued. She acidly added, 'But will the She Fiend do the same[?]'[169] In another letter, Sykes called Mina 'his evil genius' and told White that, although she would like to help Beresford, 'it is quite useless trying' since '[he] sees nothing except through the falsifying spectacles she provides'.[170] Fisher himself had a very low opinion of Mina, saying that he was 'sick of being vilified and calumniated daily, and that poisonous woman ... is a slanderer of the first water'.[171] (His reference to slander was no exaggeration. At the time of the Lady Brooke controversy, Mina circulated a booklet that was so libellous she was compelled to recall every copy to forestall legal action against her.)

By January 1908, Esher was so frustrated by the Board's refusal to act that he drew up a long memorandum on the subject for the King. Drawing on historical precedents, he sought to demonstrate that 'The Board of Admiralty is the supreme authority, wielding the powers of the King and of the Executive Government.' He pointed out that 'every great Admiral' in the past had 'had to obey ... the orders of the Board'. Of course, there was a hidden agenda in this paper since Esher was seeking to pre-empt an enquiry into the Admiralty which, he said, would be an 'abdication of the elementary functions of Government'.[172]

And so the first year of Beresford's Channel Fleet command drew to a close. Whatever it had done for Beresford, it had certainly left its mark on Fisher, as Esher noted in his journal. Fisher, he wrote, was 'among the sands and shoals', a state which had become 'periodical'. Dejected, he feared that his friend 'will get aground one of these days'.[173]

If Beresford was to be believed, all the trouble had been caused by Fisher, who, he told Bellairs, sought 'to make it a personal question' and 'to irritate and undermine me at every turn'.[174] In truth, Beresford had taken every opportunity to hit out at both Fisher and the Admiralty, although he was confused as to the difference. Like Maxse of the *National Review*, Beresford claimed that Fisher had assumed such dictatorial powers that 'there is no Board, it is all Fisher'.[175] There was, he told Bellairs, a 'dictatorship' at the Admiralty.[176]

However he phrased it, Beresford had developed a fanatical, personal hostility to the First Sea Lord. Probably no sea-going admiral ever caused so much trouble to the Admiralty in one year as did Beresford between April 1907 and March 1908. The frequency and the severity of his clashes was increasing, yet there seemed no end to their duration. In part, Tweedmouth was the trouble. As First Lord he was way out of his depth; as the man who stood between Fisher and Beresford he looked on bewildered. Under his tutelage nothing was likely to change. It was time for a new man to step in.

*Act 8*

# McKenna Calls Time

Fisher had no animus whatsoever against Lord Charles
until the latter part of 1908. – *Bacon*[1]

## Scene 1: A change of management

As Fisher sat at his desk in Whitehall in March 1908, reflecting on recent
events, there was not much to feel pleased about. The last twelve months
had been a rearguard battle with the Syndicate and Beresford, yet there
was little prospect of any respite. Only the unwavering support of the King
lay between him and dismissal.

Back in November of the previous year, however, an accident of history
had set in train a series of events that were to change Fisher's prospects.
Campbell-Bannerman, the ageing Prime Minister, had suffered yet another
heart attack whilst on a speaking engagement at Bristol. He had been out of
action until 20 January 1908, when he returned to work, only to have a
further attack on 12 February. Despite his attempts to cling to office, in
April he finally gave way to his doctors' insistence that he should resign.
There was no doubt who was to succeed him: Herbert Asquith, then
Chancellor of the Exchequer. The King summoned him to Biarritz on
4 April to kiss hands – the first and only premier to take office on foreign
soil.[2]

A new Prime Minister necessitated new ministers and no one (other than
Tweedmouth) was surprised when the First Lord was asked – in a two-line
note – to surrender his office.[3] He was offered the Presidency of the
Council but was so outraged at his dismissal from the Admiralty that he
threatened to leave the Government altogether. Fisher stepped in to persuade him that such a move 'would be construed into an admission that
your administration of the Navy had failed'.[4] Tweedmouth accepted the
advice, so smoothing the way for Reginald McKenna to become the new
First Lord. Fluent in French and German, a brilliant mathematician and a
rowing blue, McKenna was a talented man. After a successful career as a
barrister, he had entered the Commons in 1895 as a Liberal MP. When the
Liberals returned to power in 1905, McKenna became Financial Secretary
to the Treasury under Asquith, who quickly recognised his formidable

powers. After a short posting at the Board of Education, his elevation to the prestigious post of First Lord was no surprise.

Fisher, when consulted by Asquith over Tweedmouth's successor, had expressed a preference for Winston Churchill. It was difficult, after all, for him to forget how hard both Asquith and McKenna had fought against his naval estimates. However, it did not take long for him to change his mind. McKenna called on him at the Admiralty, where Fisher harangued him for three hours. When McKenna left he told Fisher that he was *'fascinated'*.[5] Whatever reservations each may have had about the other, they dissolved in a moment; it was the beginning of both a professional partnership and a lifelong friendship. Within days Fisher had forgotten all about Churchill and was telling Esher that 'he could think of no one he would prefer to McKenna' as First Lord.[6] The King's insistence that McKenna's appointment was conditional on Fisher remaining in post had proved superfluous.[7]

Within days of taking up his post, McKenna found a letter from Fisher on his desk, warning him against Beresford. He told McKenna that the Admiralty could permit no 'cavilling or criticizing' of Admiralty orders 'by officers on active service or afloat, and more especially by those in high command'. He had been driven to write the letter by an attempt by Beresford 'to dictate to the Admiralty what particular destroyers he should have'. He referred to the 'unprecedented lengths to which Lord Charles Beresford has been permitted ... to flout the Admiralty'. Whilst he did not ask McKenna for immediate action, he warned him of the need to discourage any 'disloyal' or even 'insubordinate' conduct. Apologising for writing in these terms, Fisher explained that he felt he had to do so 'before you (quite inadvertently) give any sort of recognition to what is really a most mischievous agitation'. It was a case, said Fisher, where Beresford must *'Se soumettre ou se démettre.'*[8,9]

Not to be outdone, Beresford, too, wrote to McKenna, going one better by following up his letter with *'an emissary* (Strath[10]) to warn him against Fisher'.[11]

## Scene 2: Beresford cuts Fisher

On the evening of 30 April, the Royal Academy of Arts opened its doors to the 140 guests for its annual dinner. This prestigious occasion was first held in 1771 at Somerset House when it was presided over by Sir Joshua Reynolds. To be invited as a guest was an exceptional honour. Each guest had to be nominated by a member and then survive a ballot in which two black balls sufficed for rejection. Invitations were strictly personal so if the guest were unable to attend, no substitute was allowed.[12] Beresford and Fisher, as in past years, had survived this selection process.

By 1908, the Academy had long been installed at Burlington House in Piccadilly, and the dinners took place in the large exhibition room at the top of the stairs. When Fisher and Beresford, in the company of the Prince of Wales and other illustrious members of society, passed through the main doors they found, said *The Times*, the stairs luxuriously adorned with 'white lilies and marguerites and red geraniums and roses'. On the first floor guests were greeted with a sea of tables, richly decorated 'with roses, lilies of the valley, white lilac and fern'.[13]

It was here, amongst the splendour of a great occasion in the annual social calendar, and in so public a place, that Beresford feigned to not notice his superior's outstretched hand. Fisher, refusing to be slighted, had followed the retreating Beresford around the dining room. When he finally cornered his reluctant subordinate, Fisher thrust out his hand in greeting; Beresford gave way and shook the First Sea Lord's hand. All this was observed, not least by Esher, who duly recorded it in his journal and recounted it in his correspondence.[14]

Fewer than two weeks later, Fisher and Beresford found themselves once again at a highly public function – on this occasion, one of the King's *levées*. Slade was close enough to see what happened. 'Fisher,' he wrote in his diary, 'was standing against the wall talking to Winston Churchill and Lloyd George.' Beresford arrived and shook hands with the two politicians, 'but when Sir J. put out his hand he turned his back on him'. Slade mildly remarked that Beresford 'behaves just like a naughty schoolboy'.[15] Doubtless others saw what happened since just three days later Esher told his son Maurice that 'It is all over the fleet.'[16]

No action, though, was taken and the King flew into a rage at his Government's failure to order Beresford to haul down his flag. They were, he said, 'a pack of cowards'.[17]

Beresford soon found it necessary to make his excuses and put round the story that he had failed to notice Fisher because the sun was in his eyes. As Mr Phillips, an Admiralty clerk, wryly commented to Arnold White: 'That there was no sun that day is of course quite immaterial.'[18] (It had been a dull, cloudy day in London, with just 2.8 hrs of sunshine.)[19]

In so publicly refusing to recognise his superior officer, Beresford had crossed his Rubicon. By July Viscount Midleton recorded that Beresford's actions had 'put the King against him and the whole hierarchy are determined to have him out'.[20] Beresford had neatly converted the question of 'Should Beresford go?' to 'When should Beresford go?'

## Scene 3: McKenna gives a warning

While McKenna was getting to know his new department, and Beresford was cutting Fisher in public, Fisher's attitude towards his subordinate was hardening. In April, they clashed twice and, in each case, Fisher was imprudent in his response. When Beresford asked to be supplied with some of the War College publications, Fisher instructed his staff that 'nothing should be sent to him without the sanction and authority of the Admiralty'. Slade duly noted in his diary that 'it is an impossible attitude to take up' but it was inevitable since Fisher was 'so bitter against Lord C. that anything he does or says is wrong'.[21] Two weeks later, when Beresford requested the addition of a mining vessel and some submarines to his fleet, all he received, said Slade, was 'a rude reply', a response that Fisher immediately regretted since he feared Beresford would use the lack of ships as an excuse for any failings in the next manoeuvres. In his diary Slade correctly forecast that Beresford 'will not sit down under the rebuff'.[22]

A month after McKenna had taken up his new post he received another letter from Fisher about Beresford. Fisher had heard 'via a reliable source in the Channel Fleet' that 'Beresford was about to cause *"a great upheaval"* and force the resignation of the First Sea Lord.' Coming so soon after the Academy Dinner and *levée* incidents, Fisher was in no mood to ignore such information, which, he told McKenna, was a clear sign that 'an incipient mutiny is being arranged in the Fleet'.[23]

Ten days later Fisher hastened the pace by sending McKenna a résumé of Beresford's obstinate refusal to produce war plans. He told him how the saga had begun only a month after Beresford's appointment to the Channel Fleet. The catalogue was relentless: there had been Beresford's complaint about lack of plans from the Admiralty (May 1907); his charge that the Home Fleet was a fraud (May 1907); his criticisms of his predecessor's plans (May 1907); his sketch plan (June 1907) which led the Board to issue new war orders; his refusal to produce plans (June 1907); the meeting with Tweedmouth, at which Beresford agreed a way forward with Fisher and Tweedmouth (July 1907); his follow-up letter in which he said he was now able to produce war plans (July 1907). But, said Fisher, 'from that day to this, a period of ten months, no War Plans have been submitted by Lord C. Beresford'.[24]

Where Tweedmouth had prevaricated, McKenna seemed willing to act, so Fisher put the administrative machine into action. First, he drafted a letter of dismissal in McKenna's name. Beresford was to be informed that McKenna had decided to merge the Home and Channel Fleets but that 'I do not offer you the new appointment of commander-in-chief of the Home Fleet as it is essential the officer so selected should be in agreement with Admiralty Policy and in cordial relationship with the Members of the Board of Admiralty in inaugurating a new policy.' He would 'in due course' be told the date on which he was to haul down his flag.[25]

Next, Fisher prepared a draft press statement in which the Board was to announce the disgraced admiral's departure. No diplomat, Fisher let his pen flow with abandon as the pent-up irritation of the last few years gave way to his anticipation of victory. The world was to be told that:

> The First Lord has also convinced himself that in the interests of the Service ... it is impossible to retain in his high Command afloat the present Commander-in-Chief of the Channel Fleet who admittedly and in the eyes of all the World adopts a hostile attitude towards the Board of Admiralty and its Policy ...

The public were to learn that it had been 'decided that Lord Charles Beresford should vacate his appointment' before the next manoeuvres took place.[26]

Whatever pleasure Fisher derived from drafting these two documents, neither ever went further than McKenna's desk. In his rush to push Beresford out, Fisher had overlooked the political aspect: no First Lord would dare sack Beresford without first obtaining Cabinet approval. In any case, it was Beresford who made the next move.

Smarting under Fisher's refusal of a mining vessel and submarines, and his refusal to release War College papers, Beresford wrote an eighteen-page letter to McKenna in early June. Ostensibly it was about the fighting efficiency of the fleets, but it was mostly a recapitulation of old sores. The first ten pages were devoted to the history of the Channel and Home Fleets, the long saga of his truncated command, and his attempts to produce war plans. None of this would have been new to the Admiralty staff and, though it was new to McKenna, he was not moved by it. The fact that Beresford concluded with a critique of the Admiralty's shipbuilding policy – which was none of his business, in McKenna's opinion – did not help his case.[27]

Any goodwill which Beresford might have built up with the new First Lord vanished when he treated the Board like fools over the issue of inviting journalists to witness manoeuvres. The date of the official visit to Norway and the subsequent manoeuvres in the North Sea was rapidly approaching. For years past such manoeuvres were accompanied by a mass of journalists, who reported on every trivial move of the massed ships. On this occasion, Beresford had pleaded with the Admiralty 'to exclude all correspondents'. Not long afterwards, Crease, then working at Admiralty House, noted that Beresford had decided 'to fill up the ships ... with his own friends'. This, he sarcastically noted was 'not to report the manoeuvres personally, but to assist in the agitation afterwards!'[28] The response from the Board was ruthless. Beresford was told to disembark his 'guests & civilians ... before the manoeuvres commence'.[29] To avoid a charge of vindictiveness on their part, the Board had, reluctantly, to issue the same order to the Home Fleet. With a wry smile, Crease looked forward to Beresford either disregarding the order or having to deposit his guests 'in the wilds of Norway'.[30]

It was around this time that McKenna decided that Beresford had to go. The precise date that he acted is not known, since all we have to go on are two undated documents that McKenna prepared for the Cabinet. In his evidence to the enquiry in 1909, he recalled that:

> I asked for the approval of my colleagues in taking two steps; the immediate re-organisation of the fleet in Home Waters ... [and] ... the termination of Lord Charles Beresford's command on the absorption of his fleet into the Home Fleet.

As he also recalled, 'Strong objection was taken to both steps, I think by the whole of my colleagues, without exception.'[31]

Following the Cabinet's refusal to act, McKenna did the next best thing, which was to limit the damage that Beresford could do whilst he remained afloat. What most worried McKenna was that Tweedmouth had placed Beresford in overall command in home waters in the event of war. He was convinced that Beresford was incapable of fulfilling such a command. There was only one thing to do: change the terms of his appointment. This he did in a letter of early July. On the same day, a more formal letter from an Admiralty official enclosed new war orders and confirmed that 'all previous War Orders communicated to you are to be cancelled'. The letter made it clear that 'The Board of Admiralty are solely responsible for ... the number and type of ships built, their manning and equipment ... and they alone have the responsibility of the strategic distribution of the Fleet in war.' Commanders-in-chief, such as Beresford, were responsible for 'using his utmost endeavours to defeat the enemy with the force placed at his disposal'.[32] In other words, should war break out, Beresford was not to assume that he would take supreme command in home waters – he would simply be expected to do the best he could with his own fleet.

Beresford's response was fully in character when he replied that he was 'so busy making out manoeuvre plans and drills' that he was unable to answer the First Lord.[33] Nevertheless, before he did answer at the end of the month, he had found time to send the First Lord a long critique of the Board's shipbuilding policy. This, McKenna firmly told him, was none of his business. As to the change in terms of command, Beresford made no comment.[34]

## Scene 4: Beresford humiliates Scott again

While Beresford was busy annoying Fisher and McKenna, his vendetta against Scott was never far from his thoughts. For all his viciousness

154

over the paintwork incident in the previous year and his acrimonious, self-justifying correspondence with the Admiralty, one simple fact stared Beresford in the face: Scott was still in command of the First Cruiser Squadron. This was a daily humiliation for Beresford. Although he had told the world at large that he had been in the right and that the Board had supported him, Scott still retained the confidence of their Lordships. The temptation to seek out petty squabbles with his squadron commander was to prove irresistible.

In the summer of 1908, Beresford returned to the attack. The first incident of what was to be an end-to-end sequence occurred in April. Or, at least, Beresford alleged that it occurred then, since he is the sole witness to this story. In his evidence to the enquiry, Beresford reproduced a letter that he wrote to the Board in August 1908 in which he claimed that, at a meeting of 'Lieutenant-Commanders of destroyers' at Cromarty, Scott warned them to 'be careful of your paintwork' because 'then you will get on in this fleet'.[35] Trivial as this was, Scott's repetition of his paintwork remark may well have rekindled Beresford's determination to destroy him, and so explain the succession of incidents that were to follow.

Having publicly shunned his First Sea Lord in May, Beresford now refused to recognise his rear admiral on two separate occasions. The first occasion occurred during the official visit of the French President to Britain in May 1908. In a tour packed with festive occasions, the Channel Fleet came in for its share of the dining, entertaining and dancing. On 28 May Beresford's officers were the guests of the French ship *Léon Gambetta* followed by 'international sports' between British and French officers at Dover. (Enigmatically, *The Times* reported that 'many' of the sports were 'of an amazing nature'.) In the evening it was the turn of the *King Edward VII* to act as host. The entertainment included a performance of *The Geisha* (a musical comedy) and the evening was topped off by a dinner at the Lord Warden Hotel in Dover, given by the French Consul, Baron de Belabre.[36]

Around 300 guests from the two fleets sat down to the meal and dancing was laid on to follow. It should all have been a splendid day of indulgent fun and amusement. For two men, though, the day was to end most unhappily. It all went wrong because, not for the first time, Beresford arrived late. The seating plan had placed him next to Scott, a fact that he only discovered on his arrival. He was incandescent. How could anyone have chosen to place him next to the rear admiral whom he had banned from his presence? At his insistence, Scott was placed at a decent distance from his Commander-in-Chief. It was not long before the incident reached the press which, said Scott, 'effectually fanned the smouldering embers into flames once more'.[37]

A month later, Beresford's Fleet had arrived at Christiania (now Oslo) for an official visit before the summer exercises in the North Sea. Here, yet another dinner was to play its part in riling Beresford. On this occasion it was one given by the King and Queen of Norway to the Channel Fleet on 20 June. The meal itself went off without a hitch. Beresford sat on the right of the Queen; the King proposed a toast to 'the British Fleet' and Beresford responded with one to 'the King and Queen of Norway'. After the meal Beresford received the Order of St Olav, while Scott, Milne and Rear Admiral Foley were made Knight Commanders of the same order.[38]

During the dinner someone approached Scott and asked him to 'provide some little surprise' for the following day when the King and Queen were to inspect the British Fleet. Scott recalled that 'The request rather upset my appetite as I could not think of anything.' Then, an idea came. In his memoirs he recalled how 'When I returned on board – very late – I routed out the Commander. He and a few carpenters stayed up all night.'[39] Only Scott, the commander and the carpenters had any idea what he was up to. Nothing was revealed until, as Scott told White, 'the King and Queen steamed round the Fleet in the *Surprise*. On arriving at the *Good Hope* they found written on her side "*LEVE KONGEN*" (Long live the King)'. Initially, there was no reaction. Then it dawned on the spectators that, what they took to be whitewashed letters, was in fact 'written in Men, 200 in all, 20 to a letter'.[40] Loud cheers followed and the Queen took photographs. Beresford scowled.

Fortunately we have Beresford's complaint to the Admiralty to explain why he was so upset at Scott's pleasing the royal couple. It was all to do with disobeying orders. Beresford had ordered, he told the Board, 'ships' companies to be in No. 1 dress [formal uniform for ceremonial occasions] for [the] visit of King and Queen'. Scott, on the other hand, had dressed his letter-men in No. 5 dress, that is, working uniforms. Since Beresford knew nothing of the display until the royal party 'was about a cable' (200 yards) from the *Good Hope*, he maintained that 'The position in which I was placed by the incident was invidious.'[41] A greater man might have congratulated Scott on his initiative.

The following day another incident occurred. (In Scott's record of these incidents,[42] he dates this incident as taking place on 30 June, but the *Good Hope*'s log book[43] records it as having taken place on 22 June.) This time the object of the controversy was a humble kedge anchor, that is a small anchor used when manoeuvring ships from one place to another in an anchorage. The anchor had been used to turn the *Good Hope* through ninety degrees but, on completion of the turn, it remained stuck in the mud of Christiania harbour. A cutter, which on four other occasions, alleged Scott, had been used to retrieve kedge anchors, was sent to the rescue, but was unable to dislodge it.

As the cutter struggled to heave the anchor out of the mud, a signal from the *King Edward VII* reached the *Good Hope*, commanding that the 'Rear

156

Admiral repair on board'. Scott, fearful of what to expect, climbed onto Beresford's quarterdeck where, he recorded:

> Lord Charles, in a loud and angry voice, which could be heard by my Flag Lieutenant, other Junior Officers and Seamen standing near, demanded from me what I meant by allowing a cutter to weigh a kedge anchor, and on my replying that the boat had weighed it before, he expressed incredulity.

Beresford then demanded to know why Scott had not been on deck during the operation, to which he replied that he had been there. Beresford, according to Scott, 'angrily exclaimed that he had two eyes in his head and that he did not see me'. Scott was then dismissed from the flagship with the warning that he would receive a memorandum demanding him to explain 'when and where this cutter had ever before weighed a kedge anchor'. Scott, angry at Beresford's 'publicly insulting' him was determined to 'lay the matter before the Admiralty'.[44] In his cabin, he began his letter, but before it was ready to send, two more incidents rapidly followed. The second of these was to finish Beresford's career.

On the night of 22 June, the Mayor of Christiania gave a dinner to officers of the Fleet so, once more, Beresford found himself in the presence of the rear admiral whom he had sworn to ostracise. Scott, who was most amused by the incident, wrote to White the next day. He described how Beresford had, yet again, had 'such bad luck' over a seating plan. On this occasion, it was Scott's turn to arrive late and he found that the only vacant seat was on Beresford's right-hand side. Before disaster could occur, Sir Berkeley Milne (Custance's replacement) intervened and, said Scott, 'shoved the Minister of War and himself along and so saved the situation'.[45]

The consequences of this were misread by Scott when he wrongly predicted in the same letter to White that 'The Belabre incident, coming with my not being invited to Custance's [farewell] dinner has caused much talk in the Fleet, and all sorts of rumours are afloat; everyone seems to have made up their minds that he goes in August.'[46] Beresford's position might have been insecure, but not as insecure as that.

Since April, when he twice cut Fisher, there had been five clashes between Beresford and Scott. Just one of the incidents reached the press and even that caused only minor ripples. Now the balance would shift in the other direction with an incident that was utterly trivial, but which Beresford ensured brought his competence under close and critical scrutiny and aroused the ire of both the Commons and *The Times*.

The facts of the incident are simple enough, although there was to be little agreement on their interpretation. On 1 July 1908, the Third Division of the Fleet was steaming in the North Sea. The exact position of Scott's ships is

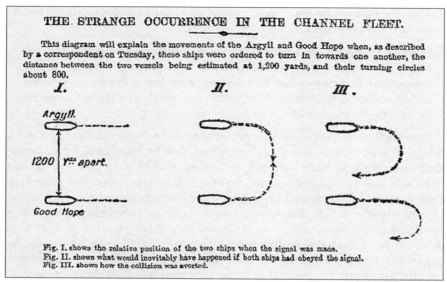

THE STRANGE OCCURRENCE IN THE CHANNEL FLEET.

This diagram will explain the movements of the Argyll and Good Hope when, as described by a correspondent on Tuesday, these ships were ordered to turn in towards one another, the distance between the two vessels being estimated at 1,200 yards, and their turning circles about 800.

Fig. I. shows the relative position of the two ships when the signal was made.
Fig. II. shows what would inevitably have happened if both ships had obeyed the signal.
Fig. III. shows how the collision was averted.

The Times diagram of the signal incident.

unclear since different accounts place them in different relative positions. What everyone agrees on – including Scott and Beresford – is that the *Good Hope* and the *Argyll* were on parallel courses about 1,200 yards apart as in position I in *The Times* diagram of the incident.

Beresford wished the Squadron to reverse its direction, so he sent two signals. The first told the squadron to turn 180° to starboard; the second ordered *Good Hope* to turn 180° to port. Had this order been executed, the *Argyll* and the *Good Hope* would have moved to the positions shown in part II of the illustration. In Scott's opinion the ships were so close that a collision was inevitable. He therefore turned to starboard, as shown in part III of the diagram, so avoiding any possible collision.

To understand the sensitivity with which this trivial event was received, we have to recall that a similar and much more catastrophic incident was fresh in every naval officer's mind: the sinking of the *Victoria* by the *Camperdown* on 23 June 1893. The scenario was identical, bar the behaviour of the subordinate officer. On that occasion, the Mediterranean Fleet under Admiral Sir George Tryon was steaming in two columns, 1,200 yards apart. He made a signal which required each column to turn inwards, even though such a manoeuvre required the columns to be at least 1,600 yards apart. Like Scott, Rear Admiral Markham, Second-in-Command of the Mediterranean Squadron, hesitated. Dare he question a signal from his irascible Commander-in-Chief? When Tryon impatiently signalled 'What are you waiting for?' Markham's courage failed him and he executed the order. It was not long before even Tryon could see that a collision between

158

the *Camperdown* and *Victoria* was inevitable. As the sharp ram of *Camperdown* sliced into the flagship, water poured in as if the ship had been opened from end to end. Within four minutes the foredeck was under water; eight minutes later, the ship keeled over and sank beneath the mirrored surface of a dead calm sea. The death toll was a staggering 358 men, including Tryon.[47]

Markham (along with other officers) was court-martialled but was acquitted since 'it would be fatal to the best interests of the Service to say he was to blame for carrying out the directions of the Commander-in-Chief present in person'.[48] Scott would have been familiar with this verdict; that he chose to ignore Beresford's order indicates that he was made of sterner stuff than was Markham.

To understand how the incident was seen by both Beresford and Scott, we have first to look at some of the technicalities of flag signalling. The normal procedure when making a signal was: (1) the signalling ship raised the signal; (2) to show that the signal had been received, the receiving ship raised an answering pennant to a position called 'the dip'; (3) only when the receiving ship had understood and accepted the signal did it raise the pennant 'close up'; (4) finally, the signalling ship would lower the signal, indicating that it was now to be carried out. Here, then, is the sequence of (abbreviated) signals on the day that was to initiate the countdown to the sacking of Beresford:

7.04 pm    Flag to 3rd Division    3rd Division turn 180-degrees to starboard.[49]
                                    *Good Hope* turn 180-degrees to port.

Scott recorded the *Good Hope* part of this signal in the ship's log book, where he also noted 'considered this dangerous therefore turned to starboard'. Beresford, seeing that the *Good Hope* was turning to starboard rather than to port, sent the signal:

7.08 pm    Flag to *Good Hope*    Did *Good Hope* take in signal to turn to port?

What had happened was explained by Scott's next signal:

*Good Hope* to Flag    *Good Hope* did not go close up before the signal was
                       hauled down.

By this, Scott meant that he had assumed that Beresford had cancelled the signal since he had lowered it *before* Scott had hoisted his pennant. Scott's thinking was that Beresford had realised that the original signal was dangerous and so had cancelled it. In response came a reassuring signal from Beresford:

7.16 pm    Flag to *Good Hope*    Did *Good Hope* take in signal to turn to port? If
                                  *Good Hope* took in the signal to turn to port and
                                  R.A. thought *Good Hope* was too close to *Argyle*
                                  [sic], R.A. was right to turn to starboard.

159

Scott then replied:

*Good Hope* to Flag

*Good Hope* took in signal to turn to port, but did not go close up as there was danger in such a turn. As the signal to turn to port was hauled down before *Good Hope* had answered it, R.A. concluded that the danger had been realised and *Good Hope* therefore acted on the General Signal to the 3rd Division to turn to starboard.

And there the incident might have ended, as just a simple case of a rear admiral using his judgement to ignore a signal that seemed to him to be too dangerous to execute. Someone, though, was determined to make mischief of the event and six days later an ominous headline appeared in *The Times*: *A Strange Occurrence in the Channel Fleet*. What followed was an essentially accurate account of the manoeuvre and the exchange of signals, but the wording of the second and third paragraphs caused Beresford to explode:

> The *Good Hope* and the *Argyll* were abeam of one another on a parallel course, 1,200 yards apart. Lord Charles Beresford made a signal to them ordering the *Argyll* to turn 16 points to starboard and the *Good Hope* 16 points to port.
>
> Had the signal been obeyed the *Good Hope* and the *Argyll* would have collided, as did the *Victoria* and *Camperdown*. The *Argyll* obeyed the signal, the *Good Hope*, to avert a collision, disobeyed the signal.[50]

There it was in black and white: Beresford had issued a dangerous signal and Scott had saved the day. The next two paragraphs aggravated the situation by implying that, whereas Markham had stupidly obeyed a dangerous signal in 1893, Scott had acted well in disobeying one in 1908.

Ironically, and most unfortunately, the very day before *The Times* article had appeared, that same newspaper had published a sharply-worded

*Good Hope's* log book showing the signal that brought Beresford's and Scott's careers to an end.

attack on Beresford from Arthur Lee, a Conservative MP and a one-time Civil Lord of the Admiralty. Whilst he admitted that 'it is not a pleasant task ... to assist in the public washing of dirty linen' he noted that 'the Commander in Chief of the Channel Fleet (who is presumably the Admiralissimo designate in the event of war) is not on speaking terms with the Admiral commanding his cruiser squadron on the one hand, or with the First Sea Lord of the Admiralty on the other'. He wished to know 'what steps the First Lord of the Admiralty, or the Cabinet, propose to take in order to put an end to a grave scandal'.[51] The furore created by this letter caused Lee so much distress that he and his wife went off on holiday.[52] The other players had no option but to remain on the scene. As Beresford was to note in *The Betrayal*, 'there appeared simultaneously in many newspapers articles assailing my character, and adversely criticising my conduct as an officer'.[53]

*The Times*, long aware of the machinations of Beresford, decided that the time had come to move in for the kill. The paper drew attention to Lee's letter which, it said, 'manifestly demands ... the prompt consideration of the Cabinet'. There then followed the clearest possible statement of the necessity to put an end to Beresford's flouting of discipline:

> We say frankly that if, as is alleged, LORD CHARLES BERESFORD is at loggerheads with the Board of Admiralty, or with any individual member of it, he is, in our judgement, *ipso facto* in the wrong.

And, turning to his relationship with Scott, the paper added 'if, as is also alleged, he is not on speaking terms with one of his flag officers, he is equally in the wrong'. It was his duty to 'do nothing to impair the discipline, good order, and good feeling of the fleet under his command'. He had, said the paper, 'set a deplorable example of indiscipline and insubordination to the Fleet' and 'must be confronted with the historic alternative *se soumettre ou se démettre*'.[54] While these accusations clearly referred back to a long sequence of Beresfordian disputes, the signal incident had acted as a trigger for an all-out assault on the unmanageable admiral.

Beresford could be forgiven for his paranoia at this sudden outburst of journalistic hostility. The next day the attacks moved to the Commons where Asquith parried calls for an enquiry into Admiralty administration and 'dissensions' in the Navy by saying that 'The Government have no knowledge, apart from unverified rumours, of the dissensions alleged.'[55] Then, on 9 July, Lea asked whether the First Lord was 'aware that the present commander of the Channel Fleet, Admiral Lord Charles Beresford, is not on speaking terms with his official superior, Admiral of the Fleet Sir John Fisher, and with his official subordinate, [Rear] Admiral Sir Percy Scott'. When Dr Thomas Macnamara, the Parliamentary and Financial Secretary to the Admiralty, replied that he could add nothing to what Asquith had said the day before, Lea responded with a supplementary question that went to the heart of the issue. He asked whether 'the rules and regulations of the Navy ... are only to apply to the humbler ranks, stokers, for example, while Lord Charles Beresford is to be allowed to break them with impunity?'[56] No answer came from the Government benches.

Lea was also on his feet to ask about the signal incident. He referred to the order given by Beresford 'which would have made collision inevitable' and reminded the House that this would have 'reproduced the disaster caused by the *Camperdown* sinking the *Victoria*'. Disaster had been avoided, he said, 'by the officer commanding the *Good Hope* disobeying the order'. He called for a court of inquiry and for the Government to 'relieve Lord Charles Beresford of his command'. The only answer that he received was that 'The Admiralty have no information on the subject' and were waiting for a report from Beresford.[57]

Beresford's situation was now becoming serious. When Lea had asked his question about the near collision, eight days had passed, during which not one word had been heard from the originator of the signals – Beresford. It was not until 12 July that he finally wrote to the Admiralty. When Macnamara opened the envelope, he must have eagerly looked forward to an explanation that would put an end to the controversy. To his surprise, all he found was a brief letter. There was not one word about the incident – no account from Beresford's point of view, no dispute of the facts as reported in the press, no attempt to extricate himself from the serious charges that had been made against him. The whole of the letter was devoted to one thing only: finding who had leaked the signals to *The Times*. He told the Admiralty that the logs of all the ships in the Fleet had been checked and that 'the only logs in which the signals quoted in *The Times* are recorded are those of *King Edward VII* and *Good Hope*'. He went on to claim that one signal was recorded at 7.08 pm in the *Good Hope* log book, but at 7.10 pm in the log book of the flagship. Since *The Times* gave the time as 7.08, he concluded that their story had originated from the *Good Hope* 'in direct contravention' of 'Article 12, King's Regulations'.[58] In his memoirs, Beresford claimed that *The Times* account of the incident 'was totally incorrect'.[59] That sits oddly with the fact that his letter of July 1908 tacitly accepted the account as correct and focused solely on the leak.

Beresford concluded by drawing the Admiralty's attention to his previous claims that information was being leaked from his Fleet in 'an attempt to injure the discipline of the fleet and my position and authority'. Now, he said, he had given them 'direct proof ... that the source of such communications is the *Good Hope*' and he invited them to 'take such action as they may think proper'.[60] (To put this hypocritical complaint into perspective, Beresford wrote twenty letters to Bellairs in 1908, most divulging information about his Fleet.)

162

Privately, Beresford had further, and much more explosive ideas as to who was at the bottom of all this: Fisher. He told the *Daily Express* journalist Blumenfeld that, on 6 July, Fisher had 'sent for Thursfield of the TIMES'. That day was, according to Beresford, 'the morning the information arrived from P[ercy].S[cott].', which, he said, was a fact 'well known to every underling at the Admiralty'. Noting that *The Times* article attacking him had appeared the next day, he drew the conclusion that Thursfield and Fisher had concocted the account in a manner 'worthy of the time of the assassins of the Doges of Venice'.[61]

The *Morning Post* also pointed the finger at Fisher, noting that 'The choice of time and method of attack seem, under all the circumstances, to be Asiatic rather than European, and they are certainly the very last to have been expected by any English gentleman.'[62] Every reader of that journal would have recognised 'Asiatic' to be a coded reference to Fisher, whose parentage was regarded by some as suspect and who was regularly denigrated on account of his non-aristocratic background.

As in the best melodramas a surprise witness now appeared on the scene. On 22 July, a Captain Morgan, serving on the *Britannia* battleship in the Channel Fleet sat down to write a letter as his ship steamed in the middle of the North Sea. Beresford was already familiar with the contents since he had met Morgan a week earlier in a chance encounter. So important was the story that Morgan had told him, that Beresford had asked him to put it in writing. Morgan recounted that he had met Scott on 10 July at a hotel at Skagen Point – the northernmost tip of Denmark. There, Scott had told him that the information in *The Times* article 'was the same which he had written to the Admiralty'.[63] Despite the ambiguity of the letter – it was by no means evident that Scott had therefore sent the details to *The Times* – Beresford was overjoyed. He immediately wrote to the Admiralty from Portland to inform them that 'I have ordered a Court of Enquiry with a view to framing charges for a court-martial.'[64]

25 July must have been a hectic day, assuming that Beresford dated his letter correctly. He had written the letter and sent it to the Admiralty – presumably by a special courier. Later in the day he was in McKenna's office to discuss the letter and, by the close of the day, he had written yet another letter, this time to McKenna. Clearly the alarming news that he had ordered a Court of Enquiry had led to an urgent recall to London. Exactly what was said in McKenna's office we do not know, since we only have two accounts, both by Beresford. One was written on the same day; the other some time in 1909 when he was preparing his evidence for the enquiry. The latter was probably embroidered to make a particular case, so the earlier account is likely to be the best we have.

Writing to McKenna after the meeting, Beresford said he had 'given the deepest consideration' to McKenna's arguments against a Court of Enquiry. He recalled that McKenna had warned that it would be 'bound to rake up a deplorable amount of scandalous matter'. Expanding his reasons for accepting McKenna's recommendation, he noted that it was McKenna's view that such an enquiry would give the impression that 'I was acting solely from vindictive and personal motives'.[65]

All this rings true, and is no doubt more or less what McKenna advised. The rest of the letter though is a typical Beresfordian muddle in which he asserts that McKenna asked him: (1) to court-martial Scott, which Beresford said he could not do since he lacked the evidence; and (2) 'to leave the matter of *The Times* communication in your hands'.[66] Given that five days later McKenna was to stand up in the House of Commons and exonerate Scott of any blame, it is hard to credit that he was determined on a court martial on 25 July. Nor did it make sense to encourage Beresford to court-martial Scott if *The Times* letter were to be excluded. In interpreting Beresford's account of his interview with McKenna, it is helpful to recall that according to Beresford, he was in the right over the *Daily Mail* letter in 1901–2, that he was exonerated over the paintwork incident in 1907 and, yet to come, the enquiry ruled totally in his favour in 1909. As an interpreter of events in which he was involved, Beresford was self-deception personified.

Some further indication of the Admiralty line comes in a letter from Fisher to McKenna three days later. The tenor of the first part of this letter suggests that McKenna had been probing Fisher on the possibility of the Admiralty issuing a statement. Fisher advised him that the Admiralty could not make a statement 'without an enquiry, but an enquiry would re-open the whole scandal'. Saying that Beresford ought 'to be satisfied with the removal of Scott [from the Channel Fleet]' Fisher thought that the affair would die out if the Admiralty were to adopt delaying tactics in responding to communications from Beresford. In the same letter Fisher denied that he had had any involvement in *The Times* leading article of 8 July. He, he said, neither 'had any conversation' with Thursfield, nor 'inspired' him to write the article.[67]

Two days later it was Scott's turn to present himself in the First Lord's office. McKenna, Scott said, 'informed me that I should no longer be troubled by Lord Charles Beresford'. Instead he was to be 'in command of a squadron of cruisers to represent the Mother Country in South Africa'.[68] As Scott was about to leave McKenna's room, the First Lord offered him the warning that 'it's dangerous to get mixed up with the press, Admiral. They'll suck you dry. And when you can't feed them any more – they'll eat *you!*'[69] Perhaps McKenna was inwardly convinced that it was Scott who had leaked the story to the press.

That same day McKenna came under fire in the Commons. Viscount Castlereagh, Unionist MP for Maidstone, wanted to know whether the Board had yet received a report from Beresford on the incident. In an ambiguous reply, McKenna indicated that the Board had, indeed, received a report. Who it was from he did not say. However, the Board was now 'satisfied that the manoeuvre was not dangerous', thus exonerating Beresford from the charge of issuing a hazardous order. At the same time, Scott 'was justified in turning the other way' since he thought the manoeuvre dangerous.[70] McKenna then drew attention to the fact that everyone seemed to have ignored ever since the incident occurred: at the time when Scott had disregarded the signal, he also had signalled his reasons to Beresford, who had accepted them. There had been no dangerous order, no insubordination – just a minor perturbation in a normal day's exercises.

Bellairs then turned the House's attention to the issue of 'the editors of those papers which had erroneously accused Lord Charles Beresford of having endangered the lives of 1,600 men'. What did the Admiralty intend to do to correct that false impression? Not surprisingly, after all the trouble that the press had caused recently, McKenna replied that 'I think it is always desirable to avoid communication with the Press.'[71]

This incident drew to a close with a long and vitriolic letter that Beresford sent to the Admiralty on 11 August. He provided eighteen reasons to justify his 'adverse remarks on the character and conduct' of Scott. He implied Scott was behind the January *John Bull* article which contained 'scurrilous and untrue attacks on my personal reputation' and was part of an 'organised campaign' against him. As to the question of Scott not being invited to official dinners, he protested that Scott 'has been asked to every official dinner given on board the *King Edward VII* since he has been present with the fleet'. (But not, presumably, to the chummy dinners which Beresford gave for his officers.) Then there was Scott's behaviour over the *Leve Kongen* incident and his 'derogatory remark' over paintwork. At Esbjerg, he said, Scott had refused an invitation to dine with the Governor of the Province, giving 'no excuse or explanation'. Turning to Scott as commander, Beresford opined he did 'not show aptitude for the command of a cruiser squadron' and went on to accuse him of incompetence at the October 1907 manoeuvres, the July 1908 manoeuvres and at the time of the signal incident. To top it all, Scott was 'disloyal' and had even been responsible, said Beresford, for 'the disgraceful personal attack on me' in *The Times* of 7 July 1908.[72]

There was nothing new here and, by the time the Admiralty received the letter, Scott was steaming in the southern oceans. Doubtless the Secretary of the Admiralty briefly noted the contents and quietly filed the letter in the burgeoning file 'Beresford – abuse received from'.

Scott never accepted that he had been fairly treated over the signal incident nor over the other Beresford-inspired clashes. His entanglement in the Beresford-Fisher feud ensured that his mission to South Africa was his last sea appointment, his flag coming down in February 1909. For years he would write sad and angry letters to anyone who would take an interest, but it was to no avail. No one ever took up his case and, by the time of the enquiry, the Government were no longer concerned with Scott's reputation, but their own.

Beresford had taken his first scalp in his war with Fisher. It would not be long before he would attempt to take the next.

## Scene 5: Managing and mismanaging the Fleet

Whilst these clashes and alarms fed the public's interest for intrigue and scandal, Beresford was still Commander-in-Chief of a powerful fleet. Despite his many absences, his ships continued to cruise around the British Isles. In April they visited Lamlash and Ballachulish before moving on to Invergordon. There were also visits to Scarborough, Lough Swilly and Oban. It is clear, though, that Beresford was bored with the routine of a peace-time fleet. Whenever possible, he would find an excuse to board the *Surprise* to take him back to Portsmouth or Portland, from where he could take a fast train to London and rejoin society.

From June onwards, there were persistent indications that all was not right in the Channel Fleet. Admiral Sir Francis Bridgeman, in charge of the Home Fleet, complained to Fisher about the 'persistent statements' in the press about his own fleet. They were, he said, 'malicious' and his officers 'think the C-in-C Channel Fleet is in some way responsible for the statements'. So disgruntled were they that they 'want him brought to book'. While Bridgeman wished to avoid a public spat with Beresford, 'if it does come to a war of words I have plenty of material with which to attack the C-in-C Channel'.[73]

Scott, even before the signal incident, also thought that something was wrong. Captain Montague Browning, the new chief of staff on *King Edward VII* from 1 February was, he told White, 'the most unpopular man in the Fleet'. He had also noted that, on board the *King Edward VII*, 'everything is done on the cheap' and there was 'very little entertaining'. He hypothesised that Beresford was 'saving up a bit before he goes'.[74] Even an admirer of Beresford, such as Frewen, could not help noticing such signs of slackness. In June he noted that Beresford was astounded to find that his fleet was 'dressed with masthead flags'. On being told that the display was for the King's birthday, Beresford responded 'Oh, is it?'[75] Perhaps the loss of Custance – he had departed the Fleet in mid-June – had left Beresford feeling isolated. Certainly his mind was turning towards the shore, where he needed to be if he were to pursue his vendetta.

There were, though, a good number of distinguished visitors to show round the Fleet. In addition to the visit to Norway's royalty, Beresford's final year afloat coincided with an official visit of the French President in May and a visit of the Maharajah of Nepal in the same month. On the occasion of the President's visit, he was able to proudly display fifty-two ships manned by 17,544 officers and men. The splendour of the visit reached a peak, noted *The Times*, on the evening of 25 May when the *King Edward VII* blazed with light as French and British officers sat down to dinner in an 'improvised dining-room' on deck. The decorations, continued the paper, were 'elaborate' and included 'twenty emblematic designs, of which each battleship and cruiser in the Fleet had sent one'. Never one to miss a chance of making a speech, Beresford took the opportunity to praise the French Navy and the 'gallantry' of its officers.[76]

During this time the visitors who most mattered to Beresford were Edward and Alexandra. Estranged from Edward since 1891, Beresford was ever seeking opportunities to rebuild that once intimate relationship. The royal inspection of the Fleet seemed to be just what was needed.

Early on the morning of 7 August, the royal party, with Fisher in attendance, left Cowes to visit Beresford's Fleet. He was determined to make it a memorable occasion for his sovereign. As the Royal Yacht approached Portland, a flotilla of Beresford's scouting vessels and destroyers came out to escort it into harbour, where Edward and Alexandra were greeted by the combined guns of the Fleet. When the yacht steamed into the Portland roads, the royal couple were able to admire the sixteen battleships and numerous other vessels lined up for inspection. On shore, huge crowds jostled to catch a glimpse of their sovereign, dressed in his admiral's uniform. The strains of the National Anthem drifted ashore, carried by the brisk north-westerly breeze. Under a fierce sun, the royal couple transferred to a pinnace to make the short trip to the flagship. As he climbed on board, Edward gave, said *The Times*, 'a hearty greeting' to Beresford, who then presented his flag admirals to the King. Scott, of course, was no longer among them, a fact that must have been of relief to both Edward and his Commander-in-Chief.[77]

Beneath the surface pomp of that day, undercurrents were at play. Nothing was quite what it seemed. Fisher had been against the visit from the start. Following so closely on the signal incident, he deprecated the royal imprimatur that was implied by a fleet inspection. However, once the visit was over, Beresford sought to profit from the goodwill that it had generated. Writing to Edward, he told him that 'I shall never forget the day' because it 'reminded me so clearly of those happy days gone by which can never be erased from my memory'.[78] This was a less than veiled allusion to their rapport before the Lady Brooke incident and was clearly a plea to Edward to return to their former closeness.

Edward's reply was ambiguous. He opened with the usual niceties, recalling 'the great pleasure and satisfaction' that he and his wife had found in seeing 'the Channel Squadron under your command'. However, in closing, he added a note of warning: 'Trusting that nothing may occur to prevent your continuing to hold the high and important position which you now occupy.'[79] Whether Beresford was able to decipher this allusion to the recent Scott incident, we do not know. On balance, the evidence suggests that he could never see what he had done wrong in his clashes with the Admiralty so we might assume that the King's warning went unnoticed. Indeed, within forty-eight hours Beresford had needlessly written again to his sovereign, foolishly making a new attempt at self-justification. He was, he said, grateful for the King's support at a time 'when my position had become exceedingly difficult'.[80] It was effort wasted, though, since Edward remained implacably on Fisher's side.

Beresford's attempts to inveigle the King into taking up his case against the Admiralty received no response. In fact, only a few days later Edward asked Lord Knollys to visit Fisher to discuss what could be done about Beresford's continued agitation amongst 'all the Dukes and Duchesses' and his persistent attacks on Edward himself.[81] Although Fisher continued to receive the King's support, he nevertheless had to accept that, for this year at least, he should not lunch with him at Marienbad when they were both there for their cures. Meanwhile, Beresford's attempt at rapprochement seems to have ended when Alexandra wrote to him later in the month. While she wished him success in his career, she nevertheless reminded him that 'one should *always* try and sacrifice personal grievances and remember Nelson's words – England expects every man to do his duty'.[82]

Despite the Board's decision to not authorise further manoeuvres, a total of 301 ships were mobilised under Beresford in July 1908 for three weeks of activity. Sir Arthur Wilson was appointed by the Admiralty to prepare a report on their progress.

Wilson was not impressed by what he saw, saying in his report that 'It should be impressed upon Admirals ... [that] the main object is to produce incidents that will give experience in the operations of war. A spirit of enterprise in making attacks on the enemy should be encouraged, and it should be considered much better for an Admiral's reputation to carry out a well considered attack and fail, than to avoid action altogether.'[83] Not only had Beresford put up a poor performance, in Wilson's opinion, but he was so slow in submitting his own report that Wilson went to work on his final report without waiting for the Commander-in-Chief's own offering.[84]

By mid-August, no longer prepared to wait for Beresford's report, the Board announced that 'Their Lordships have decided not to have any further Combined Fleet Exercises this year.' Should any further exercises be desirable, 'they themselves will initiate the orders'.[85] Beresford challenged this decision in October, but the Board refused to review its decision.[86]

Much later in the year, *The Times* published a letter from H.W. Wilson, chief leader-writer of the *Daily Mail* and a strong supporter of Beresford, in which he quoted the Admiralty claim that 'practice would be given to the British war commander in the handling of larger masses of ships in time of peace'. He then went on to point out that the booklet *The Truth About the Navy* had included the statement that the fleets 'are concentrated three times a year for manoeuvres'. He continued: 'Alas for these boasts and promises.' This showed, Wilson alleged, that 'the Admiralty has repudiated its promises' and had refused a request from Beresford 'to exercise the Home Fleet with the Channel Fleet'.[87] While some of the details of Wilson's letter might have been disputable, his fundamental point – that the Admiralty had a Commander-in-Chief who they could not trust to manage his Fleet – stood. It was an extraordinary position for the world's premier naval power to find itself in.

There was one final unpleasant incident towards the end of the year, this time involving Beresford's flag captain, Henry Pelly. At the time the fleet was practising night manoeuvres and, the ship in total darkness, Pelly was on the bridge while Beresford was on the quarterdeck. Pelly recalled that 'I received a verbal message through a signal boy instead of from the Flag Lieutenant ... which I failed to understand, not realizing that it came from the Commander-in-Chief.'[88] On failing to carry out the order, Pelly was arrested and placed in his cabin. Whereas, though, Scott's similar action led to unrelenting persecution, Pelly was released next day with an apology from Beresford for 'his loss of temper'. The differential treatment that the two men received eloquently testifies just how contemptible Beresford's vilification of Scott was.

## Scene 6: Who will free me from this turbulent Admiral?

While Beresford was writing letters in his attempt to regain the King's support, Edward was raging against the Cabinet for lacking the courage to sack both Beresford and Scott. When Beresford saw *The Times* of 6 August, he must surely have realised that, far from coming back into favour, dark forces were stacked against him. He may not have been too alarmed to read that he might, 'for reasons of ill health', leave his post 'in the autumn' but nothing would have prepared him for the bald statement that he was to go 'in March of next year'.[89] He had presumed that his appointment was for three years, so to learn from the pages of a newspaper that it would be for only two was an insult of the first order. His successor, the paper said, was to be the Second Sea Lord, Vice Admiral Sir William May.

Two days later Beresford wrote to McKenna to demand an explanation. In the circumstances he showed remarkable moderation. Noting that *The Times* report 'may or may not be authoritative' he asked McKenna whether 'will you be good enough to let me know if my command of the Channel Fleet is to terminate in March 1909, after holding the position for two years?' He maintained that 'the commands of the important Fleets have hitherto been held for three years, and my predecessor held this appointment for four years'. At this stage there were no histrionics, no threats and no recriminations. Beresford merely asked for an early reply since 'I have my private arrangements to consider in such a contingency.'[90] (While Beresford was constrained in his letter to McKenna, he was more open in writing to Long: 'If I am to be relieved in March it is monstrous that the Press as usual should be informed before me.')[91]

In his reply, McKenna was able to reassure Beresford that the article in *The Times* was 'wholly unauthorised' and 'contains much information which ... is unknown to me'. As to the period of Beresford's appointment, McKenna offered little comfort. He reminded Beresford that all such posts are 'held at His Majesty's pleasure'. Whilst he admitted that 'the commands of the important fleets have usually been held for three years' he was not prepared to promise him 'any fixed limit of time'.[92]

Although Fisher had enthusiastically drafted the press release and letter for Beresford's dismissal back in June, by September, he was having second thoughts. After a batch of troublesome letters from Beresford to the King which, said Fisher, could be summarised as '*the Board of Admiralty consists of idiots and Beresford is the one and only man!*' Fisher began to contemplate the havoc that Beresford could create on the back benches. Momentarily forgetting the location of Beresford's appointment he told Knollys that 'it's better to have him [Beresford] in the Mediterranean [Channel] than in Parliament. In the Mediterranean [Channel] we can sit upon him – in Parliament no one can!'[93]

Fisher did not believe the many rumours suggesting that Beresford was about to resign. As he told an unknown recipient, 'the fact is he thinks everyone is frightened of him, and certainly he has been treated as if this were the case'. Later in the same letter he correctly forecast that 'this [is] parleying with mutiny, and we shall have a catastrophe before long!'[94]

As to Beresford's resignation, the rumours had some substance since he had sought the advice of friends on whether to go following the signal incident and the subsequent Parliamentary outcry. One friend in particular was to have a powerful influence over his decision: Walter Long. An immensely wealthy Tory landowner with a distinguished Parliamentary career as a reformer, Long had turned down the post of First Lord when it was offered to him by Balfour in 1905. By 1908, in opposition, he was marked down as a potential leader of the Tory party. Failing that, he and Beresford envisaged a future in which Long would be First Lord, supported by Beresford as First Sea Lord. When, therefore, Long provided Beresford with blunt advice on 20 October, Beresford was inclined to listen.

If he were to resign, said Long, with his history of bad relations with the Admiralty, this might be seen as 'being an act of quasi insubordination'. Whilst Long knew 'a great many people' who were well-disposed towards Beresford, the fact was that his well-known hostility to Fisher led them to assume that this affected his judgement of his superior officer. In the circumstances he advised Beresford 'not to mention the word "resignation" again, to talk to nobody except your Chief of Staff about your relations with the Admiralty, and to devote the whole of your attention to your work as Commander-in-Chief'. This would put him in a strong position if 'the Admiralty, for their own purposes, were to supersede you'.[95]

Beresford, who was 'very touched ... by the tone of the letter', accepted this advice, adding the improbable assurance that 'I assure you that I will endeavour to remove the impression "that I am unreliable, and would do my best to upset McKenna, Fisher and the whole Board"'.[96] Who exactly Beresford intended to fool with statements like this is hard to imagine. Only one month previously he had sent Bellairs yet another long list of points on which he was to attack the Admiralty, including: 'depletion of stores', Montgomerie being 'superseded' and the weakness of the Fleet compared to Germany.[97]

Thoughts of resignation were running through Fisher's mind, too. As he told McKenna, he did not wish 'to lag superfluous on the stage'. On the other hand, he felt that he needed two more years to secure his reforms. As long as there was 'cordial harmony between the First Lord and First Sea Lord' he would stay.[98] When writing to White, though, he sounded a much more fatigued note. 'I am,' he said, 'getting sick and meditating a sudden and unexpected departure à la Elijah.'[99] Another possibility, which he put to Esher, was to 'retire next November with a Peerage'. Although, Esher noted in his journal, 'he would lose £3,000 p.a., ... he would avoid in this way an inevitable fall!'[100] A few weeks later, though, Fisher was more optimistic, having decided to stay. Esher noted 'The fact is that he cannot bring himself to say good-bye to the Admiralty, even a year hence.'[101]

## Scene 7: McKenna wields the axe

Eight months after taking office, McKenna wrote to Beresford to terminate his command. He had no desire to humiliate Beresford further than was necessary, so he made no mention of his insubordinations or his quarrels with the Admiralty. To sugar the pill, he told Beresford that he had decided 'that the present commands of the Channel and Home Fleets shall be held for a period of two years', thus suggesting that Beresford was just the innocent victim of an administrative change. Then, somewhat disingenuously, he added that 'this decision will probably not be unwelcome' given his 'continuous and distinguished tenure of chief commands lasting six years'. In practice, two years for Beresford would have meant hauling down his flag on 4 March 1909, but McKenna suggested 24 March, 'to coincide with the date on which the command of the Home Fleet will also be vacated'.[102]

171

The clearest explanation as to why McKenna chose this route for dismissal comes from a letter that Fisher wrote to McKenna three days later, in which he recounted how he had explained McKenna's thinking to Knollys. The latter had accepted that changing all the home appointments to two years was an administrative act 'in which the King has no say'. In this way, the King would be kept out of the firing line if things turned nasty. Although McKenna could have relied on precedence – many of these posts had been held for two years in the past – Fisher had explained to Knollys that McKenna had preferred an argument based on the needs of the fleets. The modern fleets in home waters, he had told Knollys, were 'in constant & continuous work' whereas in the past 'the whole Channel Fleet went deliberately into winter quarters for months at a time for the annual dockyard refit'. Nowadays, a home command was a 'sustained tension for the Commander-in-Chief'.[103]

Three days later, under the careful tutelage of Long, Beresford wrote a pained but restrained reply to his letter of dismissal. In an understatement he told McKenna that 'the termination of my command in this manner is not either convenient or pleasant to me'. Further, he reminded McKenna, as recently as 8 August he had implied that no changes to his command were then foreseen. Were such changes to be contemplated, Beresford had requested that '[you] give me early intimation of your decision in order that I might make my arrangements'.[104]

Nor was he happy about the comparative outcome between himself and Bridgeman who, he noted, would 'receive another appointment'. He then added: 'I must observe that there is a wide difference between an Officer holding an important command being placed on half pay, presumably for the remainder of his Service, and being relieved in order to take up another appointment.' In conclusion, Beresford explained that 'Under the circumstances you cannot wonder that I feel deeply that my career afloat, which has extended over very nearly fifty years, should be so abruptly terminated.'[105]

Beresford's letter to McKenna was for public consumption, hence his unusually restrained manner, whilst still making clear that he felt let down by the decision. In private, the story was rather different. When the news broke, he told Bellairs that the Admiralty 'will infer that it is I who has made all the row between the First Sea Lord and myself' but 'everybody knows it is the First Sea Lord who has attacked me'.[106] In hanging on, Beresford hoped to ensure that, in the public eye, he would appear to be the injured party. Two years later, in a letter to Sturdee, he explained how he had often felt like resigning, but noted that 'had [I] gone voluntarily I should never have received the sympathy and enthusiasm which I got when ordered to haul down my Flag'.[107]

By mid-January Beresford was beginning to see the bright side of his position. Noting that 'something has occurred to prevent the gazetting of my being compelled to haul down my Flag' he told Long that 'the opinion of my friends at the Admiralty is that they are frightened at the tone of my letter'. This raised his spirits, and his thoughts turned to what to do next. 'The future,' he said, '[is] bristling with difficulties' but he was sure that 'the Navy and my countrymen will want me to speak and inform them of the true state of the case when I go out.' However, what he really wanted was to oust Fisher. 'If I sit still and do nothing,' he pondered, would that 'prevent me getting First Sea Lord[?]' In that case, 'any use I might be to the Country would be thrown away'.[108]

Having mulled over these difficult points, Beresford told Long that '[I] shall be delighted if my Flag comes down' and that since he did not 'want to be awash neither in nor out of the water as I might be if I said nothing' he had decided 'I would rather go out and have my fight in the Country.'[109] And, with that decision, Beresford had set in motion the denouement of the feud. Unable to accept the defeat implied in the loss of his command, he was now to fight the battle on the open ground of the public stage.

In taking this risky stance, Beresford did so in the confident expectation that he would bring down the Government and so open the way to the return of Balfour and a Tory government. Then, said Esher in a letter to Knollys, provided Balfour appointed him to the post of First Sea Lord, 'he would keep quiet about the state of the Navy; otherwise, he would "stump the country and agitate"'.[110]

## Scene 8: Beresford's triumphal exit

In a letter to McKenna of 27 February, Fisher wrote 'This will make you shake in your shoes! *"Nelson's last words"* & *"Music singing"* give the graphic touch!' The occasion for this outburst of jollity was a request from Beresford to take his Fleet on one last cruise to Lough Swilly. 'In the ordinary course of events,' said Fisher, 'it would be rather silly to approve this in view of the re-arrangement of the ships on March 24' but he thought it best 'to let him have his fireworks.' He could not help, though, recalling how, when Wilson left the Fleet in April 1907 he issued 'a signal forbidding cheering or any demonstration of his departure'.[111]

On the Fleet's return to Portland from the north, Beresford was entertained at a farewell dinner given by the town of Weymouth and received the freedom of the borough.[112] It was to be his last reception as a serving admiral.

And so the final day of Beresford's sea-going career dawned. It was, said *The Times*, 'very many years' since a 'naval officer had received such a demonstration of goodwill'. As the *King Edward VII* docked at Portsmouth, Beresford was awaited by a port welcoming committee of Admiral Sir Arthur Fanshawe (Commander-in-Chief), Captain E. Hyde Parker (Flag Captain) and Vice Admiral C.G. Robinson. They boarded the flagship to witness Beresford's last farewells to his crew and then accompanied him, with Sturdee and Browning, in Fanshawe's carriage. Despite the cool, cloud-covered day, at the dockyard railway station they found 'the townsmen assembled in thousands' and a similar animated crowd awaited Beresford and his wife at the town station, where their train for London awaited them. Along the route between the two stations, *The Times* noted that they had driven through a double file of 'motor-cars decked with Union Jacks'. At the station itself, the deafening sounding of the car horns was 'almost drowned by the vociferous cheering' of the crowds.[113]

At Waterloo a few hours later, the same spirited atmosphere greeted the Beresfords. So pressing were the crowds at the station, that the police had been compelled to clear two platforms to maintain order. As the train came into view, the onlookers spontaneously erupted into the singing of *For He's a Jolly Good Fellow* and, when the train drew to halt, hundreds rushed towards it. Hemmed in by the throng, all Beresford could do was to raise his hat in response to the rapturous welcome. So desperate were the crowds to get a sight of the great admiral, that a nearby empty train was rapidly filled with spectators, leaning out of the carriage windows in eager anticipation. The roof of the train was commandeered by press photographers and the general public even occupied the engine and tender.

If the Government needed any warning of what they had taken on in confronting Beresford, these wild scenes of public frenzy were clear enough. On the other hand, if Beresford needed any warning of how isolated he was in the political establishment, he needed only to look at the great and the good who had turned out to welcome him. There was not one person of any significance in Whitehall. There were though, two names that told all: Mr Harold F. Wyatt and Mr L.G.H. Horton Smith, the founders of the Imperial Maritime League. It was as if a senior Labour politician of today found a reception committee being led by the Socialist Workers' Party or, for a Tory, found one under the banner of the UK Independence Party.

The path to his goal of First Sea Lord was not to prove as smooth as this heroic welcome might, at first glance, have implied.

# Act 9

# Maelstrom

The main object was to drive the present Board of the
Admiralty out of office. – *Beresford's admission to Hankey.*[1]

## Scene 1: Beresford writes a letter

Dismissed, disgraced in the eyes of some, a hero for others, Beresford
seethed with anger over his failed battles with the Admiralty. Well before
stepping ashore, he had been mulling over what to do next. In mid-
February, he seemed resolved to accept defeat, telling Bellairs that 'I shall
do and say nothing.'[2] This uncharacteristic mood did not last long and, six
days later, Bellairs received a voluminous letter, full of ammunition for
him to use 'to trap this untruthful man [McKenna]'.[3] On the following day,
Beresford was congratulating his tame MP on the question he had asked
about the period of Beresford's Channel appointment.[4] Not content with
McKenna's reply, Bellairs drafted a new question, which Beresford felt
'looks as if I was behind you'. He suggested amendments to avoid this,
emphasising that Bellairs should refer to Beresford's dismissal. 'Keep on
the word "DISMISSAL",' he repeated.[5]

Unsure how best to wreak his revenge, Beresford met Asquith in mid-
January to discuss the state of the Navy. He was, he told Noel, encouraged
to find that the Prime Minister already 'knew that the state of morale of the
service was very grave' and 'seemed uneasy about the Navy generally'.[6]
In the following month, after a dinner with Asquith, he was able to tell
Noel that he was even further convinced that the Prime Minister was on
his side since 'he could not help agreeing with some of the points I made'.[7]
In fact, just a week after the dinner, Asquith told his wife that he was
tempted to 'cashier' his headstrong admiral.[8] It was not to be the last time
that Beresford would misread Asquith's intentions in the turbulent year
ahead.

Beresford blamed 'a determined Government' for having cut short his
command, so it was no surprise that, by mid-February, his thoughts were
turning to renewing his Parliamentary career. He was, however, still a
serving naval officer, so, as he told Captain Troubridge, Commodore of the
Royal Navy Barracks, it was 'impossible' for him to talk openly about his

175

plans.[9] It was feasible to plot, though, as long as he was discreet, and his next port of call was Balfour.

In approaching Balfour, Beresford seems to have been less guarded, so was over-playing his hand. After bombarding him with his so familiar litany of troubles at the Admiralty, he then attempted to bribe his interlocutor. For some time Beresford had been convinced that the Liberal Government was about to fall and that Balfour would soon be once more Prime Minister. How would it be, he asked, if he agreed to say nothing about the naval failures and, in return, Balfour promised to make him First Lord?[10] It was an offer Balfour did not take up.

Whatever his intentions, the fact that Beresford had selected the Prime Minister and the Leader of the Opposition as his first ports of call was a clear sign that he had no desire to keep quiet.

On his first day on half-pay, Beresford finally made a move. Writing once more to Balfour, he told him that he had 'resolved that the country should know the whole truth' and that he proposed to 'begin a campaign'. First, though, he wanted to consult him on tactics.[11] Two days later, he once more poured out his grievances to Balfour, who listened, but declined to respond immediately. Next day, in a letter to Beresford, Balfour gave his opinion. Carefully avoiding any indication of direct support for Beresford's plans, he wrote: 'You ask me whether I see any objection to your publicly raising these points in the near future. I do not see that I can raise *any* objection,' but, he added, 'you should tell the Prime Minister what you propose to do.'[12]

Taking Balfour's advice, Beresford saw Asquith on 30 March and returned home to write the letter of his life. It took him two days to compose and ran to around 2,500 words. Dated 2 April and addressed to Asquith, the letter began with a reference to 'your recent utterances on naval affairs', but swiftly moved to Beresford's justification for writing: 'If, at this critical moment in the destinies of the Empire, I remained silent . . . I should be wanting in my duty to the Navy and the nation.'[13]

There then followed the two fundamental charges that he was to make year in and year out from that day until his death:

During the whole of my tenure of the command of the Channel Fleet proper, that force, owing to the number of vessels constantly withdrawn from it for the purposes of refit, has never, even for a day, been equal to the force which it might have to encounter in home waters. During that period the fleets in home waters have not been organised in readiness for war, and they are not organised in readiness for war now, to-day.[14]

The letter rambled on, mixing technical criticisms of naval procedures with personal complaints and gripes against Tweedmouth and others. Beresford had been careful not to ask for any specific action on the

Government's part. He well knew that his letter might be printed and circulated throughout Whitehall and, perhaps, further. Instead, he reserved his bite for a handwritten covering letter:

I do not intend to make any public statement until after the 14th April by which time you will no doubt have had leisure to verify the remarks contained in enclosure No. I [his main letter].[15]

Asquith was left to read into this letter whatever he wished, but Sykes already knew his intentions. In a letter to Arnold White, she explained that, 'He said he will give the Government till April 14 to decide whether they would act on his advice or not & if they do not do so, will then publish his letter which will reveal everything to the English people.'[16] It was pure blackmail from a servant of the Government. How should Asquith respond?

It is clear from the Sykes' letter that Beresford had talked freely about his approach to Asquith. Indeed, he even gave an interview to a Paris newspaper in which he described his 'ultimatum' to the Prime Minister.[17] This – or perhaps just coincidence – may explain why, on 6 April, Asquith was faced with a parliamentary question from the Liberal member Mr George Faber, who asked 'whether, in view of the grave and growing anxiety regarding the Navy, he will forthwith instate an inquiry into the workings of the Board of Admiralty and Naval Administration?'[18] Whatever the case, Asquith must have suspected that Beresford was mustering his forces against the possibility that there was no reply to his letter.

Fisher heard about the imminent enquiry around 8 April. His dramatic letter reporting the news to McKenna began: 'A thunder-clap half an hour after you left!' Jellicoe had met Lord Morley at their club, where he had learnt that 'an enquiry seemed imminent and unavoidable, and had gone so far that the constitution of the Commission had been fixed at six members of the House of Lords and six members of the House of Commons'.[19] Fisher was outraged to find that 'a meeting of officers on the Active List, in a room in Grosvenor Street [Beresford's house], is able to coerce a Cabinet and force the strongest Board of Admiralty to totter to its fall!'[20] Esher, in a letter to Balfour, expressed his horror at the thought that 'the Government are contemplating some sort of "Enquiry" into the Admiralty'. He had earlier tried to persuade Fisher to announce his retirement for 21 October, 'But *now*, in face of attacks, I have strongly urged him to wait till he is *turned out* by a file of marines.'[21]

Whatever actions Asquith did take – and it is not clear how widely he consulted about his response – he did consult McKenna, who offered his advice. The measured tone of that counsel suggests that McKenna had not been shown the blackmail letter and so was only able to respond to the more formal one. He was, he told the Prime Minister, in favour of his suggestion of an enquiry by the Committee of Imperial Defence. It would,

177

he said, 'be the surest way to bring immediate peace' and 'the ultimate vindication of the Admiralty'. What was more, once an enquiry had been announced, the matter would become *sub judice* so 'critics would have to keep silence'. Having commented favourably on Asquith's solution, he then proffered some advice that Asquith was to ignore, so for ever casting a shadow over the conclusions of the enquiry. The enquiry committee should, he wrote, include 'two distinguished admirals – say, Sir Arthur Wilson and Admiral Neville'.[22]

With McKenna's support, Asquith now felt able to go ahead. Replying to Beresford's letter (just inside the deadline) he told him that 'Statements so grave upon matters so vital to national safety, proceeding from an officer of your eminence and your long distinguished service, clearly call for prompt and thorough examination.' He would, he said, hold an enquiry, adding: 'I shall myself preside.' Without having thought through just how he would structure his enquiry, Asquith assured Beresford that 'I shall take steps to secure that those who are associated with me in conducting it are both impartial and competent.'[23] If he had any particular steps in mind, they have gone to the grave with him. As we shall see, he took care to *exclude* competent people from the enquiry, eschewing appropriate members and taking no steps to call relevant witnesses. (Indeed, not one witness appeared at the request of Asquith.) The casualness with which he approached this task was fully in character. He always preferred to leave stones unturned and, when forced to do so, limited himself to the minimum acceptable response.

Why exactly Asquith agreed to an enquiry so readily has always been a mystery. Known as 'Mr Wait and See', he was renowned for inaction and prevarication. If an issue could wait, it always did. So why the haste in this case? Clearly, one factor was Beresford's blackmail deadline of fourteen days, but Asquith could have negotiated over that. One explanation that is often put forward is that he was keen to wreak revenge on the Board who had burdened his budgets with heavy estimates when he was Chancellor of the Exchequer and continued to cause him problems as Prime Minister. He had, he told Campbell-Bannerman in 1906 'very little confidence in the present lot of Sea Lords'.[24] It has been suggested that, through an enquiry, he would be able to delve into the Admiralty's secrets and, perhaps, gain the upper hand over them. As we shall see, if this was his aim, he made little effort to pursue it.

Although there had still been no public announcement of the enquiry, reactions and comment were freely circulating. Knollys feared that such an enquiry 'would not confine itself into its official instructions' and would be used to 'make a scapegoat of Fisher'.[25] On the other hand, when Beresford heard there was to be an enquiry, he was 'very glad' and thought that Asquith's presidency showed 'the importance of the enquiry'.[26] The London Chamber of Commerce, who should have known nothing about the enquiry at this time welcomed it 'with great satisfaction'.[27] This they could do because, 'pledged' by Beresford 'to secrecy', he had read to them both his letter and Asquith's reply.[28]

Asquith's continuing reluctance to say anything in public was leading to increasing misunderstandings as to what was going on. Balfour was alarmed at 'anything in the nature of a *parliamentary* or even semi-public enquiry' (which Asquith never proposed) and thought a CID enquiry would be better (which was just what Asquith had decided).[29]

While all this speculation continued, Asquith at last informed the King of his decision and assured him that the enquiry membership would include Sir Arthur Wilson 'whose authority in the navy is probably greater than that of any other officer'.[30]

With just a few days to go before the enquiry started, demands began to be heard for a peerage for Beresford. Knollys suspected that Sir Thomas Brassey, a noted authority on naval affairs, had started the campaign, but Asquith quickly put a stop to the idea. Knollys agreed, saying that 'the moment is not at present opportune'. The idea that he should receive 'a high reward' just after 'the Admiralty shortened his command by a year' seemed to him, he told Asquith, 'absurd'. He could not resist adding that 'all the same it would be very amusing if he & Fisher were in the House of Lords together'.[31] Oddly, according to Esher, the King seems to have been in favour of the peerage.[32]

On 19 April, Asquith asked Esher to call on him. After showing him Beresford's letter, which he found 'very temperate and well written', Asquith told him of the proposed membership of the committee.[33] This was to be Grey, Haldane, Crewe, Wilson, Esher, with Asquith in the chair. At the same time, Asquith asked Esher to draft the terms of reference in consultation with Ottley, which he did the following day. His terms, Esher said, covered 'all the charges in Beresford's letter ... It is useless to shirk anything!'[34]

This initial membership seemed very sensible: a sprinkling of Cabinet ministers, Wilson as the revered naval authority and Esher, well-respected for his work on committees to reorganise the Army. Only Crewe was the odd man out. Just sixteen months earlier, Esher had noted in his journal that Crewe had told him that 'if the C.I.D. had insisted on examining C. Beresford, he would have retired from the Committee. He agrees to the impossibility of a Naval enquiry'.[35]

Beresford vigorously objected to the presence of Wilson and Esher on the committee. Both were promptly dropped. Esher was most relieved to find that 'I am *not* to have to adjudicate.'[36] Wilson, never one to speak a word when silence was an option, left no comment. Meanwhile, not having been told of Wilson's discharge, the King wrote to Asquith to congratulate him on his choice, saying that the selection 'is an excellent one, as his views will be of the greatest value being one of the most distinguished Officers of the Navy'.[37]

In a letter to Ponsonby, Fisher revealed his outrage at the events of the last few weeks. Asquith had conceded an enquiry to Beresford which, he said, had but one object: 'to discredit me.' He had then selected Wilson without first consulting Wilson's employer – the Admiralty; Beresford had objected 'and he is taken off the Committee'; next 'Esher is especially invited to serve' but 'Beresford objects and Esher's appointment is cancelled'. Fisher then went on to complain at the freedom that Beresford was being given to summon 'as witnesses my own personal staff'. Such behaviour, he said, would only have been tolerated by 'a pack of cowards'.[38] For all the bias that Fisher inevitably brought to the situation, he had pinpointed the weak point of the enquiry: Asquith's fear of the aristocratic Beresford. Cashiering him was Asquith's daydream – face-to-face, he surrendered to all his demands.

Just twenty-two days after Beresford had sent his letter to Asquith, *The Times* announced the formation of the committee and noted that its members would be Asquith, Grey, Haldane and Crewe. In fact the 'well-informed correspondent' who passed this story to the newspaper had omitted one member: Lord Morley, added as a make-weight when Wilson and Esher were dropped. Commenting on the membership, the article noted that 'to secure an absolutely unbiased tribunal' there would be 'no naval officer ... upon it'.[39] And so, in the interests of lack of bias, Asquith had thrown aside his commitment to ensure a competent committee. Instead, a bunch of amateurs who, throughout the fifteen days of the enquiry would struggle to understand even the basics of the issues under discussion, were left to arbitrate on matters of extraordinary technical complexity.

Asquith seems to have given no thought to witnesses, which left Beresford free to make the running. As a result, on 22 April his list of seventeen proposed witnesses landed on the Prime Minister's desk. Beresford had neatly recorded the officers he wished to call, with their ranks and the items on which they could give evidence. He had one full admiral (Custance), one vice admiral (Berkeley Milne, his late second-in-command in the Channel), three rear admirals (Sturdee, Slade and Bethell), six captains, one commander, three Admiralty clerks, one historian and one civil servant.[40] Acting as if he were in charge of the enquiry, he sent a copy of the list to Ottley, telling him that he had noted 'what I wish them to be examined upon'. He was also going to tell Asquith that Slade, then in the East Indies, 'should be ordered by telegram' to send his papers in.[41] On receiving the list, Ottley told Beresford that Asquith 'does not give you any undertaking that he will be able to hear them all'.[42] In practice, most were never called, and only Custance was heard at length.

Around this time Beresford fired off letters to various officers telling them that he was going to call them as witnesses. Milne and Captain Brock received such letters, along with a copy of the '8 heads for this enquiry'. Beresford peremptorily told Milne that 'I shall demand the presence of both of you.'[43] None of his correspondents responded with any enthusiasm. A typical, reserved reply came from Milne who declined, saying 'Considering my present position, I think it would be inadvisable to name me as a witness before the Court [sic].'[44] These were the first indications that, apart from the faithful Custance, Beresford would have to fight his battle single-handed. After all the years of bluff talk about 'every officer in the Navy' supporting him, he was to search in vain for one single active-list officer beyond Custance who would willingly second his case before the committee.

Doubtless Beresford would have put this down to fear of victimisation. When in command of the Channel Fleet, he had made extravagant claims about officers who had criticised Admiralty policy and were then overlooked for promotion. Now he raised the same charge in connection with witnesses for the enquiry. He had, he told Asquith, 'two letters from Captains' who feared that answering questions before the enquiry 'must more or less be regarded as a criticism of authority'. In consequence 'they must ask for some protection as their future career might be absolutely ruined for expressing their opinion'.[45] Asquith provided the assurance that Beresford sought, telling him that 'he might assure his friends that no prejudice of any kind to their future careers could result from their evidence – whatever that might be'.[46] The task of ensuring this was delegated to McKenna when Ottley asked him to 'take due care to safeguard their interests'.[47] Whatever care McKenna took, it was not to satisfy Beresford: his charge of victimisation would still be alive long after the enquiry was over.

Emboldened by the free ride that Asquith had given him so far, Beresford finally overstepped the mark when he despatched Custance to ask for permission to rummage through the index of the Naval Intelligence Department in search of documents that the two of them could use as evidence. Ottley's initial reaction was encouraging – 'I should imagine there will be no objection'[48] – but Asquith declared the suggestion to be 'an entirely inadmissible demand'.[49]

## Scene 2: The return of the Bacon letters

On the very day that Beresford despatched his letter to Asquith, Sir George Armstrong, proprietor of *The Globe* newspaper, gave a speech to the Constitutional Club. At first glance, this had no connection with Beresford's campaign, and there is nothing to suggest that the timing was anything other than coincidence – but it was a conjunction that was most painful to Fisher and most convenient for Beresford.

According to Widenmann, a German naval attaché, Sir George Armstrong had been discharged from the Navy in 1892 'on account of imprudent remarks about Sir John Fisher'. Forced 'to apologise publicly, he had vowed vengeance'.[50] To this end, he had steadily collected material that might be used against Fisher if and when an opportunity arose. Sensing that his moment had come, Armstrong decided to go public. His weapon was to be one of the Bacon letters of 1906 (Act 6) that had fallen into his hands.

Armstrong's speech formed part of his campaign for election as Member of Parliament for Pembroke Boroughs. After opening with a long attack on the Government's dreadnought policy, he launched into an assault on Fisher, whose 'autocratic power ... could not fail to have the most evil consequences'. It had led, he said, to 'a system of favouritism and cliquism'. After claiming that 'he did not wish to make an attack on one particular man', he then did exactly that, saying that Fisher had set up 'a system of espionage' in the Navy. Waving a document in his hand which he declared to be 'a letter written by an officer who was at the time a captain of less than six years' seniority' giving 'his opinions on various officers in the Navy who were his senior officers' he brought to light one of Bacon's long-forgotten Mediterranean letters.[51]

Fisher, in a pained letter to McKenna, described his fury at 'the cad Armstrong's quotation of ... [a] private letter to me' and Bacon, he told him, was 'distressed'. How Armstrong came to have the letter was a mystery to him. 'So far as I remember,' he told McKenna, 'I got it printed for the First Lord – obviously it was not meant for circulation.'[52] Unfortunately for Fisher the letter *was* now in circulation, although almost all who commented on it never read it. One such non-reader was the Liberal MP Captain Carr-Gomm who, in a parliamentary question, asked McKenna whether he was aware that 'the letter revealed a system of espionage, and that the captain who wrote it criticised his superior officers wholesale'.[53] McKenna rejected the charge, saying that the letter had been 'written by Captain R.M. Bacon, now Director of Naval Ordnance, an officer who has the full confidence of the Board of Admiralty. I have read the letter; it is a perfectly proper letter to have been written'. He added that 'I cannot find in it the smallest ground for any of the calumnious charges which have been made upon it.'[54]

Armstrong presented the Bacon letter as if it were just one of many such reports to Fisher. He had no evidence to support such an assertion, but then nor did Beresford. That did not stop the latter from telling Milne that 'I know several more cases which are as bad, or even worse.'[55] Such mud was liable to stick, even if Beresford never produced a jot of evidence to substantiate his charge. Fisher was bound by regulations to remain

182

silent, so it was left to McKenna to issue the denials. When Ernest Meysey-Thompson, Unionist MP for Handsworth, asked in the Commons 'if subordinate officers in the Navy have been making reports about their superior officers', McKenna replied that 'No such reports have been made.'[56]

There were more Commons questions on 11, 12, 19 and 24 May as members sought to prove that Fisher had maliciously spied on officers and circulated reports based on the information that he had collected, all at the taxpayer's expense. Beresford remained silent, but it is unlikely that he did not assist from behind the scenes. In particular, Bellairs made two interventions on 19 May. In one case he wished to know whether there were any more such letters – a piece of information Beresford was desperate to get hold of. McKenna, though, brushed the question aside saying that he declined 'to give information with regard to confidential documents'.[57]

It was on that same day that McKenna sought to put an end to the questioning by personally defending Bacon and Fisher. Of Bacon he said 'The only crime, if it be a crime, that he has committed is that he is a very able man who writes remarkably good letters.' The letters, he added, were printed 'without his knowledge'. In Fisher's case, he told the House that 'He [Fisher] regrets, and nobody regrets it more than himself, that without editing those letters first they were printed for private use.'[58] (This was a reference to the fact that one letter had, most unfortunately for Fisher, mentioned Bellairs by name.)

Day after day, questions were asked in the Commons as to who had authorised the circulation of the letters and how widely they had been distributed. McKenna had stuck to the official line that copies had been made solely for use inside the Admiralty (a normal practice before the days of office photocopiers). Inevitably, there were more Commons questions later in the day. At last, on 27 May, McKenna went on the offensive and tore apart Armstrong's whole thesis of 'systematic espionage'. How was it, he asked, that there could be such a widespread system if 'the only evidence that can be produced three years afterwards … is the production of a letter three years old[?]'[59]

And there, but for some personal bickering about exactly how Armstrong came to have the letters, the episode petered out – for now. Meanwhile, the Beresford Enquiry had been in progress for exactly one month. Charges more serious than circulating tittle-tattle had been under consideration.

## Scene 3: The Cabinet wants to know

The enquiry committee assembled on 27 April 1909, twenty-three years after Beresford had presented the Board with his paper on want of war organisation. It had been rejected without consideration and Salisbury had sought to console him with the advice that 'you must have more experience'.[60] Since then, hardly a day seemed to pass without Beresford making a disparaging comment about the Admiralty. Governments came and went, Boards came and went, yet his song never changed: the country was not organised for war. Finally, a Government had listened, admittedly only after having relieved him of his command. His spirits rose, certain that finally he would turf the Board out and soon be First Lord or, if he had to compromise, First Sea Lord.

The remit of the committee was enigmatically stated in the enquiry's ludicrously long title: *A Sub-Committee of the Committee of Imperial Defence to Inquire into Certain Questions of Naval Policy Raised by Lord Charles Beresford.* (From here onwards, the Beresford Enquiry Committee.) The committee was asked to consider eight points of dispute:

1. Whether from the 15th April, 1907, to the 24th March, 1909, the Channel Fleet has 'never been equal to the force which it might have to encounter in Home waters'.
2. Whether during that period the fleets in Home waters have been organised in readiness for war, and are so organised to-day.
3. Whether during the same period there was such a deficiency in Home waters in small craft and destroyers as to constitute a grave weakness.
4. Whether the types of British torpedo craft were unsuitable for the purposes required.
5. Whether the organisation and distribution of His Majesty's Fleets in Home waters were during the period in question strategically sound, and provided a sufficient margin of superiority, after allowing for the absence of ships in dockyard hands, to safeguard us against sudden attack.
6. Whether it is a fact that, 'whatever were the scope and nature of a strategical scheme to be put into operation on the outbreak of war, no such plan, under the existing organisation, could immediately be put into execution'.
7. Whether it is a fact that the strategical schemes and plans for the disposal of the forces under the orders of the Commander-in-Chief of the Channel Fleet in war were not transmitted to Lord Charles Beresford on his assuming that command.
8. Whether it has been the custom of the Board of Admiralty to transmit in time of peace War Plans to the Commanders-in-Chief of sea-going fleets.[61]

These were highly technical issues. To answer them, in addition to receiving 246 pages of documents, the committee heard evidence that produced 328 pages of transcripts, not to mention numerous papers which were tabled but not retained in the archives. (According to the report, over

2,600 questions were put to Beresford – a figure repeated again and again in other publications. In fact, there were far, far fewer questions, the 2,600 figure being the total of numbered paragraphs in the report.)

Any systematic account of the interminable hours of discussion would be tedious in the extreme. So, since this is a book about a feud between two men, we will concentrate on the *style* of Beresford's attack and the *style* of the Admiralty defence – a defence which was, of course, largely prepared by Fisher.

The seriousness with which the Admiralty took the enquiry can be seen in Ottley's remark to Haldane when he told him that 'for six months during which the Beresford Enquiry was proceeding the entire thinking machinery of the Admiralty was concentrated on that question'. In consequence, 'every other matter was necessarily shelved'.[62]

The five members of the committee – Asquith, Crewe, Morley, Grey and Haldane – were all experienced Cabinet ministers, who felt at home in the corridors of power, yet not one of them had the sort of forceful character that was needed to confront Beresford. They were bookish men, reserved, used to quiet conversation on great issues and much averse to bombastic display. Only in one respect could they hope to tower over Beresford: in intellect. Asquith had sailed through the City of London School and Balliol College Oxford, carrying off prizes and scholarships without the least visible effort. This he followed by a career in journalism and the bar, before entering Parliament. Crewe also enjoyed a sound academic pedigree, having been educated at Harrow followed by Trinity College Cambridge. As well as being an active politician, he wrote and translated poetry. No less lacking in distinction, Morley followed his attendance at University College School by graduating from Lincoln College Oxford, after which he took up a career in journalism and writing. Haldane could even boast attendance at two universities, having studied at both Edinburgh and Göttingen. Only Grey was less distinguished in this sense. Although he attended both Winchester College and Balliol College, Oxford, he showed no academic promise and left with a third-class degree.

Against this glittering array of talent, Beresford was soon out of his depth. His paltry education had given him no opportunity to learn that language mattered. He had grown up in a world where pompous generalities and bold assertions served for argument. His inquisitors had all, from an early age, learnt to dissect arguments, to analyse phrases, to query meaning. They used words with care; Beresford regarded them as 'just a term' – a favourite phrase of his. It was to be brains versus brashness.

Another factor that was to influence the enquiry was Asquith's chairmanship. Esher, who had had much opportunity to observe the Prime Minister's laid-back approach to meetings, said he was 'not imposing as a Chairman' and was prone to permit 'an excess of discursive talk'. He saw him as 'a timid man' who 'lacks some element of character; perhaps decision'.[63]

Esher's judgement was borne out by the enquiry. Asquith opened the first meeting by inviting Beresford 'to make an opening statement'.[64] From that moment on, for fifteen sittings, Asquith never regained control of the agenda. Occasionally he would terminate a tedious discussion or rule an item as beyond the scope of the enquiry, but he essentially allowed Beresford to treat the committee as his audience, rather than his master.

Technically this was an enquiry into naval policy, which was the responsibility of the Admiralty. The charges were put by Beresford, who was assisted by his devoted Custance and by his private secretary. Never referred to in the transcript, the role of Beresford's secretary will forever be unclear. However, the contrast between the prompt and orderly way in which Beresford presented the committee with papers and his fumbling attempt to discuss or remember their contents, suggests that the secretary had charge of all the paperwork and the mining of Beresford's records. As to Custance, even he seemed bemused as to his role since, following the first meeting, he sent a letter to Asquith, which resulted in Asquith ruling at the start of the second meeting that he was to be 'regarded ... in the light of a witness'.[65] From then on, Beresford stood alone.

On the Admiralty side were McKenna and Fisher, accompanied by Commander Crease to provide secretarial aid. Fisher was strictly forbidden from saying a word unless requested to do so – this was to prevent the enquiry turning into a slanging match between the two admirals. McKenna could have produced numerous witnesses but, using only papers ably prepared by Fisher and his colleagues, he single-handedly took on Beresford. Summoning all his past skills as a barrister, he had no trouble in quickly turning his accuser into a very uncomfortable witness. At times, Asquith was to restrain McKenna's enthusiasm. Unrestrained, the enquiry would have become a bloodbath. Although calm on the surface, McKenna boiled with fury at Beresford's accusations against him and his colleagues.

**Day one: Tuesday, 27 April**
The very first item discussed on 27 April was one raised by Beresford rather than one prescribed by the enquiry. He asked that the committee see, at that very moment, a witness who 'has had a threat as to whether he gives evidence'. The witness, Captain Arthur H. Hulbert, Assistant Director of Naval Intelligence, was called and he described how, he claimed, Rear Admiral Bethell had told him that he would have to leave the Admiralty if he gave evidence.[66] It was, of course, a misunderstanding, but one that Beresford relished since it gave him yet more confirmation of 'victimisation' in the Navy. When Bethell, who as Director of Naval Intelligence was Hulbert's superior, was called in, it transpired that all that he had done

was to point out that, since he would need Hulbert to help him prepare his evidence for the committee, Hulbert could not also act for Beresford. It was Hulbert who took this to mean he would have to leave the Admiralty.[67]

Having disposed of the Hulbert question, the committee turned to its main purpose. Things got off badly within minutes of starting, when Beresford seemed to say that he had 'nothing more to say' than was in his letter. Asquith had to coach him into starting:

| | |
|---|---|
| *Asquith* | You are prepared to deal with each head *seriatim*, are you? |
| *Beresford* | Yes. |
| *Asquith* | And to substantiate what you say under each head? |
| *Beresford* | Yes. |
| *Asquith* | I suppose that would be the most convenient way of taking it?[68] |

Asquith should, of course, have established this procedure from the start, rather than allow it to arise out of Beresford's apparent inability to begin. The point was, though, irrelevant, since Beresford never stuck to the proposed procedure and, at times, the committee had no idea which item was under discussion.

After these preliminaries, Beresford began his 'opening statement'. It soon turned into a ramble, mixing evidence on his charges with the history of his appointment and arguments about war plans. It was not long before the committee had an early warning of what was to come. He had just recounted the meeting when he finally agreed terms for the Channel Fleet.

| | |
|---|---|
| *Haldane* | Was that the interview of 5th July [1907]? |
| *Beresford* | Yes, it was. |
| *McKenna* | I do not think July was the date – it was January. |
| *Beresford* | Quite true ...[69] |

This was the first of many occasions when Beresford failed to recall his facts correctly, and had to bow to McKenna's more accurate information. On this particular occasion, the confusion was astounding. If Beresford's mind had been in full working order, he must have been aware that he took up command of the Channel Fleet on 15 April 1907 – the date was in the terms of reference – so how could the meeting to agree terms have been *after* that date?

**Day two: Wednesday, 28 April**
When the second meeting opened on 28 April, Grey and Morley showed signs of discomfort with the ramble of the previous day, Asquith having given no direction to the proceedings, driven as they were by whatever idea came into Beresford's head. Doubtless Grey and Morley, with major departments of state to run, were wondering just how long all this was going to take. In an attempt to give some focus to their work, Grey

187

suggested that 'the important point ... was whether the organisation suggested by Lord Charles Beresford, or that adopted by the Admiralty, was preferable as far as capital ships were concerned'. For Morley, the issue was even simpler: all that he wanted to know was 'whether we were at the mercy of the German Fleet during Lord Charles Beresford's tenure of command or not'.[70] These interventions were to prove to be in vain; not until McKenna began his evidence was the committee to work to any clear agenda.

Beresford was due to continue his opening statement, but first wanted to make a complaint about how his role was being portrayed. He told the committee that 'It appears to me now that there is some sort of idea that I am here in the nature of a prosecutor or on my defence or something of that sort.' If that were so, he added, 'I would rather make my case somewhere else.'[71] This threat seemed to arise from the fact that Bethell had been informed that Hulbert was to attend the Committee. Asquith made it clear that he considered this a mere act of courtesy, with no sinister implications at all. Beresford refused to let go and a bad-tempered dispute followed.

Once Asquith had been able to calm Beresford down, the latter returned to his opening statement, which he had begun the previous day. His central charge was that, all the time that he had been in charge of the Channel Fleet, the fleets in home waters had not been organised for war. The committee were puzzled as to why Beresford had accepted the command if this were true:

*Morley*     You would not have taken command if you had not been satisfied that there was a fair working arrangement?
*Beresford*  That is so.
*Morley*     Of course, you took great precaution, and naturally in dealing with Lord Tweedmouth and the Board of Admiralty, and you got an arrangement which satisfied you?
*Beresford*  Yes.[72]

Beresford tried to explain away the contradiction between his charge before the committee and his acceptance of his post in April 1907 by saying that 'the terms agreed upon were not kept'.[73] Like most of Beresford's charges, the more the committee probed, the less substance there seemed to be.

Following a long discussion as to whether the Admiralty had supplied Beresford with regular lists of ships that would be at his disposal in war, Beresford said 'I have finished all that I have got to say ... as a statement.' Then, without any explanation or warning, he launched into an attack on the committee and the Admiralty, saying 'I object to these officers being called witnesses.'[74] Who he meant, he did not make clear, but since it was Beresford himself who first used the word 'witness' of those who appeared before the committee, how could he blame others for following his lead?

When Beresford asked 'I hope I have made myself quite clear', Asquith wearily replied 'Quite clear' and passed on to other business.[75]

The 'other business', though, was a further attempt by Beresford to manipulate the committee. This time he wanted to order an admiral home from his post as Commander-in-Chief in the East Indies:

Beresford    One more thing I must ask – that you recall [Rear] Admiral Slade. [Rear] Admiral Slade will tell you everything ... [Rear] Admiral Slade should be immediately telegraphed to send every paper that he possesses on this question of war organisation ...

Haldane    What difference would that make to us?

Beresford    He was the head of Naval Intelligence Department ...

Haldane    Why should we attach so very great importance to [Rear] Admiral Slade's views if we can get the facts?[76]

Grey, always one to smooth over a difficulty, suggested that Slade could be sent some questions to answer in writing, to which Beresford agreed. Asquith promptly asked Beresford to draft the questions, once more demonstrating his lack of interest in the committee proceedings and his indifference to the outcome. If he had really wanted Slade's expert view, then surely the task of drawing up the questions would have been handed to a member of the CID staff. To pass the task to the very admiral who had been so recently relieved of his command, and who had demonstrated such virulent hostility to the Board, showed how confused the committee was as to its role and who was supposed to be in charge. At least, though, Asquith consented to allow the Admiralty to suggest some questions.[77]

Only a few days after the committee had heard Beresford's views on the distribution of the fleets and Beresford had requested Slade's return home, Meysey-Thompson was on his feet again in the Commons. He requested, in a question to the Prime Minister, that the sub-committee 'inquire into the disposition and organisation of the Home Fleets' and asked whether the report was to be submitted to the Commons.[78] Asquith declined to answer either question. He must surely have seen Beresford's hand behind this intervention. Perhaps the latter had hoped that, by provoking discussion in the Commons, he could yet force Slade's recall. As for Asquith's refusal to comment on publication, this was just one more sign of his indecision as to what he was seeking from the enquiry. Reluctant as he had been to tell the Commons of the existence of the committee, he was to prove even more recalcitrant over the question of publication.

**Day three: Thursday, 29 April**
On the third day Beresford continued his opening statement. A good deal of the discussion was around the war plans that he had been handed in April 1907. These came in four parts – there would be much dispute as to

whether he had received all the parts at the same time – but most of the dispute that day concerned Part 1, which Beresford derogatively called 'the pedagogue's plan'. 'Pedagogue' here referred to the fact that it had been prepared by the naval historian, Sir Julian Corbett. In fact the war plans themselves were in Parts 2, 3 and 4 – Part 1 was an overview only, but it suited Beresford to pretend this was part of the war plans:

> Beresford    As a literary effort everything contained in it was sound common sense, but it would be of no use when I want to fight.
> Asquith    This is what you call the pedagogue's plan?
> Beresford    Yes ...

Later:

> Beresford    The pedagogue's plan is a splendid thing to read to school-children – excellent ...[79]

This was the sort of knockabout fun that Beresford had enjoyed for years as he criticised the Board with his friends and supporters. He was soon to find that such colourful generalisations were not enough to satisfy the committee.

## Day four: Tuesday, 4 May

On the fourth day, there was a sudden change of tone when McKenna, without any apparent reason, began an unpleasant attack on Beresford's sea-going career, about which he seemed to know a lot more than Beresford:

> McKenna    Your first appointment as a commissioned officer was, I believe, as a sub-lieutenant in the 'Clio' in January 1866?
> Beresford    I am afraid I cannot remember ...
> McKenna    You were appointed Rear-Admiral on 16th September, 1897?
> Beresford    That I cannot remember ...
> McKenna    During the thirty-one years between your appointment as a sub-lieutenant and your appointment as Rear-Admiral, your experience at sea, apart from service in a Royal Yacht, amounted to eight years 250 days?
> Beresford    That I cannot tell you ...

Later:

> Beresford    I should think that is incorrect; but I will get it for you.[80]

It was to be the first of many occasions when Beresford could not remember key facts and would request that the topic be deferred to another day.

It was on that same day that one of Beresford's more stupid evasions took place. This was occasioned by his accusation that he had not been issued with war plans when he took over the Channel Fleet. The argument went back and forth until it became obvious that Beresford was in the wrong. McKenna then laid into him, sharply putting Custance into his place:

McKenna   I put it to you that the universal practice of the Navy, without question, so far as history goes back, has been for the Admiralty to issue War Orders to the Commander-in-Chief, and for the Commander-in-Chief to draw up his detailed War Plan to execute them – I do not want Sir Reginald Custance to answer this question, please; I want Lord Charles to answer it – it was for the Commander-in-Chief to draw up a plan upon those War Orders and submit his War Plan to the Admiralty?

Beresford could only fall back on the ludicrous prevarication of pretending he did not know what the term 'war plan' meant:

Beresford   I must understand what you mean by the War Plan.
McKenna   I will give you a copy of a War Order.
Beresford   This was the War Plan you refer to . . .
McKenna   These are the War Orders transmitted to you when you took command of the Channel Fleet. When the Channel Fleet was turned over to you, did you find these War Orders left by your predecessor? [Beresford was then handed the document of 24 June 1905.]
Beresford   I do not remember them . . .
McKenna   Those were the War Orders?
Beresford   They are not headed War Orders.[81]

Beresford steadfastly refused to admit that the Admiralty had never – prior to April 1907 – issued war plans to home fleets in peace-time. His resulting evasions reduced the enquiry to a farce. If the so-recently most senior admiral afloat were to maintain that he did not know what the term 'war plan' meant, what hope was there for a serious discussion of his charges?

McKenna knew that he had Beresford cornered and, for once, Asquith allowed him to continue questioning. McKenna held out the very same war orders that had been handed to Beresford in 1905:

McKenna   Is that the kind of document that the Commander-in-Chief would receive from his predecessor . . ., which would be known under the name of War Orders?

191

*Beresford*   Yes; but I do not think it would be known under the name of War Orders.

*McKenna*   Under what name?

*Beresford*   I could not tell until I look at my papers.[82]

Rather than admit that war orders had always been called war orders, and nothing else, Beresford hid behind the pretence that he needed to check his records before answering.

It was not long before Beresford got himself into another corner on this difficult day, this time trying to deny that he had received documents that he clearly had been given. This was no academic point since the Admiralty knew that Beresford had received the war plans under dispute in 1907 – indeed Beresford's own critique of the plans, dated April 1907, was reproduced in the enquiry appendices.

*McKenna*   When did you receive War Plans, Parts 2, 3, and 4?

*Beresford*   I cannot remember until I look at my papers ...[83]

Beresford then tried to insist that Fisher had given him Part 1 ('the pedagogue's plan') on an earlier occasion.

*McKenna*   Do you seriously dispute that the whole of these parts were handed to you at one time, bound together?

*Beresford*   No. I do not remember. They may have been ...[84]

Asquith then pressed Beresford to admit that he had already talked about receiving all four parts at the same time. Beresford's answer made no sense at all.

*Beresford*   Certainly I did not get the pedagogue's plan first and the others some days afterwards – of that I am perfectly clear. Whether I got them the same day or not, of that I am not quite sure. I think I was there [at the Admiralty] on two days.[85]

What the committee concluded from that is hard to imagine.

Beresford had made great play about not having had a sufficient force at his command to face the German threat. As he talked, McKenna realised that Beresford had very confused ideas as to what force the Germans might put to sea, so he decided to probe Beresford's understanding of his adversary:

*McKenna*   What is the constitution of the German High Sea Fleet?

*Beresford*   I have given it in the paper. I think it is eighteen battleships.[86]

*McKenna*   Can you tell me what the organised German High Sea Fleet which our fleet will have to meet consisted of?

192

| | |
|---|---|
| *Beresford* | I can tell you what it might be and what it is at this minute. |
| *McKenna* | Will you tell me what it is at this minute? |
| *Beresford* | I have put it in writing, and it has gone in. |
| *Crewe* | You said just now, I think, that eighteen battleships were together for eight months and were trained all together; I should like to know if that is so? |
| *Beresford* | They can be, because they all refit all their ships together; they have got about four months off.[87] |

Whether Beresford really did not know, or just could not be bothered to reply to McKenna, is not clear. Whatever was the case, McKenna seized his opportunity for a barrister's put-down:

| | |
|---|---|
| *McKenna* | If you do not know these things as an expert, I will not put the question to you. Do you wish it to go in before the Committee that the High Sea Fleet consists of eighteen battleships, six armoured cruisers and six small cruisers?[88] |

Defeated, Beresford fell back on an answer that he would often use to end an argument that he could not win:

| | |
|---|---|
| *Beresford* | The 'High Sea Fleet' is a term.[89] |

McKenna, seeing the weakness of Beresford's stand, did not let up:

| | |
|---|---|
| *McKenna* | The point that I am endeavouring to establish now is that in April 1907, when Lord Charles Beresford took charge of the Channel Fleet, the constitution of the German Navy was such that the Channel Fleet gave absolute security to this country, even under Lord Charles. |
| *Beresford* | Fourteen battleships, four armoured cruisers, and three un-armoured cruisers; we should have to fight the German Fleet with that force. |
| *McKenna* | No. |
| *Beresford* | But that was the Channel Fleet. |
| *McKenna* | The constitution of the Channel Fleet gave security to this country, coupled as it was with the Atlantic Fleet and the Home Fleet ... you say the country was in danger; in April 1907, what was the condition of Germany for fighting at that time?[90] |

Beresford gave an evasive reply.

| | |
|---|---|
| *McKenna* | Are you aware that in the organization of the German Fleet the High Sea Fleet consisted in April 1907, of twenty-five ships only? |
| *Beresford* | I dare say ... but that has nothing to do with my point ...[91] |

This was the first intimation the committee had that, when Beresford compared his fleet to others, he discounted any of his vessels that were in dock, even if only for an hour or so, but assumed every German ship was instantly available, even including those away in the Baltic. His non-sensical comparisons would be torn further apart by McKenna in due course.

The terrible fourth day continued as McKenna then set about Beresford's contradictory arguments over the possibility of a surprise attack by Germany – a 'bolt from the blue'.

It took McKenna four attempts to get Beresford to answer 'yes' or 'no' to the simple question: 'are you assuming that the Germans would attack us in a time of profound peace, without warning?' Finally, Beresford answered 'yes'.[92] McKenna knew full well that Beresford did not keep his fleet in a state of alert which was compatible with such a belief, so he set about to demonstrate the gap between Beresford's rhetoric and his behaviour:

*McKenna*  Would you keep steam ready?

*Beresford*  Don't ask such questions as that.

*McKenna*  I only want to know.

*Beresford*  You have always got steam ready when you are out ...

*McKenna*  Would you have officers' and men's leave stopped in the High Sea Fleet [presumably McKenna meant the Channel Fleet]?

*Beresford*  If you are going into these questions I am afraid I must decline to answer anything so absurd.

*McKenna*  Did you institute a practice in the Channel Fleet of giving Friday to Monday leave to half the crews on two weeks in each month?

*Beresford*  Certainly ...

*McKenna*  On your supposition of a bolt from the blue, I suppose that if the Germans were aware of the practice they would have chosen a Friday or a Saturday for their attack.

*Beresford*  I really could not tell you what the Germans might or might not do.

*McKenna*  Is it not the fact that that practice of giving week-end leave would prevent the ships being ready to take part in war for at least twenty-four, and possibly forty-eight hours?[93]

Beresford gave a contradictory reply to this question in which he both claimed that the ships would go to sea immediately in such an emergency and that he could get the men back.

*McKenna*  I only want to show that your own action as Commander-in-Chief indicates that you yourself believe that we should

194

always have twenty-four hours or forty-eight hours before
the ships of war would be required ...

*Beresford*   I think you are putting words into my mouth ...[94]

The committee must have been flabbergasted by Beresford's insolent
replies to his superior. In a world where deference to rank and position
was the order of the day, what they were witnessing was unheard of.

At the end of the fourth day, Beresford had suffered a grilling such as he
had never before had in his life. Faced with McKenna's courtroom skills
and his mastery of detail, Beresford's case looked weaker by the hour. It is
no surprise to find that Fisher was feeling more cheerful as a result. In a
letter to Ponsonby, he described Beresford's performance under 'cross-
examination' that day, saying that the committee had 'roped him in on
every single point so far'. However, Fisher was concerned at 'the obvious
desire of the committee to get him out of his mess'. Beresford, he continued, 'refuses to answer questions when we get him into a tight place ...
or else he says the question is too absurd to answer – and the Committee
let him have his way and don't insist on his answering'.[95]

Meanwhile, Fisher told Ponsonby, he had to keep silent as he listened to
Beresford's 'most malignant misstatements' and, 'when we bring him to
book, he appeals to Asquith' who, complained Fisher, 'glosses over the
matter'.[96] It was a deeply painful experience for him. As he told Hurd, 'I
am eating dirt and undergoing humiliation' but, he added, 'I am going to
stick it, and stick to it in silence.'[97]

### Day five: Thursday, 6 May

The fifth day opened with Beresford on the attack over McKenna's
apparent slur on his sea time. What had it to do with the case 'unless ... it
was to discredit the witness?' Then, tabling a sheaf of figures, he declared
that his sea service amounted to thirty years – rather more than the eight
years 250 days suggested by McKenna. To bolster his case, he declared 'I
commanded more ships at sea than any man.'[98] Whether this was true or
not, over half of the ships that he 'commanded' were simply ones he took
to sea for trials of a few days when he was in charge of the steam reserve at
Chatham in 1893–6.

The sea-time dispute was left unresolved and was followed by a clash
between Beresford and McKenna over the latter's charge that Beresford
had failed to produce a war plan when ordered to do so in 1907. After
some bickering over dates and plans, McKenna bluntly reminded Beresford what his charge was:

*McKenna*   My statement was that the order was given to you on the
14th June, 1907, and that the order was not obeyed until the
1st June, 1908.[99]

195

Beresford then took the committee on a long digression, referring to plans he submitted on 14 May, 1 June and 6 June – all *before* the order, and so all irrelevant to the point under discussion. In effect, Beresford offered no explanation for his failure to obey the order.

Having got as far as he could on that point, McKenna now raised the question of Beresford's having carried out manoeuvres in 1907 on a plan which the Admiralty had rejected:

*McKenna*   You carried out the manoeuvres of October 1907 on your plan of May?

*Beresford*   By the approval of the Admiralty.

*McKenna*   This is what you told us at the last meeting.

*Beresford*   ... I was doing it under the Orders which I had got in writing.

*McKenna*   Will you produce the Orders we gave you in writing?

*Beresford*   Which?

*McKenna*   The Orders for carrying out the manoeuvres of 1907 ...[100]

Beresford then deflected the discussion away to other plans and documents and it was some time before McKenna could bring him back to the point:

*Beresford*   ... when I took that plan to the First Sea Lord I asked him if I could make out the manoeuvres on it, and he said Yes ...

*McKenna*   I understood you to say you were going to produce it in writing?

*Beresford*   Yes; I will if I can.[101]

He never did.

It was a sad performance and must have been painful for the committee to watch. Beresford's pompous charges evaporated under McKenna's questioning. To the charge that he had failed to produce a war plan for a whole year, all Beresford could do was to huff and puff, and then refer to earlier plans. To the charge that he carried out manoeuvres on a plan rejected by the Board, his response was that they had approved it in writing. Pressed to produce the document, he fell back on Fisher having authorised the manoeuvres verbally.

Within minutes of having made a fool of himself over war plans, he then repeated the same bizarre behaviour over his accusation that the Admiralty had not provided him with a strategic plan. Once more, McKenna's persistent questioning soon revealed that a serious charge made by Beresford had no foundation whatsoever:

*McKenna*   ... You begin by saying, 'When Lord Charles Beresford took over the command of the Channel Fleet in March 1907, he immediately asked for the strategic plans ... After repeated requests ... a plan ... was sent in April 1907.' The first question I ask you is, were you not in America in March 1907?

Beresford  I dare say; I cannot remember. It may have been in April, but that is a small detail ...

McKenna  I put it to you that you did not return from America till the month of April? [He arrived back on 10 April 1907.]

Beresford  I dare say.

McKenna  That on your return you called at the Admiralty?

Beresford  Yes.

McKenna  That you had made no requests for plans until you called at the Admiralty?

Beresford  I should think certainly not. Are you driving at the date, whether it was March or April? Do you want to know whether this is correct or incorrect?[102]

McKenna's increasing frustration with Beresford's evasions finally burst out:

McKenna  I want to know whether a single fact that you allege in this statement is true. I am going to show you that not one is true ...[103]

McKenna then went on to produce the plans that Beresford said he had not been given, despite repeated requests. The evidence against him was so clear that, in the end, Asquith intervened, ruling that 'there is no doubt' that Fisher gave Beresford the plans when he visited the Admiralty. He then promptly undermined his support of the Admiralty case by declaring 'it is not in the least important'.[104] How it could be 'not important' that Beresford had made grossly inaccurate charges against the Admiralty is not clear.

Having declared that the arrangement of the fleets had been a danger to the country, Beresford proposed a different arrangement of the fleets. Given the importance that Beresford attached to his proposed new organisation, the committee must have been surprised at the lack of detail. He wanted, he said, two divisions. McKenna asked him to give details of one division, but Beresford was unable to give a clear answer. Asquith felt he had to intervene:

Asquith  Give us one division, Lord Charles.

McKenna  That is what I am endeavouring to get from him, but he declines to give me one division.

Beresford  I decline nothing.

Asquith  Come on – eight battleships?

Beresford  Eight battleships, six armoured cruisers, and about six un-armoured.

197

| McKenna | This is a well-thought out scheme of distribution of the ships? |
|---|---|
| Beresford | I have not thought it absolutely out. I prefer to give it to you another day.[105] |

After some further prevarication by Beresford, McKenna pressed him for some more detail:

| Beresford | You shall have it tomorrow. |
|---|---|
| McKenna | You have not got it prepared at this moment? |
| Beresford | No. I do not keep these things in my head.[106] |

This was an astounding performance. The centre of Beresford's charges was that the *distribution* of the fleets was wrong and that he had a better arrangement which would offer greater security. Yet, when asked what that arrangement was, he could not reply.

Having found Beresford hazy about one of his key proposals, the committee were perhaps not surprised that he confessed ignorance about the current distribution of the fleets in home waters:

| McKenna | Do you think the country is not safe at this moment? |
|---|---|
| Beresford | From what? |
| McKenna | From foreign attack. |
| Beresford | From your bolt from the blue? |
| McKenna | From foreign attack in the event of war?[107] |

It then turned out that Beresford thought McKenna was asking about the time when he was in command of the Channel Fleet. McKenna clarified this:

| McKenna | I am speaking of what is now. |
|---|---|
| Beresford | How am I to know what is now ... |
| McKenna | Don't you know what is now? |
| Beresford | How am I to know? |
| McKenna | It is not very difficult to read. |
| Beresford | I read the newspapers. |
| McKenna | The Parliamentary Papers have declared what it is.[108] |

This inane argument continued until Asquith intervened to remind Beresford of what he had written in his letter of 2 April:

| Asquith | The statement in your letter is this ... 'During that period [his command] the fleets in Home waters have not been organised for war, and they are not organised in readiness for war now, to-day.'[109] |
|---|---|

In other words, on 2 April Beresford knew enough about the fleet distribution to declare it unsafe; by 6 May, all he could say was 'How am I to know what is now?'

So far the committee's discussions had wandered from topic to topic, often seeming to be far from Beresford's main accusation: that his fleet 'has never, even for a day, been equal to the force which it might have to encounter in home waters'.[110] With relish, McKenna set out to disprove this statement.

Beresford had foolishly specified certain dates on which his fleet lacked the force necessary to meet a German attack. Choosing the date which Beresford had maintained was the worst in his two years (23 September 1908),[111] McKenna began a forensic analysis of the two fleets on that day. He started with the Channel Fleet:

McKenna  ... you put to sea actually with six battleships?
Beresford  Yes, that is right.[112]

Later:

McKenna  ... On that date, 23rd September, you had six ships which you took with you on a visit to Scarborough?
Beresford  I really do not remember where I went.
McKenna  It was to Scarborough. The other two ships you had sent to calibrate?
Beresford  Yes, that is right.
McKenna  So, though you went to sea with six ships, it was your own doing, because you had sent the two other ships to calibrate?
Beresford  No, I did not send them. You sent them.[113]

This was disingenuous since Beresford himself had written to the Admiralty, asking them to issue the order for the ships to calibrate their guns.

McKenna steadily worked through the other ships that Beresford alleged had not been available to go to sea, until he had proved his point:

McKenna  So that in the case you suppose, of your sailing with six ships, there were, in fact, eleven ships available?
Beresford  I really do not know, Mr Asquith, what I am wanted to say.
Asquith  This is most material; I cannot imagine anything more important. You gave us an illustration –
Beresford  That I went to sea with five [sic] ships – yes, quite true.
Asquith  You gave us as an illustration of the constant shortage that you once went to sea with six battleships out of fourteen, four armoured cruisers out of six, four unarmoured cruisers out of four, and fifteen out of thirty destroyers?
Beresford  That is a fact.[114]

A fact, yes. But Beresford, in writing to Asquith, in briefing journalists, in talking in the London salons and in giving evidence to the committee, had

199

made no mention of the other ships that were there to call on in an emergency. Was he genuinely ignorant of this fact? Or, if not, did he really believe that he could mislead the committee to the point of supporting his case? Whatever the truth, by the fifth day Asquith must have begun to wonder whether he had been duped. If Beresford's most serious and central charge were so devoid of truth, what might that imply for the subsidiary charges? It was too late, though, to pull out. The committee would have to endure another ten sittings, of much the same character.

**Day six: Friday, 7 May**
The sixth day ranged over many topics, to no clear purpose. At the start of the meeting, Beresford tried once more to discuss whether he had received all the four parts of the war plans at the same time but Asquith declared 'It is really not worth labouring.'[115]

The committee then went on to further explore Beresford's knowledge of the German Fleet, but found him to be as hazy as on previous days.

Next, Beresford tried to restart discussions as to whether he had or had not been authorised to carry out the October 1907 manoeuvres. McKenna reminded him that he had promised to produce the written order, but Beresford now admitted 'There was no letter.'[116]

In cunning mood, McKenna then played the barrister's trick of leading a witness into a trap via a series of apparently innocuous questions:

*McKenna*   You have spoken more than once in the course of your evidence of military analogies; the military analogy you have spoken of consists of infantry, cavalry, and artillery?
*Beresford*   Yes.[117]

After further questioning, McKenna continued:

*McKenna*   If I take the destroyers as the infantry, the cruisers as the cavalry, and the battleships as the artillery, we shall have a fair analogy ...?
*Beresford*   Yes, for comparison.[118]

Shortly afterwards, Beresford became uncomfortable with the direction of the questioning:

*Beresford*   ... you must not put words into my mouth and say that catchers are infantry, that would look rather funny.
*McKenna*   Yes, it would, I agree.
*Beresford*   I never said so.
*McKenna*   Consequently, I put it to you that any inferences you draw from military analogy must always be taken with great caution ...[119]

200

Beresford became increasingly annoyed with McKenna, but was still not sure what all this was leading up to. Then, McKenna pounced:

*Beresford*  I distinctly demur to calling the catchers infantry ...

*McKenna*  ... but after you had agreed that the battleships were artillery, you had no alternative. I think this is rather a lesson, and we must be very cautious in accepting the military analogies ...[120]

It was cruel, since Beresford was an innocent in the hands of the intellectual McKenna.

After the sixth meeting, there was a weekend break, which Beresford chose to spend in the north-west, where he made speeches at St George's Hall, Liverpool and then in Southport. He confined himself to talking about the nation's 'physical deterioration' and the need for more physical training.[121]

The following day he told Bellairs that 'the Cabinet Com[tee] is going very well at present'. If this was his genuine assessment then he failed to read the committee. There had not been one single issue on which McKenna's grilling had not exposed the weakness of Beresford's claims. Meanwhile, the rest of the committee, although more polite than McKenna, and even somewhat deferential, were showing few signs of conviction. Perhaps, though, Beresford hinted at some recognition of his lack of progress when he told Bellairs that 'I have a great many more proofs of my statement in papers and by officers.'[122]

The King, meanwhile, was keeping a vigilant watch over Fisher and, on his return from a Mediterranean cruise, summoned him to an audience. According to Lady Fisher, the King had told Fisher that 'his conduct ... had been Dignified and Courageous' which, she felt was 'no small compliment from the King'.[123]

## Day seven: Tuesday, 11 May

There was a desultory start to the seventh day, with no clear agenda. Then McKenna brushed aside one of Beresford's papers, in a manner that provoked Beresford to a reply which was both insulting and condescending:

*McKenna*  I do not propose to examine Lord Charles on Appendix 6 ... [which includes] a series of statements to the Committee which I think I shall be able to show the Committee – you will forgive my saying the word – are almost entirely devoid of sense.

*Beresford*  I quite forgive you. Knowing that you know nothing whatever about it, I do not mind what you say.[124]

201

Relations between the two men were not helped by the fact that McKenna followed the clash over Appendix 6 by a further attack on Beresford's sea time. This was provoked by the latter's having handed in details of his claim to thirty years of sea time.

McKenna    With regard to his sea time, I will only hand in to the Committee the record of Lord Charles's service ... as a commissioned officer up to his appointment as Rear-Admiral, exclusive of harbour time and leave ...[125]

Excluding his service with Lord Wolseley in the Sudan and his time on the Royal Yacht, the total sea time came to eight years 250 days – rather short of the thirty years claimed by Beresford.

Beresford    I must ask the opinion of the Committee as to what this is being brought in for.
McKenna    I can explain it.
Beresford    What is my sea time being brought in for? ... It is to discredit me.
McKenna    I will explain, if you desire.[126]

Beresford's reply was interesting since it exposed an un-discussed oddity about the proceedings – just what was the role of McKenna?

Beresford    You must not think of cross-examining me in any way, or inferring in any way. I am doing this to help the Committee.[127]

Strictly speaking McKenna was a witness, just as Beresford was, but he had been vigorously cross-examining the admiral since the fourth day, just as if he were a member of the committee. Beresford was right to sense an unevenness in the treatment of the two sides. It would seem clear that Asquith had not thought about this aspect of the enquiry when he chose its structure. That neither he nor the rest of the committee took any steps to constrain McKenna in his dual role is simply explained: if they had not allowed him a free rein, they would never have been able to challenge a single thing that Beresford said. The 'unbiased' committee that Asquith had put together was totally dependent on McKenna's expertise (or, rather, Fisher's in disguise) to expose the vacuity of Beresford's charges. Only he could pose relevant and sufficiently penetrating questions. Only he could expose inconsistencies and evasions in Beresford's replies.

McKenna now revealed why he had raised the sea-time issue:

McKenna    The reason is that I shall call other naval officers, whose evidence on questions of naval policy will be diametrically opposed to that of Lord Charles Beresford, and I want to show, when I shall call them and ask them as to their experience at sea, that their experience as a naval officer in the ranks below that of an Admiral is far superior to that of Lord Charles Beresford.[128]

Asquith was not impressed and said he would not be 'much influenced ... by the comparative length of service of the different officers'.[129] And, since McKenna never called any witnesses, the hours spent disputing sea time proved pointless for both parties.

Beresford had submitted a bulky set of documents concerning Rear Admiral Montgomerie's command of the torpedo and submarine craft, variously attached to the Home Fleet and the Channel Fleet at different times. The quantity of such craft, their distribution and their command were all issues about which Beresford had made strong representations, but the issue that flared up on day seven was his charge that Montgomerie had his command reduced as a result of a letter that he wrote to the admiralty about defects in torpedo craft. Despite submitting eight pages of detailed data to support this allegation, Beresford denied that he had made any such charge:

> *McKenna* ... you say; 'Return showing Rear-Admiral Montgomerie's command before and after he sent his letter of the 6th July, 1907.' I wish to ask you whether by that statement ... you intend the Committee to understand that Admiral Montgomerie's command was reduced in consequence of his letter?
>
> *Beresford* I do not intend the Committee to understand anything except what I have written. You can take it any way you like. I have written a certain thing, which is a fact. I do not make inferences; I do not say 'if' and 'because' and 'suppose'.[130]

Yet for what other reason would Beresford have included the phrase 'before and after he sent his letter' other than to suggest that the letter was germane?

In any case, Beresford had his facts wrong since, as McKenna was able to demonstrate, Montgomerie's command was reduced on 3 June, whereas his letter of complaint was written on 6 July:

> *Beresford* What is the difference in time?
> *McKenna* The 3rd June comes before the 6th July.
> *Beresford* It is such a tremendous point ...[131]

After seven days of listening to Beresford's complaints, the committee might have been rather surprised to hear that he never made complaints. He explained this conundrum as follows:

> *McKenna* You complain in your paper ...

*Beresford*  Is the word 'complaint' in?

*McKenna*  I use the word 'complaint'. I will ask you if you do complain?

*Beresford*  No. I make definite statements of fact with regard to my duty, but I make no complaints.[132]

McKenna then established that Beresford did not approve of the organisation of the destroyers. When he attempted to get Beresford to admit that this constituted a 'complaint', Beresford resorted to an amusing evasion:

*McKenna*  Then I am justified in saying that you use the word 'complaint' of that organisation?

*Beresford*  No, I do not complain. I make a statement. Housemaids complain, not men.[133]

One reason that Beresford gave for not drawing up a war plan as ordered was that he did not receive fortnightly 'Orders of Battle' – lists of ships that were available should an emergency occur – from the Admiralty. These came, he said, every three months. McKenna then tabled the relevant orders, to show that they had been sent monthly.

*Asquith*  I think you must have been mistaken about the three months, Lord Charles.

*Beresford*  Very likely.[134]

This did not prevent his then contradicting himself only a few minutes later:

*Beresford*  I think you will find I am right about the three months.[135]

McKenna pursued the battle order question and exposed a further jumble of contradictions in Beresford's evidence:

*McKenna*  ... So far as the destroyers in the Home Fleet were concerned, you were also aware every Sunday morning how far they were ready, and what their condition was?

*Beresford*  Every Sunday morning?

*McKenna*  Yes; every Sunday morning you knew the condition of the destroyers in the Home Fleet?

*Beresford*  I do not think so. (Lord Charles' secretary made a communication to him.)

*McKenna*  I think Lord Charles is capable of answering the questions.

*Beresford*  Yes; he is very capable of answering, but he wants a little time. I will tell you that tomorrow.[136]

But the committee had no need to wait since Beresford had already provided the information, which McKenna then read out from Beresford's opening statement on day one. There, he had said that he updated the information every week, just as did Montgomerie. So, now the committee knew that, from Beresford's evidence of 27 April, he checked the condition of the destroyers once a week, but from his evidence of 11 May that he had no idea whether he did or did not carry out such checks.

However, since the central point under investigation at this moment was his accusation that the Admiralty did not supply up-to-date information on the ships of the Home Fleet, the committee were curious to know why he did not just ask Bridgeman for the details.

> *McKenna*  Did you ever ask the Commander-in-Chief of the Home Fleet?
> *Beresford*  No.
> *McKenna*  Why not?
> *Beresford*  Because I told the Admiralty that I refused to do anything of the sort ... he very rightly did not like to be interfered with ...[137]

Why Beresford should have thought that Bridgeman would have been affronted by such a request was beyond McKenna's comprehension. As he pointed out to Beresford, when Bridgeman was appointed he had been ordered to 'be in continuous and full communication' with Beresford, who had received a copy of this letter. The nearest that Beresford could get to explaining this was that Bridgeman 'would not have done it because we were friends; but if we had not been friends he certainly would have done it'.[138]

McKenna then asked him whether he asked his Intelligence Officer to get this information. When Beresford said he did not, McKenna probed further:

> *McKenna*  Are the Committee to understand that, although you said it was of vital importance that you should know which ships are ready at any given moment, you neither asked the Commander-in-Chief of the Home Fleet to inform you as to his ships, nor did you ask your Intelligence Officer at the Admiralty ...
> *Beresford*  I have told you that I was not going messing about with another Commander-in-Chief's fleet. It would have made friction ...[139]

Beresford had submitted a paper on small cruisers and torpedo craft and had alleged that Britain was inadequately supplied with such craft compared to Germany. McKenna sought to clarify this statement:

> *McKenna*  I want to understand from you wherein the danger lies ... You said that our torpedo boats were unable to work at any great distance from their bases?[140]

Beresford, though, was very unclear as to what he had said:

| | |
|---|---|
| *Beresford* | The catchers [destroyers]. |
| *McKenna* | Our torpedo boats [torpedo launchers]? |
| *Beresford* | Not the boats. |
| *Asquith* | The destroyers, you mean? |
| *Beresford* | The destroyers. |
| *McKenna* | You say the torpedo boats also. |
| *Beresford* | Was I talking about boats or catchers? |
| *McKenna* | The torpedo boats are, you say, unable to work at any great distance from their bases; and you also say the destroyers. |
| *Beresford* | It was the catchers I meant, probably; or was I referring to boats then? |
| *McKenna* | You were referring to torpedo boats. Is that true of the thirty-six ex-coastal destroyers? |
| *Beresford* | Yes.[141] |

This was a monumental display of incompetence. After making a very serious allegation about small craft, when questioned about it, Beresford could not even remember which boats he had been referring to. When he finally decided that it was the destroyers that he was discussing, he then went on to admit that he had no experience of them but was sure that 'from their make and shape that they would not do'.[142]

There was, though, a much more serious point behind McKenna's questioning. German destroyers were also unsuited to working far from their bases, yet Beresford insisted on Britain preparing for a bolt from the blue attack. How was Germany to stage such an attack unless her destroyers first crossed the North Sea? When challenged by Asquith as to the logic of this argument, Beresford replied 'We ought to be so organised that it does not matter what they do.'[143]

Having condemned destroyers, which he said he had no experience of, Beresford then made a similar attack on submarines.

| | |
|---|---|
| *McKenna* | You attach no importance to submarines …? |
| *Beresford* | I attach no importance to things that are not practically proved to be right. Now in regard to a submarine, the one thing which beats a British seaman when he is on top of the water is a fog, and the submarine is always in a fog [i.e. could not see where it was going].[144] |

Later:

| | |
|---|---|
| *McKenna* | Have you ever been in one of the later submarines? |
| *Beresford* | I have seen them, but not away at sea …[145] |

This gave Beresford the chance to refer to his letter of 11 April 1908 when he had requested 'a mining vessel and a division of submarines'. The

Admiralty had declined on the grounds that 'the training of these branches ... is ... sufficiently provided for by the periodical combined exercises'.[146] Momentarily, Beresford had the advantage over the committee but, instead of following up the Admiralty's failure to allocate him some submarines, he cheekily responded to McKenna's next point:

> McKenna  Are you aware that only last week a section of our sub-
> marines made a run of 600 miles at full speed in rough
> weather?
>
> Beresford  I dare say they could go a thousand.[147]

That is, having declared that submarines were 'always in a fog', Beresford now happily admitted that they might be able to navigate 1,000 miles. Still, he was not converted to them:

> Beresford  ... but fancy trusting to submarines! You have covered all
> our coasts with submarines – with thirty or forty sub-
> marines – and we have not got the small cruisers and
> catchers upon which we shall depend in war.[148]

In Beresford's defence, many other senior officers underestimated the value of submarines at that time. Only when Germany made such deva-stating use of them in the First World War did the Royal Navy belatedly realise their potential.

The seventh day was lightened by an amusing incident when McKenna was able to resurrect the Dogger Bank affair of 1904 in which Beresford's proposed 'chivalrous' approach to dealing with the Russian fleet had earned him a reprimand (Act 5). That McKenna (who was not then First Lord) was able to bring in this incident must have been due to Fisher's masterly briefing behind the scenes.

The basis of the tiff was the debate between concentration (keeping all the home vessels together) and dispersion. After McKenna had established that Beresford was for concentration without exception at all times, he seized his moment:

> McKenna  May I remind you of what occurred in October 1904 ...
> You proposed then, in the event of your fighting Russia, to
> dismiss half your fleet and to fight them with the other
> half.[149]

Beresford put up a spirited defence, but, as McKenna pressed his case, his temper rose. In the end, he could contain himself no longer:

> Beresford  ... Well, Mr. McKenna, you give me enormous advantages
> by your cross-examination – enormous. Everything you
> have given me I have been able to knock into a cocked
> hat.[150]

207

At which point was commented:

*Asquith*  It is very pleasing to see that this is the demeanour of the witness.[151]

The, by now, ill-tempered atmosphere was further aggravated by McKenna making another attempt to question Beresford's version of his own career. First, McKenna sought to disprove Beresford's claim that he set up the Naval Intelligence Department. Asquith brushed this aside. Then McKenna set out to disprove Beresford's claim that he had resigned in 1888 'on the question of the strength of the fleet'.[152] Asquith dismissed this on the grounds that this was 'at some remote date', hoping to cool the atmosphere.

There was, though, to be no let-up as the debate became increasingly personal. This time, the subject was Fisher's war plans when he was Commander-in-Chief in the Mediterranean. Beresford had made statements that clearly implied that it was he, not Fisher, who had been responsible for those plans:

*McKenna*  ... [is] the Committee to infer from that statement that you initiated the plan of war made out for the Mediterranean Fleet by Sir John Fisher?
*Beresford*  ... I infer nothing. I tell you what happened. I spoke to Sir John Fisher about the plan, and he made out the plan ...[153]

McKenna pressed him as to whether the plan was 'a consequence' of his talking to Fisher, to which he would only reply:

*Beresford*  ... I spoke to him about a plan, and he made a plan.
*McKenna*  It is a very ambiguous phrase.[154]

For once Asquith came in to support McKenna, and insisted that the phrase 'is open to either construction'.[155] He tried to persuade Beresford to agree 'that we will take it that Sir John Fisher made the plan on his own initiative'. Beresford would not agree that this was the case, at which point Fisher made one of his rare interventions in the enquiry:

*Fisher*  I want to state that I made that plan without Lord Charles saying one single word to me ...
*Beresford*  Then I state exactly the opposite ...[156]

Whilst none of those present round the table knew it, Beresford's behaviour on that day was a perfect echo of his performance twenty-three years ago as Junior Naval Lord. According to then First Lord, Lord George Hamilton, Beresford repeatedly briefed the press lobby with claims to Admiralty reforms which were nothing to do with him. The 'atmosphere of friction' which he created led to the point where Lord George feared that, if Beresford did not go, the two senior Naval Lords would resign. The view was that Beresford was kept on because he was 'a Member of Parliament and a popular pet'.[157] Nothing had changed in 1909.

After the seventh day there was an eight-day break in the meetings, during which Beresford carried on his public life. It was an active time for him as he was elected a Fellow of the Royal Colonial Institute, announced as the guest of honour at a forthcoming Australian annual banquet, was received by the King and was present at the Royal Navy and Military Tournament, where he occupied the royal box. However badly things were going at the enquiry, there was no diminution in his immense popularity with the public. Fisher, meanwhile, with a major department of state to run was less in the public eye, although he too attended the tournament – but not on the same day as Beresford.

### Day eight: Wednesday, 19 May
The eighth day saw the closing elements of Beresford's evidence, with the emphasis on the errors which he alleged McKenna had made in his comments. One of these was the now notorious eight years and 250 days of sea time which, Beresford said, should be ten years and twenty-five days – astoundingly less than the thirty years he had previously insisted on. A lively and rather personal discussion followed, which led Beresford to ask Asquith to 'forgive me if I am a little warm'. Asquith made no reply, turned to McKenna and said 'Will you proceed, Mr. McKenna?'[158]

And so began the Admiralty fight-back against the eight days of rambling charges and accusations from Beresford.

It must be admitted that from here on the enquiry makes very dull reading as page after page of carefully prepared evidence flowed from McKenna. There were few interruptions and few disputes, and, said Sandars, 'Charlie B. made no resistance to it that was worth a moment's consideration.'[159] (Exactly how Sandars, who was not present, knew this is not clear.)

McKenna began by explaining how he would proceed. He would, he said, 'confine myself strictly to the terms of reference', clearly implying that Beresford had not done so, adding, 'I do not propose to call any witnesses.'[160] This was presumably a change of plan. After all, he had justified his exploration of Beresford's career on the grounds that he was going to call officers with greater sea time than Beresford, who would testify against his views. Not having left any clue as to this change in tactics, we can only guess at his motives. Perhaps he realised that he had more than enough ammunition to demolish Beresford's charges; or perhaps he feared clashes of officer against officer if conflicting professional views were allowed to enter into the argument.

He proposed, he said, to consider just two issues. First, 'whether the organisation in fact secured safety if war had taken place'; and second, 'whether the organisation was the best obtainable, having regard to the circumstances'.[161]

After the rambles of Beresford's presentation, McKenna's systematic evidence must have been a relief to the committee. He began on 'whether safety was secured'. To consider this, he had asked Asquith to choose four random dates. For each of these days – 6 October 1907, 19 January 1908, 7 June 1908 and 21 March 1909 – the Admiralty staff had tabulated the fleet strengths; in all there were twenty-two pages of dense tables.[162]

Using these tables, McKenna was able to demonstrate that, on each occasion, the fire-power of the available British ships was superior to that of the available German ships. Beresford haggled over a ship here and ship there, but made no attempt to challenge McKenna's central point: safety had been secured. So, Beresford's main charge had simply crumbled to nought.

As Beresford sat through the eighth day, he must have become aware that the whole tenor of the enquiry had fundamentally changed. Bickering dispute had given way to smooth presentation; questioning members had turned to dutiful listeners. It was a world in which he was not able to operate – the world of calm intellect and rational discussion.

That Beresford was aware of this sudden turn is shown by what happened as the meeting broke up. Beresford had conversed casually with Ottley and within earshot of Hankey. What Hankey heard so staggered him that he went straight to his desk to record the conversation, signed the note, and then took it to Ottley, asking him to countersign it as a true record of what Beresford had said. One of these two witnesses then took the trouble to deposit this single sheet of handwritten foolscap in one of the enquiry's administrative files, where it still lies today. (There is no evidence to show that either of them ever showed it to anyone else.)

Talking to Ottley, Beresford first tried to dismiss the importance of the day's proceedings, saying: 'The statement made by Mr. McKenna, relating to "ships, tons, and guns" were [sic] quite irrelevant and could easily be controverted.' Beresford then said that 'These matters, however, were not ... the real issue' and 'So far as he himself was concerned the main object was to drive the present Board of the Admiralty out of office.' The Hankey account continued:

He was inclined to think that the Sub-Committee would think as he did in this matter, but if the Government themselves did not decide to enforce the resignation of the Board of Admiralty, he (Lord Charles Beresford) himself would appeal to the public, and compel the Board to resign.[163]

So much for the several occasions during the enquiry when he had told the committee that he was only there to help the Board.

## Day nine: Thursday, 20 May

A good deal of the ninth meeting was taken up with comparisons of the relative strengths and modes of operation of the British and German fleets.

Beresford asked a few questions and made the occasional challenge, but he basically allowed McKenna's evidence to flow without interruption. The committee must have been startled to find how strong the Royal Navy was in comparison with the wilting violet that Beresford had described for eight days. In home waters, McKenna explained, British 12-inch guns dominated German 11-inch guns in a ratio of 3:1; a similar level of dominance occurred with the smaller guns:[164]

|                     | 12-inch | 11-inch | 10-inch | 9.2/9.4-inch |
|---------------------|---------|---------|---------|--------------|
| Home waters fleets  | 124     |         | 4       | 88           |
| German fleet        |         | 46      |         | 36           |

In arriving at these figures McKenna had even been cautious enough to compare British ships ready for instant use against the full paper strength of the German fleet.

The day after this meeting, Beresford gave a speech to the Australian annual banquet. Whereas, in speaking at Liverpool earlier in the month, he had kept off subjects that might have compromised the enquiry, this time he showed no such restraint. While fully supporting the then popular demand for eight dreadnought battleships to be built that year, he attacked the dreadnought concept, which he blamed for an increase in German shipbuilding. Bethell seems to have been present since he sent Fisher a detailed critique of Beresford's remarks, correcting what, he told Fisher, were various false statements.[165]

The days of the enquiry were hard for Fisher to bear, so he would have welcomed news from Esher that the King had 'spoke[n] *most warmly* to me of McKenna's fine performance during the last two days'. He thought his First Lord to be *'first rate'*.[166] Beresford, on the other hand, must have been delighted to hear that Madame Tussaud's had just unveiled a new figure of him.[167]

**Day ten: Tuesday, 25 May**
The tenth meeting began with just the five members of the committee and their secretariat. Asquith read out Slade's reply to the committee's questions and the committee decided that, for time being, its contents should remain secret. The rest of the day was largely taken up by a detailed technical defence of Beresford's charges about war plans and orders of battle.

At the end of the tenth day, Fisher was much more optimistic, telling Stead that 'All is going splendid[ly] as regards the Committee.' Beresford, he said, was 'mad', as was Custance.[168] The next day, he told Edward Goulding, a Conservative MP, that 'I see victory all round', while the rumours of his forthcoming resignation were without 'a particle of truth' and simply put about by Beresford 'to cover his defeat in [the] Committee of Enquiry'.[169] Far from being on the brink of resigning, Fisher now saw himself staying in post until 1911, side by side with McKenna. 'The Peerage can go to the Devil,' he told McKenna, '[since] I want to stick to you now till the day you leave office no matter when that is.'[170]

Despite this optimism, Knollys was concerned at the way 'that rotten lot "London Society"' were 'trying to "hound him [Fisher] down"', so he invited him to dinner at Brooke's, telling Esher that 'I want to show him this little attention just now.'[171]

Meanwhile, another cloud had appeared over Fisher's horizon when he heard news about a possible libel action against him over the Bacon letters. He had heard from Esher that Armstrong had some more letters of his. He could remember nothing about them since 'I was fighting night & day then and no time to think of consequences!'[172]

### Day eleven: Tuesday, 8 June

After a long break, the enquiry recommenced on 8 June. For Beresford, there was the welcome news that he would be able to see Slade's letter. It was the nearest that he was able to come in his campaign to put Slade in front of the committee.

Where he had failed with Slade, Beresford succeeded with Custance, who was the next witness. Like his master, he was not able to launch straight into his statement, without first meticulously recalling his correspondence with Asquith of April, in which he protested that he was not to be regarded as a 'prosecutor'.[173]

Having cleared up his status, Custance launched into a lengthy statement on fleet organisation and war plans, wandering back as far as 1803. (Or, as King-Hall, drawing on a conversation with Drury, put it: 'Custance never got beyond the 15th Century.')[174] Since Asquith had, earlier in the enquiry, ruled that plans as early as 1905 were hardly relevant for conditions in 1909, Custance's predilection for meticulous historical detail can hardly have impressed the committee.

Three days later, writing to Esher at 4.30 am, Fisher described how 'we sat till nearly 7.00, with Custance spitting venom all the time at the First Sea Lord'. He was concerned that Beresford might be blackmailing Asquith since 'Beresford requested a private interview with Asquith at the end of the meeting.'[175] Nothing came of this though, and, a few days later, Fisher was organising a secret visit of Asquith to the Admiralty, who was to use 'the back door of Admiralty as nearest to Wireless room'.[176] What was discussed we do not know.

### Day twelve: Tuesday, 15 June

On the twelfth day, Custance completed his presentation, concluding that 'The uncertainty which has been shown to exist in orders, plans, organisations, and training, would probably have resulted in confusion in the event of war.'[177] Beresford agreed with this, and the committee moved on to hear evidence from Captain H.H. Campbell. 'Moved on' turned out to be 'attempted to move on' since first, Beresford, who had called Campbell as a witness, turned out to not even know which post he held. He had to turn to Ottley, who did not even work for the Admiralty, to confirm that Campbell was 'Head of the Trade Division' and 'an Assistant Director of Naval Intelligence'.[178]

Before hearing Campbell, Asquith, by now almost certainly irritated with Custance's long and dreary lecture on war plans and war organisation, wished to assure himself that Campbell could add to what was already before the committee in Slade's letter. Turning to Beresford, he politely enquired:

Asquith    I think, Lord Charles, that you have seen the answer which Admiral Slade sent to the questions?[179]

In response, Beresford took the opportunity to show offence and unnecessarily irritate the committee:

Beresford    Yes; but I did not get till a fortnight afterwards.
Asquith    Nobody did; we kept it to ourselves for a time.
Beresford    You gave it to me eventually.
Asquith    You got it as soon as the Admiralty got it ...
Beresford    I am not complaining.[180]

When Asquith further pressed Beresford as to whether Campbell could really 'add something' to what Slade had said, Beresford replied with yet another gratuitous attack on the committee:

Beresford    I do not propose to bring anybody else, unless Mr. McKenna produces his Admiral, I think it is Sir Michael Culme-Seymour, and for any Admiral he produces, of course, I am prepared to produce four ...[181]

To which Asquith cuttingly commented:

Asquith    It would be a very unedifying exhibition.[182]

With reluctance, Asquith asked the committee whether there was any reason why they should not see Campbell. No objections were raised, but McKenna emphasised that trade routes – the area of Campbell's expertise – were outside the terms of reference of the enquiry. Beresford exploded:

Beresford    That will not do ...[183]

and launched into a lengthy account of the various letters in which he had voiced concern about protection of the trade routes. In this outburst, he showed no understanding of the difference between the scope of the terms of reference (which he had accepted) and the varying contents of his multitudinous letters of complaint to the Board and to ministers. McKenna insisted:

> *McKenna* Of course the terms of reference speak for themselves.[184]

Asquith then ruled, by means of an ingenious explanation, that trade protection was within the remit. The rest of the meeting was then taken up with some preliminary discussion of the trade protection issue.

Five days later, on Sunday, 20 June, Fisher turned his mind to the next meeting on Thursday, 24 June, and he sat down to write a briefing note for McKenna. He had, he said, woken 'with the all-pervading sense of victory'. This was because Asquith had arranged for McKenna to speak before Beresford, giving him an opportunity to 'get in your "crowning-of-the-edifice" speech', which, Fisher said, should be based on Wilson's comments, demolishing Campbell's arguments and showing up the errors in Beresford's comments on the scrapping of ships. Fisher then gave McKenna detailed advice on how to plan his week:

> saturate yourself on Sunday with the subject, and to give it to us on Monday in the Bovril [condensed] form, for on Tuesday and Wednesday you won't have time – Defence Committee, Cabinet, etc. Wednesday evening I suggest you keep free to consider Beresford's speech made that afternoon at London Chamber of Commerce.[185]

In fact, none of this was relevant, since the enquiry was, to all intents and purposes, over. Campbell was to be heard, followed by Wilson. The former was to have almost no influence over the committee, while the opinion of the latter was to prove crucial.

## Day thirteen: Thursday, 24 June

Before the main business of the day began, Beresford made a statement to the committee, handing in papers on both the ship-scrapping policy and the Scott incidents. The former had already been ruled as irrelevant; the latter was shortly to suffer the same fate. Meanwhile, the committee turned its attention to Campbell.

Campbell then gave a prepared statement of the vulnerability of the mercantile marine to a sudden attack. The detail does not matter, but the whole of the Campbell case (and hence, Beresford's) on trade protection depended on their assumption that German merchant ships were armed. The Admiralty had clear evidence that they were not, which rather undermined Campbell's position. This section of evidence, though, was to prove explosive for another reason and led Campbell to regret his participation in the enquiry for the rest of his life. It all began with an apparently innocent question:

*Beresford*   I should like to ask whether there is any documentary evid-
           ence from the Commander-in-Chief on the Cape of Good
           Hope station as to this question – whether he is satisfied
           with what he possesses for trade protection ... I should
           like to know whether there are any letters from Admiral
           Egerton on this point which the Committee should see; do
           you know, Captain Campbell?
*Campbell*   Yes. There is a letter which points out very distinctly to my
           mind that Admiral Egerton considers it impossible to
           defend the trade.[186]

How fortunate that the very letter Beresford hoped might exist actually
did exist. What a coincidence! Or was it coincidence? The truth was that
Beresford and his friends had arranged for Egerton to write the letter, as
Hurd revealed much later in the year.[187] At the time, the committee
suspected nothing, but even when they began to have qualms, they never
found out the full truth. For Campbell, though, there would be consequences in 1910.

Finally Wilson – the very man whom Asquith had appointed and then
ejected after Beresford's protestations – appeared before the committee.
Having confirmed that he had read the enquiry papers, he told the
committee that 'I do not wish to take my place as a judge. I am ready to
answer any questions.'[188]

There was nothing startling in what Wilson told the committee, but then
he was the most sober of men, who would never have startled anyone.
Cumulatively, however, his evidence failed in any way to support
Beresford's claims of imminent national disaster. Like Beresford, he had
not always had direct command of the destroyers. Like Beresford, he had
had only occasional manoeuvres of the combined fleets. Like Beresford, he
had been 'very short of unarmoured cruisers'. Like Beresford, he had 'no
reports' on other ships – just the 'monthly list of all the ships that were
available in reserve'. He too thought that there were not enough small
craft. But, unlike Beresford, he declared that the fleet arrangements in his
time were 'quite satisfactory – at least, not unsatisfactory'.[189] There were
no histrionics, no attacks on the Admiralty, no forecasts of Armageddon.

On two points, he fundamentally disagreed with Beresford. First, on the
issue of the use of small craft off the German coast, where he agreed that
there were too few craft, but he differed in that he did not *want* to work off
the German coast. Despite Beresford's attempts to get him to express such
a wish, Wilson replied that 'I say I would work on our side in the North
Sea.'[190]

His second disagreement was over war plans. While Beresford had
complained again and again that the Admiralty had not supplied him with
war plans, Wilson simply doubted their value. He was reported as saying

that 'any plan drawn up in peace would not be carried out in war, and the value of drawing up plans was educational'. As to the idea of 'a plan of campaign in which every ship was stationed and told off by name for its duties' (which was what Beresford had asked for), he declared this to be 'practically impossible'.[191]

Beresford tried to persuade Wilson to agree that detailed ship numbers were needed to draw up a war plan.

*Wilson*      But that is a different thing from your plan which you wanted to fill up every Sunday morning.

*Beresford*   Pardon me, my plan of every Sunday morning was not a plan at all.

*Wilson*      That seemed to me pedantic.

*Beresford*   What I wanted every Sunday morning was to know every ship that was ready during the week. That had nothing whatever to do with the Plan of Campaign.

*Wilson*      You said you could not draw up a plan until you had got it, and you could not draw up a plan because you had not got it.[192]

At this point, Asquith fell in behind Wilson, saying to Beresford:

*Asquith*     Because you had not that information.[193]

And so, while Wilson had escaped having to 'judge', he had nevertheless come down more on the Admiralty side than on Beresford's.

Following Wilson's statement, Beresford asked Asquith 'Are you going to close to-day?' Explaining that he had 'certain things' that he still wanted to raise, Beresford leapt straight back into the discussion of his sea time. In reply, Asquith told him 'Don't bother about your time ... We know you are an Admiral of very great experience and authority.'[194]

There was then a break of a week, during which time Beresford attended the Imperial Press Conference where he spoke on the fairly safe subject of imperial and dominion defence. More questionably, he was the key speaker at a meeting of the London Chamber of Commerce on 30 June, where his subject was trade protection. He told his audience that the enquiry had now completed its evidence and, whilst admitting that its work was *sub judice* and that he had been told to be restrained, he confessed 'I have no intention whatever of being reticent. I will tell my country what I believe to be the case.' He then went on to attack the Government's trade protection policy and its shipbuilding programme. The situation was 'more serious than is generally known', he said, and then he listed what he said were 'extensive arrears of shipbuilding'.[195] It was as if he sensed that the enquiry would find against him and, in anticipation, was attacking in advance of the report.

**Day fourteen: Thursday, 1 July**

Between 24 June and 1 July, the committee had brooded on Beresford's rather too well-informed question about the Egerton letter and had come to the conclusion that he already knew the answer before asking it. But who had leaked this information? Asquith led the interrogation:

| | |
|---|---|
| *Asquith* | ... The Committee desire to know from you how you obtained the information that Admiral Egerton had written any letter on the subject [trade protection] to the Admiralty. |
| *Beresford* | I certainly was told, but I forget at the moment who told me. |
| *Asquith* | Try and refresh your memory. |
| *Beresford* | I should think it was either Captain Campbell or Captain Hulbert. |
| *Asquith* | Two gentlemen both in the Intelligence Department. |
| *Beresford* | Yes. But I should say it was in reference to a question I asked them. |
| *Asquith* | What do you mean? |
| *Beresford* | That I asked a question. |
| *Asquith* | Did you go to those gentlemen and ask whether Admiral Egerton had written a letter or not? |
| *Beresford* | No. What I expect I did – I do not remember exactly – was to say 'Has any information been sent from these people abroad on the question?' |
| *Asquith* | What do you mean by 'these people'? |
| *Beresford* | People who command. |
| *Asquith* | Did you go to officers of the Intelligence Department and ask them that question? |
| *Beresford* | It is very likely I did. |
| *Asquith* | 'Very likely' – you either did or did not. |
| *Beresford* | I really cannot remember, but I will think it out, if you will give me a moment. What was it I said to the Committee?[196] |

Asquith gave a long response in which he demonstrated how Beresford had given away in his replies that he knew what to ask for.

| | |
|---|---|
| *Beresford* | Your question is, How did I know? |
| *Asquith* | How did it come into your mind that Admiral Egerton had communicated with the Admiralty? |
| *Beresford* | It is very reasonable it should come to my mind. Why shouldn't it? |
| *Asquith* | I ask how it came. |
| *Beresford* | It is only common sense, from my point of view.[197] |

After much further insistent questioning by Asquith, Beresford finally offered an explanation:

217

> *Beresford*  I think I said both to Captain Hulbert, and to Captain
> Campbell, 'I am going to ask for evidence from the
> Commander-in-Chief of the Cape' – I think I probably said
> other Commanders-in-Chief – 'if there are any letters', and
> I think very likely that they said to me, 'Yes'.[198]

Asquith kindly ended this embarrassing exchange by accepting this explanation.

Beresford's role was coming to an end. He made a further long statement, going over much ground that had already been covered. In passing, he regretted that neither May nor Bridgeman had been called 'because I am satisfied that if I had asked them the question, "Is it a fact that the Home Fleet was ready as a striking force for instant action without an hour's delay ...?", they would have said, "No"'.[199]

In the long interval between the penultimate and ultimate meetings, Ottley asked McKenna to find out whether either May or Bridgeman were 'disposed to make a communication on the subject'.[200] May declined, saying that as far as he was concerned, the recent manoeuvres had 'shown that the organisation for mobilisation has been most successful'. He had had 'eighty-three ships completed from nucleus crews ... and [they] have done all the work the other ships have had to do to my entire satisfaction'.[201]

## Day fifteen: Tuesday, 13 July

Bridgeman chose to appear before the enquiry on its last day. He categorically refused to support Beresford's assertion that he, Bridgeman, would deny that the Home Fleet was ready for instant action: 'I never made such a statement, and I could not possibly make such a statement.' As to Beresford's assertion that it took six months for a ship 'to become fit for active work', Bridgeman replied: 'Good gracious, no! ... We are quite ready to fight, even with a nucleus crew, at a pinch.'[202]

It was fitting that Bridgeman, the admiral with whom Beresford was commanded to cooperate, but to whom he felt unable to address even a simple request for a list of ships, should close the enquiry with a series of resounding refutations of some of Beresford's assertions.

It was now time to write the report. Asquith had, on four occasions, refused to give any information to the Commons (3 May, 17 June, 1 and 7 July) on what form the report would take and when it would be available. Even as late as 15 July, when the sittings were complete, the best that he could tell the House was that 'The results of the investigation will in due course be made public, and the exact scope of the enquiry will then become apparent.'[203] Asquith appeared to have no idea what sort of report he wanted, which may explain why three drafts were needed before he approved it.

It fell to Ottley and Hankey to draft the report. The first draft is an odd document, short, curt, almost an apology for a report. It has no title, no date and no signature, but lies, carefully placed in the administrative file for the enquiry. As to who put it there, that surely must have been Ottley, who would have been in charge of the file, so perhaps he was the author. A clue to this being the case comes in Hankey's account of the enquiry. He refers to two drafts, the first one being rejected 'as too detailed and elaborate'.[204] No one could call the early draft either detailed or elaborate, so it would seem Ottley had his own stab at a first draft, which he never showed to Hankey.

It its conclusions this 'Ottley' draft noted that 'Lord Charles has failed to prove his case' and, in most undiplomatic language, concluded:

> If, therefore, the Committee adopt the view of Admiral of the Fleet Sir Arthur Wilson, who is universally admitted to be free from bias, and a sailor of exceptional capacity and insight, they cannot fail to Report that at no time was the country placed in a position of insecurity or grave disadvantage by the action of the Board of Admiralty.[205]

Whoever wrote this version, they cannot have hoped to have had it published. There were none of the circumlocutions of Whitehall language, being more likely to reopen the dispute rather than to close it down.

After the 'too detailed' draft (which no longer exists), Hankey recalled that he and Ottley 'produced a bowdlerised version, which passed muster'.[206] It was Fisher's view that Haldane had persuaded Asquith 'to alter the Beresford Report into a d___d milk and water fizzle, instead of pulverising Beresford out of existence, as first drafted'.[207] Hankey recalled that 'The Committee's aim was to produce a document which, without bringing discredit on Beresford and his colleagues, would show clearly that the Admiralty had retained the confidence of the Government.' Vainly, they had hoped for 'a golden bridge' to help heal the divisions in the Navy.[208] The committee's attempt to mollify both sides was to lead to both Beresford and his adversaries claiming victory, yet leaving all parties feeling let down.

On 12 August, the report – short and bland – was presented to Parliament. The first three pages reprinted Beresford's letter of 2 April to Asquith; then followed a page describing the committee's structure; the report then summarised Beresford's criticisms and the Admiralty's responses in a mere three pages – around 300,000 words of talk and papers reduced to nearer 1,500; and finally, less than half a page was devoted to its conclusions.

The most striking aspect of the report was its brevity. That in itself said a lot. Had there been any significant basis to Beresford's charges, the committee would have had to discuss those issues in more depth and report more fully on them. It was not just brief; it was disdainfully brief, both in its body and in its 'General Conclusion':

> In the opinion of the Committee, the investigation has shown that during the time in question no danger to the country resulted from the Admiralty's arrangements for war, whether considered from the standpoint of the organisation and distribution of the fleets, the number of ships, or the preparation of War Plans.
>
> They feel bound to add that arrangements quite defensible in themselves, though not ideally perfect, were in practice seriously hampered through the absence of cordial relations between the Board of Admiralty and the Commander-in-Chief of the Channel Fleet. The Board of Admiralty do not appear to have taken Lord Charles Beresford sufficiently into their confidence as to the reasons for the dispositions to which he took exception; and Lord Charles Beresford, on the other hand, appears to have failed to appreciate and carry out the spirit of the instructions of the Board, and to recognise their paramount authority.
>
> The Committee have been impressed with the differences of opinion amongst officers of high rank and professional attainments regarding important principles of naval strategy and tactics, and they look forward with much confidence to the further development of a Naval War Staff, from which the Naval members of the Board and Flag Officers and their staffs at sea may be expected to derive common benefit.[209]

Had Ottley and Hankey avoided bringing 'discredit on Beresford' and, at the same time, shown 'clearly that the Admiralty had retained the confidence' of the Government? Time would tell, but, reduced to its bald outline, the committee's conclusions were: (1) There was not one iota of truth in Beresford's allegations; (2) Beresford and the Board did not get on with each other; and (3) the Naval War Staff needed beefing up. A first reading would suggest that Beresford had suffered a catastrophic defeat, while the Admiralty had received little comfort, if, at the same time, little blame.

It was now time for all the parties to put the enquiry behind them. That would not prove easy to do.

## Act 10

# Consequences

Only Beresford himself can explain how a scheme which in April was a danger to the country can now be cited as the fruits of his judgment and sagacity. – *Manchester Guardian*[1]

### Scene 1: Winners, losers and uncertainty

Beresford put on a brave face when the report revealed that all his charges had been rejected. In a letter to *The Times*, he had the gall to claim that the Admiralty had accepted many of his criticisms and he listed eight reforms for which he claimed credit. In fact, there had been no significant changes at the Admiralty since the day in April when he wrote to Asquith. Continuing his letter, Beresford said that he had not been 'guilty of disloyalty' and that the only part of the report to which he took exception was the charge that he had not followed 'the spirit of the instructions' of the Admiralty.[2]

He was similarly sanguine when he told Sturdee that 'I am satisfied in the main with the finding of the Committee.'[3] Indeed, he was so convinced that the report had found in his favour that he told Long that 'J.F. ought to have been drummed out of the Adl[m] on the evidence.'[4] None of this gives the impression that he had been chastened by the committee's unremitting grilling and McKenna's pitiless questioning. Indeed, Balfour found him 'in ecstasies' at the outcome, claiming that 'he had won all along the line'.[5]

Some blamed this reaction on the report's blandness, but Knollys saw it as inevitable: whatever the report had concluded, he told Esher, 'Beresford ... would have given out that he had proved his case' since 'his effrontery, vanity & conceit are beyond belief'.[6]

If Asquith had hoped that he could silence his recalcitrant admiral simply through a fifteen-day enquiry, he was to be thoroughly deceived.

At the time that the report was published, Fisher was taking his annual cure in the South Tyrol, so it was difficult for him to engage in the debate. However, in his first letter to McKenna after publication, his bitterness erupted. The report was, he wrote, '*a cowardly document*'. As for 'the five men who signed it', he had been 'bitterly mistaken'; having thought them 'great men', he now thought that they were 'great cowards!' He called the final recommendation on the Naval War Staff 'poisonous' and bemoaned the total lack of any 'commendation for the Nucleus Crew System'.[7] (Fisher highlighted nucleus crews since they had saved the Government millions of pounds. That no gratitude was shown was hurtful to him.)

Writing to Crease a few days later, he lambasted the committee for the 'dirty trick' of saying that 'the Admiralty had not given its confidence to Beresford', given that he 'had abused that confidence within twenty-four hours of hoisting his flag!' He was, Fisher said, 'very sick of it all'.[8] Then, in a letter to Esher, he began to brood on his isolation – doubtless enhanced by his remoteness from London – saying that 'McKenna is powerless' since '[the] Prime Minister and the rest of them [are] dead against him now'. Lamenting the lack of 'one word of commendation for the Admiralty for its unparalleled work in gaining fighting efficiency', he concluded that 'Asquith won't do anything for *justice*' since 'only *fear* moves him'. This bitter letter was signed 'Yours for ever, but *disappointed* and *disgusted!*'[9]

Two days later, looking beyond the immediate impact of the report, Fisher suggested to Ottley that, by 'not squashing Beresford when they had the chance' the committee had 'given Beresford a fresh lease of insubordinate agitation'.[10]

There was much criticism of the supine nature of the report. Knollys told Esher that he was 'not surprised' at its 'colourless' nature. For him that was an inevitable outcome of 'the composition of the Committee which I always thought an absurd one'. Its members, he claimed, had been 'terrified at C. Beresford ... especially Asquith'. It was this fear of Beresford, he said, that led the Admiralty to make 'one grave mistake': prevarication in the face of his 'mutinous conduct'. They should either have recalled him at the start of his insubordinations, or let him 'complete his command'.[11] As it was, they had both allowed him to consistently thwart the authority of the Admiralty *and* suffered from all the consequences of an enquiry.

Ponsonby, too, thought that the report had been watered-down by 'the five just men' because 'Beresford contemplates going into Parliament and this probably frightened them'.[12]

No close reading of the report was needed to see that it showed little public support for the Board. It was, Sandars told Esher, 'equivocal'. As far as he was concerned, 'the Admiralty have made out their case against C.B.' but the Government had lacked 'the moral courage to give the Admiralty that clean verdict which they deserved'. He drew attention to the sad irony of the outcome. Just at the moment when the Board finally took 'a disciplinary step in the matter of Charlie B's command', and truncated his post, 'a Cabinet Cttee of unprofessionals' came in and undid the good work by returning 'a verdict which appears to be of ingenious balance'.[13]

While Beresford himself shrugged off the report's conclusions and bounced back within days of its publication, his supporters were less ready to come to terms with what they saw as a lack of vindication of their hero. In the lead, naturally, was Bellairs, who said in a speech at Westminster that the report 'was spread over with a copious use of whitewash, but revealed some very black streaks indeed'. He had not expected any other outcome since 'it was an inquiry by the Cabinet into preparations for which they are responsible'. They were not going to condemn themselves, he said, although, contradicting himself, he claimed that 'Lord Charles and the Admiralty were both found fault with' but only Beresford had been 'punished'.[14] Maxse, the editor of *The National Review* was reported as thinking that the report 'substantially justifies the action taken by Lord Charles, and is a scarcely veiled vote of censure on the Fisher régime'.[15]

Several commentators attributed the outcome to Beresford's aristocratic influence. Most of these suggestions were made in private letters, but *The Referee* was prepared to make the charge in public. The paper asked: 'Had Lord Charles Beresford not belonged to an old family, does anyone imagine that he could with impunity to himself have written to the Prime Minister in April that everything was wrong with the Navy, and to *The Times* on Aug. 17 that everything was right?'[16]

One of the few people who had no fear of Beresford was the King, who fumed at the Government's failure to take firm action against him. In a *'Most Confidential'* postscript in a letter to Fisher he wrote: 'I trust the Board of Admiralty will consider most seriously C.B.'s outrageous conduct.'[17]

Whichever way the report was read, one thing was obvious to almost everyone: nowhere was there any resounding, overt support for Fisher. The implications of this were quickly spotted by the likes of Esher and Knollys, who realised that Fisher's position had been severely undermined. Esher had found the report, he told Balfour, 'very cold and judicial' although 'perfectly sound'. However, it lacked 'any warm appreciative touch of Jackie's great services'. In his view, 'Jackie will be hurt at the want of direct support given to him', which was an accurate assessment. (His forecast of Beresford's reaction was, though, wide of the mark, suggesting that he 'will be furious'.) In this way, he wrote, 'I suppose the Report fulfils all "political" requirements.'[18]

The King, too, saw his friend as vulnerable and expected moves to oust him, but declared 'Fisher shall not be kicked out, in spite of the Cabinet, the Press, and C.B.'[19] In Esher's view, what was needed was a fleet circular to bolster Fisher's position. It was to warn 'sailors that all criticism must cease, and King's regulations must be observed' and should be backed up by 'some honour *at once*' for Fisher. The Government should then 'let him

223

alone for a year, after which he could retire'.[20] McKenna, though, thought discreet silence was more appropriate.

It was one thing for Fisher's friends to note his isolation, but quite another to do something positive about it. In the case of Sandars, he was to make very heavy weather over a simple request from Esher. On 24 August, Esher sent him a gossipy letter about reactions to the report. He had, he told Sandars, 'just read a letter from poor Jackie to the King'. Fisher was 'frightfully sore'; the Government had not shown 'conspicuous courage'. It was gloom all round. Casually, he added, 'You might write Jackie a friendly line of comfort.'[21] It was obvious what sort of letter Esher had in mind, but not so obvious to Sandars. At first, there was no problem: 'I will gladly write to him,' he told Esher, flippantly adding 'he may wish to print and circulate my letter?!!!'[22] Two weeks later, though, the letter remained unwritten. Sandars had begun to have 'doubts' and had consulted Balfour, who had raised all sorts of objections. 'The letter,' said Sandars, 'would be taken for an opinion unfavourable to C. Beresford in the issue between him and the Government.' Also, Balfour had told him, that 'any letter from me is equivalent (he says) to one from him'.[23] And so, it was never written. It was an ominous sign. If even Fisher's friends could not arrange a simple note of sympathy, what hope was there for his retaining his post?

For those who saw the verdict as an outright defeat for Fisher, the outcome was a matter for rejoicing. Frewen spoke for many when he wrote in his diary: 'so the Fisher regime, damn it, totters to its fall, thank Heaven.'[24] In the case of Maxse, editor of *The National Review*, the feeling was one of vindication. He described himself as one of 'the very few who for the last three or four years have been fighting against Fisherism'. In the past they had been vilified as 'simple maniacs' but with the publication of the report it could be seen that 'the strongest things ever said in the "National Review" on the subject, pale beside the actual reality'.[25] He added that, 'Should it come to hanging' Fisher 'will be entitled to the nearest lamp post' for his 'crime' of having reduced the estimates in the last years of the Unionist government.[26]

Some, though, saw the report as an outright defeat for Beresford. When Crease attended a City dinner and Fisher's name was mentioned in the toasts, there was, he told Fisher, a wave of enthusiastic support. But Beresford's name was greeted 'with a roar of laughter'. The City magnates, Crease claimed, 'no longer treated [him] seriously'.[27] A few months earlier, the roles would have been completely reversed.

## Scene 2: Fisher's fall

Fewer than two weeks after the report was published, and while Fisher was still abroad, Sandars was writing to Esher to share his doubts over

Fisher's capacity to continue in office. 'Has he really,' he asked, 'the strength & vigour of mind and body' to continue or was 'his genius spent?' Nostalgically, he recalled that 'Jackie in his prime ... would soon set these grave issues on right lines.' Now, though, he thought that Fisher was 'struggling with more than a man at his age can tackle'. All this was 'very very sad' and he hoped they would see 'our old friend making his bow, honoured in any way he would wish at the hands of the King'.[28]

Fisher, however, was bursting with confidence on his return from the South Tyrol. He told his daughter Beatrix that he was 'feeling most extraordinarily fit and well' and was like 'a giant refreshed'. He was ready for 'fierce fighting at the Admiralty'. This was probably mere bravado since, later in the same letter, he admitted 'I've had about enough of it now. I should have gone last year, except for the King.'[29]

However confident Fisher felt about continuing in post, his enemies wanted him drummed out, whilst friends advised him to leave gracefully. Only two days after his bouncy letter to Beatrix, he hinted to White that the pressure was on him to go, telling him that 'I am getting tons of kindly advice. I am invited to perform hara-kiri!' He was resisting, he said, 'For the sake of the greatest of all things – *Discipline*.'[30]

Amongst those who pressed him to stay, the King was foremost. Knollys, in a letter to Esher, reported that 'The King ... says that if he can help it Fisher shall not be "kicked out" ... in spite of the Cabinet.'[31] Fisher would have been pleased to hear similarly encouraging views from Lionel Yexley, a naval journalist, who had just returned from Portsmouth where, he said, '[I] addressed five good meetings [of] Ships' Stewards, Warrant Officers, Chief Petty Officers, Artisan ratings and Marines.' The name of 'Jacky Fisher,' he wrote, 'was never mentioned without eliciting emphatic exclamations of approval.' For added comfort, he added that 'Bellairs is so very much approved [of]' that 'the Ward Room and lower deck' called him 'Windy Bill'.[32]

Within three months of the report's publication, Fisher bowed to the inevitable and announced his retirement. Esher had urged this on him in early September, but had noted that 'McKenna objects to this, and is asking him to stay.'[33] Sandars approved of Esher's plan. If only Fisher would name a date, he told Esher, 'I believe there would be a strong reaction in his favour and his finale would be all that his friends could wish.' In that event, 'his errors and indiscretions would be forgotten and his great achievements would be on everyone's lips'. There would, he added, be the bonus of 'an immediate slump in C.B. stocks'.[34]

Fisher set the date for 25 January 1910 – his sixty-ninth birthday. He brushed aside those who would have preferred to help him to stay in office since, as he told James Remnant, a Conservative MP, 'Nothing would induce me to let you help me. I ruin every man and woman who does so.' He had, he said, 'told the King I had led a dog's life, but yet every dog has had his day!'[35] Beresford was delighted that 'the evil one has gone' but less pleased that '[he] will still intrigue as he is on [the] Council of Defence'.[36]

Sir Arthur Wilson was selected to take over from Fisher. McKenna chose him despite Fisher's initial coolness at the idea. But, by 8 November, he was won over, telling McKenna 'I must congratulate you on getting Wilson! *It's a great coup!*' He was the obvious choice because, in contrast to the turbulent years of Fisher, the man who did too much, Wilson would provide a period of calm and be the man who did too little. McKenna had, as Fisher reminded him, said that what was needed was 'a stonewall' for two years.[37] The result was not a success and, in the opinion of one of Fisher's biographers, Wilson's tenure 'was the greatest administrative catastrophe suffered by the Royal Navy in this century'.[38] Known as 'ard heart', Wilson was a taciturn and reserved man. Although Bridgeman accepted him as 'the best solution' he told Fisher that 'there is no joy to be found in serving either with him or under him! Deadly dull! ... impatient in argument, even to being impossible!'[39]

After Asquith's failure to support Fisher at the time of the enquiry, he belatedly offered him the olive branch of a baronetcy. In his letter he at last found himself able to use the words that were so markedly missing from the enquiry report:

> I desire ... to express to you the sincere and grateful acknowledgements of His Majesty's Government for the great work – unique in our time – which you have accomplished in developing and strengthening the Navy, and assuring the maritime supremacy of Great Britain.[40]

Yes, there, finally, were the words: 'maritime supremacy'. Fisher knew that he had secured it; Beresford and the Syndicate disputed it; finally, Asquith had admitted it – but only in a private letter.

Fisher sent the letter to the King, who found it '[a] charming letter in every respect', adding his own praise to that of the Prime Minister: 'Nobody deserves the thanks of your Sovereign and your Country more warmly than you do.' He hoped that Fisher would remain on the CID: 'You possess too much vitality to "lie fallow"!'[41]

The baronetcy was honour, but not honour enough for Fisher, who wished for a viscountcy. As he told Ponsonby, 'I've been urged to demur being a common and [sic] garden Peer like the man who makes linoleum or lends money for elections.'[42] If the brewer Edward Guinness could become *Viscount* Iveagh, he argued, surely an admiral of the fleet should not count for less?

Fisher's hopes of a higher honour came to nothing, as did his battle over his title. He had favoured being 'Lord Fisher of Packington', the small village where his ancestors had possessed a manor house from 1544 to 1729. 'There are three tiers of Fishers in black marble tombs at Packington,' Fisher scrawled on a press cutting that claimed that he preferred the title

Kilverstone, 'I think that is more appropriate.'[43] There was also a tussle over the arms and, if Fisher can be believed, 'Garter King at Arms' came to his bedside to persuade him 'to discard the ancient Fisher arms'. On a lighter note, he continued, 'Some wag has sent me Beresford and Custance standing on their heads upside down as supporters' as a suggestion. It was at the same meeting that Garter King at Arms turned down Fisher's chosen motto – dreadnought – and suggested the phrase that is now forever associated with his name: 'Fear God and Dread Nought.'[44] The announcement of his baronetcy appeared in *The Times* on 18 November: 'Baron Fisher of Kilverstone.'[45]

As the last few weeks slipped by, Fisher and McKenna both mourned their parting. 'I would have dearly liked to be with you to the end,' Fisher told McKenna.[46] In a letter to Fisher, written on Christmas Day, McKenna looked back over the year, thinking of the 'many tough and victorious fights in which we have been comrades'. He thought that their 'most powerful weapon' had been their 'perfect unanimity'. And, in a final tribute to Fisher's genius he wrote: 'I recall with feelings of the most affectionate friendship how firmly you stood by me in my Cabinet troubles. The victory was due to you.'[47]

And so came the last day – for some reason it was 18 and not 25 January. 'I've parted from my moorings this morning,' he told Mrs Meynell, 'and the Admiralty knows me no more!' He had already decided to lie low so, although both Esher and White had visited him that morning, 'both girding at me to speak and blast my enemies' he told Mrs Meynell: '*I will not.*'[48]

## Scene 3: Beresford reborn

On 20 August 1909, Beresford left Liverpool for a political tour of Canada and the United States. It was a dramatic way to announce 'business as usual' after the drubbing he had received from the enquiry. His speeches in North America continued the very same attacks on Government and Admiralty policy which had so recently been rejected by the enquiry. He pressed the need for more cruisers, rather than dreadnoughts, saying: 'We want cruisers, and will have them ... Armed tramps are what we fear' and he told his Canadian audiences that he wanted to be back in the Commons 'as soon as possible' since 'the whole responsibility for this naval matter rests on my shoulders'.[49] Despite speeches such as this, *The Times* strangely reported that Beresford had been 'singularly reticent and discreet' on his tour.[50]

When Asquith opened his *Times* on the morning of 25 October 1909, he must have cursed the day he ever decided to treat with Beresford. There, displayed to the world, was their correspondence, dating back to 21 April. In an explanatory letter in the paper, Beresford told his readers that he

227

found it 'deplorable that it is necessary to make public this correspondence'. Not so deplorable, though, for him to have held back.[51]

Ostensibly, the publication of the correspondence was all to do with Hulbert, although as it progressed, its scope widened. Beresford started with Asquith's letter of 21 April, in which he had assured him that there would be 'no prejudice of any kind' against those who gave evidence. In a Beresford letter of 20 July, *Times* readers learnt how Hulbert had been 'given leave of absence from 1 July' after his position in the NID had been made 'exceedingly difficult by his superiors'. He had also been passed over for other appointments by 'four junior officers'.[52] On 9 August, Asquith had replied, telling Beresford that Hulbert's leave was just the result of organisational changes and that 'his professional prospects and future are not going to be in any way impaired by anything that happened in connection with our inquiry'.[53]

There was then a pause in the correspondence of over two months before another letter landed on Asquith's desk. This time, Beresford claimed that 'certain officers referred to in our previous correspondence have been placed on half-pay'.[54] Two days later, Asquith provided more details of the changes in the Admiralty which had resulted in both Hulbert and Campbell being sidelined. Campbell's division, which dealt with trade, 'was not worth its cost' and had been closed. For different reasons, Hulbert's department had been merged with another area of work. None of these changes, Asquith said, had anything to do with their having given evidence, and both were now awaiting appointments as captains of a ship.[55]

Not for one moment did Beresford accept this account. Writing to Asquith two days later he insisted that Hulbert's career 'has already been "prejudiced" by the unjust and humiliating treatment' of being suspended from his post. In a moment of hyperbole, excessive even by Beresford's standards, he said that this 'was tantamount to placing him under arrest for incompetency or misconduct', adding that it had been 'an attempt to intimidate a witness'. He concluded that the 'real reason for carrying out the "reorganisation" was the removal of the two officers who were called by me to give evidence'. The same letter also suggested that Sturdee had been passed over for a posting by 'seven officers junior to [him]'.[56]

This letter was an astounding piece of arrogance, since it effectively accused both the Prime Minister and the First Lord of lying, and, in the case of the latter, of reorganising his department with the sole purpose of persecuting officers who had disagreed with Admiralty policy. These were serious charges, which demanded answers. Yet, before Asquith had had time to breathe, he was reading the same letter in *The Times*.

In reply, Asquith reprimanded the still untamed admiral, regretting 'that an officer of your experience and distinction should have allowed himself to become responsible for the publication of such a letter'. This he found 'hard to reconcile with the best traditions of a great service'.[57]

Meanwhile, Asquith had passed a copy of Beresford's letter of 23 October to McKenna, who replied to him on 29 October, the letter appearing in *The Times* the next day. McKenna's relaxed opening revealed his cool approach to Beresford's outrageous charges:

> As I am convinced [he told Asquith] that you would not advise the retention of a Board of Admiralty capable of the misconduct imputed to it by Lord Charles Beresford, I am satisfied that you do not attach the slightest credence to his allegations. You have not, indeed, invited me to reply to them ...[58]

But he did reply. It was the McKenna of the enquiry all over again: calm, methodical, precise ... and devastating.

Was it true that the NID reorganisation was carried out to get rid of Hulbert and Campbell? No, since, as he pointed out to Asquith, the reorganisation had been planned long before either officer had appeared to give evidence, and Asquith had received regular updates on the proposed changes.

Was it true that Hulbert had been sent on leave because he gave evidence? No, it was 'for disciplinary reasons', the details of which McKenna could provide if required.

Was it true that Sturdee had been passed over? No, and he had talked to Sturdee, who had no complaints.

Was it true that five captains associated with Beresford had been held back in their careers? No; in fact they were all captains who had to qualify by seniority, i.e. they needed to serve more sea time as captains before they became eligible for promotion.

And then McKenna listed all the officers who had served with Beresford in 1907 and 1908 – the very group who Beresford said were being victimised – and demonstrated the extraordinary number of promotions (eight out of fourteen) in this group. Ignoring those officers too junior to be considered for promotion, the list was impressive:

| Officer | Rank (1907) | Rank (1909) |
| --- | --- | --- |
| Sturdee | Captain | Rear Admiral |
| Brock | Captain | Flag Captain |
| Booty | Commander | Captain |
| Roper | Lieutenant | Commander |
| Royds | Lieutenant | Commander |
| Silvertop | Lieutenant | 'Important appointment at the Admiralty' |
| Fullerton | Lieutenant | HM Yacht *Victoria and Albert* |
| Browning | Captain | Captain, HMS *Britannia* (a 1st class battleship) |

| Hulbert | Commander | Captain |
|---|---|---|
| Thring | Commander | Moved to War College at own request |
| Gibbs | Lieutenant | No change |
| Pelly | Captain | Captain Superintendent of contract-built ships – the highest-paid captain in the Navy |
| Baird | Commander | Captain |
| Scarlett | Lieutenant | Commander |

Although not intended for publication, the letter's appearance in *The Times* was a public relations triumph. There was really nothing that Beresford could say in reply. His bluster and his wild accusations had been overwhelmed by facts and analysis.

There was one interesting postscript to this. In April 1910, Campbell entered into a lengthy correspondence with the Admiralty to try to clear his name over the leaked letter. He was convinced that his Admiralty file contained accusations of dishonourable conduct. When McKenna's private secretary told him that the Board had 'no record whatever official or unofficial in which any reason is given for the termination of your appointment' he was far from satisfied.[59] He wanted, he said, a letter from the First Lord 'which would make it clear that I am innocent' of the charge of having leaked a letter to Beresford.[60] When McKenna finally wrote to Campbell, he told him that 'There is no ground whatsoever for supposing that in the course of the proceedings of the Beresford Committee you showed a Confidential Document to Lord Charles Beresford … Your appointment to HMS *Hindustan* is of itself sufficient proof that the Board of Admiralty had no belief in this allegation.'[61]

Still unhappy, Campbell recommenced his correspondence. In reply, an exasperated Troubridge foolishly added a personal comment to his official reply of 25 May, saying, 'I tell you quite frankly as a sea officer myself, and I may add, an hereditary sea officer, that I believe you to be wrong in this.'[62] This provoked a bitter retort from Campbell and, on 31 May, Troubridge's patience gave out. 'I have,' he told Campbell, 'decided to end the correspondence.'[63]

There remained the question of Beresford's naval career. Technically he was still an admiral on the active list, ready for service and receiving half-pay. What was to be done with him until retirement in 1911? There were discreet demands that he should be removed from the Navy List, which would have been a drastic step and would have undoubtedly brought opprobrium on the Government. Knollys observed, in a letter to Esher, that 'Whatever the [he] may say or do' Asquith would not agree to his removal.[64] Fisher, on the other hand, favoured his removal, even though there was 'a danger of making Beresford a martyr'.[65]

It is unlikely that Beresford even wanted to return to a posting – bar one: First Sea Lord. He had succeeded in ousting Fisher and Scott, but failed in his aim to take the former's place. In September, just one month after the report's publication, he was closeted with Long at the latter's country seat in Wiltshire, where, alleged Fisher, they were plotting the future management of the Navy. 'Walter Long,' he said, 'hopes to be First Lord ... with Beresford as First Sea Lord!'[66]

The King was not at all happy that no action had been taken against Beresford after the enquiry. He wanted the Board to 'consider most seriously C.B.'s outrageous conduct' and hoped that '"serious action" will be taken!'[67] Nothing, though, was done.

If the enquiry had left any doubt that Beresford's naval career was over, his letter of 23 October removed any remaining uncertainty. He had already decided that he would return to politics if other routes were blocked, so it was convenient that, just a week later, the Unionist Party in East Marylebone, London, voted to invite him to become their parliamentary candidate. With rumours of an early general election in the air, it seemed likely that Beresford would be back in the House within months. He had already agreed to stand on condition that 'the invitation is unanimous'.[68] Four days later the nomination meeting took place and Beresford spoke 'at great length' on various subjects, including tariff reform, of which he approved.[69] He was selected unanimously.

Meanwhile, a rival Unionist candidate had appeared, also a tariff reformer. It was not unusual to find competing Unionist candidates at that time since the party was hopelessly split between tariff reformers (i.e. those who favoured protective taxes on imports) and free-traders. However, two rival tariff-reformers must have been unusual. Beresford's 'unanimous' election began to look less secure than it first appeared.

Before the East Marylebone situation could develop much further, a by-election vacancy arose in Portsmouth. The local Unionist party already had a candidate, but he promptly resigned in order to allow Beresford to take his place, because he said there was 'a very serious crisis in the history of the Navy ... [and] no greater blow could be delivered to the Government than the return of Lord Charles for Portsmouth'.[70] Fisher was distraught at the news: within days of McKenna's crushing letter in *The Times*, Beresford was about to be resurrected. 'Nothing,' Fisher told Pamela McKenna, 'could be more disastrous. It is the apotheosis of insubordination!'[71]

At Portsmouth Beresford had, once again, landed a nomination where there were rival Unionist candidates – two this time – but both quickly gave way in a telegram to him. As he boarded the train on 18 November to attend his nomination meeting he can hardly have anticipated the reception that lay ahead. It was a repeat performance of his landing on 24 March. Once more the station overflowed with well-wishers; once more the Town Hall square was a seething mass of people. As the train pulled into the station, there were 'prolonged and lusty cheers' and, said *The Times*, 'the enthusiasm increased as his carriage, drawn by blue-jackets, left the station yard'.[72] After a wide-ranging address to the party, Beresford was adopted as the Unionist candidate for Portsmouth. He was now the official candidate for two constituencies.

Beresford quickly extricated himself from his commitment to East Marylebone, giving as his reason 'the unsatisfactory state of the Royal Navy, upon which the destiny of the British Empire depends'. It was his duty, he said 'to accept the [Portsmouth] candidature'.[73]

The campaign began immediately and within days Beresford received an offer from his old friend, Bellairs, to assist him. Beresford thanked him for his offer, but declined it since his presence might 'be regarded as a direct attack on the Admiralty and Fisher'. He had been advised that he needed 'to stand clear of all questions about the Admiralty or Fisher'. At the back of his mind was York, 'where I only won by eleven votes' in 1898.[74]

Although Beresford was undoubtedly keen to be elected, his campaigning style was relaxed to the point of lethargy. From the start, his supporters, said *The Times*, were concerned about 'his abstention from open-air meetings', particularly since the other candidates were 'zealous open-air speakers'.[75] Next, he refused to 'canvass the electors individually', saying that he had 'too much respect for their intelligence'. In reporting this, *The Times* journalist added that 'fortunately for him his agents have no such high-minded qualms'.[76] Doubtless such indifference led to criticism, so it is not surprising that Beresford soon found a way of exonerating himself: 'his medical adviser', he said, had forbidden him 'to address open-air meetings'.[77] (By contrast, Daisy Warwick, his great love, was able to address 'five open-air meetings in drizzling rain' in one day when she stood as a Labour candidate in 1923, aged sixty-one.)[78]

Fisher keenly followed the election, praying for Beresford's defeat. He grabbed at any passing rumour that sustained his hope. So much so that he became convinced that 'Beresford is going to be beaten at Portsmouth' and that he wanted to 'cut and run'.[79] We shall never know the truth since, on 1 December, the Government announced that they would not move the writ for the by-election. Their battle with the House of Lords over the budget was to go to the hustings: there would be a General Election in January 1910.

Meanwhile, Beresford had been active on a wider political front. In early November, he sent a letter of support to a Mr Harold Lloyd, a Unionist Parliamentary candidate in the Rhondda Valley. The letter, which appeared in *The Times* on 6 November flatly stated that his charges had been vindicated by the enquiry committee. 'The report,' Beresford told Lloyd, 'conclusively shows that my statements were correct.' Then, forgetting that he had accused the Admiralty of stealing all his ideas, he continued: 'The

Navy is not properly organised or trained for war, and no plan of campaign can be effective unless the ships are there to carry the plan out.'[80]

A month later, as the General Election campaign developed, Beresford stomped the country in support of Unionist candidates. At North Shields, he told a meeting that 'If the papers which he put before the Cabinet Committee were made public there would be riots.'[81] He did not add that the committee had utterly rejected his charges. Later that month he was campaigning on behalf of Sir George Armstrong, the man who had released the Bacon letter. Pressing the need to spend more on the Navy, he told his Welsh audience that 'The public had not been told the truth about the Navy.'[82] This 'truth', of course, referred to the false charges that should, by now, have been laid to rest.

Polling took place in January and February 1910. Beresford's great hope – a Unionist victory – was not to be. The Liberal Party scraped home with 273 seats, just twenty ahead of the Unionists. With eighty-two Irish Nationalists ready to keep the Liberals in office in return for a Home Rule bill, Beresford's hopes of the post of First Lord or First Sea Lord were finally annihilated. In consolation though, he was elected Unionist member for Portsmouth. Interestingly, Conan Doyle declined to stand for the seat in 1891 because he would have had to answer 'a hundred letters a day'.[83] The conscientious Doyle would have handled these personally. Doubtless Beresford left that to his secretary.

And there Beresford's career came to a dead end, despite pressure for him to be made an Admiral of the Fleet. In December, Long had heard rumours that 'Charlie [was] being passed over.'[84] Meanwhile, Beresford had been preparing a dossier on those admirals who had been specially promoted to Admiral of the Fleet so that they could remain on the active list – these included Richards (1898), Kerr (1904) and Wilson (1907). He was, he told Long, 'naturally anxious to remain on the Active List'.[85] No offer came; the Government had no further use for him.

There remains the question as to why no action was ever taken against Beresford. He himself bragged that he had had more reprimands than any other officer and, for once, it is a believable Beresford claim. Yet, there was little tolerance of officers' insubordinations in the Navy generally. As a contrast to the Board's endlessly elastic tolerance of Beresford, we need look no further than what happened to three officers after a minor squabble fewer than two decades after the enquiry.

In late 1927 the *Royal Oak*, of the Second Battleship Squadron in the Mediterranean, found itself with three new officers: Rear Admiral Collard, Captain Dewar and Commander Daniel. Within weeks, relations between the arrogant, self-important Collard, the taciturn and withdrawn Dewar, and the rather too clever Daniel had broken down. On 12 January 1928 Collard, dissatisfied with the playing of the ship's band at a dance on board ship, viciously humiliated Percy Barnacle, the Bandmaster. In a thundering voice, clearly audible to officers and their guests, Collard called him a 'bugger' and pronounced that he was to be dismissed from the ship the next day. Further incidents followed, culminating in an occasion when the admiral refused to return the salutes of the ship's officers. Humiliated and angry, Daniel and Dewar wrote letters of complaint to Vice Admiral Kelly. Within the day, Collard had been put ashore at Malta and Daniel and Dewar had been sent back to England. Following the courts martial in London of Dewar and Daniel (held at their own request), the two men were severely reprimanded, but not dismissed from the service. Collard, who escaped a court martial, was forcibly retired.[86]

Had times simply changed from Beresford's days, or was there more to the Beresford case? The latter seems likely. In varying degrees at different points in Beresford's naval career, he was protected by his aristocratic birth, his political influence, and his public popularity from the treatment that would have been meted out to a lesser man.

Beresford's political activities also helped to protect him. From the day that he first entered Parliament, he was never without an offer of a seat. Although he was an indifferent performer in the House – where, in practice, he had little influence – and a poor party member, he could always get himself elected when he chose. Successive Boards of Admiralty were ever mindful of this when choosing between a sea command and half-pay for Beresford. At times, sea lords and first lords admitted amongst themselves that sending Beresford to sea was the lesser of two evils. There was, therefore, great pressure within the Admiralty to live with the problem rather than to offer Beresford the martyrdom that he perhaps craved. From the point of view of successive Cabinets, they too perhaps preferred to keep him at sea rather than to suffer his abusive tirades from the back benches.

And finally, there was his popularity. 'Charlie B' was a national hero. From the days in 1882 when the cry of 'Well done, *Condor!*' first went up in the assembly halls of England, Beresford was assured of a tumultuous welcome wherever he chose to speak. His reception on landing at Portsmouth on 24 March 1909 and that when he returned there in November were enough to make any politician think twice before taking him on.

And what was he up against? Sir John Fisher, a genius according to many, and certainly far more talented than Beresford, but a man who rarely went out into society, who dined out infrequently and avoided politicians except when duty demanded that he made use of them. Fisher simply never had the public influence that was Beresford's. He would never have survived the onslaughts of Beresford and the Syndicate from 1906 to 1909 had it not been for the King's unfaltering support. He could, and did, put up a mighty defence of his works, but he was not able to mount a mighty *attack*. He repeatedly told correspondents that he was determined not to react, to stay silent and to keep out of the fray. Whether this was the best tactic is hard to say.

234

# Beresford's decline and Fisher's return

His genius was deep and true.
– *Winston Churchill on Fisher*[1]

If the story had ended with Fisher's retirement and Beresford's election to the Commons, we would be left with the impression that Beresford was the victor and Fisher the victim. Things were to turn out rather differently.

Beresford's bounce was just an illusion – a last burst of ebullience before a long, embittered decline. Although he remained an MP until his elevation to the peerage in 1916, he had little political influence. He never admitted that his charges had been rejected by the committee and year in, year out, repeated them in varied forms. He even published a book in 1912, *The Betrayal*, which, he claimed was 'a statement of facts'.[2] Many of those 'facts', though, were the very same charges rejected by the enquiry committee. Its general tone can be gauged from the concluding chapter in which Beresford said 'the naval policy of the years 1902 to 1909 was mistaken in every important particular. From the beginning the great body of naval opinion held that the new policy was wrong'.[3] This was to conveniently forget how strongly he had first supported Fisher's reforms. He repeated the charge that 'several' of the officers who joined him in criticising Admiralty policy … have been placed on half-pay and kept without employment, or their Service careers have been summarily terminated.'[4] He gave no names or details, so no one could check this 'fact'; nor did he mention the numerous promotions detailed in McKenna's letter of 29 October 1909. On the book's publication, *The Times* noted that 'the country at large' had already rejected these claims and expressed 'regret that Lord Charles Beresford has seen fit to publish his book'.[5] Its style, said *The American Journal of International Law* was 'impetuous'.[6]

During the First World War, he waited anxiously for the call to serve the nation. None came. Meanwhile, he bombarded Asquith with voluminous letters which criticised his conduct of the war. He was still, in 1917, raging against Fisher and even claimed in a letter to Bellairs that he was 'mainly responsible for the war'.[7]

In the last years of his life, the old hatreds kept returning. McKenna was to blame for his wilderness years when he forced him to haul down his flag, '& proceed ashore'. It was, he told Hurd in April 1919, 'the McKennas, Churchills, J. Fishers' who were responsible for all 'my gallant dead ship-mates'.[8] It was no wonder that he died of apoplexy five months later.

Fisher's career, on the other hand, took a strange turn.

On leaving office, he went abroad and was away on and off until June 1912. His intention was to keep out of Wilson's way, but his pen was as active as ever as he bombarded friends, colleagues and politicians with long, vigorous letters. He was, he said, like a mole: 'unseen but recognised by upheavals.'[9] Meanwhile, he continued to be a member of the CID, although avoided attending its meetings since he did not wish to upstage Wilson. Although he was pestered by people who pressed him to return home, including McKenna, who was disillusioned with Wilson, he refused to move.

Then, in October 1911, politics suddenly turned in Fisher's favour. The Asquith Government was beset by social and domestic problems, many of which were in the domain of the Home Office. In Asquith's opinion, Churchill was, as Home Secretary, rather too forceful and high-handed, so he decided to swap him with the more staid McKenna. The latter was bitterly disappointed at the change, but from Fisher's point of view it was providential since the young, inexperienced Churchill felt in need of a mentor. Four days after Churchill's appointment, Fisher was secretly recalled for a clandestine conference with Churchill and other Government officials. So hush-hush was the meeting that he was not allowed to even tell his family why he was in England, nor explain his failure to visit them at Kilverstone Hall.

Further secret meetings and much correspondence ensued, including an occasion when Asquith and Churchill, travelling in the Admiralty yacht *The Enchantress*, turned up at Naples to consult with Fisher. In part, the meeting was designed to lure him back home – 'I was very nearly kidnapped and carried off in the Admiralty Yacht!' he told the journalist Gerald Fiennes, adding 'The Prime Minister is "dead on" for my coming back, and he has put things so forcibly to me that, with great reluctance to enter the battlefield, I probably shall do!'[10]

On his return, he was appointed Chairman of the Royal Commission on Oil Fuel and Oil Engines, his first public activity since leaving the Admiralty eighteen months earlier. His rehabilitation had begun.

On 4 August 1914, Britain declared war on Germany. In anticipation of this, the Fleet had gone to its battle stations. It was, to all intents and purposes, Fisher's fleet and it was his fleet that held the German High Sea Fleet at bay for four years, until it was ignominiously scuttled at

Scapa Flow in 1919. Strong as the Fleet was, the public refused to give it their confidence as long as Prince Louis of Battenberg was First Sea Lord. A Briton of unquestionable loyalty, he was widely seen as a traitorous German. After two months of vicious public vilification, he retired a broken man. Churchill unhesitatingly recalled Fisher.

The combination of the irrepressible Churchill and the demonic Fisher was widely forecast to be short-lived. And so it was. Throughout the early months of 1915 they clashed over the running of the Dardanelles campaign. On Saturday 15 May, Fisher turned up for work at his usual early hour. After reading the telegrams that Churchill had prepared the night before, ready to be sent to the Mediterranean Fleet, Fisher knew he could take no more. He picked up his pen for the very last time in Admiralty House to tell Churchill that 'After further anxious reflection, I have come to the regretted conclusion I am unable to remain any longer as your colleague.' He was, he said, 'in the position of continually vetoing your proposals' which was 'not fair to you'. Wishing to avoid any further discussion of their differences, Fisher added 'I am off to Scotland at once.'[11]

Two days later, the Government fell. Fisher was not the sole cause, but he gave it the final push. By the end of the week, Churchill was gone too. It was the end of the Fisher era.

Fisher lived on until July 1920, carrying out small public functions, but increasingly a private man who sought consolation in religion.

One other player in this story remains to be accounted for: Walter Long. He had refused the Admiralty in 1905 but was offered it again by Lloyd George in 1919. Although he took the post, the fire had gone. He was, he recorded in his memoirs 'too old, too much worn by the responsibilities of office and by domestic sorrow to be able to bring to the discharge of my duties the freshness and vigour of my earlier days'. What was worse though, was that rather than 'build up a great navy' he had been put there 'to reduce the splendid Force which had been brought to such wonderful strength and efficiency by my predecessors'.[12] What a humiliation it must have been after all the bold talk of how the Long-Beresford partnership would abolish inefficiency and create a mighty Navy.

On the deaths of Beresford in 1919 and Fisher in 1920, *The Times* obituary writers chose to overlook the feud. In the case of Beresford, there was a brief reference to his 'exaggerated or ill-founded'[13] criticisms of the Admiralty and, in the case of Fisher, it was noted that his reforms 'aroused much bitter antagonism and much painful controversy'.[14] Neither Fisher nor Beresford chose to discuss the feud in their memoirs. Scott, too, glossed over almost all his controversies with Beresford.

Despite this, the feud must remain the defining feature of Beresford's life. For all his courage, for all his skill as a seaman, for all his popularity, he was a man of feeble intellect and poor judgement. However unjust some of Fisher's actions may have been (and even that is hard to determine),

Beresford turned competition for high office into a vendetta. In doing so, he took on the Admiralty and the Government, and lost.

In Fisher's case, the feud was just an incident in a life of staggering achievements. At times he acted harshly, at times he was careless of the effect of his policies and actions on others. Yet, throughout his life, he acted only to promote the long-term interests of the Navy and the country. His memorial was the great Fleet that protected Britain throughout the First World War and safely transported millions of soldiers to and fro across the Channel.

Yet, for all their faults and quarrels, Fisher and Beresford were giants. Sadly, they were giants who were destined to clash.

# Reprimands and Expressions of Disapproval of Beresford

The following is a list of the twenty-three (including the double reprimand of 1901) known reprimands and expressions of disapproval that Beresford received. Almost certainly there were many more, of which no record survives.

| Date | Ship | Details |
|---|---|---|
| c.1860 | *Britannia* | Promoted to the rank of cadet captain. Demoted the same day.[1] |
| c.1861 | *Marlborough* | Secretly prepared a sail in order to gain advantage in a contest. 'Severely reprimanded' for 'staining the character of a ship'; disrated to cadet.[2] |
| c.1863 | *Defence* | Tried to steal (for the *Defence*) a length of rope. Caught by a dockyard policeman and reported for stealing Government property.[3] |
| 1877 | *Thunderer* | Criticised the Navy in Parliament while being a serving officer. The Board told him that he had to choose between the Navy and Parliament and he was kept on half-pay for five years.[4] |
| 1879 | Half-pay | Wrote to the press, commenting on the reasons for the *Thunderer* gun explosion, without waiting for the enquiry report. Board condemned him for his 'impudence'.[5] |
| 1882 | *Condor* | First Lord 'proposed to order the immediate arrest of Lord Charles and his trial by naval court martial' following his communications with journalists.[6] |

| | | |
|---|---|---|
| 1885 | Service in Sudan | Unclear criticism of Beresford in connection with his 'relinquishing command of the Naval Brigade' in the Sudan.[7] |
| 1890 | *Undaunted* | Was reprimanded in connection with watch-keeping following the loss of the *Undaunted*'s steam cutter.[8] |
| 1893 | *Undaunted* | Acquitted after a court martial. (The *Undaunted* had touched the bottom of the sea.)[9] |
| 1895 | Half-pay | Reprimanded in connection with his complaints after being passed over for an ADC appointment.[10] |
| 1900 | *Ramillies* | Reprimanded for allowing captains 'to handle and manoeuvre the Squadron under my watchful care'.[11] |
| 1901 | *Ramillies* | Fisher twice reprimanded him after newspaper reports 'in which my name was mentioned as revolutionising the squadron'.[12] |
| 1902 | *Ramillies* | Reprimanded for 'having published in the *Daily Mail* of 21 June 1901 a letter on the subject of war organisation of the Med$^n$ Fleet'.[13] |
| 1902 | Half-pay | Reprimanded for his letter to *The Times* of 8[14] April 1902.[15] |
| 1903 | *Majestic* | Reprimanded 'for the near-loss of a battleship by holding night manoeuvres with lights out' and accused of 'a crazy new-fangled' practice.[16] |
| 1903 | *Caesar* | Reprimanded for criticising the Board for having delayed (in his opinion) the introduction of telescopic sights on guns.[17] |
| 1904 | *Caesar* | Reprimanded for his 'chivalrous' plan for intercepting the Russian Fleet on its way from the Baltic to the Far East.[18] |
| 1904 | *Caesar* | Reprimanded for remarks on prize-firing returns, April 1904.[19] |
| 1907 | *King Edward VII* | Reprimand for press remarks which 'tend to propagate alarmist rumours of national danger'.[20] |

| 1907 | *King Edward VII* | Reprimanded for asking the Commanders-in-Chief at Chatham and Devonport to address him officially in a different manner to that authorised by the Admiralty.[21] |
| 1908 | *King Edward VII* | Reprimanded for inviting personal friends to join his fleet for manoeuvres, after having asked the Admiralty to ban journalists from the same manoeuvres.[22] |
| 1908 | *King Edward VII* | Reprimanded for circulating a memorandum which criticised officers of the Home Fleet.[23] |

# Notes

**Abbreviations:** BL, British Library; CCA, Churchill College Archives; NA, National Archives; NMM, National Maritime Museum; ODNB, Oxford Dictionary of National Biography.

## Prologue: The Roots of the Feud

1. Quoted in Marder, 1965, pp. 240–1.
2. Jenkins, 1994, p. 95.
3. ODNB.
4. NA CAB 16/9 A, p. 1.
5. Dorling, 1929, p. 263.
6. ODNB.
7. The term Sea Lord replaced the term Naval Lord in October 1904.
8. Fisher, 1919a, p. 36.
9. CCA FISR 8/4.
10. Bosanquet to White, 26 May 1907. NMM WHI/75.
11. Crease to White, 28 and 30 June 1908. NMM WHI/76.
12. Royal Navy. http://www.royal-navy.mod.uk.
13. Lambert, 2008, p. 311.

## Act 1: Giants in the Making

1. Bennett, 1968, p. 86.
2. Three biographies of Fisher, and his own memoirs, state that his father was ADC to the Governor of Ceylon. There is no documentary evidence to support this, William Fisher being nowhere mentioned in the official record of ADCs. See British Imperial Calendar 1831–1841.
3. *The Victoria History of the Counties of England.*
4. Fisher, 1919b, p. 2.
5. Captain Fisher to Fisher, 14 January 1862. CCA FISR 15/1/2/1.
6. Fisher, 1938, pp. 16–22.
7. R. Ussher and M.E. Ussher, November and December 1933. CCA FISR 15/3/2/5.
8. Fisher, 1919b, pp. 4–5.
9. Marder, 1952, p. 24.
10. Fisher, 1919b, p. 10.
11. CCA FISR 15/1/2/1.
12. CCA FISR 9/1.
13. Fisher, 1919b, pp. 11–12.
14. Ibid., p. 13.
15. CCA FISR 9/1.

16. Fisher to Mrs Warden, 28 June 1859. CCA FISR 15/1/1.
17. Fisher to Mrs Warden, 21 October 1859. CCA FISR 15/2/6.
18. Moorhouse [later Meynell], 1940, p. 78.
19. Fisher to Mrs Warden, 21 October 1859. CCA FISR 15/2/6.
20. Fisher 1919b, p. 14.
21. Fisher to Mrs Warden, 5 February 1860. CCA FISR 15/2/6.
22. Fisher to Mrs Warden, 24 March 1860. CCA FISR 15/2/6.
23. Ibid.
24. Fisher to Mrs Warden, 9 April 1860. CCA FISR 15/2/6.
25. CCA FISR 15/3/2/6.
26. Edmunds to 2nd Lord Fisher, 26 October 1920. CCA FISR 15/3/2/6.
27. Fisher, 1919a, p. 229.
28. Fisher to his wife, 13 June 1870. CCA FISR 15/1/2/2.
29. This is the version of Mrs Fisher's maiden name as confirmed by her son. CCA FISR 15/3/1/2.
30. Moorhouse [later Meynell], 1940, p. 75.
31. Fisher to his wife, 4 December 1870. Quoted in Marder, 1952, p. 69.
32. Fisher to his wife, 5 February 1872. CCA FISR 15/1/2/2.
33. CCA FISR 13/17.
34. CCA FISR 10/8.
35. CCA FISR 9/26.
36. Ibid.
37. NMM PHI/120.
38. Bennett, 1968, Chapter 1.
39. Beresford, 1914, p. xiv.
40. Quoted in Bennett, 1968, p. 147.
41. ODNB.
42. Bennett, 1968, p. 29.
43. Beresford, 1914, p. 5.
44. Ibid., p. 6.
45. Ibid., p. 8.
46. Ibid., pp. 26–7.
47. Ibid., p. 41.
48. Ibid., p. 64.
49. Ibid., p. 64.
50. Ibid., p. 539.
51. ODNB.
52. Beresford, 1914, p. 45.
53. Ibid., p. 64.
54. Ibid., p. 71.
55. Ibid., p. 113–14.
56. Bennett, 1968, pp. 70–1.
57. Beresford, 1914, p. 157.
58. Quoted in Lee, 1927, p. 379.
59. Bennett, 1968, p. 53.
60. Ibid., p. 66.
61. ODNB.
62. Bennett, 1968, p. 63.
63. Beresford, 1914, p. 142.
64. Wemyss to his wife, 11 June 1906. CCA WMYS 7/6.
65. Bacon, 1929, p. 186.

## Act 2: Giants into Action

1. Quoted in Bennett, 1968, p. 142.
2. Hopkins to Fisher, 27 August 1897. CCA FISR 1/1.
3. Clowes, 1903, pp. 321–2.
4. Quoted in Bennett, 1968, pp. 76–7.
5. Ibid., pp. 76–7.
6. Quoted in Lee, 1925, p. 456.
7. Magnus, 1964, p. 174.
8. Quoted in Lee, 1925, p. 456.
9. CCA FISR 9/1.
10. Bacon, 1929, pp. 74–7; Mackay, 1973, pp. 152–4.
11. Fisher, 1919a, p. 156.
12. Ibid., p. 156.
13. Fisher to his wife, 12 June 1882. Quoted in Marder, 1952, p. 105.
14. Clowes, 1903, p. 323.
15. Sydenham of Combe, 1927, p. 36.
16. Clowes, 1903, p. 328.
17. A breathless account of the *Condor*'s action can be found in Chapter 6 of Fraser, 1904.
18. Beresford, 1914, p. 187.
19. Ibid., p. 188.
20. Ibid., p. 189.
21. Clowes, 1903, p. 331.
22. Ibid., pp. 336–7.
23. *The Times*, 7 August 1882.
24. Wilson, 10 August 1882. Quoted in Bradford, 1923, pp. 71–2.
25. Beresford, 1914, p. 193.
26. Marling, 1931, pp. 72–3.
27. Beresford, 1914, p. 180.
28. *The Daily News*, 19 August 1882. FISR 11/1.
29. Fisher, 1919a, pp. 156–7.
30. Bennett, 1968, pp. 92–3.
31. Fisher, 1919a, p. 156.
32. Fisher to Lord Alcester. Quoted in Marder, 1952, pp. 112–13.
33. Quoted in Bennett, 1968, p. 94.
34. Beresford, 1914, p. 210.
35. Bennett, 1968, p. 74.
36. Beresford, 1914, p. 228.
37. Ibid., p. 235.
38. Bennett, 1968, p. 106.
39. Ibid., pp. 105–6.
40. Quoted in Bennett, 1968, p. 107.
41. There are many spelling variants for Metemmeh. I have used the one adopted by Beresford on his elevation to the peerage in 1916.
42. Bennett, 1968, p. 110.
43. Beresford, 1914, pp. 263–4; Asher, 2006, pp. 220–1.
44. Asher, 2006, p. 226.
45. Newbolt was mistaken about the type of gun. He was also mistaken about the Colonel, who did not die until some days later.
46. No relation of the Wilson at Alexandria.
47. Beresford, 1914, p. 288.
48. The name is spelt differently in different texts. I have used Beresford's spelling.
49. Beresford, 1914, p. 296.

50. Ibid., Chapter XXXI.
51. Ibid., p. 312; Bennett, 1968, p. 199.
52. NA ADM 196/83/86.
53. Fisher to his wife, 22 January 1883. FISR 2/1.
54. Fisher to his wife, 5 February 1884. CCA FISR 2/1.
55. Article on Stead from untitled magazine, around 1903. FISR 11/11.
56. *Pall Mall Gazette*, 15 October 1886.
57. Fisher, 1919b, pp. 57–8.
58. Quoted in Bennett, 1968, p. 132.
59. Bennett, 1968, p. 132.
60. Ibid., p. 134.
61. Ibid., p. 479.
62. Ibid., p. 336.
63. Ibid., p. 344.
64. Hamilton, 1922, p. 88.
65. Beresford, 1914, p. 347.
66. Bennett, 1968, p. 135.
67. Ibid., p. 144.
68. Beresford, 1914, p. 350.
69. Bacon, 1940, p. 54.
70. *The Times*, 27 July 1887.
71. Bennett, 1968, p. 141.
72. Quoted in Bennett, 1968, p. 142.
73. Bennett, 1968, p. 146.
74. *The Times*, 30 January 1888.
75. *The Times*, 27 January 1888.
76. Bennett, 1968, p. 145.
77. Bennett, 1968, p. 148.
78. Beresford, 1914, p. 360.
79. Ibid., p. 385.
80. Lambert, 2008, p. 283.
81. Beresford, 1914, p. 364.
82. Anand, 2008, pp. 38–9.
83. Magnus, 1964, pp. 231–2.
84. Bennett, 1968, pp. 168–9.
85. Magnus, 1964, p. 235.
86. Bennett, 1968, pp. 168–9.
87. Beresford, 1914, pp. 378–82.
88. Ibid., pp. 384, 393.
89. Ibid., p. 394.
90. Ibid., p. 395.
91. Bennett, 1968, p. 199.
92. Beresford, 1914, pp. 414, 416; Bennett, 1968, p. 198.
93. Bennett, 1968, pp. 202–3.
94. Beresford, 1914, p. 462.
95. *The Times*, 10 January 1900.
96. ODNB.

## Act 3: Friendship and Rivalry in the Mediterranean

1. CCA FISR 3/1.
2. *The Daily News*, 29 July 1899.
3. Ibid., 29 July 1899.

4. CCA FISR 1/2.
5. Scott, 1919, pp. 60–1.
6. Ibid., pp. 28–9.
7. Jameson, 1962, p. 144.
8. Beresford, 1914, p. 20.
9. Jameson, 1962, p. 105.
10. Smith, 1936, p. 127.
11. Chatfield, 1942, p. 35.
12. Hankey quoted in Roskill, 1970, p. 47.
13. Maurice Hankey to Hilda Hankey, 26 September 1899. Quoted in Roskill, 1970, p. 47.
14. King-Hall's diary, 20 April, 25 November and 25 December 1900.
15. Ibid., 12 October 1901.
16. Quoted in Bacon, 1940, p. 122.
17. Balfour to Beresford, 4 January 1900. BL Add. Mss. 49713.
18. *The Times*, 10 January 1900.
19. Ibid., 11 January 1900.
20. Guide to the Naval Review. Navy League, 1897, p. 2.
21. NMM Beresford's notebook, p. O5.
22. Beresford to Balfour, 8 April 1900. BL Add. Mss. 49713.
23. Ibid.
24. Ibid.
25. Ibid.
26. Lady Charles to Sandars, 27 April 1900. BL Add. Mss. 49713.
27. Magnus, 1964, p. 292.
28. NMM Beresford's notebook, p. O5.
29. Ibid.
30. NA ADM 50/390.
31. Beresford to Balfour, 8 April 1900. BL Add. Mss. 49713.
32. CCA WMYS 7/6.
33. NMM Beresford's notebook, p. S8.
34. Ibid., p. C11.
35. *Daily Mail*, 25 June 1901.
36. NMM Beresford's notebook, p. B12.
37. Ibid., p. P4. n.d., after 31 December 1900.
38. Ibid., p. 6.
39. Beresford to Bellairs, nd. McGill Bellairs archive.
40. Beresford to Bellairs, 9 December 1900. McGill Bellairs archive.
41. NMM Beresford's notebook, p. O5, n.d., but before 18 March 1901.
42. Ibid., c.14 March 1900.
43. King-Hall's diary, 19 March 1900.
44. Ibid., 25 December 1900.
45. NMM Beresford's notebook, p. O5. Dated 27 August 1900.
46. Ibid.
47. King-Hall, 1935, p. 313.
48. Hankey, 1961, p. 20.
49. Quoted in Roskill, 1970, pp. 56–7.
50. *The Times*, 4 October 1900.
51. Lambert, 1999, p. 187.
52. CCA FISR 3/1.
53. Bacon, 1929, p. 152.
54. Jameson, 1962, p. 85.
55. Bennett, 1968, pp. 230–1.

56. King-Hall's diary, 6 June 1901.
57. Beresford to First Lord, 26 June 1901. BL Add. Mss. 50288.
58. Beresford to Bellairs, 6 April 1901. McGill Bellairs archive.
59. Beresford to Bellairs, 24 May 1901. McGill Bellairs archive.
60. Fisher to White, 8 January 1901. CCA FISR 15/2/1/1.
61. Fisher to Thursfield, 8 January 1901. Marder, 1952, pp. 179–80.
62. Bacon, 1929, p. 136.
63. *Daily Mail*, 25 June 1901.
64. Ibid., 11 June 1901.
65. NMM Beresford's notebook, November 1901.
66. Bennett, 1968, p. 239.
67. Beresford to White, 4 May 1901. NMM WHI/18.
68. Beresford, 1914, p. 466.
69. Beresford's notebook, p. U12, n.d.
70. Ibid., 14 November 1901.
71. NA ADM 1/7507.
72. Beresford, 1914.
73. Ibid., p. 462.
74. NMM Beresford's notebook, p. Z15A, n.d.
75. Penn, 2000, p. 76.
76. Fisher to his wife, 29 September 1900. Marder, 1952, pp. 161–2.
77. *Navy League Minutes*, 30 September 1901.
78. Fisher to his wife, 29 September 1900. Marder, 1952, pp. 161–2.
79. Fisher to Selborne, 15 September 1901. Marder, 1952, pp. 207–8.
80. Fisher to Cecil Fisher, 15 May 1902. CCA FISR 15/1/3/1.
81. CCA FISR 1/2.
82. NMM Beresford's notebook, p. O5.
83. Beresford, 1914, p. 465.
84. Penn, 2000, p. 71.
85. Bennett, 1968, p. 228.
86. Penn, 2000, p. 71.
87. Chatfield, 1942, p. 41.
88. Hankey, 1961, p. 20.
89. Chatfield, 1942, p. 41.
90. Bacon, 1929, pp. 134–5.
91. Hankey, 1961, p. 20.
92. NA ADM 50/390.
93. Chatfield, 1942, p. 41.
94. Bennett, 1968, p. 235.
95. King-Hall's diary, 22 October 1901.
96. Fisher to Thursfield, 28 November 1901. Marder, 1952, pp. 215–17.
97. Hankey, 1961, p. 61.
98. Fisher to his wife, 7 July 1899. Marder, 1952, p. 143.
99. King-Hall's diary, 27 June 1901.
100. NA ADM 1/7507.
101. NA ADM 1/7597.
102. BRI/15. Quoted in Penn, 2000, p. 80.
103. Custance to Bridge, May 1902. NMM, BRI/15.
104. Beresford to Bellairs, 27 December 1900. McGill Bellairs archive.
105. Beresford to Bellairs, 9 December 1900. McGill Bellairs archive.
106. Beresford to Bellairs, 25 December 1901. McGill Bellairs archive.
107. 'The Objects of the Navy League' in *Guide to the Naval Review*, Navy League 1897.

108. NMM Beresford's notebook, p. N5, 20 July 1901.
109. Fisher to Thursfield, 21 July 1901. NMM THU/1.
110. Hankey, 1961, p. 20.

## Act 4: The *Daily Mail* Letter

1. *Daily Mail*, 10 June 1901.
2. Mina Beresford to White, n.d., c. 21 June 1901. NMM WHI/7.
3. Beresford to Balfour, 8 April 1900. BL Add. Mss. 49713.
4. Bacon, 1929, p. 136.
5. *Parliamentary Debates*, 4th Series, XCV, 24 June 1901.
6. ODNB.
7. Magnus, 1964, p. 349.
8. *The Times*, 13 March 1909.
9. *Parliamentary Debates*, 4th Series, XCV, 24 June 1901.
10. Beresford to White, 4 May 1901. NMM WHI/18.
11. *Navy League Minutes*, 20 May 1901.
12. *Daily Mail*, 11 June 1901.
13. CCA FISR 11/11.
14. *Navy League Minutes*, 10 June 1901.
15. White to Beresford, 16 May 1902. NMM WHI/19.
16. *Daily Mail*, 21 June 1901.
17. White to Arnold-Forster, 25 June 1901. BL Add. Mss. 50288.
18. Ibid.
19. King-Hall's diary, 21 July 1901.
20. CCA FISR 11/11.
21. *Daily Mail*, 27 June 1901.
22. Beresford to White, 27 June 1901. NMM WHI/18.
23. Arnold-Forster to Fisher, 4 July 1901. BL Add. Mss. 50288.
24. NA ADM 1/7465C.
25. Ibid.
26. Fisher to Fawkes, 27 June 1901. Marder, 1952, p. 197.
27. *National Review*, July 1901.
28. *Navy League Minutes*, 1 July 1901.
29. Ibid., 2 July 1901.
30. *National Review*, July 1901.
31. *Parliamentary Debates*, 4th Series, 96, 3 July 1901.
32. *Navy League Minutes*, 3 July 1901.
33. Beresford to White, 27 June 1901. NMM WHI/18.
34. Fisher to his wife, 5 July 1901. FISR 2/2.
35. Fisher to unknown, 23 July 1901. CCA FISR 2/2.
36. NMM Beresford's notebook, p. Z29, 5 August 1901.
37. *Parliamentary Debates*, 4th Series, 96, 9 July 1901.
38. Ibid.
39. Beresford to White, 9 July 1901. NMM WHI/18.
40. Ibid.
41. NMM Beresford's notebook, p. Z24, 11 July 1901.
42. Fisher to Thursfield, 16 July 1901. Marder, 1952, p. 199.
43. *Navy League Minutes*, 22 October 1901.
44. Fisher to Thursfield, 28 November 1901. Marder, 1952, pp. 215–17.
45. Beresford to Bellairs, 5 February 1902. McGill Bellairs archive.
46. There is, though, no mention of this in *The Times* report of 15 March 1902.

47. Fisher to Selborne, 26 March 1902. Marder, 1952, pp. 234–7. Fisher's mix of 'Naval Lord' and 'Sea Lord' reads oddly, but is in the orginal letter.
48. *The Times*, 9 April 1902.
49. Ibid., 22 April 1902.
50. Beresford, 1914, p. 479.
51. *The Times*, 25 April 1902.
52. Ibid., 29 April 1902.
53. Beresford to White, 29 April 1902. NMM WHI/19.
54. *The Times*, 2 May 1902.
55. Ibid.
56. Fisher to his wife, 2 May 1902. FISR 2/2.
57. *The Times*, 5 May 1902.
58. NA ADM 1/7450B.
59. Fisher to Thursfield, 27 April 1900. Quoted in Marder, 1952, pp. 155–6.
60. Secretary of the Admiralty to Fisher, 1 July 1901. NA ADM 116/900B.
61. *Parliamentary Debates*, 4th Series, 97, 5 May 1902.
62. King-Hall's diary, 6 May 1902.
63. *Parliamentary Debates*, 4th Series, 98, 14 May 1902.
64. Ibid.
65. Ibid.
66. Ibid.
67. Ibid.
68. Ibid.
69. Ibid.
70. Ibid.
71. Ibid.
72. *The Times*, 15 May 1902.
73. Beresford to Arnold-Forster, 2 May 1902. BL Add. Mss. 50288.
74. White to Beresford, 16 May 1902. NMM WHI/19.
75. Admiralty to Beresford, 22 May 1902. BL Add. Mss. 50288.
76. Fisher to Cecil Fisher, 15 May 1902. CCA FISR 15/1/3/1.
77. Note by Fisher, 16 Apr 1902. BL Add. Mss. 50288.
78. White to Scott, 16 July 1902. NMM WHI/2.

## Act 5: Fisher Takes the Prize

1. *Review of Reviews*, March 1909.
2. Fisher to unknown, 31 December 1901. Quoted in Bacon, 1929, p. 155.
3. Fisher to Beresford, 22 February 1902. Quoted in Marder, 1952, pp. 231–4.
4. Fisher to Earl Spencer, 28 March 1902. Quoted in Marder, 1952, pp. 237–8.
5. Selborne to Fisher, 9 February 1902. Quoted in Marder, 1952, p. 222.
6. Kerr to Selborne, 17 December 1901. Quoted in Boyce, 1990, pp. 137–9.
7. Fisher to Cecil Fisher, 10 April 1903. Quoted in Marder, 1952, p. 272.
8. Recollections of Sir Charles Walker. CCA FISR 15/3/2/1.
9. Fisher to Cecil, 12 September 1902. CCA FISR 15/1/3/1.
10. Recollections of Sir Charles Walker. CCA FISR 15/3/2/1.
11. Ibid.
12. Ibid.
13. Ibid.
14. NMM RIC 1/6.
15. *Cmd. 1385*. December 1902.
16. Tria Juncta in Uno to *The Times*, 14 January 1901.
17. *The Times*, 17 January 1903.

18. Ibid.
19. A relative of Captain Wemyss, see Act 3.
20. *The Times*, 14 January 1903.
21. Ibid., 1 January 1903.
22. Beresford to Fisher, April 1903. CCA FISR 8/18.
23. *Navy League Annual Report*, May 1903.
24. ODNB.
25. *The Times*, 19 February 1903.
26. *The Times*, 8 April 1903.
27. Fisher to Cecil, 6 March 1903. CCA FISR 15/1/3/1.
28. Now in the National Portrait Gallery.
29. *The Times*, 2 May 1903.
30. NMM RIC 1/6.
31. Beresford, 1914, p. 488.
32. Pelly, 1938, pp. 55–8.
33. Beresford, 1914, p. 486.
34. NA ADM 116/3108.
35. *The Times*, 22 May 1903.
36. Beresford, 1914, p. 489.
37. Pelly, 1938, p. 90.
38. *The Times*, 10 June 1904.
39. Quoted in Bennett, 1968, p. 257.
40. Beresford to Bellairs, 13 July 1903. McGill Bellairs archive.
41. James, 1956, pp. 100–1.
42. *The Times*, 19 January 1904.
43. *The Times*, 26 April 1904.
44. *The Times*, 23 April 1904.
45. Beresford, 1914, p. 490.
46. Ibid., p. 492.
47. Frewen, 1961, p. 51.
48. Bennett, 1968, p. 260.
49. Beresford to Admiralty, 3 December 1903. NA ADM 116/3108.
50. Minute by Kerr, 2 March 1904. NA ADM 116/3108.
51. Admiralty to Beresford, 11 April 1904. NA ADM 116/3108.
52. NA ADM 196/83/86.
53. Beresford to Balfour, July 1904. BL Add. Mss. 49713.
54. In practice Fisher started on 20 October but since 21 October was the anniversary of the Battle of Trafalgar, Fisher always maintained that it was the day he started.
55. Fisher to Esher, 17 May 1904. Quoted in Marder, 1952, p. 316.
56. King-Hall's diary, 15 October 1903.
57. CCA FISR 15/1/4/2.
58. *Daily Telegraph*, 20 June 1904.
59. *Daily Mail*, 21 October 1904.
60. Marder, 1961, pp. 26–7.
61. Fisher to Esher, 28 July 1904. Quoted in Fisher, 1919a, p. 181.
62. Hough, 1969, p. 179.
63. Fisher to Cecil, 1 September 1904. CCA FISR 15/1/3/1.
64. Fisher to Esher, 4 October 1904. Quoted in Marder, 1952, pp. 329–400.
65. Fisher to Esher, 11 September 1904. Quoted in Marder, 1952, pp. 327–8.
66. Fisher to Esher, 25 September 1904. Quoted in Marder, 1952, pp. 328–9.
67. Moorhouse [later Meynell] 1940, pp. 67–8.
68. Hough, 1969 p. 189; Bacon, 1929, p. 63.

69. King Edward VII to Fisher, 8 January 1905. FISR 1/4.
70. Fisher to Churchill, 13 March 1912. Quoted in Marder, 1956, pp. 440–2.
71. James, 1956, p. 116.
72. Fisher to Selborne, 25 October 1904. Quoted in Marder, 1956, pp. 45–6.
73. Battenberg to Clarke, 1905. Quoted in Jameson, 1962, p. 131.
74. Clarke to Battenberg, 16 March 1905. Quoted in Bacon, 1929, p. 96.
75. Fisher to the Prince of Wales. Quoted in Marder, 1956, pp. 60–1.
76. King-Hall's diary, 15 October 1903.
77. *Cmd. 2335*. December 1904.
78. *Naval Necessities*, ii, p. 463.
79. *Naval Necessities*, i, November 1904.
80. Fisher to Balfour, March 1905. BL Add. Mss. 49710.
81. Beresford to Pakenham, 13 August 1905. NMM PKM/2/21.
82. Wood, 1911, Chapter 22.
83. Quoted in Mackay, 1973, p. 316.
84. Bacon, 1929, p. 60.
85. Fisher to his wife, c. 1 November 1904. Quoted in Marder, 1956, p. 47.
86. Fisher to Lord Selborne, 29 October 1904. Quoted in Marder, 1956, pp. 46–7.
87. *The Times*, 26 October 1904.
88. *The Times*, 29 October 1904.
89. Pelly, 1938, p. 91.
90. Marder, 1940, p. 440.
91. Hough, 1969, p. 208.
92. Marder, 1940, p. 441, fn. 10.
93. Beresford to Sykes, 16 November 1904. NMM PKM/2/20.
94. Pelly, 1938, pp. 91–2.
95. Marder, 1940, p. 439.

## Act 6: An Uneasy Truce

1. Hay to Fisher, 8 January 1906. NA ADM 116/3108.
2. King-Hall's diary, 3 March 1905.
3. Ibid.
4. Beresford to Bellairs, 12 December 1905. McGill Bellairs archive.
5. Pakenham to Sykes, 3 December 1905. NMM PKM/2/20.
6. Beresford, 1914, p. 509.
7. Ibid., pp. 508–17.
8. Ibid., p. 510.
9. Kerr, 1934, p. 180.
10. Wemyss, 1935, p. 86.
11. Ibid.
12. NA ADM 196/83-86. The precise details of the third event are no longer readable on the microfilm record.
13. Bridgeman to Fisher, July 1907. CCA FISR 1/5.
14. Chalmers, 1951, pp. 88–9.
15. Lambert, 2008, p. 343.
16. Bacon, 1940, p. 121.
17. Ibid., p. 124.
18. Pelly, 1938, p. 85.
19. Wemyss to his wife, late 1905. CCA WMYS 7/4.
20. Wemyss to his wife, 19 June 1906. CCA WMYS 7/6; Wemyss, 1935, p. 86.
21. Bacon, 1940, p. 124.
22. Frewen, 1961, p. 100.

23. Magnus, 1964, p. 363.
24. Penn, 2000, p. 147.
25. Wemyss to his wife, 11 June 1906. CCA WMYS 7/6.
26. Wemyss to his wife, 7 July 1906. CCA WMYS 7/6.
27. Wemyss' journal, 16 January 1906. CCA WMYS 12/1.
28. Schurman, 1981, p. 65.
29. Custance to Noel, 31 August 1905. Quoted in Schurman, 1981, p. 64.
30. Fisher to Cawdor, 23 January 1906. Quoted in Marder, 1956, p. 67.
31. Fisher to Corbett, 12 May 1906. FISR 1/6.
32. Wemyss to his wife, 4 April 1906. Quoted in Wemyss, 1935, p. 81.
33. Esher, 1934, p. 269.
34. Fisher to the Prince of Wales, 15 April 1906. Quoted in Marder, 1956, pp. 78–9.
35. Ibid.
36. Beresford to Bellairs, 24 March 1906. McGill Bellairs archive.
37. Fisher to Thursfield, 31 December 1906. NMM THU/1.
38. Jameson, 1962, pp. 294–5.
39. Fisher to unknown, 3 January 1907. Quoted in Marder, 1956, pp. 111–12.
40. Magnus, 1964, p. 285.
41. *The Times*, 6 December 1905.
42. Crease to Bacon, 9 July 1928. CCA FISR 15/3/1/2.
43. Beresford to Bellairs, 2 January 1906. McGill Bellairs archive.
44. Beresford to Bellairs, 4 February 1906. McGill Bellairs archive.
45. Battenberg to Fisher, 24 July 1906. CCA FISR 1/5.
46. Crease to Troubridge, 16 May 1906. NMM TRO/300/5.
47. Troubridge to Crease, 17 May 1906. NMM TRO/300/5.
48. Troubridge to Fisher, 24 May 1906. Quoted in Kemp, 1960, p. 401.
49. Penn, 2000, pp. 145–6.
50. Beresford, 1912, p. 22.
51. Bacon, 1940, p. 126.
52. Bacon to Fisher, 31 March 1906. CCA FISR 15/3/1/1.
53. Bacon to Fisher, c. 12 April 1906. CCA FISR 8/17.
54. Ibid.
55. Bacon to Fisher, 15 April 1906. Quoted in Marder, 1956, pp. 75–7.
56. Bacon to Fisher, 24 April 1906. CCA FISR 8/17.
57. Beresford to Knollys, 27 September 1906. Quoted in Bennett, 1968, p. 279.
58. Beresford correspondence with Tweedmouth. Quoted in Bennett, 1968, p. 279.
59. Fisher to Tweedmouth, 4 October 1906. Quoted in Marder, 1956, pp. 93–5.
60. Fisher to Tweedmouth, 11 October 1906. Quoted in Marder, 1956, pp. 98–9.
61. Ibid.
62. Knollys to Esher, 23 October 1906, Quoted in Marder, 1961, p. 72.
63. Battenberg to Thursfield, 23 January 1907. Quoted in Morris, 1981, p. 45.
64. Kerr, 1934, pp. 225–6.
65. Lambert, 1999.
66. NMM RIC/1/7.
67. Admiralty minute Home Fleet Creation, 23 October 1906. NA ADM 116/1037.
68. Telegram Beresford to Admiralty, 8 December 1906. NA ADM 116/3108.
69. Fisher minute to the Board, 9 December 1906. NA ADM 116/3108.
70. Ibid.
71. Ibid.
72. *The Spectator*, 12 January 1907.
73. *The Times*, 11 June 1910.
74. Quoted in Bennett, 1968, p. 279.

75. Beresford to Tweedmouth, 22 January 1907. NA CAB 16/9 A.
76. Bennett, 1968, p. 280.
77. Fisher to Lambert, 21 January 1907. Quoted in Marder, 1956, p. 115.
78. Beresford to Tweedmouth, 22 January 1907. NA CAB 16/9 B.
79. Fisher to unknown, 24 January 1906. Quoted in Marder, 1956, pp. 116–17.
80. Mina Beresford to Bellairs, n.d. McGill Bellairs archive.
81. Ibid.
82. Ibid.
83. Frewen, 1961, p. 128.
84. Fisher to Knollys, 27 January 1907. Quoted in Marder, 1956, p. 117.
85. Esher to Fisher, 4 February 1907. Quoted in Esher, 1934, pp. 219–20.
86. NA ADM 116/3108.
87. Wemyss' journal, 17 January 1907. CCA WMYS 12/1.
88. Fisher to White, 19 January 1907. Quoted in Marder, 1956, p. 114.
89. *New York Times*, 7 July 1907.
90. Woods, 1990, p. 117.
91. Ibid., pp. 116–17.
92. Fisher to Arnold White, 19 January 1907. Quoted in Marder, 1956, p. 114.
93. *The Times*, 21 and 23 March 1907.
94. Bennett, 1968, p. 279.

## Act 7: Beresford Declares War

1. Magnus, 1964, p. 370.
2. Fisher's suggested title of a projected autobiography. Quoted in Marder, 1961, p. 100.
3. Fisher to Beresford, 8 March 1907. NA ADM 116/3108.
4. Marder, 1961, p. 91.
5. Tweedmouth to Fisher, 8 June 1907. Quoted in Marder, 1956, pp. 125–6.
6. ODNB.
7. CCA SDEE 1/17.
8. Quoted in Bennett, 1968, p. 284.
9. Dawson, 1933, pp. 55–6.
10. Quoted in Bennett, 1968, p. 284.
11. *Daily Despatch*, 7 August 1907.
12. Quoted in Bennett, 1968, p. 284.
13. Pelly, 1938, pp. 106–7.
14. *Memorandum on the Relations of the Commander-in-Chief, Channel Fleet, and the Board of Admiralty*, July 1907. NA ADM 116/3108.
15. CCA FISR 1/5.
16. Fisher to Beresford, 22 April 1907. Quoted in Marder, 1956, p. 121.
17. Beresford to Fisher, 22 April 1907. Quoted in Marder, 1956, pp. 121–2. Emphasis added.
18. Bacon, 1929, p. 31.
19. Esher's journal, 19 January 1908. CCA ESHR 2/11.
20. Beresford to Admiralty, 21 May 1907. NA ADM 116/1037.
21. Bellairs, 'Impending Naval Crisis' in *National Review*, October 1907, p. 310.
22. Ibid., p. 308.
23. Beresford to Bellairs, 8 November 1907. McGill Bellairs archive.
24. Beresford to Bellairs, 13 February 1908. McGill Bellairs archive.
25. Beresford to Bellairs, 9 March 1908. McGill Bellairs archive.
26. Fisher to Beresford, 8 March 1907. NA ADM 116/3108.
27. Fisher to Beresford, 30 April 1907. Quoted in Marder, 1956, p. 122.
28. Beresford to Fisher, 2 May 1907. Quoted in Marder, 1956, p. 123.

29. *Memorandum on the Relations of the Commander-in-Chief, Channel Fleet, and the Board of Admiralty*, July 1907. NA ADM 116/3108.
30. Fisher to Beresford, 4 May 1907. NA ADM 116/3108.
31. Beresford to McKenna, 8 May 1907, in *Extracts from Official Correspondence, &c, between the Admiralty and Lord C. Beresford*, April 1907 to January 1908. NA ADM 116/3108.
32. Fisher to McKenna, 26 May 1908. Quoted in Marder, 1956, pp. 177–9.
33. *War Arrangements, June 1907*. NA ADM 116/3108.
34. *Memorandum on the Relations of the Commander-in-Chief, and the Board of Admiralty*, June 1907. NA ADM 116/3108.
35. Beresford to Knollys, 21 May 1907. Quoted in Bennett, 1968, pp. 286–7.
36. Admiralty to Beresford, 5 June 1907. CCA FISR 8/42.
37. Tweedmouth to Fisher, 8 June 1907. Quoted in Marder, 1956, pp. 125–6.
38. Beresford to Admiralty, 14 June 1907. NA ADM 116/1037.
39. Referred to in Fisher to McKenna, 26 May 1908. Quoted in Marder, 1956, pp. 177–9.
40. *Memorandum on the reply of the Commander-in-Chief, Channel Fleet, to War Orders*, June 1907. NA ADM 116/3108.
41. Minutes of 5 July meeting. NA ADM 116/3108.
42. Sir F. Ponsonby to Fisher, 8 October 1907. CCA FISR 1/5.
43. Minutes of 5 July meeting. NA ADM 116/3108.
44. Bridgeman to Fisher, July 1907. CCA FISR 1/5.
45. Thomas to Beresford, 5 July 1908. NA ADM 116/3108.
46. Fisher to Beresford, 6 July 1907. Quoted in Hough, 1969, p. 220.
47. Beresford to the Admiralty, 16 July 1907. NA ADM 116/3108.
48. Beresford to Fisher, 16 July 1907. Quoted in Marder, 1956, p. 127.
49. Beresford to the Admiralty, 16 July 1907. NA ADM 116/3108.
50. *The Times*, 5 June 1907.
51. Scott, 1919, pp. 198–9.
52. *Daily Mail*, 7 August 1907.
53. *Daily Despatch*, 7 August 1907.
54. *The Times*, 7 August 1907.
55. Beresford to Blumenfeld, n.d., c. 8 August 1907. PA BLU/1/2/BERE.3.
56. *The Times*, 9 July 1907.
57. *The Times*, 30 July 1907.
58. *The Times*, 13 August 1907.
59. Ponsonby, 1951, p. 132.
60. Beresford's Admiralty record. NA ADM 196/83/86.
61. Ibid.
62. *Reasons for the Omission of Combined Tactical Exercises in 1908*, 18 May 1909. NA ADM 116/3108.
63. Beresford to Admiralty, 9 December 1907. ADM 116/3108.
64. Admiralty to Beresford (draft), 16 December 1907. NA ADM 116/1037.
65. *The Times*, 20 October 1924. This account states that the hit rate was eighty-seven per cent, but Scott gives it as eighty per cent – see Scott, 1919, p. 88.
66. Quoted in Padfield, 1966, p. 28.
67. *Leeds Mercury*. Quoted in Padfield, 1966, p. 171.
68. Padfield, 1966, p. 15.
69. Bacon, 1940, p. 155.
70. Padfield, 1966, p. 161.
71. Scott's account of the incidents, February 1909. CCA FISR 5/16.
72. *The Times*, 24 November 1902.
73. Scott's account of the incidents, February 1909. CCA FISR 5/16.
74. Scott, 1919, p. 202.

75. Scott's account of the incidents, February 1909. CCA FISR 5/16.
76. Beresford, 1914, p.561.
77. NA ADM 53/21378.
78. Padfield, 1966, p.163.
79. Beresford's evidence on the Scott incidents, June 1909. NA ADM 116/3108.
80. Beresford's evidence on the Scott incidents, June 1909. NA ADM 116/3108.
81. Dawson, 1933, p.60.
82. Dawson, 1933, p.61.
83. Beresford's evidence on the Scott incidents, June 1909. NA ADM 116/3108.
84. Dawson, 1933, p.61.
85. Ibid.
86. Beresford, 1914, p.561.
87. Beresford's evidence on the Scott incidents, June 1909. NA ADM 116/3108.
88. Ibid.
89. Scott to White, 15 December 1907. WHI/170.
90. Beresford's evidence on the Scott incidents, June 1909. NA ADM 116/3108.
91. Scott to White, 17 November 1907. NMM WHI/170.
92. Beresford's evidence on the Scott incidents, June 1909. NA ADM 116/3108.
93. Ibid.
94. Ibid.
95. Frewen, 1961, p.139. No date given, but was immediately after the paintwork incident.
96. *The Times*, 12 November 1907.
97. *The Times*, 11 November 1907.
98. Fisher to Corbett, 4 December 1907. Quoted in Marder, 1956, p.152.
99. *The Times*, 17 December 1907.
100. Scott to White, n.d. NMM WHI/172.
101. Penn, 2000, p.188.
102. Beresford's evidence on the Scott incidents, June 1909. NA ADM 116/3108.
103. Ibid.
104. *John Bull*, 19 January 1908. Quoted in Morris, 1981, p.59.
105. Beresford to Carson, 21 January 1908. Quoted in Marder, 1961, p.99.
106. Esher's journal, 19 January 1908. CCA ESHR 2/11.
107. Beresford's evidence on the Scott incidents, June 1909. NA ADM 116/3108.
108. Ibid.
109. Ibid.
110. *Parliamentary Debates*, 4th Series, Vol.185, 9 March 1908.
111. Scott, 1919, p.204.
112. Lellenberg, 2008, p.617.
113. ODNB.
114. Hay to Fisher, 8 January 1908. NA ADM 116/3108.
115. Admiralty statement, 15 August 1907. CCA FISR 1/5.
116. Admiralty to Beresford, 22 August 1907. NA CAB 16/9B.
117. Beresford to Admiralty, 12 November 1907. NA ADM 116/3108.
118. Admiralty to Beresford, 21 November 1907. NA ADM 116/3108.
119. Fisher to Clarke, 12 September 1907. Quoted in Marder, 1956, pp.131–3.
120. Fisher to Ottley, 18 September 1907. CCA FISR 1/5.
121. Repington to Esher, 7 October 1907. Quoted in Morris, 1999, pp.122–5.
122. Repington to Lord Roberts, 22 October 1907. Quoted in Morris, 1999, pp.127–8.
123. Repington to Esher, 22 October 1907. Quoted in Morris, 1981, p.58.
124. Repington to Roberts, 24 November 1907. Quoted in Morris, 1999, pp.132–3.
125. NMM CBT/6/4.
126. Esher, 1934, p.262.

127. Marder, 1961, p. 97.
128. Bridgeman to Fisher, 4 January 1908. CCA FISR 1/6.
129. Ibid.
130. Fisher to Bridgeman, c. 5 January 1908. Quoted in Marder, 1956, p. 154.
131. NA ADM 116/3108.
132. Beresford to Admiralty, 12 November 1907. NA ADM 116/3108.
133. Draft Parliamentary Question from A Naval Man, n.d. McGill Bellairs archive.
134. Beresford to Admiralty, 12 November 1907. NA ADM 116/3108.
135. Ibid.
136. Marder states that these two letters were sent to Beresford, (Marder, 1961, p. 96) but the Admiralty record account says they were sent to the C-in-C Home Fleet (NA ADM 116/3108) so Beresford may never have seen them.
137. Admiralty to Beresford, 30 July 1907. NA ADM 116/1037.
138. *The Times*, 3 September 1908.
139. Beresford to Admiralty, 12 November 1907. NA ADM 116/3108.
140. Admiralty to Beresford, 21 November 1907. NA ADM 116/3108.
141. *The Times*, 1 November 1909.
142. Fisher to Cawdor, 25 November 1907. Quoted in Marder, 1956, pp. 151–2.
143. Fisher to Cawdor, 25 November 1907. Quoted in Marder, 1956, pp. 151–2.
144. *The Proposed Inquiry into Admiralty Policy*, 16 January 1908. NA ADM 116/3108.
145. Fisher to Tweedmouth, 23 January 1908. Quoted in Marder, 1956, pp. 157–9.
146. Fisher to Grey, 23 January 1908. Quoted in Marder, 1956, pp. 155–7.
147. NA ADM 116/3108.
148. Esher's journal, 24 January 1908. CCA ESHR 2/11.
149. Fisher to Cawdor, 27 January 1908. Quoted in Marder, 1956, p. 159.
150. Marder, 1961, p. 101.
151. Fisher to McKenna, 18 April 1908. CCA FISR 5/14.
152. *The Times*, 1 February 1908.
153. *The Times*, 19 July 1907.
154. *The Times*, 28 January 1908.
155. Esher to Wyatt and Horton Smith, 22 January 1908. CCA FISR 15/3/3/4.
156. Scott to White, 19 February 1908. NMM WHI/2.
157. NA CAB 16/9A.
158. *The Times*, various issues.
159. Beresford to Bellairs, 13 February 1908. McGill Bellairs archive.
160. Scott to White, 23 February 1908. NMM WHI/2.
161. NA ADM 53/22747.
162. Scott to White, 1908. NMM WHI/2.
163. Fisher to Esher, 7 October 1907. Quoted in Marder, 1956, pp. 144–6.
164. Ibid.
165. Drury to Fisher, 30 October 1907. Quoted in Marder, 1956, p. 151, fn. 1.
166. Ponsonby, 1951, p. 132.
167. Unknown to Dear Mr. ___, 16 January 1908. CCA FISR 1/6.
168. Slade's diary, 13 January 1908. Quoted in Morris, 1981, p. 60.
169. Sykes to White, February(?) 1908. NMM WHI/76.
170. Sykes to White, 11 February 1908. NMM WHI/76.
171. Fisher to Cawdor, 25 November 1907. Quoted in Marder, 1956, pp. 151–2.
172. Esher memorandum, 25 January 1908. CCA FISR 1/6.
173. Esher's journal, 15 April 1908. CCA ESHR 2/11.
174. Beresford to Bellairs, 20 October 1907. McGill Bellairs archive.
175. Beresford to Bellairs, 13 February 1908. McGill Bellairs archive.
176. Ibid.

## Act 8: McKenna Calls Time

1. Bacon, 1929, p. 30.
2. Jenkins, 1994, pp. 177–8.
3. Wilson, 1973, p. 629.
4. Fisher to Tweedmouth, c. 11 April 1908. Quoted in Marder, 1956, pp. 171–2.
5. Esher's journal, 22 April 1908. CCA ESHR 2/11.
6. Ibid.
7. King Edward to Fisher, 14 April 1908. Quoted in Marder, 1956, p. 172, fn. 1.
8. 'Submit or resign' – a classic phrase associated with the French Third Republic, when the President tried to override the will of the electorate.
9. Fisher to McKenna, 16 April 1908. Quoted in Marder, 1956, pp. 172–3.
10. Possibly William H.D. Strath, Chief Boatswain attached to the C-in-C, Nore.
11. Esher's journal, 22 April 1908. CCA ESHR 2/11.
12. Sandby, W., 1862.
13. *The Times*, 1 May 1908.
14. Esher, 1934, p. 307.
15. Slade's diary, 11 May 1908. Quoted in Mackay, 1973, p. 400.
16. Esher, 1934, p. 312.
17. Magnus, 1964, p. 370.
18. Phillips to White, 6 July 1908. NMM WHI/76.
19. *The Times*, 12 May 1908.
20. Midleton to Selborne, 9 July 1908. Quoted in Morris, 1981, p. 79, n. 104.
21. Slade's diary, 11 April 1908. Quoted in Mackay, 1973, p. 399.
22. Slade's diary, 24 April 1908. Quoted in Mackay, 1973, p. 399.
23. Fisher to McKenna, 16 May 1908. Quoted in Marder, 1956, pp. 176–7.
24. Fisher to McKenna, 26 May 1908. Quoted in Marder, 1956, pp. 177–9.
25. McKenna to Beresford, draft letter prepared by Fisher, c. 25 May 1908. CCA MCKN 3–4.
26. Fisher minute, 27 May 1908. CCA FISR 5/14.
27. Beresford to McKenna, 5 June 1908. NMM MLN/227.
28. Crease to White, 23 June 1908. NMM WHI/76.
29. Crease to White, 30 June 1908. NMM WHI/76.
30. Ibid.
31. McKenna's evidence to the 1909 inquiry. NA ADM 116/3108.
32. Thomas to Beresford, 1 July 1908. CCA FISR 1/6.
33. Beresford to McKenna, 6 July 1908. CCA MCKN 3/8.
34. Beresford to McKenna, 29 July 1908. CCA MCKN 3/8.
35. Beresford to Admiralty, 11 August 1908. NA ADM 116/3108.
36. *The Times*, 29 May 1908.
37. Scott's account of the incidents, February 1909. CCA FISR 5/16.
38. *The Times*, 22 June 1908.
39. Scott, 1919, p. 209.
40. Scott to White, 23 June 1908. NMM WHI/2.
41. Beresford to the Secretary of the Admiralty, 11 August 1908. NA ADM 116/3108.
42. Scott's account of the incidents, February 1909. CCA FISR 5/16.
43. NA ADM 53/21377.
44. Scott's account of the incidents, February 1909. CCA FISR 5/16.
45. Scott to White, 23 June 1908. NMM WHI/2.
46. Scott to White, 23 June 1908. NMM WHI/2.
47. Massie, 1991, pp. 393–5.
48. Quoted in Gordon, 1996, p. 274.
49. Signals based on Scott's account of the incident, Beresford's account and Padfield, 1966.
50. *The Times*, 7 July 1908.

51. *The Times*, 6 July 1908.
52. Clark, 1974, p. 100.
53. Beresford, 1912, p. 29.
54. *The Times*, 8 July 1908.
55. *Parliamentary Debates*, 4th Series, Vol. 191, 8 July 1908.
56. Ibid., Vol. 192, 9 July 1908.
57. Ibid.
58. Beresford to the Secretary of the Admiralty, 12 July 1908. NA ADM 116/3108.
59. Beresford, 1912, p. 29.
60. Beresford to the Secretary of the Admiralty, 12 July 1908. NA ADM 116/3108.
61. Beresford to Blumenfeld, July 29 1908. PA BLU/1/2/BERE.6.
62. *Morning Post*, 9 July 1908. Quoted in Penn, 2000, p. 195.
63. Captain Fred Morgan to Beresford, 22 July 1908. NA ADM 116/3108.
64. Beresford to the Secretary of the Admiralty, 25 July 1908. NA ADM 116/3108.
65. Beresford to McKenna, 25 July 1908. CCA MCKN 3–8.
66. Beresford to McKenna, 25 July 1908. CCA MCKN 3–8.
67. Fisher to McKenna, 28 July 1908. Quoted in Marder, 1956, pp. 184–6.
68. Scott, 1919, p. 210.
69. Padfield, 1966, p. 188.
70. *Parliamentary Debates*, 4th Series, Vol. 193, 30 July 1908.
71. Ibid.
72. Beresford to Admiralty, 11 August 1908. NA ADM 116/3108.
73. Bridgeman to Fisher, June(?) 1908. CCA FISR 1/6.
74. Scott to White, 23 June 1908. NMM WHI/2.
75. Frewen, 1961, p. 167.
76. *The Times*, 27 May 1908.
77. *The Times*, 8 August 1908.
78. Beresford to Edward VII, 7 August 1908. Quoted in Magnus, 1964, p. 371.
79. Edward VII to Beresford, 8 August 1908. Quoted in Lee, 1927, p. 600.
80. Quoted in Bennett, 1968, p. 298.
81. Fisher to McKenna, 11 August 1908. Quoted in Marder, 1956, p. 187.
82. Quoted in Bennett, 1968, p. 298.
83. *Memorandum on Fleet Exercises in the North Sea*, July, 1908. CCA FISR 5/15.
84. Fisher to McKenna, 11 August 1908. CCA MCKN 3/4.
85. Greene to Beresford, 11 August 1908. CCA MCKN 3–4.
86. Admiralty to Beresford, 24 October 1908. NA ADM 116/1037.
87. *The Times*, 6 November 1908.
88. Pelly, 1938, p. 115.
89. *The Times*, 6 August 1908.
90. Beresford to McKenna, 8 August 1908. CCA FISR 1/7.
91. Beresford to Long, 18 October 1908. BL Add. Mss. 62407.
92. McKenna to Beresford, 11 August 1908. CCA FISR 1/7.
93. Fisher to Knollys, 8 September 1908. Quoted in Marder, 1956, pp. 192–3.
94. Fisher to unknown, 16 September 1908. CCA FISR 1/7.
95. Long to Beresford, 20 October 1908. BL Add. Mss. 62407.
96. Beresford to Long, 21 November 1908. BL Add. Mss. 62407.
97. Beresford to Bellairs, 11 October 1908. McGill Bellairs archive.
98. Fisher to McKenna, 28 October 1908. Quoted in Marder, 1956, p. 199.
99. Fisher to White, 2 November 1908. Quoted in Marder, 1956, p. 200.
100. Esher's journal, 2 November 1908. CCA ESHR 2/11.
101. Esher, 1934, p. 357.
102. McKenna to Beresford, 19 December 1908. BL Add. Mss. 62407.

103. Fisher to McKenna, 22 December 1908. CCA MCKN 3/4.
104. Beresford to McKenna, 23 December 1908. CCA MCKN 3/8.
105. Ibid.
106. Beresford to Bellairs, 26 October 1908. McGill Bellairs archive.
107. Beresford to Sturdee, 21 October 1910. CCA SDEE3/2.
108. Beresford to Long, 14 January 1909. BL Add. Mss. 62407.
109. Ibid.
110. Esher to Knollys, 23 February 1909. Quoted in Marder, 1961, p. 189.
111. Fisher to McKenna, 27 February 1909 (wrongly dated 1908). CCA MCKN 6/2.
112. *The Times*, 21 March 1909.
113. *The Times*, 25 March 1909.

## Act 9: Maelstrom

1. Hankey memorandum, 19 May 1909. NA CAB 17/7.
2. Beresford to Bellairs, 12 February 1909. McGill Bellairs archive.
3. Beresford to Bellairs, 18 February 1909. McGill Bellairs archive.
4. Beresford to Bellairs, 19 February 1909. McGill Bellairs archive.
5. Beresford to Bellairs, 23 February 1909. McGill Bellairs archive.
6. Beresford to Noel, 17 January 1909. NMM NOE/5.
7. Beresford to Noel, 11 February 1909. NMM NOE/5.
8. Quoted in Marder, 1961, p. 161.
9. Beresford to Troubridge, 20 February 1909. NMM TRO/300/5.
10. Marder, 1961, pp. 188–9.
11. Beresford to Balfour, 24 March 1909. BL Add. Mss. 49713.
12. Balfour to Beresford, 27 March 1909. BL Add. Mss. 49713.
13. Beresford to Asquith, 2 April 1909. NA CAB 16/9B.
14. Ibid.
15. Beresford to Asquith, 2 April 1909, 2nd letter. NA CAB 17/7.
16. Jessica Sykes to White, 3 April 1909. NMM WHI/2.
17. Fisher to McKenna, c. 8 April 1909. Quoted in Marder, 1956, p. 242.
18. *Parliamentary Debates*, Vol. 3, 6 April 1909.
19. Fisher to McKenna, c. 8 April 1909. Quoted in Marder, 1956, p. 242.
20. Fisher to Esher, 13 April 1909. Quoted in Marder, 1956, pp. 211–12.
21. Esher to Balfour, 13 April 1909. BL Add. Mss. 49719.
22. McKenna to Asquith, n.d., but shortly after 8 April 1909. Quoted in McKenna, 1948, pp. 86–7.
23. Asquith to Beresford, 14 April 1909. NA CAB 17/7.
24. Asquith to Campbell-Bannerman, 20 December 1906. Quoted in Rowland, 1968, p. 186.
25. Knollys to Esher, 13 April 1909. CCA ESHR 10/51.
26. Beresford to Asquith, 14 April 1909. NA CAB 17/7.
27. LCC statement, 14 April 1909. NA CAB 17/7.
28. Beresford to Asquith, 16 April 1909. NA CAB 17/7.
29. Balfour to Esher, 16 April 1909. CCA ESHR 5/30.
30. Asquith to King Edward VII, 19 April 1909. Quoted in Lee, 1927, p. 601.
31. Knollys to Asquith, 16 April 1909. NA CAB 17/7.
32. Esher's journal, 15 April 1909. CCA ESHR 2/12.
33. Esher to Sandars, 20 April 1909. BL Add. Mss. 49719.
34. Esher to Balfour, 20 April 1909. BL Add. Mss. 49719.
35. Esher's journal, 24 January 1908. CCA ESHR 2/11.
36. Esher to Sandars, 24 April 1909. BL Add. Mss. 49719.
37. King Edward VII to Asquith, 25 April 1909. Quoted in Lee, 1927, p. 602.
38. Fisher to Ponsonby, 24 April 1909. Quoted in Marder, 1956, p. 247.

39. *The Times*, 24 April 1909.
40. Beresford's proposed witnesses, 22 April 1909. NA CAB 17/7.
41. Beresford to Ottley, 24 April 1909. NA CAB 17/7.
42. Ottley to McKenna, 27 April 1909. NA CAB 17/7.
43. Beresford to Milne, 25 April 1909. NMM MLN/227.
44. Milne to Beresford, c.29 April 1909. NMM MLN/227.
45. Beresford to Asquith, 21 April 1909. NA CAB 17/7.
46. Asquith to Ottley, 21 April 1909. NA CAB 17/7.
47. Ottley to McKenna, 27 April 1909. NA CAB 17/7.
48. Ottley to Custance, 29 April 1909. NA CAB 17/7.
49. Asquith to Ottley, 29 April 1909. NA CAB 17/7.
50. Widenmann to Tirpitz, 22 July 1909. Quoted in Marder, 1961, p.190.
51. *The Times*, 3 April 1909.
52. Fisher to McKenna, 5 April 1909. CCA MCKN 6/2.
53. *Parliamentary Debates*, Vol.3, 6 April 1909.
54. Ibid.
55. Beresford to Milne, 25 April 1909. NMM MLN/227.
56. *Parliamentary Debates*, Vol.3, 6 April 1909.
57. *Parliamentary Debates*, Vol.5, 19 May 1909.
58. Ibid.
59. *Parliamentary Debates*, Vol.5, 27 May 1909.
60. Beresford, 1914, p.347.
61. NA CAB 16/9 B, p.1.
62. Ottley to Haldane, 11 December 1909. Quoted in Lambert, 1999, p.195.
63. Esher's journal, 28 November 1907. CCA ESHR 2/10.
64. NA CAB 16/9A, p.2.
65. Ibid., p.25.
66. Ibid., p.3.
67. Ibid., p.22.
68. Ibid., p.4.
69. Ibid., p.12.
70. Ibid., p.25.
71. Ibid., p.26.
72. Ibid., p.43.
73. Ibid., p.43.
74. Ibid., p.47.
75. Ibid., p.48.
76. Ibid., p.48.
77. Ibid., p.48.
78. *Parliamentary Debates*, Vol.3, 1 May 1909.
79. NA CAB 16/9A, p.61.
80. Ibid., pp.66–7.
81. Ibid., pp.68–9.
82. Ibid., p.69.
83. Ibid., p.74.
84. Ibid., p.75.
85. Ibid., p.75.
86. Ibid., p.91.
87. Ibid., p.91.
88. Ibid., p.91.
89. Ibid., p.92.
90. Ibid., p.93.

91. Ibid., p. 93.
92. Ibid., p. 93.
93. Ibid., pp. 94–5.
94. Ibid., p. 95.
95. Fisher to Ponsonby, 4 May 1909. Quoted in Marder, 1956, p. 248.
96. Fisher to Ponsonby, 4 May 1909. Quoted in Marder, 1956, p. 248.
97. Fisher to Hurd, 5 May 1909. Quoted in Hough, 1969, pp. 292–3.
98. NA CAB 16/9A, p. 98.
99. Ibid., p. 99.
100. Ibid., p. 100.
101. Ibid., p. 101.
102. Ibid., pp. 106–7.
103. Ibid., p. 107.
104. Ibid., p. 109.
105. Ibid., p. 110.
106. Ibid., p. 111.
107. Ibid., p. 114.
108. Ibid., p. 114.
109. Ibid., p. 114.
110. NA CAB 16/9B, p. 2.
111. NA CAB 16/9A, p. 11.
112. Ibid., p. 117.
113. Ibid., pp. 117–18.
114. Ibid., p. 120.
115. Ibid., p. 131.
116. Ibid., p. 138.
117. Ibid., p. 140.
118. Ibid., p. 141.
119. Ibid., p. 141.
120. Ibid., p. 141.
121. *The Times*, 10 May 1909.
122. Beresford to Bellairs, 9 May 1909. McGill Bellairs archive.
123. Quoted in Bacon, 1929, p. 57.
124. NA CAB 16/9A, p. 165.
125. Ibid., p. 165.
126. Ibid., p. 165.
127. Ibid., p. 165.
128. Ibid., pp. 165–6.
129. Ibid., p. 166.
130. Ibid., p. 166.
131. Ibid., p. 167.
132. Ibid., p. 168.
133. Ibid., pp. 168–9.
134. Ibid., p. 171.
135. Ibid., p. 172.
136. Ibid., p. 172.
137. Ibid., p. 173.
138. Ibid., p. 174.
139. Ibid., p. 175.
140. Ibid., pp. 183–4.
141. Ibid., pp. 183–4.
142. Ibid., p. 184.

143. Ibid., p. 187.
144. Ibid., p. 187.
145. Ibid., p. 187.
146. Ibid., p. 188.
147. Ibid., p. 188.
148. Ibid., p. 189.
149. Ibid., p. 191.
150. Ibid., p. 192.
151. Ibid., p. 192.
152. Ibid., p. 192.
153. Ibid., p. 193.
154. Ibid., p. 193.
155. Ibid., p. 193.
156. Ibid., p. 193.
157. Hamilton, 1922, p. 91.
158. NA CAB 16/9A, p. 198.
159. Sandars to Esher, 15 August 1909. CCA ESHR 5/3.
160. NA CAB 16/9A, p. 198.
161. Ibid., p. 198.
162. NA CAB 16/9B, Appendix 22.
163. Hankey memo re Beresford, 19 May 1909. NA CAB 17/7.
164. NA CAB 16/9A, p. 223.
165. Bethell to Fisher, 22 May 1909. CCA MCKN 3/4.
166. Esher to Fisher, 23 May 1909. CCA FISR 1/8.
167. *The Times*, 24 May 1909.
168. Fisher to Stead, 26 May 1909. CCA STED 1/27.
169. Fisher to Edward Goulding, 28 May 1909. Quoted in Marder, 1956, p. 250.
170. Fisher to McKenna, 28 May 1909. CCA MCKN 6/2.
171. Knollys to Esher, 31 May 1909. CCA ESHR 10/51.
172. Fisher to Stead, 26 May 1909. CCA STED 1/27.
173. NA CAB 16/9A, p. 259.
174. King-Hall's diary, 23 September 1909.
175. Fisher to Esher, 12 June 1909. Quoted in Marder, 1956, pp. 251–2. Bacon (1929c, p. 54) claims that this letter refers to the last day of the enquiry. This is inconsistent with the date of the letter and its contents.
176. Fisher to McKenna, 14 June 1909. CCA MCKN 6/2.
177. NA CAB 16/9A, p. 286.
178. Ibid., p. 286.
179. Ibid., p. 286.
180. Ibid., pp. 286–7.
181. Ibid., p. 287.
182. Ibid., p. 287.
183. Ibid., p. 287.
184. Ibid., p. 287.
185. Fisher to McKenna, 20 June 1909. Quoted in Marder, 1956, pp. 253–4.
186. NA CAB 16/9A, p. 300.
187. Fisher to Hurd, 3 March 1910. CCA HURD 1/14.
188. NA CAB 16/9A, p. 304.
189. Ibid., pp. 304–6.
190. Ibid., p. 314.
191. Wilson's evidence. CCA FISR 5/15.
192. NA CAB 16/9A, p. 315.

193. Ibid., p.315.
194. Ibid., p.315.
195. *The Times*, 1 July 1909.
196. NA CAB 16/9A, pp.317–8.
197. Ibid., p.318.
198. Ibid., p.319.
199. Ibid., p.322.
200. Ottley to McKenna, 7 July 1909. NA CAB 16/9B, p.227.
201. May to Ottley, 11 July 1909. NA CAB 16/9B, p.227.
202. NA CAB 16/9A, pp.326–7.
203. *Parliamentary Debates*, Vol.7, 15 July 1909.
204. Hankey, 1961, p.74.
205. NA CAB 17/7.
206. Hankey, 1961, p.74.
207. Fisher to White, 13 November 1909. Quoted in Marder, 1956, pp.277–8.
208. Hankey, 1961, p.75.
209. Cmd. 256, 12 August 1909. HMSO.

## Act 10: Consequences

1. Quoted in Marder, 1961, p.200.
2. *The Times*, 17 August 1909.
3. Beresford to Sturdee, 17 August 1909. CCA SDEE 3/2.
4. Beresford to Long, 12 September 1909. BL Add. Mss. 62407.
5. Balfour to Esher, 16 August 1909. CCA ESHR 5/31.
6. Knollys to Esher, 23 August 1909. CCA ESHR 10/51.
7. Fisher to McKenna, 19 August 1909. Quoted in Marder, 1956, p.260.
8. Fisher to Crease, 22 August 1909. CCA FISR 1/8.
9. Fisher to Esher, 27 August 1909. CCA FISR 1/8. (Marder, 1956, pp.260–2, incorrectly dates this letter as 28 August.)
10. Fisher to Ottley, 29 August 1909. Quoted in Marder, 1956, pp.262–3.
11. Knollys to Esher, 23 August 1909. CCA ESHR 10/51.
12. Ponsonby to Fisher, 21 August 1909. CCA FISR 1/8.
13. Sandars to Esher, 8 September 1909. CCA ESHR 5/31.
14. *The Times*, 16 August 1909.
15. *The Times*, 1 September 1909.
16. Quoted in Marder, 1956, n. 1, pp.270–1.
17. Edward VII to Fisher. Quoted in Marder, 1956, p.275.
18. Esher to Balfour, 15 August 1909. Quoted in Esher, 1934, pp.399–400.
19. Magnus, 1964, pp.376–7.
20. Esher to Sandars, 26 August 1909. BL Add. Mss. 49719.
21. Esher to Sandars, 24 August 1909. BL Add. Mss. 49719.
22. Sandars to Esher, 25 August 1909. CCA ESHR 5/31.
23. Sandars to Esher, 8 September 1909. CCA ESHR 5/31.
24. Frewen, 1961, p.179.
25. Quoted in Morris, 1981, p.67.
26. *National Review*, September 1909.
27. Crease to Fisher, 26 November 1909. CCA FISR 1/8.
28. Sandars to Esher, 25 August 1909. CCA ESHR 5/31.
29. Fisher to Mrs Reginald Neeld, c.10 October 1909. Quoted in Marder, 1956, pp.270–1.
30. Fisher to White, 12 October 1909. Quoted in Marder, 1956, p.271.
31. Knollys to Esher, 23 August 1909. CCA ESHR 10/51.
32. Yexley to Fisher, 9 October 1909. CCA ESHR 10/43.

33. Esher to Sandars, 15 September 1909. BL Add. Mss. 49719.
34. Sandars to Esher, 16 September 1909. CCA ESHR 5/31.
35. Fisher to Remnant, 29 October 1909. Quoted in Marder, 1956, p. 274.
36. Beresford to Balfour, 12 December 1909. BL Add. Mss. 49713.
37. Fisher to McKenna, 8 November 1909. CCA MCKN 3/4.
38. Hough, 1969, p. 277.
39. Bridgeman to Fisher, 21 November 1909.
40. Asquith to Fisher, 26 October 1909. CCA MCKN 6/2.
41. King Edward to Fisher, 29 October 1909. Quoted in Marder, 1956, p. 275.
42. Fisher to Ponsonby, 29 October 1909. Quoted in Marder, 1956, p. 275.
43. CCA ESHR 10/43.
44. Fisher to Mrs McKenna, 14 November 1909. Quoted in Marder, 1956, pp. 278–9.
45. *The Times*, 18 November 1909.
46. Fisher to McKenna, 23 November 1909. Quoted in Marder, 1956, p. 283.
47. McKenna to Fisher, 25 December 1909. Quoted in Marder, 1956, p. 287.
48. Fisher to Mrs Meynell, 18 January 1910. Quoted in Marder, 1956, p. 291.
49. *The Times*, 30 August 1909.
50. *The Times*, 14 September 1909.
51. *The Times*, 23 October 1909.
52. Beresford to Asquith, 20 July 1909. *The Times*, 25 October 1909.
53. Asquith to Beresford, 9 August 1909. *The Times*, 25 October 1909.
54. Beresford to Asquith, 18 October 1909. *The Times*, 25 October 1909.
55. Asquith to Beresford, 21 October 1909. *The Times*, 25 October 1909.
56. Beresford to Asquith, 23 October 1909. *The Times*, 25 October 1909.
57. Asquith to Beresford, 30 October 1909. *The Times*, 1 November 1909.
58. McKenna to Asquith, 29 October 1909. *The Times*, 1 November 1909.
59. Troubridge to Campbell, 27 April 1910. NMM MLN/211/2.
60. Campbell to Troubridge, 1 May 1910. NMM MLN/211/2.
61. McKenna to Campbell, 19 May 1910. NMM MLN/211/2.
62. Troubridge to Campbell, 25 May 1910. NMM MLN/211/2.
63. Troubridge to Campbell, 31 May 1910. NMM MLN/211/2.
64. Knollys to Esher, 10 September 1909. CCA ESHR 10/51.
65. Fisher to Ponsonby, 3 November 1909. Quoted in Marder, 1956, p. 276.
66. Fisher to Esher, 13 September 1909. CCA ESHR 10/43.
67. King Edward to Fisher, 29 October 1909. Quoted in Marder, 1956, p. 275.
68. *The Times*, 1 November 1909.
69. *The Times*, 5 November 1909.
70. *The Times*, 15 November 1909.
71. Fisher to Pamela McKenna, 16 November 1909. Quoted in Marder, 1956, pp. 279–80.
72. *The Times*, 18 November 1909.
73. *The Times*, 19 November 1909.
74. Beresford to Bellairs, 22 November 1909. McGill Bellairs archive.
75. *The Times*, 23 November 1909.
76. *The Times*, 24 November 1909.
77. *The Times*, 26 November 1909.
78. Anand, 2008, p. 251.
79. Fisher to McKenna, 29 November 1909. CCA FISR 1/8.
80. Beresford to Lloyd, n.d. *The Times*, 6 November 1909.
81. *The Times*, 14 December 1909.
82. *The Times*, 20 December 1909.
83. Lellenberg, 2008, p. 411.
84. Long to Mina Beresford, 14 December 1910. BL Add. Mss. 62407.

85. Beresford to Long, 19 December 1910. BL Add. Mss. 62407.
86. Glenton, 1991.

## Epilogue: Beresford's decline and Fisher's return
1. Churchill, *The World Crisis, 1911–1918*, 1941, p. 230.
2. Beresford, 1912, p. v.
3. Ibid., p. 163.
4. Ibid., pp. 163–4.
5. *The Times*, 29 January 1912.
6. *The American Journal of International Law*, Vol. 7, No. 1, January 1913, pp. 203–5.
7. Beresford to Bellairs, 24 February 1917. McGill Bellairs archive.
8. Beresford to Hurd, 5 April 1919. CCA HURD 1/5.
9. Fisher to Hurd, 2 April and 8 August 1910. Quoted in Morris, 1981, p. 51.
10. Fisher to Fiennes, 28 May 1912. Quoted in Marder, 1956, p. 465.
11. CCA FISR 1/19.
12. Long, 1923, p. 267.
13. *The Times*, 8 September 1919.
14. *The Times*, 12 July 1920.

## Appendix
1. Beresford, 1914b, p. 8.
2. Ibid., pp. 26–7.
3. Pears, 1960, pp. 170–1.
4. Beresford, 1914b, p. 142.
5. Bennett, 1968, pp. 70–1.
6. Magnus, 1964, p. 174.
7. NA ADM 196/83–86.
8. Ibid.
9. Ibid.
10. Ibid.
11. Beresford to Bellairs, 9 December 1900. McGill Bellairs archive.
12. Beresford's notebook, p. O5, n.d., but before 18 March 1901.
13. NA ADM 196/83–86. See also BL Add. MSS. 50288, ff. 116, 22 May 1902.
14. This seems to be a clerical error, since there is no Beresford letter in *The Times* of that date, although he published a letter the following day. Whichever letter is intended, the reprimand was related to his recent LCC speech.
15. NA ADM 196/83–86.
16. Frewen, 1961, p. 51.
17. Adm letter to Beresford, 11 April 1904. NA ADM 116-3108. See also NA ADM 196/83–86.
18. Marder, 1940, p. 441, fn. 10.
19. NA ADM 196/83–86.
20. Admiralty to Beresford, 5 June 1907. CCA FISR 8/42.
21. Fisher to White, n.d. (1907?). NMM WHI/75.
22. Crease to White, 30 June 1908.
23. Admiralty selection of Beresford correspondence.

# Bibliography

Anand, S., *Daisy. The Life and Loves of the Countess of Warwick*, London, Piatkus, 2008.

Asher, M., *Khartoum. The Ultimate Imperial Adventure*, London, Penguin Books Ltd., 2006.

Bacon, R., *From 1900 Onward*, London, Hutchinson and Co., 1940.

Bacon, R., *The life of Lord Fisher of Kilverstone*, 2 vols, London, Hodder and Stoughton, 1929.

Bennett, G.M., *Charlie B.: A Biography of Admiral Lord Beresford*, London, Peter Dawnay Ltd., 1968.

Beresford, C., *The Memoirs of Admiral Lord Charles Beresford*, 2 vols, London, Methuen and Co., 1914.

Beresford, C., *The Betrayal: Being a Record of Facts Concerning Naval Policy and Naval Administration from the Year 1902 to the Present Time*, London, P.S. King and Son, 1912.

Boyce, D.G. (ed.), *The Crisis of British Power: The Imperial and Naval Papers of the Second Earl of Selborne, 1895–1910*, London, The Historians' Press, 1990.

Bradford, Admiral Sir E., *Life of Admiral of the Fleet Sir Arthur Knyvet Wilson*, London, Murray, 1923.

Chalmers, W.S., *The Life and Letters of David, Earl Beatty*, London, Hodder and Stoughton, 1951.

Chatfield, Lord, *The Navy and Defence*, London, William Heinemann Ltd., 1942.

Churchill, W.S., *The World Crisis 1911–1918*, London, Macmillan, 1941.

Clark, A., *A Good Innings: The Private Papers of Viscount Lee of Fareham*, Murray, 1974.

Clowes, Sir W.L. et al., *The Royal Navy: a History, Vol. VII*, London, Sampson Low, Marston and Co., 1903.

Dawson, Lionel. *Flotillas. A Hard-lying Story*, London, Rich and Cowan Ltd., 1933.

Dorling, T., *Men o' War*, London, P. Allen and Co., 1929.

Esher, R.B., *Journals and letters of Reginald, Viscount Esher, Vol. II*, London, Nicholson and Watson, 1934.

Fisher, Admiral Sir F., *Naval Reminiscences*, London, Frederick Muller, 1938.

Fisher, Lord, *Memories*, London, Hodder and Stoughton, 1919a.

Fisher, Lord, *Records*, London, Hodder and Stoughton, 1919b.

Fraser, E., *Famous Fighters of the Fleet*, London, Macmillan, 1904.

Frewen, O., *Sailor's Soliloquy*, London, Hutchinson, 1961.

Glenton, R., *The Royal Oak Affair. The Saga of Admiral Collard and Bandmaster Barnacle*, London, Leo Cooper, 1991.

Gordon, A., *The Rules of the Game*, London, John Murray, 1996.

Hamilton, Lord George, *Parliamentary Reminiscences and Reflections 1886–1906*, London, John Murray, 1922.

Hankey, M., *The Supreme Command 1914–1918, Vol. I*, London, George Allen and Unwin Ltd., 1961.

Hough, R., *First Sea Lord: An Authorized Biography of Admiral Lord Fisher*, London, George Allen and Unwin Ltd., 1969.

James, Admiral Sir W., *A Great Seaman: The Life of Admiral of the Fleet Sir Henry F. Oliver*, London, Witherby Ltd., 1956.

Jameson, W., *The Fleet That Jack Built*, London, Rupert Hart-Davis, 1962.

Jenkins, R., *Asquith*, London, Papermac, 1994.

Kemp, P.K. (ed.), *The Papers of Admiral Sir John Fisher, Vol. I*, Greenwich, Naval Records Society, 1960.

Kerr, M., *Prince Louis of Battenberg: Admiral of the Fleet*, London, Longmans, 1934.

King-Hall, L. (ed.), *Sea Saga: Being the Naval Diaries of Four Generations of the King-Hall Family*, London, Victor Gollanz Ltd., 1935.

Lambert, A., *Admirals. The Naval Commanders who Made Britain Great*, London, Faber and Faber, 2008.

Lambert, N.A., *Sir John Fisher's Naval Revolution*, Columbia, University of South Carolina Press, 1999.

Lee, Sir S., *King Edward VII. A Biography, Vol. I*, London, Macmillan and Co. Ltd., 1925.

Lee, Sir S., *King Edward VII. A Biography, Vol. II*, London, Macmillan and Co. Ltd., 1927.

Lellenberg, J. et al., *A Life in Letters: Arthur Conan Doyle*, London, Harper Perennial, 2008.

Long, W., *Memories*, London, Hutchinson and Co., 1923.

Mackay, R.F., *Fisher of Kilverstone*, Oxford, Clarendon Press, 1973.

Magnus, P.M., *King Edward The Seventh*, London, John Murray, 1964.

Marder, A.J., *British naval policy, 1880–1905: The Anatomy of British Sea Power*, London, Putnam and Co., 1940.

Marder, A.J., *From The Dreadnought To Scapa Flow. The Royal Navy In The Fisher Era, 1904–1919, Vol. I*, London, Oxford University Press, 1961.

Marder, A.J., *From The Dreadnought To Scapa Flow. The Royal Navy In The Fisher Era, 1904–1919, Vol. II*, London, Oxford University Press, 1965.

Marder, A.J. (ed.), *Fear God and Dread Nought: The Correspondence of Admiral of the Fleet Lord Fisher of Kilverstone, Vol. I*, London, Jonathan Cape, 1952.

Marder, A.J. (ed.), *Fear God and Dread Nought: The Correspondence of Admiral of the Fleet Lord Fisher of Kilverstone, Vol. II*, London, Jonathan Cape, 1956.

Marling, Col. Sir P., *Rifleman and Hussar*, London, John Murray, 1931.

Massie, R.K., *Dreadnought: Britain, Germany and the Coming of the Great War*, London, Pimlico, 1991.

McKenna, S., *Reginald McKenna 1863–1943*, London, Eyre and Spottiswoode, 1948.

Moorhouse (later Meynell), E.H., *A Woman Talking*, London, Chapman and Hall, 1940.

Morris, A.J.A., 'A not so silent service', *Moira: Journal of the School of Philosophy, Politics and History* (University of Ulster Polytechnic), 1981; 6:42–81.

Morris, A.J.A., *The Letters of Lieutenant-Colonel Charles à Court Repington*, Stroud, Sutton Publishing Ltd., 1999.

Padfield, P., *Aim Straight: A Biography of Admiral Sir Percy Scott*, London, Hodder and Stoughton, 1966.

Pears, Commander Randolph, *Young Sea Dogs: Some Adventures of Midshipmen of the Fleet*, London, Putnam, 1960.

Pelly, Sir H.B., *300,000 Sea Miles. An Autobiography*, London, Chatto and Windus, 1938.

Penn, G., *Infighting Admirals. Fisher's Feud with Beresford and the Reactionaries*. Barnsley, Lee Cooper, 2000.

Ponsonby, Sir F., *Recollections of Three Reigns*, London, Eyre and Spottiswoode, 1951.

Roskill, S., *Hankey, Man of Secrets, Vol. I*, London, Collins, 1970.

Rowland, P., *The Last Liberal Governments: The Promised Land 1905–1910*, London, Barrie and Rockliff, 1968.

Sandby, W., *The History of the Royal Academy, Vol. II*, London, Longman, 1862.

Schurman, D.M., *Julian S. Corbett, 1854–1922*, London, Royal Historical Society, 1981.

Scott, Sir P., *Fifty Years in the Royal Navy*, London, John Murray, 1919.

Smith, H.H., *An Admiral Never Forgets*, London, Seeley, Service and Co. Ltd., 1936.
Sydenham of Combe, *My Working Life*, London, John Murray, 1927.
Wemyss, V.W., *The Life and Letters of Lord Wester Wemyss*, London, Eyre and Spottiswoode, 1935.
Wilson, R.J.M., *A Life of Sir Henry Campbell-Bannerman*, London, Constable, 1973.
Wood, W., *North Sea Fishers and Fighters*, London, Kegan Paul and Co., 1911.
Woods, L.M., *British Gentlemen in the Wild West*, London, Robson, 1990.

# Index

271

273